To Heather,

With ♡

From Mom.

12/25/97

The Ultimate Household Reference Guide

By
Dr. Myles H. Bader

THE ULTIMATE HOUSEHOLD REFERENCE GUIDE

ISBN: 0-9646741-4-9

Published by:
Northstar Publishing Company
1818 Industrial Rd. Suite 209
Las Vegas, Nevada 89102
(702)383-8511
Order Line - 1 (800)717-6001

Printed in the United States of America
First Printing 1996

Illustrations

By

Deborah Rose Peek

A WORD ABOUT THE AUTHOR

Dr. Myles H. Bader (known by many as the "Doctor of Food Facts") has been interviewed on over 1600 radio and television talk shows internationally. These shows have included; The Oprah Winfrey Show, America's Talking, Help at Home, The "Home Matters Show" on the Discovery Channel, Crook and Chase on TNN, Mike and Maty, QVC, and The Morning Exchange in Cleveland to mention only a few.

Dr. Bader received his Doctorate Degree from Loma Linda University majoring in Public Health and is Board Certified in Preventive Care. He has practiced in major medical clinics in California and has established numerous prevention programs for a number of Fortune 500 companies, governmental agencies, and safety departments.

While in practice he has written numerous books and protocols in the areas of fitness, weight control, general nutrition, stress management, and cardiac rehabilitation.

Presently, he lectures extensively throughout the United States and Canada in all areas of wellness. He is regarded as one of the leading authorities in the field of prevention and wellness with over 3,000 presentations and seminars.

His current books include; "To Supplement Or Not To Supplement," "6001 Food Facts and Chef's Secrets," "The Wellness Desk Reference," and his latest "The Ultimate Household Reference Guide" with over 8,000 household hints, food facts, stain removal tips, and grandmother's kitchen secrets.

Lendon Smith, M.D., better known as the Good Morning America Doctor for many years has this to say of Dr. Bader, "He is highly knowledgeable in the areas of health, nutrition, and preventive care."

THIS BOOK IS DEDICATED

TO PAULETTE

A TRUE FRIEND WHEN ONE WAS REALLY NEEDED

TABLE OF CONTENTS

Chapter 1

Household and Entertaining Tips

BATTLING THE BUGS

"KEEPING THE CRITTERS AT BAY"
Bay leaves or cloves should be placed in all kitchen drawers, the flour and sugar containers, and anywhere you wish to keep the crawling insects away from.

"INTO THE WILD BLUE YONDER"
If you have a problem with flying insects, especially flies and mosquitoes, try keeping a basil plant or two around the house. Keep the plant well-watered from the bottom, this will cause the plant to release additional aroma.

"JUST HANGING AROUND"
Hanging small muslin bags with dried basil will also repel flying insects.

"YOU WON'T NEED THE ROD AND REEL"
To get rid of silverfish, try mixing 1 part of molasses in 2 parts of white vinegar. Apply the mixture to cracks and holes where they reside. Treat the baseboards and table legs as well.

"FASTER THAN RABBITS"
Garbage pails and trash compactors can produce 1,000 or more flies a week unless they are sealed tight.

"AROMATHERAPY FOR FLIES"
Flies are repelled by oil of lavender. Soak a sponge with the oil and leave in a saucer. Other natural fly repellents are oil of cloves and mint sprigs.

"FLEA SUCTION"
Fleas can be eliminated by vacuuming with a high powered vacuum cleaner (Preferably Electrolux) with a good sealing bag. Remove the bag and dispose of immediately after vacuuming.

"ODOR CONTROLLER"
Citronella oil candles will rid your home of mosquitoes. The smell is pleasant and not at all offensive.

"MOTH TRAPPER"
Moths can be trapped by mixing 1 part of molasses with 2 parts of white vinegar and placing the mixture in a bright yellow container.

"SNAIL ZAPPER"
Place stale beer in a shallow container just below ground level. The beer tends to have a diuretic effect, causing the liquids in the snail to be released.

cheek '91

"LE PEW"
Mice can't stand the smell of fresh mint or peppermint. Plant it around your home to repel any type of rodent. Oil of peppermint may be placed on a cotton ball and placed in any location in the home to chase the critters away.

"GETTING METHODICAL"

Ants – Method 1: To keep ants away, place whole cloves or sage around the windows and doors or anywhere else they appear.

Ants – Method 2: For a quick ant kill, mix two cups of borax with one cup of sugar in a quart jar. Punch holes in the lid and sprinkle around the outside of the house.

Ants – Method 3: To get rid of ants, pour Ivory Liquid Soap around. This is the only liquid soap that seems to work.

Ants – Method 4: To eliminate ants from your kitchen counters, try washing the counter with equal parts of water and white vinegar.

Ants – Method 5: If you have an area that ants travel the most, just sprinkle a small amount of baby powder in the area. Ants will never cross baby powder.

Ants – Method 6: Cucumber peelings will repel ants outside the house.

Ants – Method 7: If the first 6 methods fail, call Hertz and rent an Aardvark.

Roaches as well as ants will be repelled by cucumber peelings.

If you place a border of bone meal around a plant it should keep the ants away.

A good roach killer can be made from 35% borax, 15% white flour, 10% powdered sugar, and 40% cornmeal.

"WON'T WORK ON MEXICAN WEEVILS"
If you want to keep weevils and other crawling insects out of your grits and legumes, try placing a hot dried red pepper in with them.

A solution of weak tea, ammonia, and dish soap placed in a spray bottle and sprayed on plants will keep most bugs away.

"NO MERCY"
If you have a roach problem, fill a large bowl with cheap wine and place it under the sink or ?. The roaches will drink the wine, get drunk, fall in and drown. Go ahead and laugh, but this really works.

MISCELLANEOUS FACTS

Keep an empty plastic soda bottle handy in case you ever need a hot water bottle. Just fill it up with hot water and wrap it in a towel.

Vinegar, The All Around Helper

"BE-WARE"
Never use a painted plate for serving a food containing vinegar dressing. Vinegar will corrode the paint off the plate and may release harmful toxins into the food.

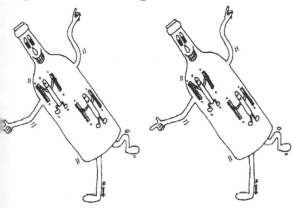

To remove an unsightly residue buildup from inside a flower vase or wine bottle, try using a solution of 1 tablespoon of salt and 1 cup of white vinegar. If you still have some residue left, add some rice and shake.

Use warm vinegar to remove old decals. Just allow the vinegar to soak for a few minutes then sponge off the decal.

If the sun is shining on your windows, do not wash them until they are in the shade. When they dry too fast they tend to show streaks.

"PUT A LID ON IT"
A fire in a pan can easily be put out by just placing a lid over the fire and cutting off the oxygen supply.

"A SLOW BURN"
Candles should be stored in the refrigerator or freezer. This will reduce dripping and make them burn slower.

Black soot marks on candles are unsightly and can be removed with rubbing alcohol.

A nick on the rim of a glass can be removed with an emery board.

Peanut butter will remove gum from a persons hair.

Egg white sponged on leather will revive its luster.

A few drops of vanilla extract placed in a bottle top in the refrigerator will remove odors.

Dry mustard will remove onion odors from your hands or cutting board. Rub in then rinse off.

To prevent windows from steaming up, rub then with equal amounts of glycerin and methyl alcohol.

"I WONDER WHERE THE YELLOW WENT"
Stale milk or leftover milk makes an excellent cleaner for plant leaves.

Mayonnaise can be used to oil wood.

Salt is handy for sopping up wine spills. Pour the salt on the spill, wait until it dries, then vacuum it up.

"DO THE TWIST"
Pour oil and vinegar into the remains on the bottom of a ketchup bottle, shake vigorously to make a great salad dressing.

Don't buy dustcloths that are treated to attract dust, just dip a piece of cheesecloth in a solution of 2 cups of water and 1/4 cup of lemon oil, then allow to dry.

Leftover tea will clean varnished furniture.

"BEATS IRONING"
Sheer curtains will come out of the washer "wrinkle-free" if you dissolve a package of unflavored gelatin in a cup of boiling water and add it to the final rinse.

After you polish your furniture, sprinkle a small amount of cornstarch on and rub until you get a high gloss. The cornstarch will absorb oil and leave a great shine.

For a brighter shoe shine, place a few drops of lemon juice on your shoes when you are polishing them.

Lemon juice and salt will remove mold and mildew.

Glue on containers can be removed by using vegetable oil.

Diamonds and gold can be cleaned using a solution of vinegar and water. Never place opals, emeralds, or pearls in the solution or any other soft stone or costume jewelry.

Costume jewelry can be cleaned with a weak solution of baking soda and water. Scrub lightly with a toothbrush.

"EXTINGUISHING THE OLD FLAME"
Baking soda makes an excellent fire extinguisher. It smothers the flames by cutting off its oxygen supply.

"A POPPER OUTER"
If you have a problem removing a nut or bolt, just pour some carbonated soda on it and allow it to sit for 15 minutes.

Battery posts can be cleaned with a thick solution of baking soda and water. Allow it to soak for 10-15 minutes before washing it off. Baking soda is a base and will neutralize a weak acid.

To remove unwanted grass from between sidewalk and driveway cracks, try using vinegar and salt.

An inexpensive method of cleaning dentures is to soak them overnight in white vinegar.

Vinegar can be used to clean pipes.

White rings on furniture may be removed by using a paste of vegetable oil and salt. Allow the solution to stand for a few hours then remove.

Baking soda added to furniture oil may remove stains from woodwork. Adds just the right amount of a mild abrasive.

"SMOKERS BEWARE"
To remove cigarette smoke from a room, try soaking a towel in a solution of vinegar and water, ring out completely, then wave it in a circular motion around the room. Accidentally hitting the smoker may also help.

"STEAK SHAKE?"
To tenderize meat when barbecuing, add green papaya to the barbecue sauce. Don't leave the meat in too long or it will start to break down and liquefy.

Buttermilk can be used to soften dry cheese.

Pecans, walnuts or peanuts can be used to mask scratches on furniture. Use a broken edge of the nut.

Along with your detergent, add a bottle of cola to a load of greasy work clothes. It will help loosen the serious dirt.

"BETTER THAN SOME TV SHOWS"
Instead of throwing leftover colas down the kitchen sink, dump them down the toilet bowl and watch what happens. After it has soaked for awhile the toilet bowel should be sparkling clean.

Lemon extract will remove black scuff marks from shoes and luggage.

Stains from ball point pens can be removed with hair spray or milk.

"ELIMINATING A CRACK-UP"
A simple method of removing cracks in china cups is to simmer the cup in milk for 30-40 minutes, depending on the size of the crack. If the crack is not too wide, the protein in the milk will seal it.

White vinegar will help eliminate the odor from a dog's accident on the carpet. Try a small area in a corner first, to be sure the carpet is colorfast.

To make your hair shiny, try a teaspoon of vinegar in your final rinse.

Oven Guard used on a clean car bumper before a trip will make it easy to remove the bugs.

"GREAT, GRATER TIP"
If you have a problem cleaning the grater after grating cheese, try rubbing a raw potato over it before washing. Also, using an old toothbrush to clean the grater works well.

A few drops of ammonia should be dropped into greasy pots before pouring in hot water. This will make them easier to clean.

Place a piece of chalk in a silver chest to absorb moisture and slow tarnishing.

"A LITTLE DIP WILL DO YA"
If you want your fingernails to be whiter, dip them in lemon juice. The acidic nature of the lemon will bleach them. Always keep a small plastic baggie handy when you have both hands in any food you are mixing. If the phone rings, just slip your hand into the baggie.

"AH CHOO"
To keep plant eating pets or varmints out of your garden or from potential poisonings, place red or black pepper on the leaf tips of plants, especially African violets and other toxic plants.

"FOILED AGAIN"
To keep animals away from your plants, try placing tin foil around them. Most animals will stay clear.

"LUCKY FOR YOU"
The reason you can place your hand into a 500 degree oven and not into a pot of boiling water at 212 degrees is that air does not transfer heat well.

"MESSY!"
Run a warm iron over contact paper and it should peel right off. Provides just enough heat to soften the glue.

"SEASON YOUR CARPET"
Carpet colors will be more livelier if you sprinkle a small amount of salt on before vacuuming.

Empty plastic ketchup and mustard containers are great for holding icings and oils.

"KITCHEN COPTER"
To get the last drop out of a ketchup bottle, grasp the bottom of the bottle <u>firmly</u> and swing it in a circular motion from your side. The remaining ketchup will go to the top.

"CRUMMY SOLUTION"
Keep a jar handy for leftover crumbs from empty low-sugar cereal or low-salt cracker boxes. When you need crumbs they will be there for you.

SPRAY ANY VEGETABLE OIL ON YOUR SNOW SHOVEL AND THE SNOW WILL SLIDE RIGHT OFF.

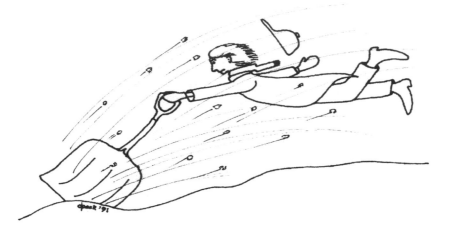

"A SINKING FEELING"
To unclog a drain, try using a cup of salt mixed with a cup of baking soda (no liquid). Pour the dry solution into the drain followed by a pot of boiling water.

Odor Eaters

To eliminate refrigerator odors, try using a small amount of vanilla on a cotton ball.

If you boil several cloves in a cup of water, it will rid the house of unwanted food odors.

Cloves can also be combined with cinnamon, wrapped in a piece of cheesecloth and placed in boiling water to give off a pleasant fragrance.

Coffee grounds kept in an open jar will help absorb odors.

For an efficient refrigerator deodorizer, try using a few charcoal briquettes on a small plate.

"AN UPLIFTING EXPERIENCE"
To raise the nap of carpeting after heavy furniture has matted it down, place one or two ice cubes on the area overnight. By morning the carpet should be back to normal.

"A PERKER UPPER"
Dry eggshells in the oven then pulverize them in a blender and make a high calcium meal for your plants. Banana skins and eggshells make an excellent fertilizer.

Club soda that has lost its fizzle, has just the right chemicals left to add vigor and color to your plants.

To save washing extra cups and spoons, first measure all dry ingredients then place them on waxed paper, then use the same cup or spoon for measuring the liquids.

Save all microwave containers, place leftovers in them and freeze for later use.

"MICROWAVE SAVVY"
To check to see if a container is safe for microwave use, place the container next to a cup that is half-full of water. Use full power for 1 minute. If the container is hot to the touch, it cannot be used in the microwave, if its warm it may be used to reheat, and if cool its OK for any use.

To grease a pan easily, try using a soft bread crust spread with butter or ?

FOR THE KIDS

"CHILD'S PLAY"
The formula for a play dough is to mix together 1/2 cup of salt, 2 tablespoons of alum, 2 tablespoons of vegetable oil, then add the mixture to 2 cups of boiling water, mix well and knead.

"A BUBBLE TO BURST"
The formula for bubble solution is to mix 1 tablespoon of glycerin with 2 tablespoons of a powdered detergent in 1 cup of water. A straw works as well as an empty spool to blow the solution through.

A natural food color may be added to any of the above formulas to give it color.

"GET A GRIP ON"
Wide rubber bands placed around drinking glasses give children a better grip.

"PLUG THE DIKE"
If you place a marshmallow on the bottom of an ice cream cone, the ice cream will not leak through.

When traveling with small children, carry a bottle of powdered milk instead of regular milk which easily spoils. Add water to the powdered milk and shake.

"REJUVENATION"
To bring ping pong balls back to life and remove the dents, just place them in hot water for 15-20 minutes.

"COLD STORAGE"
Keep plastic wrap in the refrigerator to prevent it from sticking to itself when handled.

Hydrogen peroxide won't lose its fizzle if kept in the refrigerator.

Nail polish should be stored in the refrigerator. It will go on smoother and have a longer life.

"MIXER UPPER"
Keep a shaker of mixed salt and pepper near the range. Use 3/4 part salt to 1/4 part pepper.

If food is scorched, place the pot immediately in cold water to stop the cooking action, this will save the food that was not scorched from acquiring the burnt taste.

If you overdo the mayonnaise, add bread crumbs to absorb it.

"REVIVAL"
To bring the bounce back into tennis balls, place the can in the oven with the lid removed overnight. The heat from the pilot light will expand the air inside and revive them.

A thin layer of fresh baking soda should be placed on the bottom of a litter box before adding litter.

"THE NOSE, KNOWS"
A small amount of baking soda applied to you armpits will replace your deodorant.

Baking soda works great in place of toothpaste.

To repair a nail hole in woodwork, just mix a small amount of instant coffee with spackling paste or starch and water.

Mirrors can be brightened by rubbing them with a cloth dampened with alcohol.

"TROUBLE WAKING UP? TRY THIS ON"
Pantyhose will last longer if they are placed in the freezer
for the first night only. It will strengthen the fibers, but
make sure you thaw them out before wearing then, unless you
are having trouble waking up.

"NUTRAPET"
Water from boiled potatoes and vegetables should be saved
and mixed with you pets food to give them added nutrients.

"TASTE BUD ALERT"
To check your salt intake, eat a piece of bacon, if it
doesn't taste salty you're probably eating too much salt.

Tin coffee cans make excellent freezer containers for
cookies.

To cool a hot dish more rapidly, place it in a pan of salted
cold water. It will cool faster than if placed in just cold
water.

To keep milk from sticking to a pot, massage a little butter
on the bottom of the pot.

Lightly grease a gelatin mold before using. It will make it
easier to remove the mold.

Add raw rice to the salt shaker to keep the salt free-
flowing.

"SHOW STOPPERS"
To prevent carbonated beverages from fizzing up over the top
of the glass, just place the ice cubes in the glass and
rinse them with water, pour the water off, pour the soda in
and it will not fizz up. Washing the ice cubes changes the
surface tension of the ice.

Place a hot dog in plastic wrap, then put it into a thermos
of soup or coffee. When lunchtime arrives, place the hot dog
in a bun.

Sugar bags can be used to store ice cubes. They are much
thicker than plastic bags.

Small marshmallows can be used for candle holders on cakes.

Sandwiches will not become limp and soggy as readily if you
spread the butter or mayonnaise to the edge of the bread.

Floor tiles should be used instead of contact paper on
kitchen shelves. They last longer and are easier to clean.

"SLICK IDEA"
To prevent mildew from forming in the refrigerator, try spraying the insides with a vegetable oil spray after you defrost it. It will make the job easier next time.

Blenders and egg beaters should be lubricated regularly. Use mineral oil instead of vegetable oil to avoid corrosion.

If you use a small amount of oil on the threads of a syrup bottle it will stop the syrup from running down the sides of the bottle.

When you measure sticky liquids, try wiping the inside of the measuring cup with a small amount of oil. The liquids will flow freely.

To prevent ice cube trays from sticking to the bottom of the shelf, place a piece of waxed paper underneath the tray.

A hair dryer will help defrost a freezup in the ice maker.

When glasses are stuck together, just fill the top one with ice cold water and dip the bottom one in hot water.

The secret to keeping butcher block in good shape is to wash then dry, then cover with salt to draw the moisture out of the wood. Then treat the wood with mineral oil for a smooth surface.

For clear ice cubes just boil the water first. This eliminates a number of minerals that cause the cloudiness.

When grating, chef's always grate the softest items first, than the firmer ones. This will keep the grater clean.

"STUCK UP"
When postage stamps have stuck together, try placing them in the freezer for 10 minutes, they will come apart with no damage.

"A PENNY SAVED"
Save money by purchasing the least expensive dishwasher soap, then add a few teaspoons of vinegar to the dishwasher. The vinegar cuts the grease and leaves the dishes spot-free and sparkling.

When washing greasy dishes, add 1/2 cup of baking soda to the water to cut the grease faster.

To clean an electric coffee pot, place 1 teaspoon of dish soap in the pot and boil.

When you fill a thermos bottle or small mouth container, use a funnel.

To help a semi-solid soup slide right out of the can, try shaking the can first and then open it from the bottom.

"NUKED"
Never lean on a microwave door, It may become misaligned and leak radiation. An inexpensive device is available at most supermarkets to check whether you have a leak or not.

ENTERTAINING TIPS

"FILLER UPPERS"
Use a large green pepper as a cup for dips. Cut off the top, scrape the pepper clean of ribs and seeds.

Cucumber make an excellent holder for dips, When cutting, leave a handle in the middle, it will look like a basket.

Use a hollowed melon, orange or grapefruit as a cup to fill with cut-up fruits.

"THE NOSE, KNOWS"
Before your guests arrive, give your home that "somethings baking" fragrance by sprinkling some cinnamon and sugar in a tin pie pan and cooking it on high heat for a few minutes.

When making small finger sandwiches, use an electric knife to cut them and the filling won't run all out.

To keep pizza crust crispy, try placing the cheese on before the tomato sauce.

To keep ice from melting, place a container of dry ice underneath the ice.

Champagne is best if not chilled for too long a period and should only be chilled up to the neck of the bottle, any higher and the cork may be more difficult to remove.

To save leftover wines, freeze them in your ice cube trays. They can be used for any dish that you would normally season with wine or for use in wine coolers.

"SPRINKLER HEAD ALERT"
For a flaming pudding, soak sugar cubes in orange or lemon extract. Place them on the pudding and light.

Cottage cheese can be used in place of sour cream when making dips. Just place it in the blender until it is creamed.

"THE SANDWICH OF MANY COLORS"
Cream cheese can be colored with powdered or liquid food coloring and used as a filler in dainty rolled sandwiches.

Try a different color for each layer, then slice as you would a jelly roll.

To stop hard candy from sticking together, just sift a little cornstarch on it.

"PARTY CUBES"
Freeze red and green maraschino cherries in ice cubes. You can also use cocktail onions or green olives for martinis.

Freeze different colors of grapes for punches.

Freeze lemon peels in ice cubes for use in water glasses.

Use large ice cubes made from milk cartons for punches. The larger the ice cube the slower it melts.

"A CHILLING SUBJECT"
If you ever wondered how much ice to buy for a party, the rule of thumb is 1 pound per person.

"JOLLY GOOD SHOW"
Use crescent dinner rolls as a quick and easy pastry to prepare Beef Wellington.

To make a quick and unusual dip or spread, try pureeing a can of well drained white beans and a package of herb flavored soft cheese together.

Leftover sandwiches can be brushed with butter and cooked in a shallow pan.

"IT'S ZOO TIME"
When making sandwiches for the children, try using your animal-shaped cookie cutters for a unique treat.

Place a damp paper towel over the meat or cheese Hors d'oeuvres to help retain the moisture. Slows down the drying out time.

"A REAL DE-CORKER"
To remove a cork from inside an empty wine bottle, pour some ammonia into the bottle, set in a well ventilated location. In a few days the cork will be disintegrate.

To make your own Easter egg dyes, boil the eggs with grass for green, onion skins for yellow, and beets for red.

When you buy ice cubes in the bags, you will get about 10 cubes per pound. The average person at a party will go through 10-15 ice cubes depending on the type of drink.

For attractive butter servings, squeeze butter through a pastry bag or plastic bag onto a cookie sheet, then set in the refrigerator until it hardens.

"MEDICAL MIRACLE"
To preserve a Halloween pumpkin, just spray the inside and outside surfaces with an antiseptic spray to kill the bacteria and keep the pumpkin from deteriorating too rapidly. Do not eat the pumpkin after it has been sprayed.

"DOUBLE DECKER"
Salads and dips can be kept chilled by using two bowls. Place the salad or dip in the smaller bowl, partially fill the larger bowl with water and freeze. Then place the smaller bowl on top of the larger bowl and serve.

"WHOA"
When using a tray, place a damp napkin or towel under the dishes to stop them from moving around.

"A LITTLE DAB WILL DO YA"
If red wine is spilled on the carpet, it may be cleaned with shaving cream or club soda, then just sponge off with water.

After the holidays, purchase the large chocolate eggs, bunnies or ? They are usually 1/2 price, freeze them and use them for recipes to save money.

If vodka is kept refrigerated it will be more flavorful.

"PEEK-A-BOO"
If a watermelon needs to be removed from the refrigerator and sit for a while before being cut, place it in a double brown bag and it will stay cold longer.

"AN OLDIE BUT GOODIE"
To fancy up the top of a cake, cookies or pastry, try placing a wide-patterned doily on top then sprinkle powdered sugar over it and remove.

"SMART MOVE"
If your table is set with candles, it would be wise to place a small amount of salt around the top to eliminate wax droppings on the tablecloth.

Chapter 2

Miscellaneous Tips and Hints

YARD & GARDEN

"PLANT FOOD"
Banana skins will provide an
excellent source of plant
nutrients if buried just below
the surface. It is especially
good for flowers.

"GLUB, GLUB"
When cutting flowers from your garden, be sure and cut them
only in the late evening or early morning. Have a bucket of
water with you and use very sharp shears. After you cut the
flowers, place the stem under water and cut the stem again
on the diagonal, the stem will them take in water and not
air.

"HOW DRY I AM"
When transplanting, always use pre-moistened soil and peat
moss to help retain the moisture.

"A CLEAN LEAF IS A HAPPY LEAF"
If you want your plant's leaves to shine, try placing a
small amount of glycerin and water on them. Mix 1 tablespoon
of glycerin to 1 quart of water. Another method is to just
dip a cotton ball in milk or mineral oil and clean the
leaves.

"BUG KILLER"
If you place a few drops of liquid detergent in your water
that is being used to clean the plant's leaves, it will keep
the bugs off and if they go into the soil at night they will
die.

Never place a clay pot on wooden furniture, water seeps
through and can damage the wood.

"GOOD STUFF"
Egg shells should be pulverized for fertilizer, they add
lime to the soil.

If you are going to plant in window boxes, try whitewashing
them first. This will deter insects and reduce the risk of
dry rot.

1/2 gallon milk carton cut in half make an excellent seed starter flat.

"PLANT SAVER"
If you are going a a long vacation and are unable to find someone to care for your plants, try placing a large container of water near your plants, place pieces of yarn in the water and then lay the ends across the stalks of the plants. Capillary action will keep the plants in good shape until you return.

"PITHY TO THROW IT OUT"
An onion that has become pithy and has started to sprout should be placed in a pot on a window sill and as it continues to sprout just snip off pieces of the sprout for salad seasoning.

"GETTING POTTED"
If you are going to re-pot a plant, try placing a small coffee filter on the bottom of the pot to eliminate the soil from leaking out.

Be sure and place a 1/2 inch layer of gravel on the top of the soil in window boxes to prevent splattering when they are watered.

"ESPECIALLY HARD ROCK ONES"
Broken cassette tapes make excellent ties for plants.

Old ice cube trays make excellent herb starters.

"GETTING A LEG UP"
Nylon stocking or pantyhose make excellent storage holders for storing bulbs during the winter. Air is able to circulate avoiding a problem with mold. Hand in a cool dry location.

Styrofoam cups make excellent plant starters and are easy to break apart when you decide to plant the plant in the garden.

"POOR BAMBI"
Hanging small pieces of a deodorant bar soap on trees will keep the deer away. Works excellent on fruit trees.

HEALTH CARE AT HOME

"COOOOL"
Place an ice cube on a splinter a few seconds before removing it. This will deaden the area, just work fast.

A slice of cold onion placed on a bee sting should stop the pain and swelling.

To cure the hiccups, try sipping a cup of dill leaf tea slowly.

Aged wine and cheeses contain the substance tyramine. In sensitive individuals it may cause migraine headaches.

Meat tenderizer can be used to relieve the pain and itching from insect bites. Dissolve 1/4 - 1/2 teaspoon in a small amount of water. Another method is to make a thick paste of baking soda and water.

Chigger bites respond to a thick paste of a few aspirin tablets with water. Should ease the pain and itching.

"OR KISS A CUBE"
If you burn your tongue, try sprinkling a few grains of sugar on it for instant relief.

A minor burn can be relieved by rubbing a slice of raw potato on the burn gently.

To stop a sunburn from blistering, try using a small amount of white vinegar.

"ONLY THE REAL THING"
Vanilla extract will relieve the pain of a grease burn.

Headaches may be relieved by taking the herb "Feverfew."

CAR CARE

Chrome on a car can be cleaned with dampened aluminum foil.

The lids from 1 pound coffee cans will fit a can of opened motor oil to stop the dust or debris from contaminating it.

"LOCKS, NOT LOX"
A hairdryer will defrost your car lock in the winter.

If you get stuck in snow or mud, try using your car floor mat or a blanket kept in the trunk for traction.

If you run your air conditioner for 4-6 minutes during the winter it will keep the seals in good shape for the summer.

"NO NIPPING, IT'S POISON"
If your windshield wipers are smearing the windows, try wiping them with rubbing alcohol.

To make your own windshield washer fluid, try mixing 1 quart of rubbing alcohol, 1 cup of water, and 2 tablespoons of a liquid detergent together.

Old milk containers can be filled with old candle wax and kept in the car for emergencies.

"TRY, SODIUM PHOSPHATE"
TSP will remove grease stains from concrete after you scrape off the excess.

"RUB-A-DUB-DUB"
To prevent the rubber around your cars doors from freezing, try rubbing the rubber moldings with vegetable oil.

"BE GENTLE"
Steel wool pads make an excellent white wall cleaner.

"HERE, KITTY, KITTY"
To remove a grease stain from your concrete driveway, try rubbing kitty litter into the stain and allow to stand for 1-2 hours before sweeping it up. Don't let the cat out.

Old milk cartons make excellent sand containers if your stuck on ice.

If you place a sheet of fabric softener under your car seat it will keep your car smelling fresh.

PETS

To rid your pet of fleas, cut a strip of cloth about an inch larger than the size of your pets neck, fold it over so that there is an opening in the center and sew one end shut as well as placing a seam down the strip, use a funnel and fill the opening with a combination of 50/50 rosemary and oregano, then sew or tape a piece of Velcro to close the open end and attach to pet using the Velcro closure.

"FLEA B-GONE"
Brewers yeast rubbed on a dog or cats fur will repel fleas. Giving them a vitamin B supplement approved by your Vet will also help.

"HER FIDO, HERE FIDO, WHERE FIDO?"
To ward off fleas from a pet's sleeping area, try sprinkling a few drops of oil of lavender in the area. Fleas hate oil of lavender, hopefully your dog won't.

Chapter 3

Home Maintenance and Repair

"MODERATION, A MUST"
If you are going to paint cabinet doors, try rubbing a small amount of Vaseline on the hinges, it will make removing the paint easier.

"PAINT DROPS KEEP FALLING ON YOUR HEAD...."
If you are going to paint a ceiling, try cutting a tennis ball in half and placing a half on the brush to catch the drips.

If you are sure you will use up all the paint in a can, try punching a few holes near the rim you are removing the paint from. The paint that is wiped off the brush will go back into the can.

"NOT A SHOCKING EXPERIENCE"
To remove a broken light bulb, turn off the electricity, then try placing a raw potato or small apple into the broken base and screwing out.

"CALL SMOKY"
If you have a charcoal filter in your rangehood it can be recharged by placing it in a 450^0 F. oven for 30 minutes after completely cleaning the frame. If there is any grease left on the frame it may catch on fire or smoke up the house.

When painting anything, make sure you dip a 3 X 5 index card into the paint to make it easier to match it at a later date if needed.

Old nuts and bolts make excellent sinkers when you are going fishing.

"STATIC ELECTRICITY"
If a pin or needle will not penetrate an article, try rubbing it in your hair before trying it again.

"I CAN SEE A RAINBOW"
If you want to add color to a campfire, try soaking pinecones in a solution of 1/2 gallon of water and 1/2 pound of Borax.

"REAL SHARPIE"
An easy way to sharpen scissors is to fold a piece of aluminum foil 3-4 times, then cut through it several times.

"BUY A NEW LID"
If you lose a top knob to a saucepan lid, try placing a screw with the thread side up into the hole then attaching a cork on it.

"NO NEED FOR THE TANNING LOTION"
If your flashlight batteries are becoming weak while on a camping trip, try placing them in the sunlight for 6-8 hours, this should give them back some additional life.

Hair dryer cords can be kept neat using ponytail holders.

Place salt on fireplace logs to reduce the soot in the house.

"A SWEETER YULE"
To preserve your Christmas tree for a few extra days, try adding a small amount of sugar or Pinesol to the water.

"SMOOTHIE"
When applying wallpaper, try using a paint roller instead of a sponge to smooth the paper out.

"HOP, SCOTCH"
If you need to paint steps, try painting every other step, when those are dry go back and paint the rest. This will allow you continued access to the upstairs.

"COLA WORKS GREAT TOO"
If your having a problem with a rusty nut or bolt, try placing a few drops of ammonia or hydrogen peroxide on it for 30 minutes.

"MAY HAVE A NEGATIVE EFFECT"
If you run out of salt or sand to deice you walkway, try using kitty litter. Keep the cat in the house!

"FOR SAFETY'S SAKE"
If you want to fireproof your Christmas tree, try spraying a mixture of 8 ounces boric acid in one gallon of water on the tree then allow to dry.

If you need to clean your gutters, try using an old fan belt. It has excellent flexibility, and is firm enough to do the job without scrapping the paint off.

Linoleum or floor tiles are excellent for covering the tops of picnic tables.

Electrical cords should be stored in cardboard tubes from rolls of paper towels. Then label them as to which appliance they go to.

Windows will slide more easily if you slide a bar of soap across the track occasionally.

"RUST PREVENTION"
If you place a few mothballs, a piece of chalk, or a piece of charcoal in your toolbox you will never have any rust on the tools.

To reduce fireplace smoking, try placing a brick under each leg of the grate.

"OUCH"
Use a split piece of old garden hose to cover the blades of a saw when storing it to be safe.

"GOING DOWN?"
If you need to use a ladder on soft earth, try placing a coffee can under each leg.

If you need to store furniture or chairs outdoors, place a large plastic bag over them.

"IT WON'T MAKE THE ICE GROW"
A lawn seeder or fertilizer spreader make an ideal unit for scattering sand or salt on ice.

"FILLER UP"
If you have a small hole in a window screen, try using a number of layers of clear nail polish.

"MR. CLEAN"
If you place masking tape on the rim of a paint can before pouring the paint out, you can remove the tape later and the rim will be clean.

"LUMPLESS PAINT"
If you have lumps in your paint can, try cutting a piece of screen the size of the can and allowing it to settle to the bottom, it will carry the lumps to the bottom.

When painting ceilings, try wearing a pair of old plastic goggles.

Squeaky door and cabinet hinges as well as sticky locks can be sprayed with a non-stick vegetable spray.

"FOUR EYES"
If you need to get a closer look at your roof or second story, try using a pair of binoculars instead of a ladder.

"FINDING A REAL STUD"
If you don't have a stud finder, try using a compass, holding it level with the floor and at a right angle to the wall. Then slowly move the compass along the surface of the wall, when the needle moves that's where you will find a stud.

"HOW TO GET A RUN IN YOUR PANTYHOSE"
Whenever you are using sandpaper to finish a wood surface, try placing an old nylon stocking over your hand and running it over the surface, the slightest rough spot will be found.

Before you shovel snow, try rubbing candle wax on the shovel. This will cause the snow to slide off easier, it's a toss up between this and the vegetable oil.

To avoid getting locked out of your house, try placing an extra key in a plastic baggie and placing it under a rock in the garden or bury it behind a plant or tree.

"DRIP, DRIP, DRIP"
If your worried about your water lines freezing just leave one of the taps running very slightly to avoid the problem. If you have a two story house, open one on the first floor.

Using a hand moisturizer when painting or doing other dirty chores, will prevent dirt and paint from seeping into your skins pores making personal cleanup easier.

"HANDY RULER"
Remember a dollar bill is 6 inches long and almost 3 inches wide.

Varnish never needs stirring. Stirring only creates air bubbles which may ruin a smooth finish.

"ODE DE CEDAR CHEST"
If you would like the original cedar odor from an old cedar chest, try rubbing the inner surface lightly with a fine sandpaper.

"ALL-PURPOSE, OF COURSE"
If you are paining old woodwork that has small holes that need patching, try filling the holes with flour and some of the paint, it will harden and will not be noticeable.

If you are having problems with sticky drawers, try rubbing a candle along the tops of the runners.

"A CHILLING SOLUTION"
If you don't feel like cleaning a roller. place it in a plastic bag and place in the freezer. This will keep it moist and usable for a few days.

"AND A LONNNNG EXTENSION CORD"
If your pipes freeze and do not burst, try using a hair dryer to defrost them.

Lightweight materials that need to be glued together are easily held in place with spring clothespins.

When your paint brushes harden, try softening them by soaking them in full strength white vinegar them cleaning with a comb.

Empty nail polish bottles make excellent holders for touch-up paints.

If you have grease spots after removing old wallpaper, try applying a coat of clear varnish to the spots. The grease won't soak through to the new paper.

"BALLOONING"
If you are going to store a partially used can of paint, try placing a blown-up balloon the size of the space in the can. It will reduce the air in the can and keep the paint fresher longer.

"SUN-DRYING YOUR BOTTOM"
If you have a cane-bottomed chair that has loosened, try applying very hot water to the underside and allowing the chair to stand in direct sunlight until it dries.

"A WASTE OF A COOL ONE"
If you wish to "frost" a bathroom window, use a solution of 1 cup of "Lite" beer mixed in 4 tablespoons of Epsom salts. Paint the mixture on the window, it will wash off easily.

Bathroom fixtures should be painted with a special epoxy paint because of exposure to moisture.

"A SHINING EXAMPLE"
Enamel or oil paint can easily be removed from your hands with paste floor wax then washing with soap and water.

To prevent a skin forming on top of the paint, try placing a piece of waxed paper the size of the opening on top of the paint.

After you clean out a paint brush rub a few drops of vegetable oil into the bristles to keep them soft.

"I WONDER WHERE THE YELLOW WENT...."
If you add 7-10 drops of black paint to each quart of white paint it will not yellow.

"TILL YOUR OLD AND GRAY"
If you "weather" wood before applying stain, the satin will last years longer.

"DON'T CRACK-UP"
To prevent plaster walls from cracking when driving a nail in for a picture hanger, try placing a small piece of tape over the spot before hammering in the nail.

Chapter 4

General Cleaning and Stain Removal

GENERAL RULES TO REMOVE STAINS

Never wash any fabric before attempting to remove the stain, Washing in a detergent may actually set the stain and make it impossible to remove later.

Stains on washable fabrics should be treated as soon as possible. Remember, fresh stains will come out more easily than old ones. Non-washable items that normally go to the cleaners should be taken to the cleaners as soon as possible. Identify the stain for the dry cleaner. If you know what the stain is be sure and tell them.

When trying to remove stains at home, make sure you do it on a clean, well-lighted work surface. Always use fresh clean rags or a towel.

REMOVING STAINS WITH FOOD

Clothing Stains

"RHUB-A-DUB-DUB"
Rust stains on clothing can be removed with rhubarb, just use the hot juice from 5-6 stalks.

Cornstarch will remove blood stains. Use a paste, then wash in warm, soapy water.

Rust stains can be removed by wetting the areas with lemon juice, then sprinkle with a small amount of salt and allow to sit in direct sunlight for 30-45 minutes.

A scorch can be removed by rubbing a raw onion on the scorched area and allowing the onion juice to soak in thoroughly for at least 2-3 hours before washing.

Blood stains may be cleaned with club soda.

Tomato juice will remove ink spots on clothing. Allow to soak for 20 minutes before washing.

A slice of white bread will often remove makeup smudges from dark clothing.

"THE BUNDY SOLUTION"
If your white socks are getting dingy, just boil a pot of water, add 2 slices of lemon or 1/2 teaspoon of lemon juice and soak for 10 minutes. Then wash as you normally would.

Any cloth material that has chewing gum stuck to it can be placed in the freezer for about an hour. The gum should easily be removed.

Food Related Stains

Fruit and berry stains can be removed by pouring very hot water with salt added on the stain as soon as possible. The longer the stain remains, the more difficult it will be to remove. Wash the area with milk before placing it in the washing machine, Milk is a natural bleaching agent.

Fruit juice can be removed from almost any fabric by pouring at least 3 quarts of boiling water slowly on the stain.

Egg stains will respond to cold water only, hot water will only set the stain.

Coffee and tea stains can be removed with white vinegar or egg yolk mixed with warm water.

Grease stains can be removed with talcum powder if they are fresh. You can also try rubbing the stain with lard before washing in a detergent.

Grease in your carpet may be removed by rubbing cornmeal into the stain and allowing it to stand for 12 hours.

Juice, coffee and tea stains may be removed by scrubbing them vigorously with a paste made from baking soda and water. This may also work on cigarette stains.

To control the mold in your breadbox, try washing it occasionally with a mild solution of vinegar and water.

Stains Around The Kitchen

If your dishwasher has stains, try filling your dispenser with powdered Gatorade and run it through a cycle.

Water in which onions have been cooked will clean brass pots.

Orange juice can be used to clean chrome.

To make your porcelain sink look like new, place paper towels on the bottom and sides, then saturate with household bleach. Clean after 1/2 hour to 1 hour.

To remove water spots from stainless steel, place alcohol or white vinegar on a cloth and rub.

"BLACK-OUT"
Margarine or a paste of baking soda and water will remove tar or heel marks off vinyl surfaces.

To clean stains from aluminum pots, try boiling rhubarb in the pot until the stain disappears. Never use the rhubarb leaves, only the stalks.

"SQUEAKY CLEAN"
A good cleaner that won't leave a film on tile is a mixture of white vinegar and water. Use approximately 1/4 cup of vinegar to 1 gallon of warm water.

Lime deposits can be removed from teapots by filling the kettle with equal parts of vinegar and water, bringing it to a boil and allowing it to stand overnight.

After boiling potatoes, use the water to polish silver. Just place the silver in the warm water. Place a washcloth on the bottom of the pot.

Wash silver or silverplate soon after it comes in contact with eggs, salad dressing, olives, vinegar, and other foods that have been seasoned with salt. These foods will cause silver to tarnish faster.

Your oven can be cleaned easily with baking soda.

Clean crayon marks off the walls with baking soda on a damp cloth, it has just enough abrasive action to do the job without causing damage.

To remove stains from enamel pots, mix bleach with water and boil in the pot until the stain is gone.

Corningware cookware can be cleaned by filling them with water and then dropping in two denture cleaning tablets. Allow to stand for 30-45 minutes.

"ANTI-FREEZE"

In winter, add denatured alcohol to your window cleaning solution to prevent freezeups.

Woodwork is easily cleaned with cold tea.

Silver polish will remove coffee stains from plastic cups.

To clean an oven spill, sprinkle the area with salt immediately, then when the oven has cooled, just clean with a damp cloth.

An excellent way to clean a butcher block is with a plastic window scraper.

To shine chrome fixture, try rubbing them with newspaper while they are still damp. Baby oil and a soft cloth works well.

If plastic has burned on an appliance, try cleaning it with lighter fluid.

Stainless steel pots will remain shiny if you rub them with a piece of lemon rind, then wash in warm soapy water. If you have a problem, try adding a small amount of salt to the lemon.

If you coat the bottom of pots used over an open fire with shaving cream before using, the black marks will come off easier.

If you are going to use a commercial stain removal substance, be sure and follow directions carefully.

Always test a stain remover on an area of the fabric that will not show to be sure of the colorfastness of the fabric. Allow the product to stand on the area for at least 3-5 minutes before rinsing off. If there are any changes in the fabrics color, do not use.

When treating a spot, it should be placed face down on paper towel, then apply the stain remover to the underside of the garment, allowing the stain to be forced to the surface and not back through the fabric. The paper towel should be replaced a number of times if it is a tough stain to remove.

If you are going to use a bleach product, never use it on a colored garment. It is necessary to bleach the whole garment to avoid uneven color removal. If there is a change in color it will at least be uniform.

As soon as the stain is removed, launder immediately with your favorite laundry detergent. This will also remove the residues from the stain remover.

STAIN REMOVAL PRODUCTS

Prompt treatment is the key to stain removal, and it would be wise to have the supplies on hand at all times. The following list are some of the more common ingredients needed for most stain removal, however, more natural stain and general cleaning preparations are recommended.

BLEACHES	MISCELLANEOUS REMOVERS
Chlorine bleach	*Ammonia*
Fabric color remover	*Rust stain remover*
Non-chlorine, all fabric	*White vinegar*
bleach	

DETERGENTS	SOLVENTS
Enzyme detergent	*Dry cleaner spot remover*
Enzyme presoaker	*Nail polish remover*
Liquid detergent	*Rubbing alcohol*
	Turpentine

SOAPS	SUPPLIES
Laundry detergent	*Clean white cloths*
White bar soap	*Paper towels*

Any of the above products that cannot be found at the supermarket will be found at any drug store.

CAUTION

Some stain removal materials are inflammable, while others are poison or toxic. Store them safely and use with care.

Keep stain removal supplies out of reach of children. They should be stored in closed containers with childproof lids and in a cool, dry location away from any food products.

Read the labels and follow directions. Heed all label warnings and always try to store them in their original containers.

Empty and wash all containers immediately after using them. It is best to store stain removal supplies in glass or unchipped poroclain containers. Solvents will ruin plastic containers. Rusty containers should never be used.

Be careful, never allow chemicals near your face and especially your eyes. Wash any spilled chemicals off your hands as soon as possible.

Use chemicals that give off vapors in a well ventilated location, preferably outside. Try not to breathe the vapors.

Never use a solvent near an open fire or an electrical outlet.

Never add solvents directly into the washing machine. Always allow a solvent-treated fabric dry before washing or placing it into the dryer.

Never mix stain removal materials with each other, especially ammonia and chlorine bleach. If it necessary to use both, make sure one is thoroughly rinsed out before adding the other.

RECIPES FOR SAFE CLEANING PRODUCTS

The following recipes are safe when mixed in the quantities indicated below. The mixing of other household chemicals may be dangerous.

All-Purpose Household Cleaner

Add 1 teaspoon of any liquid soap and 1 teaspoon of trisodium phosphate (TSP) to 1 quart of warm water.

This is a very effective cleaner for many cleaning jobs including countertops and walls. However, try an area of the wall that will not show before using in case your walls are painted with a poor quality water-based flat paint.

Chlorine Bleach

Best to use a hydrogen peroxide-based bleach.

Degreaser (engines, etc.)

Best to use a water-based cleaner that is well diluted instead of kerosene, turpentine, or a commercial engine degreaser. These are available in part stores and the label should read *"nonflammable," "nontoxic,"* or *"store at temperatures above freezing."* These will be water-based products and will do the job.

Degreaser (kitchen, grill)

Add 2 tablespoons of TSP to 1 gallon of hot water or use a non-chlorinated scouring cleanser with a scouring or steel wool pad.

Fabric Softener

Fabrics produced from natural fibers do not need fabric softeners only synthetics.

Floor Cleaner

Vinyl Floors - Use 1/2 cup of white vinegar to 1 gallon of warm water.

Wood Floors - May be damp moped with a mild liquid soap.

Furniture Polish

Mineral oil may be used, however, most wood surfaces may be cleaned with a damp cloth.

Oven Cleaner

Mix 2 tablespoons of baking soda or TSP in 1 gallon of warm water and scrub with a very fine steel wool pad (0000). Rubber gloves should be worn and the area rinsed well. For difficult baked-on areas, try scrubbing with a pumice stone.

If all of the above fails, try using an oven cleaner that states *"no caustic fumes"* on the label.

Glass Cleaner

Use a 2-3 cup spray bottle with 1/2 teaspoon of liquid soap, 3 tablespoons of white vinegar and 2 cups of water.

If the windows are very dirty, try using more liquid soap.

Laundry Detergent

Use laundry soap in place of the detergents. Washing soda may be used in place of a softener. An alternate would be to use detergents with no added bleaches or softeners. Bleach should be used in moderation when needed.

Mildew Remover

Scrub the area with baking soda or if very stubborn with TSP.

Scouring Powder

Baking soda will work well in most instances.

Toilet Bowl Cleaner

Use a non-chlorinated scouring powder and a stiff brush. To remove hard water deposits, pour white vinegar or a commercial citric acid-based toilet bowl cleaner into the toilet and allow to sit for several hours or overnight before scrubbing.

NOTE: Washing soda and TSP are caustic and should be kept out of the reach of children.

FABRIC ADVICE

It is best to know the fiber content in clothing items. If sewn in labels are to be removed a note should be made as to which item it was removed from.

Any durable press or polyester fabric such as a Dacron, holds soil very well and especially stains. A dry cleaning solvent will work the best. If the stain remains after the first treatment, try once more. If the fabric has been washed or has been placed in a dryer, the stain may never come out.

Never use chlorine bleach on silk, wool, or Spandex.

Never remove a stain from leather, take it to a dry cleaners to send to an expert.

STAIN REMOVAL FROM WASHABLE FABRICS

A number of stains can be removed right in your washing machine. Laundry detergents that state that they contain enzymes will provide the best cleaning and stain removal. Enzyme presoak products provide extra cleaning and stain removal for fabrics that may have a more difficult stain.

An enzyme detergent or enzyme presoak product should be able to remove the following common stains:

Blood	*Gravy*	*Body soils*	*Egg*
Fruits	*Milk*	*Chocolate*	*Grass*
Cream soups	*Baby formula*	*Puddings*	*Vegetables*
Baby foods	*Ice cream*	*Most food soils*	

Yellowed fabrics can be restored and even old unknown stains may be removed by first soaking in an enzyme presoak product (Proctor & Gamble has excellent ones) such as Biz and then laundering.

Remember, even the best enzyme detergent or enzyme presoak product is not capable of removing all types of stains. A number of grease soils and highly colored stains may require special pretreatment before laundering. Since many stains require a variety of different soil removal treatments and techniques, it is important to identify a stain before trying to remove it. A number of stains may actually be set if the wrong method is used.

The following stains will usually be removed with the following recommended methods:

STAIN	METHOD OF REMOVAL
BEVERAGE	Sponge the area with cold water or soak then sponge again. Launder with oxygen bleach and the hottest water that is safe for the fabric.
BLOOD	Soak the fabric in cold water as soon as possible. If the stain persists, soak in warm water with a presoak product before laundering.
CANDLE WAX	The surface wax should be removed with a dull knife. The item should then be placed stain face down on paper towels and then sponge the remaining stain with dry cleaning solvent. Allow to dry and the launder. If traces of color from the wax remains, try soaking it in Biz or an oxygen bleach before laundering again. If the color is still present, try laundering again using chlorine bleach, if the fabric is chlorine bleach safe.
CATSUP\TOMATO PRODUCTS	Remove excess with a dull knife, then soak in cold water then launder using the hottest water the fabric will stand.

CHEWING GUM **ADHESIVE TAPE** **RUBBER CEMENT**	First apply ice to the stain to harden it. Remove excess stain material with a dull knife. Place the item face down on paper towels and sponge with a dry cleaning solvent.
CHOCOLATE\COCOA	Soak in cold water then launder with oxygen bleach using the hottest water the fabric will stand.
COFFEE/TEA	Best to soak in Biz or an oxygen bleach using the hottest water that is safe for the stained fabric then launder. If the stain persists, try laundering again using chlorine bleach if it is safe to do so.
COSMETICS	Dampen stain and rub gently with a white bar soap, then rinse well and launder.
CRAYON	If there are only a few spots they can be treated the same as candle wax. If there are many items that are stained, first wash the items with hot water and laundry soap (e.g. Ivory Snow) and 1 cup of baking soda. If the spots remain, have the clothes dry cleaned.
DEODORANTS AND **ANTIPERSPIRANTS**	Apply white vinegar, then rub and rinse. If the stain remains, try saturating the area with rubbing alcohol, rinse then soak in Biz or an oxygen bleach and launder. If the stain remains wash in chlorine bleach if safe for fabric.
DYE TRANSFER	If you have white fabrics that have picked up dye from a colored garment that "bled", try restoring the white by using a fabric color remover. Launder if any of the dye remains using chlorine bleach, if it is safe for the fabric.
EGG/MEAT JUICE	Remove excess with a dull knife then soak in cold water. Launder in oxygen bleach in very hot water.
FABRIC SOFTENERS	These stains usually result from accidental spills and can be removed by rubbing the area with a piece of cloth moistened with bar soap then launder.

FORMULA   Soak in warm water then launder with oxygen bleach and the hottest water that is safe for the fabric.

FRUIT\FRUIT JUICES   Soak in cold water before laundering.

GRASS   The green area should be sponged with denatured alcohol before washing in very hot water and oxygen bleach.

GREASE STAINS   The stained area should be placed face down on paper towels. Dry cleaning solvent should be placed on the back side of the stain and then brushed from the center of the stain to the outer edges using a clean white cloth. Moisten the stain with warm water and rub with a bar soap or a mild liquid detergent, then rinse and launder.

GUM   Rub with ice and carefully remove the gum with a dull knife before laundering.

INK STAINS   For removal of ball point stains, place the stain face down on paper towels and sponge the back of the stain with dry cleaning solvent. If there is some ink left, try rubbing the area with moistened bar soap, rinse and then launder.

For any other type of ink stains, just try and remove the stain with a dampened cloth and bar soap, rinse and soak in Biz or an oxygen bleach using very hot water. If the stain won't come out, try using chlorine bleach, if the fabric is safe. Some permanent inks may never be removed.

INK, FELT TIP   Rub the area with Fantastic or Mr. Clean, rinse and repeat if necessary. May be impossible to remove.

IODINE   Rinse the fabric from the underside with cool water, then soak in a solution of fabric color remover, rinse and then launder.

LIPSTICK   The stain should be placed face down on paper towels and then sponged with dry cleaning solvent replacing the paper towels frequently while the color is being removed. Moisten the stain with cool water and then rub with bar soap, rinse and launder.

MILDEW   The fabric should be laundered using chlorine bleach if it is safe for the fabric. If not, try soaking it in oxygen bleach and then laundering.

MILK   The fabric should be rinsed in cold water as soon as possible, then washed in cold water using a liquid detergent.

MUSTARD   Moisten stain with cool water, then rub with bar soap, rinse and launder using a chlorine bleach, if it is safe for the fabric. If not soak in Biz or an oxygen detergent using very hot water, then launder. It may take several treatments to remove all of the stain.

NAIL POLISH   The fabric stain should be placed face down on paper towels then sponge the back of the stain frequently and repeat until the stain disappears then launder. Never use nail polish remover on fabric, best to have them dry cleaned.

PAINT   Try to treat the stain while it is still wet. Latex, acrylic, and water based paints cannot be removed once they have dried. While they are wet, rinse in warm water to flush the paint out then launder.

Oil-based paints can be removed with a solvent that is recommended on the paint can. If it does not give this information, try using turpentine, rinse and rub with bar soap, then launder.

PERSPIRATION Moisten the stain and rub with bar soap. Be gentle as perspiration may weaken some fibers, especially silk. Most fabrics should be presoaked in Biz or an enzyme detergent and then laundered in hot water and chlorine bleach, if the fabric is safe.

PERFUME	Same as beverages.
RUST	Never use chlorine bleach on rust, apply a rust stain remover, rinse then launder. You can also use a fabric color remover and the launder or if the stain is really stubborn, try using 1 ounce of oxalic acid crystals dissolved in 1 gallon of water, mixed in a plastic container, then rinse and launder.
SCORCH	Soak the fabric in a strong solution of Biz and an oxygen bleach using very hot water if safe for the fabric, then launder. If the scorch remains, it will be necessary to repeat the procedure using chlorine bleach, if the fabric will take it.
SHOE POLISH	Try applying a mixture of 1 part rubbing alcohol and 2 parts of water for colored fabrics and only the straight alcohol for whites.
SUEDE	Rain spots can be removed by lightly rubbing the area with an emery board. If there are grease spots, try using white vinegar or club soda then blot out the stain. Afterwards brush with a suede brush.
TAR	The area should be rubbed with kerosene until all the tar is dissolved, then wash as usual. Test a small area first to be sure it is color fast.
TOBACCO	Moisten the stain and rub with bar soap, rinse and then launder. If the stain persists, try soaking it in Biz or an oxygen detergent, then launder. As a last resort use chlorine bleach, if the fabric is safe.
URINE, VOMIT, MUCOUS	Soak the fabric in Biz or an enzyme detergent, launder using chlorine bleach, if safe for the fabric. If not use an oxygen bleach with a detergent.
WINE/SOFT DRINKS	Soak the fabric with Biz or an oxygen bleach using very hot water then launder. Use chlorine bleach if need and the fabric is safe.

If you wish to use less detergent and save money, try using slivers of old soaps placed in a sock with the neck tied. Place the sock into the washer and you will use less detergent.

To colorfast a possible problem garment, try soaking the colored garment in cold, salty water for 30 minutes before laundering.

After washing apiece of clothing with a zipper that has given you problems, try rubbing beeswax on the zipper to resolve the problem and remove any grime that has accumulated.

"THE OLD BUBBLE MACHINE"
Placing too much soap in the washing machine can cause problems. If this happens, just pour 2 tablespoons of white vinegar or a capful of fabric softener into the machine to neutralize some of the soap.

"BEGONE OLD SOAP"
When washing clothes, to be sure that all the soap has been removed, try adding 1 cup of white vinegar to the rinse cycle. The vinegar will dissolve the alkalinity in detergents as well as giving the clothes a pleasant fragrance.

"THE GREEN, GREEN, GRASS OF HOME"
Grass stains will be easily removed with toothpaste, scrub in with a toothbrush before washing. Another method is to rub the stain with molasses and allow to stand overnight, then wash with regular dish soap by itself. If all else fails, try methyl alcohol, but be sure the color is set, best to try an area that won't show first.

Spic and Span placed in the washer is a great grease remover, 1/4 cup is all that is needed.

To avoid ironing many different types of clothes, just remove them from the dryer the second it stops and fold or hang up immediately.

Washing colored material for the first time may be risky unless you wash it in Epsom salts. One gallon of water to 1 teaspoon is all that is needed. The material will not run.

An excellent spot remover can be made using 2 parts of water to 1 part rubbing alcohol.

To remove difficult dirt, such as collars, mix 1/3 cup of water with 1/3 cup of liquid detergent and 1/3 cup of ammonia. Place the ingredients in a spray bottle. Rubbing shampoo into the area may also work.

To keep corduroy garments from retaining lint, turn them inside out when washing.

To avoid hairballs on acrylic sweaters, turn them inside out when washing them.

Iodine stains can be removed using a mixture of baking soda and water. Allow to remain on for about 30 minutes rub with mild action.

Butter will remove tar from clothing, just rub until its gone. The butter is easily removed with any type of spray and wash product.

Rubbing alcohol may remove a number of ink pen stains.

If you wash slipcovers, be sure and replace them when they are still damp. They will fit better and will not need to be ironed.

If sweater cuffs are stretched, dip them in hot water and dry with a hairdryer.

Tea stains on tablecloths can be removed with glycerin, try leaving it sit overnight before washing.

Candle wax on tablecloths can be removed by freezing with ice cubes.

Lace doilies should be hand washed in sour milk for the best results.

If you have a problem with small burrs on sweaters, try using a disposable razor to remove them.

If you are washing a wool garment, be careful not to pull on it. Wool is very weak when wet. Lay the garment on a towel and roll it up and squeeze the excess water out.

If you have a difficult blood stain, try making a paste of meat tenderizer and cold water. Sponge on the area and allow to stand for 20-30 minutes. Rinse in cold water, then wash. Hydrogen peroxide may also work.

Corn starch will remove most grease spots. Just rub it into the area and leave for 10-15 minutes.

To clean stuffed animals that cannot be placed in the washer, just place them in a cloth bag and add baking soda, then shake.

White flour will clean white gloves, just rub.

Lipstick stains will clean out of clothes by using Vaseline.

If you shrink a woolen garment, try soaking it in a hair cream rinse. This will usually make them easy to stretch back into the original size. Another method is to dissolve 1 ounce of Borax in 1 teaspoon of hot water then add it to 1 gallon of warm water. Place the garment in, stretch back to shape then rinse it in 1 gallon of warm water with 2 tablespoons of white vinegar added.

When you are doing a small wash load tear the fabric-softening sheet in half for the same results.

"A SOLID FACT"
To make your own spray starch, purchase 1 bottle of liquid starch concentrate and mix one part of liquid starch to 1 part of water, use a spray bottle.

If you lose buttons regularly on children's clothing, try sewing them on with dental floss.

If your iron is sticking, try running it over a piece of paper with sprinkled salt on it.

"WELL SEASONED CURTAINS"
Water stained fabrics should be placed in salt water and soaked until the stain is gone.

If you prefer not to use bleach, try substituting 3 tablespoons of hydrogen peroxide to the washload.

Always remove buttons before discarding a garment. They may come in handy at a later date.

Cleaning silk flowers is easy if you place them in a plastic bag with 2 tablespoons of salt and shake vigorously while holding on to the stems. Salt tends to attract the dust.

When ironing, always iron the fabrics that require a cool temperature first as the iron heats up.

Mildew on shower curtains can be removed with a mixture of 1/2 cup bleach, 1/2 cup powdered detergent, and 1 gallon of water. To prolong the life of shower curtains add 1 cup of white vinegar to the final rinse.

To prevent jeans from fading (if you want to) soak the jeans in 1/2 cup of white vinegar and 2 quarts of water for 1 hour before you wash them for the first time.

Blue jeans should only be washed in cold water then placed in a moderate heat dryer for only 10 minutes. Then they should be placed on a wooden hanger to continue drying.

If you would like to save dollars on dry cleaning of wool blankets, try washing them in a mild dishwasher soap on a very gently cycle then air fluff to dry.

"NO ONE WILL EVER KNOW"
If you scorch a garment, try removing the scorch with a cloth that has been dampened with vinegar. Only use a warm iron, not too hot. Cotton scorch marks tend to respond better to peroxide.

A sheet of aluminum foil placed underneath the ironing board cover will allow the heat to be retained for a longer period of time.

"BUTTON, BUTTON...."
Always remember to place a small amount of clear nail polish in the center of every button on a new garment. This seals the threads and they will last longer.

"A SHOCKING SITUATION"
Pipecleaner dipped in white vinegar should be used to clean the holes in the iron after it is completely cool. Make sure it is unplugged.

Glass cleaner sometimes makes an excellent spot remover if you need something in a hurry.

Washing machines should be cleaned occasionally with warm water and 1 cup of vinegar. A short cycle is all that is needed.

If you want to whiten your whites, try adding a cup of dishwasher detergent to the washer. Even whitens sweat socks.

A sticky zipper will respond to a rubbing with a lead pencil. Does an excellent job of lubricating it.

If a button comes off, try reattaching it with the wire from a twist tie.

If you use a thimble to sew or sort papers, try wetting your finger before you place the thimble on. This creates a suction and holds the thimble on.

When you wash you sneakers, spray them with a spray starch to help them resist becoming soiled.

"DIRTY BOTTOM"
If the bottom of the iron gets dirty, just clean it with a steel wool soap pad. If you want to make it shiny again, just run a piece of waxed paper over it.

Rust marks on clothing can be removed with lemon juice and a small amount of salt easily rubbed in and then allowed to sit in the sun for 2 hours.

Red wine can be removed from a tablecloth by wetting the area with club soda and allowing it to stand for 20 minutes before washing.

To dry the insides of shoes or sneakers, try placing the blower end of the vacuum hose inside.

If you have problems with your shoelaces becoming undone, just dampen them before tying them.

Silk clothing should be hand washed using cool water with Ivory liquid soap. When you rinse, try adding a small amount of lanolin to help preserve the material. Always drip dry, never place the garment in the dryer, then iron using a soft piece of cloth.

Cold water should always be used in the rinse cycle to help the clothes retain their shape and color.

Chapter 5

Personal Grooming Hints

"SLIPPERY WHEN WET?"
For an inexpensive bath oil, try using sunflower oil and either lavender or rose petal herb.

"A REVIVAL"
Hair brushes and combs may be revived by soaking them in a pot of warm water and 1 tablespoon of baking soda or ammonia.

"REFLECTING"
If you lose a contact lens, turn the lights off and use a flashlight, the len will reflect the light.

"RING AROUND THE FINGER"
If you are unable to remove a ring, try placing your hand in a bowl of very cold water for a few seconds.

If you would like to keep dirt from getting under your nails when you are working in the garden, just rub your nails over a bar of soap before starting work.

Laundry detergent makes an excellent hand cleaner for very hard to clean hands.

"A CUP OF JOE"
If you have red hair or are a brunette, try rinsing your hair with black coffee, then clear water to add luster.

"FEET ADE"
If you want to freshen your feet, try using a few fresh lemon slices. Just rub them in.

"TASTES GOOD TOO"
An inexpensive facial treatment is as follows: for normal to somewhat oily skin, use 1 cup of yogurt, 1 teaspoon of fresh lemon juice, 1 teaspoon of fresh orange juice, and 1 teaspoon of carrot juice. Blend all ingredients well and apply to your face for 10-15 minutes then rinse with warm water.

"NOT VERY APPETIZING"
Miracle Whip Salad Dressing will remove dry, dead skin from elbows, knees, and feet easily.

"NEW USE FOR BREAKFAST FOOD"
For a great facial scrub, try using a paste of oatmeal and water. Apply the paste then allow to dry until your skin feels tight. Then remove it with your fingers with a back and forth motion to remove the dead skin.

Perfume should be stored in the refrigerator if your not going to use it up over a reasonable period of time, approximately 30 days.

"GREAT FOR HALLOWEEN"
A great facial can be had by mashing 1/2 avocado and spreading it thickly on your face. Wait 20 minutes, then wash off with warm water.

Place a small amount of vegetable oil on the threads of nail polish bottles and the lid won't stick.

"YUK!"
To make your own deodorant, mix 2 teaspoons of baking soda, 2 teaspoons of petroleum jelly, and 2 teaspoons of talcum powder.

"FRUITPASTE"
To remove the yellow from your teeth, try using mashed fresh strawberries to brush with.

For a bad sunburn, try making a paste of baking soda and water, works almost as good as the white vinegar.

If you want to make a bar of soap last longer, try unwrapping it before you use it and allow it to dry out.

To add shine to your hair and to remove shampoo buildup, try adding 2 tablespoons of apple cider vinegar to the rinse water.

Before polishing your nails, try applying a small amount of white vinegar to your nails. They will stay shiny longer and it will clean them.

Baby oil will do the same job as a fancy cleansing cream at about a third of the price.

For puffy eyes, place slices of cucumber on your eyes.

If you want your perfume to last longer, try applying a small amount of petroleum jelly first on the area.

"SKIN-ADE"
Skin blemishes can be cleared up quickly by dabbing them with lemon juice 4-6 times per day.

If you want to restore the natural acid balance to your skin, try using 1/2 cup of apple cider vinegar in a basin of water. Splash it on your face the allow it to dry before removing with a towel.

To make an inexpensive shampoo mix 1/2 cup white vinegar, 1/2 cup dish detergent, 1/4 cup water with 2 teaspoons of mayonnaise (not low-cal).

To remove garden stains from your hands, try placing about 1/2 teaspoon of sugar with the soap lather when you wash your hands, you will be amazed how easy the stains are removed.

"THE MAD SCIENTIST"
The formula for a good liquid hand soap is: 1 4oz.. bar of soap, preferably one that has a moisturizing cream, and 3 cups of water. Grate the soap as fine as possible then add the water. Microwave on high till dissolved stirring every few minutes, then allow to cool before using.

If you want your makeup to last longer, try spraying your face first with mineral water and allowing it to dry.

If you break your lipstick, try heating the broken ends over a matchstick until they are soft, place them together and place in the freezer.

If hangnails are bothersome, try rubbing vitamin E oil around the cuticles.

"SHADES OF LAWRENCE WELK"
To make your own bubble bath liquid, try placing soap slivers in a porous drawstring bag. Attach the bag to the tap while the water is filling the tub and instant bubble bath. Place herbs in the bag for a pleasant fragrance.

Chapter 6

Fitness and Excercise

METABOLISM, WHAT IS IT?

Metabolism is the process by which the body releases energy derived from nutrients. It is the sum of all chemical reactions of the body's cells. The cells produce the energy in the form of heat, or in muscle cells in the form of mechanical work.

The basic fuels are proteins, carbohydrates, and fats which are converted into glucose by the liver, then travel to the cells for chemical processing by way of the Krebs cycle (complex biochemical pathway) and turned into usable energy.

Metabolic rates vary from individual to individual dependent on a person's age, sex, body size, activity level or thyroid activity. Metabolism is first in line when the body distributes the energy it produces, the body must have energy to run the heart, etc. before anything else. Physical activity energy is only available after the more important needs are met.

A common question asked physicians is how to increase the metabolic rate as we age. There is still no magic pill that has been invented that will raise the metabolic rate naturally. Recently, a number of supplement companies claim to have invented a number of different herbal combinations and special nutrients, but none have ever proved true in double-blind studies performed by a major university or testing laboratory.

Unfortunately for women, men tend to have a higher metabolic rate throughout their lives. This may be due to the male's greater percentage of lean tissue. The more muscle tissue a person has will also increase their metabolic rate.

The thyroids gland level of activity has a direct influence on the basal metabolic rate. The thyroid secretes a hormone, thyroxin, the lower the amount secreted, the lower the energy requirement for the running of the body.

The following is an example of the total energy output by a moderately active homemaker:

Energy for basal metabolism	1,400 calories
Energy for moderate physical activity	500 calories
Energy to burn 2,000 calories	<u>200 calories</u>
	2,100 calories

When more calories are burned than are ingested weight loss will occur.

THE ENERGY BALANCE

Approximately 70% of all food consumed is utilized in keeping the essential life processes going, such as the heart pumping, liver functioning, etc. The other 30% is turned into "external energy" and used in conscious activities, such as walking, playing sports or working.

The actual energy value of foods are determined by their caloric content. A Kilocalorie is a measure of heat needed to raise the temperature of a liter of water one degree centigrade (a single calorie is a thousandth of a Kcal).

When we discuss energy balance the input/output theory of weight control usually comes up. This simply means if you burn more calories than you take in you will lose weight. This is of course, a true statement, however, it is still the type of calories you consume that will ultimately determine your actual level of health.

EXERCISE

Exercise is a must for everyone, regardless of your age. The type of exercise you do should be one you enjoy doing and one you will continue for an extended period of time. Many people have the initial motivation and good intentions in starting a program but end up doing exercise they don't enjoy and would never stick with.

It is not the intention of the following information to suggest one form of exercise over another, you need to choose the one that fits your lifestyle and one you will stick to for a long period of time. The easiest for most people is walking and this chapter will provide you with guidelines of a walking program.

Before starting any exercise program it would be best to have a complete physical from your physician, not just a series of tests by a local athletic club. If you will be walking, swimming, jogging or any very active exercise, a treadmill stress test is a must. A resting cardiogram is a poor test in detecting early heart disease or how your heart will respond to the exertion of exercise.

BENEFITS OF EXERCISE

Cardiovascular System
Exercise increases the efficiency of the cardiovascular system in several ways:

The heart grows stronger and pumps more blood with each stroke, reducing the number of strokes necessary.

It increases the number and size of your blood vessels as well as your total blood volume. Enhances oxygenation of your cells.

It increases your body's maximal oxygen consumption by increasing the efficiency of the red blood cells. By doing this, it improves the overall condition of the body, especially the heart, lungs, and blood vessels.

It improves the muscle tone of your blood vessels, changing them to strong and firm tissue, possibly reducing blood pressure.

Lungs
Improves the efficiency of the lungs, making them capable of processing more air with less effort.

Aging
Slows the aging process and physical deterioration that accompanies it.

Stress
Helps you relax more easily and develop a better self-image. Relieves the tension and stress of daily living.

Job
Allows you to get more work done at a lower fatigue level.

HEART RATE RESPONSE TO EXERCISE

Resting Heart Rate
The rate will vary widely from individual to individual and also within the individual from one observation to another. It is therefore meaningless to speak of a "normal heart rate." We may say that the average heart rate is 72 beats per minute, but cannot imply that a variation from this figure in either direction is borderline or abnormal.

To determine your own resting heart rate; first take your pulse, 3 times, either radial (side of wrist), or your carotid (side of neck), and count for a total of 60 seconds, average the three figures to give you, your resting pulse rate.

After 10 days of exercising, repeat the procedure to determine your new resting heart rate, If your new rate is lower than the first one, you are experiencing a positive training effect and are staring to get in condition.

Factors Affecting Heart Rate

AGE

Resting heart rate at birth is approximately 130 beats per minute. It gradually decreases until the teens where it averages out to about 72 beats per minute.

SEX

Resting heart rate in adult females is 5-10 beats faster than the average male.

SIZE

Resting heart rate in animals vary inversely with the size of the species. A canary may have a heart rate of 1,000 beats per minute, while an elephant is only 25 beats per minute.

POSTURE

A change from a sitting to a standing position may increase the heart rate 10-12 beats per minute.

FOOD

The ingestion of food affects the resting heart rate as well as the exercising heart rate. Both rates are higher during digestion than in the pre-consumption period.

EMOTIONS

Increases resting heart rate as well as exercising heart rate. It also tends to slow the recovery rate.

ENVIRONMENT

An increase in ambient temperature causes an increase in the exercising heart rate.

SMOKING

Even one cigarette will cause an increase in the resting heart rate.

Aerobics and Fitness

The term "aerobics" refers to the type of metabolism utilizing oxygen in the production of energy. It relates to modes of training that are designed to improve the efficiency of the body's oxygen exchange system. Thus, delivering more oxygen to the cells while improving the efficiency of the cardiovascular system (heart, lungs, and blood vessels).

The degree to which the cardiovascular system becomes more efficient (and healthier) is dependent upon the total work performed by a particular exercise and its effect on the system.

By gradually increasing the amount and intensity of an exercise program, your fitness level will increase accordingly.

The following is a listing of the most realistic aerobic activities for the average person in their order of aerobic value. Remember, however, these are <u>not recommended</u> prior to a physical evaluation.

EXERCISE	DURATION (MIN.)	TIMES PER WEEK
JOGGING 6 MPH	20	4
BICYCLING 12 MPH	30	5
SWIMMING 25-50 YD/MIN.	20	4
WALKING 4 MPH (O ELEV.)	30	5
ROWING MACHINE	20	5
TENNIS (SINGLES)	45	4
HANDBALL (SINGLES)	30	4
SKATING (ICE OR ROLLER)	45	5
RACQUETBALL (SINGLES)	25	4

FAST AND SLOW TWITCH MUSCLE FIBERS

Slow-Twitch Muscle Fibers

These muscle fibers are usually utilized first during a sport or exercise until the body determines the need for the "fast twitch muscles." The following are facts apply to the slow twitch muscles fibers:

   Aerobic type muscles, which must burn glucose in the presence of oxygen to produce needed energy.

   Used for long distance endurance, exercises, or sports.

   The number of slow-twitch muscles and the intensity of their movement is usually determined by heredity.

The size and strength of the fibers can be improved with exercise.

They are also capable of burning fatty acids which reduces the body's fat stores.
The leg muscles of a long distance runner may contain up to 90% of the slow-twitch fibers.

Fast-Twitch Muscle Fibers

Activated when sudden bursts of energy are needed, such as in a "dash" or other fast movement. The following are facts related to fast-twitch muscle fibers:

These muscles are for the most part anaerobic and burn fuel without the presence of oxygen.

The leg muscles in world-class tennis players may contain up to 70% fast-twitch muscle fibers.

As with slow-twitch muscle fibers, the number of fast-twitch muscle fibers is controlled by heredity.

With training the size of the fibers can be increased and provide faster response.

SPECIAL EXERCISE CALORIE CHART

```
Beating around the bush.................. 75
Jogging your memory......................125
Jumping to conclusions...................100
Climbing the walls.......................150
Swallowing your pride.................... 50
Passing the buck......................... 25
Grasping at straws....................... 75
Beating your own drum....................100
Throwing your weight around......... 50-300
Dragging your heels......................100
Pushing your luck........................250
Making mountains out of molehills........500
Spinning your wheels.....................175
Flying off the handle....................225
Hitting the nail on the head............. 50
Turning the other cheek.................. 75
Wading through paperwork.................300
Bending over backwards................... 75
Jumping on the bandwagon.................200
Balancing the books...................... 23
Beating your head against the wall.......150
Running around in circles................350
Chewing nails............................200
Eating crow..............................225
Fishing for compliments.................. 50
```

HOME FITNESS EQUIPMENT

Rowing Machines
These are an all-around exerciser, involving the activity of numerous muscle groups. They are excellent for the legs, upper body, and arms. However, they are not recommended for person who are not in condition. They also do not provide the best aerobic workout.

Treadmills
An inexpensive method of exercising by either walking or jogging. Employs a moving belt which may be motorized. Most motorized models will allow you to adjust both the speed and elevation. The most frequent complaint is that they tend to become boring after a short period of time. Earphones with music or a TV to watch seems to solve the problem. Computerized models are best.

Mini-Trampolines
A fun way to exercise indoors or out. They provide an inexpensive aerobic alternative to jogging. Can be used by almost any age group and can provide a fairly good workout if sufficient time is spent.

Stationary Bike (Ergometer)
This by far the most popular piece of exercise equipment. It provides good aerobic training without the problems that may be caused by the continual pounding of jogging, especially for the unfit. Combining workouts on the rowing machine and the bicycle will provide a well-rounded exercise program.

The cost of the bicycle in most cases will determine the overall quality, ease of making adjustments and the degree of comfort. Many of the less expensive models do not have adjustable handlebars which is a comfort feature. Computerized models tend to hold your interest better and give you feedback.

Multi-Gyms
Usually expensive but competition has brought the prices down in recent years. Incorporates a multitude of different exercises into one unit which makes it handy for home use. Best to try out a unit before buying one, either in a store or a gym. Many of the more unusual units will not hold your interest too long. Be wary of some of the new ones advertised on TV unless you can send it back if you don't like it. Watching a person on TV using the unit is different from you using it in many instances.

FITNESS FACTS

INJURIES AND PREVENTION

Blisters

Blisters are a common problem, particularly when breaking in a new pair of shoes. Prevention begins with properly fitting shoes and socks that stay in place and do not creep or bunch up. When blisters occur, puncture the edge of the blister with a sterile needle, drain the fluid and apply a topical antiseptic solution, then cover with a bandaid.

Arch Conditions

Painful arches are usually the result of improperly fitting shoes, overweight, excessive activity on a hard surface, faulty posture or fatigue. The symptoms are divided into three stages:

1. Slight soreness in the arch area.

2. A chronic inflammatory condition that includes soreness, redness, swelling, and a slightly visible drop in the arch. See your physician.

3. A completely fallen arch, accompanied by extreme pain, immobility, and deformity. See your physician.

Caring for arch disorders should include the following suggestions:

   Shoes should be properly fitted.
   Whirlpool hydrotherapy.
   Ultrasound deep therapy.
   Arch orthotics.
   Exercise program, if detected early.

Sprained Ankle

Generally caused by a lateral or medial twist that results in external and internal joint derangement. Sprains may be classified as first, second or third degree. The majority of ankle sprains are the inversion type, resulting in the stretching or tearing of the lateral ligaments. In handling a sprained ankle, these first aid measures should be followed:

1. The ankle should be compressed with an ice pack and then elevated for 24 hours.

2. If swelling is more than minor or if a fracture is suspected, a physician should be contacted for x-rays.

3. With severe ankle sprains, continue cold applications through the second or even the third day.

4. Apply heat therapy if swelling has subsided by the third day.

Knee Problem

Although the knee is the largest joint in the body, it is extremely vulnerable to traumatic injuries because of poor bony arrangement. Knee injuries fall mainly into four categories: compression injuries, lateral and medial sprains, torsion injuries, and hyperextending injuries. See your physician.

Lower Back Pain

Lower back pain is usually the result of poor flexibility, weak abdominal and back muscles, and poor posture. Stretching and strengthening exercises, with a conscious effort to improve posture, improves the problem in the majority of cases.

Muscle Soreness

Engagement in activities different from those to which one is normally accustomed often produces muscular soreness. In some cases pain has been reported to occur during the latter stages of high-intensity exercise. More often, it occurs as many as 24-48 hours after the activity. This type of pain is less understood than immediate pain, but it most commonly occurs after an endurance workout. Reports show that the delayed pain to be caused by alterations in the muscle connective tissue (stretching of the elastic components). Recovery from this type of soreness can be enhanced by warm compresses or warm baths, accompanied by light exercise to help prevent adhesions during the healing process.

Side Stitch

A side stitch usually develops in untrained individuals during aerobic activities. Manifested in mild to agonizing pain in the area of the lower rib cage and may be on either side of the body, but usually the right side. There are several explanations for this occurrence, none of which is completely satisfactory. It is probable that all of the following factors contribute to the discomfort:

1.   Accumulation of metabolic wastes (lactic acid) in the diaphragm.

2.   Severe shaking of the abdominal contents, which causes pain in the supporting structures.

3.   Formation of gas in the ascending colon.

4.   Reduced blood flow to the affected area due to the rerouting of blood to other areas.

Relief is usually accelerated by the application of pressure on the affected side while the exercise is continued. If the pain becomes too severe, the alternative is to terminate the workout and rest.

Achilles Tendon Rupture

This usually follows a history of chronic inflammation and gradual degeneration caused by microtears. When the rupture occurs, the individual complains of a sudden snap or that something has hit them in the lower leg. Severe pain, point tenderness, swelling, and discoloration are usually associated with the trauma. Signs of a rupture are obvious indentations at the tendon site or a positive Thompson Test.

Achilles Tendon Bursitis and Tendinitis

Bursitis and tendinitis usually occur from the overstretching of the Achilles tendon, resulting in a constant inflammatory condition of the Achilles bursar. The condition is chronic, developing gradually over a period of time, and takes many days to heal. An excellent therapeutic approach is ultrasound (electrical heat transfer). Activity should be held to a minimum, and heel lifts should be placed in the shoe to relieve the Achilles tendon of as much tension as possible. After a workout, the tendon should be cooled with ice packs or ice massage. Gradual heel cord stretching is recommended.

Shin Splints

These are characterized by pain and irritation in the shin region of the leg, and are usually attributed to an inflammation localized mostly in the tendon of the tibialis posterior and the flexor digitorum longus. Inflammation in this area is often a mystery. Speculation of cause include: faulty posture alignment, falling arches, muscle fatigue, overuse stress, body chemical imbalance or a lack of reciprocal muscle coordination between the anterior and posterior aspects of the leg. All these factors singly or in combination, may contribute to shin splints.

While rest is the only sure cure, limited exercise is possible with an ice massage and a leg wrap. Prevention of shin splints can be accomplished by using proper footwear, running on soft surfaces, stretching, and strengthening the surrounding musculature.

WALKING NECESSARY TO WALK OFF COMMON SNACK FOODS

The following information will provide the walking distance required to work off the calories of a number of common snacks and foods.

SNACK	SERVING	CALORIES	MILES
THAT LITTLE SANDWICH			
Ham	1/2 oz. w/butter	335	5.8
Cheese	1/2 oz. w/mayo	400	6.7
Peanut Butter/jelly	2 Tbs. peanut butter	425	7.4
	1 Tbl. jelly		
Hamburger on bun	3 inch patty	445	8.0
Tortilla w/cheese	1 oz. cheese	190	3.2
BEVERAGES			
Carb. soft drink	12 oz. can	160	2.7
Chocolate malt	12 oz. glass	485	8.2
Ice cream soda	12 oz. glass	290	4.7
Milk/whole	8 oz. glass	160	2.7
Tea or coffee	8 oz. cup	90	1.6
(w/2T cream & 2t sugar)			
Beer	12 oz. can	165	2.8
High Ball	8 oz. glass	140	2.8
(w/ginger ale)			
Martini	Average	160	2.7
Manhattan	Average	175	3.0
Sherry	4 oz. glass	120	2.1
Scotch, Bourbon,	1 shot glass	80	1.3

FRUITS

Apple	1 medium	90	1.5
Orange	1 medium	85	1.4
Pear	1 medium	100	1.7
Grapes	25 medium	70	1.2
Banana	1-6 inch long	100	1.7
Date	1 medium	27	0.4

SALTED NUTS

Almonds	10	130	2.2
Pecans	10	150	2.5
Cashews	10	60	1.0
Walnuts	1 oz. shelled	175	2.9
Peanut	1 medium	6	0.1

CANDIES

Chocolate bar	1 1/4 oz.	185	3.1
BonBon	1 pc.	90	1.5
Caramel	1 pc. 3/4 inch	40	0.7
Jelly Bean	1 avg.	6	0.1

DESSERTS

Doughnut	1 medium	140	2.3
Ice Cream Cone	1 scoop	190	3.2
Ice Cream Sundae	2 scoops w/toppings	400	6.7
Cake (layer)	1 avg. piece	290	4.8
Pie (fruit)	1/6 pie	340	5.7
Cream Puff	4 inch diameter	365	6.1
Brownie	1 medium	300	5.0
Graham Cracker	1	42	0.7

MISCELLANEOUS

Potato Chips	10 medium	115	1.8
Popcorn(w/o butter)	1 cup	60	1.0
1 tablespoon butter modest amount for popcorn	1 Tbl.	85	1.4
Saltine Crackers	4	50	0.8

MIDNIGHT ICE BOX RAID

Piece of chicken	1 oz.	105	1.8
Chicken leg	1 average	85	1.5
Hard Boiled Egg	1 medium	80	1.3
Jello	1/2 cup	70	1.2

EXERCISE AND CALORIES

The purpose of the following information is to create an awareness of which foods are higher in calories and the number of _minutes_ needed to work off the foods. The information is based on a 150 pound adult.

	Calories	Walking 3 MPH	Bicycling 15 MPH	Jogging 5 MPH
BREAD & CEREALS				
Raisin Bran (1/2 cup)	73	15	7	10
Special K (1/2 cup)	30	6	3	4
Cornbread (2" sq.)	107	21	10	13
White Bread (1 sl.)	62	12	6	8
WW Bread (1 sl.)	56	11	5	7
Donut, iced (1 med.)	150	30	14	19
Blueberry Muffin	110	22	10	14
Cinnamon Bun	158	32	14	20
Pancake (med.)	110	22	10	14
Waffle (med.)	165	34	15	20
White Rice (3/4 cup)	103	21	9	13
Egg Noodles (1/4 cup)	70	14	6	9
Air Popcorn (1 cup)	54	11	5	7
Popcorn/oil (1 cup)	82	16	7	10
Graham Cracker (1)	30	6	3	4
Macaroni/cheese(1 C)	530	110	57	70
Spagh/meat balls (1 C)	310	68	35	46
Taco/beef (3 oz.)	195	45	22	30
Saltine Cracker (1)	14	3	1	2
MEATS				
Bacon/cooked (2 sl.)	100	20	8	12
Beef Hash (1/2 C)	230	46	21	29
Reg. Hamburger	225	45	20	28
Lean Hamburger	140	28	13	18
Beef Pot Pie (med.)	445	90	40	55
Chili/beans/meat(5 oz)	185	39	17	25
Hot Dog/plain	125	25	12	16
Ham Slice (2 oz)	185	35	18	22
Lamb (3 oz)	300	60	25	35
Meat Loaf (3 oz)	285	61	30	40
Chicken TV dinner	542	108	49	68
Bologna (1 sl)	66	13	6	8
Sausage (1 reg link)	95	19	9	12
T-Bone Steak (4 oz)	175	35	22	22

FISH/SHELLFISH

Deviled Crab (1)	188	38	17	24
Baked Flounder (3 oz)	200	41	19	28
Broiled Lobster(1 med)	310	62	28	39
Fried Oysters (7)	235	48	22	30
Broiled Salmon (4 oz)	200	45	23	29
Fried Shrimp (3 oz)	205	40	16	22
Tuna/water (4 oz)	127	26	11	16
Tuna/oil (4 oz)	205	49	19	29
Anchovies (3)	21	4	2	3

POULTRY

Fried Chicken (1/2)	460	100	45	58
Fried Chicken Leg	150	30	13	19
Roast Turkey (1 sl)	80	16	8	10

NUTS

Almonds (14)	90	18	8	11
Cashews (7)	84	17	8	11
Peanuts (1 Tbl)	86	18	8	11
Peanut Butter (1 Tbl)	88	19	9	12
Pecans (6)	100	21	9	13
Sunflower Seeds (3 oz)	502	110	50	65

PREPARED SALADS

Coleslaw (1 cup)	79	21	10	15
Carrot/Raisin (3 oz)	150	31	14	19
Macaroni Salad (1 cup)	335	67	30	41
Potato Salad (1 cup)	200	40	19	24
Salad Dressing (1 Tbl)	71	14	6	9

DAIRY PRODUCTS

Milk/whole (1 cup)	160	32	14	20
Milk/non-fat (1 cup)	105	21	10	13
Buttermilk (1 cup)	88	18	8	11
Amer. Cheese (1 oz)	110	21	10	14
Cottage Cheese(1/2 C)	120	29	14	18
Ice Cream (1/2 cup)	225	41	20	27
Yogurt/non-fat (1 C)	122	24	11	15

SOUPS

Cream of Mush. (1 C)	150	30	14	19
Chicken Noodle (1 C)	60	12	7	8
Split Pea (1 C)	120	24	11	15
Tomato (1 C)	73	15	7	9

SWEET TREATS

Chocolate Bar	215	44	20	27
Milky Way (reg)	285	57	26	37
Choc. Chip Cookies (3)	150	30	14	19
Banana Split (2 scoop)	600	120	54	74
Eclair	300	60	27	37
Apple Pie (1 slice)	390	79	35	48
Brownie (1 sq.)	150	30	14	19

BEVERAGES

Beer (12 oz)	230	42	20	53
Lite Beer (12 oz)	100	20	9	13
Brandy (3 1/2 oz)	75	15	7	9
Martini (3 1/2 oz)	140	28	13	18
Wine (4 oz)	110	22	10	14
Champagne (4 oz)	85	17	8	10
Milkshake (8 oz)	420	85	38	55
Eggnog (8 oz)	235	48	22	29
Cola Soda (12 oz)	155	31	14	21

RESTAURANT SANDWICHES

Club (3 sl bread)	600	120	59	78
Egg Salad	280	56	25	35
Tuna Salad	280	56	25	35
BLT	285	58	27	39

VEGETABLES

Asparagus (1/2 cup)	17	3	2	3
Broccoli (1/2 cup)	26	5	3	3
Cabbage (1/2 cup)	20	4	2	3
Sweet Corn (1 ear)	96	20	9	12
Sweet Pickle (1 lg)	140	30	14	18
Baked Potato (1 med)	100	20	10	14
French Fries (10 avg)	140	30	12	17
Mashed Pot. (1/2 cup)	90	16	7	10
Potato Chips (sm bag)	115	22	10	14

FRUITS

Apple (med)	50	10	4	6
Banana (1 sm)	88	17	8	12
Cantaloupe (1/4 melon)	45	9	4	6
Grapefruit (1/2 sm)	40	8	4	5
Orange (1 sm)	50	10	5	7
Watermelon (1 cup)	45	9	4	6

Chapter 7

Fruits and Vegetables

FRUITS

When choosing fruits it is always best to choose the healthiest looking and if possible check the original box it came in to see if the fruit was graded "U.S. Grade No.1" or at least has a USDA stamp on the box or crate.

To preserve the nutritional content of fruits, leave them in their original packaging material if frozen. This will reduce the risk of exposure to air which may result in a loss of flavor and cause discolorization.

To reduce the amount of fruit discolorization, slice bananas, apples, plums, and peaches with a stainless steel knife, then either combine them with any citrus fruit or sprinkle them with lemon or pineapple juice. Refrigerate as soon as possible.

Brown areas on fruits mean that oxidation has taken place from exposure to the air of the more sensitive inner flesh and that the vitamin C content has been lost. The citric acid from the lemon or pineapple alleviates the problem.

"PEELING IT OFF"

To peel thin-skinned fruits and vegetables, place them in a bowl and cover them with boiling water, allow to stand for 1 minute, then remove their skin with a sharp paring knife. Another method is to spear the food with a fork and hold it over a gas flame until the skin cracks.

To peel thick-skinned fruits or vegetables, cut a small portion of the peel from the top and bottom then set the food on an acrylic cutting board and remove the balance of the peel in strips from top to bottom.

A tasty dressing for fruits can be prepared by grating an orange rind and adding it to orange juice and low-fat sour cream.

"DON'T BE FOILED"
Aluminum foil wrap should never come in contact with acidic fruits or vegetables such as; lemons, oranges, tomatoes, grapefruits, etc. A chemical reaction may take place and it is possible that it will corrode through the aluminum foil.

two of the most nutritious fruits are papaya and cantaloupe.

Wash all fruits and vegetables in cold water or a quality organic vegetable cleaner to remove any pesticide or fertilizer residue. Never soak or store foods in water, since a number of vitamins are water soluble and may be lost.

When any fruit or vegetable is cooked, the natural enzymes will be destroyed. These enzymes are need by the body to initiate biochemical reactions.

When your foods are being bagged in the supermarket, be sure and ask the clerk not to place your fruits and vegetables in the same bag with any type of meat product. The slightest amount of leakage may ruin the food.

Since nobody likes mushy fruit, many recipes ask you to add sugar to the recipe. This strengthens the cell walls and brings the water back into the cells that the cooking has removed.

Fruit consumption in the United States has risen from 101 pounds per person in 1970 to 130 pounds in 1995.

"IT'S THE PITS"
Certain fruits, such as, apricots, apples pears, cherries, and peaches contain a small amount of the chemical "amygdalin" which tends to release the deadly poison cyanide when crushed and heated.

Coconut water found in the center of coconuts is almost fat-free and high in vitamin K. Coconut flesh and the oil is high in saturated fat.

DRIED FRUITS

Dried fruits lose most of their vitamin C when dried, however, they do retain other vitamins and almost all of their mineral content.

Dried fruits may contain sulfites, check the label and avoid any that contain this preservative. It may cause an allergic reaction in susceptible individuals.

Dried fruits are graded; extra fancy, fancy, extra choice, choice and standard is the lowest grade. The grading is based on size, color, condition after being dried, and water content.

Dried fruits, if frozen in a liquid, should be thawed in the same liquid to retain the flavor.

Dried fruit kept in airtight containers will keep for up to 6 months if placed in a cool, dry location and 1 year if refrigerated. Refrigeration places the fruit cells in a state of suspended animation and causes them to retain their flavor. Best to allow the fruit to remain at room temperature before eating for about 30 minutes to acquire the best taste.

To make raisins plump, wash them, place them in a shallow dish and bake covered in a pre-heated 350^0 oven for 8 minutes.

Prunes are a natural laxative, they contain the chemical "diphenylisatin."

Order of the nutritional quality of fruits

1. Fresh, if brought to market in a short period of time.
2. Dehydrated, if Grade A or 1.
3. Freeze Dried, if packaged at the site where grown.
4. Frozen, if packaged within 12 hours of harvest.
5. Canned.

When pouring cream over fruits, try adding a small amount of baking soda to the cream to stop the possibility of curdling. Baking soda will reduce the acidity which may cause curdling.

When cooking fruits for preserves and jellies, add a small pat of butter and there will be no foam to skim off the top. The fat tends to act as a sealant which does not allow the air to rise and accumulate on top as foam. The air just dissipates harmlessly in the product.

If you have problems with fruit jelly setting-up, try placing the jars in a shallow pan half-filled with cold water, then bake in a moderate oven for 30 minutes. This will reduce the moisture content of the jelly enough to set them up.

THE "WILD" SIDE

The Aborigines' favorite fruit in Australia is the "green plum" which contains 3,000mg. of vitamin C in a 4 ounce serving. Compare that to our orange at 70mg. per orange.

The Hadza hunters in Tanzania enjoy the "kongoroko fruit" which contains 526mg. of calcium. Compare that to an 8 ounce glass of milk which only has 290mg. of calcium.

The South African cape buffalo contains 1.5% Omega-3 fatty acids. American beef only have a small trace. Cod liver oil which is considered one of the best sources contains only 5%.

The more surface of a fruit or vegetable you expose to the air and light, the more nutrient loss will occur. Especially, vitamin C.

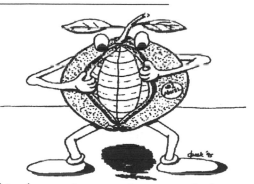

To ripen fruit, place the fruit in a brown bag and in a dark location for a few days. Most fruit gives off ethylene gas which if trapped in the bag provides a higher level of the gas which speeds up the ripening.

AKEE

Grown in Jamaica and very popular throughout the Caribbean. When mature the fruit splits open exposing the edible white aril, the outer covering of the seed.

APPLES

Certain varieties of apples may have a different taste depending on the time of year it was purchased. If you are buying large quantities, it would be best to purchase a few and taste them. They should be firm, have no holes, should not be bruised, and have a good even color. If the apple is not ripe, leave it at room temperature for a day or two, but not in direct sunlight.

Apples are capable of lasting 3-5 weeks under refrigeration and still retain its vitamin C content. Most apples are tart flavored. The best and sweetest eating apples are the red and golden delicious varieties. There are many varieties of apples, many of which are available year round.

APPLE VARIETIES

Akane

These do not store well and have a sweet-tart flavor. The skin is thin and usually tender. They retain their shape well when baked and have maintain their tartness.

Braeburn

These store exceptionally well. The skin is tender, moderately tart and they keep their shape well when baked.

Cortland

Fragile and needs to be stored carefully. High in vitamin C and resists browning. Thin-skinned with a slight tart-sweet taste. Keeps its shape well when baked.

Criterion

Yellow apples that are difficult to handle without bruising. High in vitamin C and resists browning. The skin is tender, but the flavor is somewhat bland when baked.

Elstar

Stores well with their tart flavor mellowing with storage. They have tender skin and retain their flavor and shape well when baked.

Fiji

Stores well and has a tangy-sweet flavor. Will retain its shape well when baked, but will take longer to bake than most apples. Looks like an Asian pear.

Gala

Choose apples with pale-yellow background and light reddish stripes. Sweet, with slight tartness and have tender skin. They hold their shape well when baked, however, they tend to lose flavor.

Golden Delicious

Stores well but spoils fast at room temperature. Should be light-yellow, not greenish. Skin is tender and the flavor is sweet. High in vitamin C and tends to resist browning. It retains its shape well when baked.

There are 150 strains of Red and Golden Delicious apples grown worldwide.

Granny Smith

Best color is light green, not intensely green and could even have a slight yellow tint. High in vitamin C and resists browning. Nicely balanced sweet-tart flavor. Cooks into excellent thick applesauce, but is not recommended for baking.

Idared

They keep exceptionally well and become sweeter during storage. Resembles Johathans and has tender skin. When cooked they will retain their full flavor.

Jonagold

Has a good sweet-tart balance. A very juicy apple with tender skin. When cooking, peel then strain.

Jonathan

Found in California around mid-August. They become soft and mealy very quickly. Thin skinned, they cook tender and make a good applesauce. Retain shape well when baked.

McIntosh

Most come from British Columbia. Be careful when selecting as they tend to get mushy and mealy easily. The skin is tough and will separate from the flesh. Tend to fall apart when baked in pies.

Melrose

Normally found in the Northwest. Store very well and flavor actually improves after 1-2 months of storage. Well-balanced sweet and tart flavor. Retains shape well when cooked in pies.

Mutsu

Also known as Crispin looks like a Golden Delicious but is greener and irregular in shape. Stores well and has a sweet but spicy taste with fairly coarse texture. For applesauce, cook, peel and strain.

Newton Pippen

Sometimes picked too green, wait until light green for sweetest flavor. They keep their shape well when baked or used in pies. makes a thick applesauce.

Northern Spy

A tart, green apple that is excellent for pies.

Red Delicious

Ranges in color from red to red-striped. Stores for up to 12 months but will not last long at room temperature, best to refrigerate. Avoid any bruised ones. They are normally sweet and mellow with just a hint of tartness. When cooked they do hold their flavor well.

Rhode Island Greening

Best choice for pies, but not very available. Only available October and November on the East Coast.

Rome Beauty

Do not store for long periods, they tend to get bland and mealy. Very mild and have a low acid level. The skin is fairly thick, but tender. Excellent for baking and hold its shape well.

Spartan

Will not store for long periods and gets mushy and mealy easily. Sweet-flavored and very aromatic, but flavor becomes very weak when cooked.

Stayman Winesap

Stores well. Has a spicey-tart flavor and is a good crisp apple. It has a thick skin which will separate easily. When cooked they will retain flavor well making them good for baking and pies.

APPLE FACTS

Apples will spoil 10 times faster at room temperature. After they are ripe it is best to store them in the refrigerator.

Apples will float because 25% of their volume is made up of air between the cells.

The soft texture of cooked apples is caused by the heat collapsing the air spaces between the cells.

Apple butter contains no fat if prepared properly with cinnamon and allspice.

Pare apples by pouring scalding water on them just before peeling them. This will make the skin loosen and it will be easier to peel.

To avoid wrinkled skin on apples when baking them, just cut a few slits in the skin to allow for expansion.

Apples will store for a longer period of time if they do not touch each other. The area that touches becomes warmer and mold starts to grow.

If the apples are losing their moisture and taste, try slicing them up, placing them in a dish and pouring cold apple juice over them and refrigerating for 30 minutes.

For winter storage, wipe apples dry and pack in dry sand or sawdust. Keep in cool, dry location such as a cellar.

Fresh apple juice will only last for a few weeks, even if refrigerated.

Most of an apple harvest ends up being made into pasteurized apple products or frozen to preserve it. When pasteurized at temperatures of 170-190 degrees F. microorganisms are destroyed and the juice has a stable shelf life of up to one year.

If you purchase frozen apple concentrate, it will only last for a few weeks after it is thawed.

The tartness of an apple is derived from the balance of malic acid and the fruit's natural sugars.

Commercially prepared sweetened applesauce can contain as much as 77% more calories than unsweetened varieties.

Nutritionally, there is no difference between "natural" and "regular" apple juice, even the fiber content is the same.

Apple juice is not high on the nutritional scale. It contains only a minute amount of vitamin C unless it has been added.

FDA testing can only detect 50% of the approved 110 pesticides that are used on apples. The worst ones are; Captan and Phosmet, both can be removed with washing or cooking.

Apple juice and cider should not be purchased from a roadside stand unless you are sure that the whole apple was not used in their preparation. The pits contain a poison.

"AN APPLE A DAY....."
Americans consume approximately 22 pounds of apples per person annually. Pesticides were identified as being present in 33% of all apples tested by the USDA. Fourty-three different pesticides were detected and identified.

If you store apples along with green tomatoes, they will ripen faster. Green tomatoes give off ethylene gas that speeds ripening. Apples give off the same gas but not as much.

REPORTED HEALTH BENEFITS

Studies have shown that apples will stimulate all body secretions. Apples contain malic and tartaric acids, which may aide in relieving disturbances of the liver and general digestion.

In populations that drink unsweetened apple juice on a regular basis, kidney stones are unknown.

The low acidity level of apples tends to stimulate salivary flow and stimulates gum tissue.

Studies indicate that consuming apples daily will reduce the severity of arthritis and asthma.

The skin of the apple contains an excellent level of pectin which is active in raising HDL levels (good cholesterol).

APRICOTS

Apricots are usually the first fruit of the summer season. A relative of the peach and in one ounce they contain enough beta-carotene to supply 20% of your daily vitamin A requirement. Astronauts ate apricots on the Apollo moon mission.

They were originally grown in China over 4,000 years ago and were brought to California by the Spanish in the late 18th century. California is still the largest producer of apricots and over half the apricots grown are canned due to their short season.

Apricots that are not ripe will ripen quickly at room temperature, then should be refrigerated.

"BE GENTLE"
Apricots bruise easily and need to handled delicately.

Dried apricots are over 40% sugar. When purchasing dried apricots, it is best to purchase the unsulfured ones.

REPORTED HEALTH BENEFITS

Apricots contain a high level of iron making it a beneficial fruit for cases of anemia, TB, asthma and blood impurities. may be effective in destroying intestinal worms, relieving diarrhea, and pimples.

ATEMOYA

This fruit is grown in Florida and are available from August through October. They are a pale-green fruit that should not be purchased if it is cracked open. Looks like an artichoke and has a cream-colored flesh that is sweet and almost fat and sodium-free. It is an excellent source of potassium.

AVOCADOS

Originated in Central America and were first grown in the United States in the 1800's in Florida and California. California produces 90% of all avocados sold. The most popular varieties are the Fuerte and Hass from California. The Florida variety has half the fat of the California varieties and only 2/3 of the calories.

Approximately 71-80% of the calories in avocados come from fat. However, most of the fat is of the monounsaturated type, the same type found in olive oil and Canola oil and in some studies have shown to lower cholesterol.

They are available year round and should be fresh in appearance with colors ranging from green to purple-black. They should feel heavy for their size and be slightly firm. Avoid ones with soft spots and discolorizations. Refrigerate and use within 5 days after purchase.

Avocados will ripen in a short period of time if placed in a brown paper bag and set in a warm location. They will ripen even faster if you place them in a wool sock.

The "old wives tale" about leaving the pit in the guacamole to retard the browning is just that. The guacamole will stay fresher longer and retain its color if it is covered in an airtight container, since it is the air and subsequent oxidation that causes the browning. The area under the pit doesn't brown because it lacks oxygen. Another method of reducing the blackening is to crush a few chewable vitamin C tablets, mix them in cold water and place the mixture in a spray bottle. Shake well and spay the guacamole every 20-30 minutes.

"EN GUARDE"
To remove an avocado pit, just thrust the blade of a sharp knife into the pit, twist slightly and the pit comes right out.

If an avocado is too hard and needs to be used, try placing it in the microwave using high power for 40-70 seconds. Make sure and rotate it half way through. This procedure won't ripen it only soften it.

REPORTED HEALTH BENEFITS

Used for inflammations of mucous membranes, especially in the intestines.

BANANAS

Available all year round. They should be plump and the skin should be free of bruises as well as brown or black spots. Bananas should be purchased green and allowed to ripen at home. They may be ripened at room temperature until they turn yellow, then they should be refrigerated to slow down the ripening process and the development of sugars. Refrigeration may turn the skin black, but this will not affect the inside of the fruit.

The new miniature bananas have more taste than many of the larger ones.

Excellent spices to use on bananas are cinnamon and nutmeg.

Banana chips are usually fried in coconut oil and should not be considered a nutritious snack. It would be best to choose an air-dried chip. One ounce of fried banana chips can have as much as 150 calories and up to 10 grams of fat, most of which is saturated.

Americans consume 25 pounds of bananas per person annually.

Bananas contain less water than most other fruits. They are a type of berry from a tree classified as an herb tree which can grow up to 30 feet high, and are the largest plant in the world with a woody stem.

If you wish to ripen bananas more quickly, wrap them in a wet paper towel and place them into a brown paper sack or place a green banana next to a ripe banana. More ethylene gas is released from the green banana. If you place an apple next to a banana it will also ripen very quickly, since apples give off more ethylene gas than other fruits.

Bananas will freeze for about 6-7 months if left in their skins.

To test for ripeness, stick a toothpick in the fruit at the stem end. If it goes in and out clean and with ease, the fruit is ripe.

VARIETIES

Cavandish

This is the standard banana that we normally purchase, the majority of which is imported from South America.

Manzano

Known as the "finger banana" and tends to turn black when they are ripe.

Plantains

A very large green banana which has a high starch content and are usually cooked like a vegetable. They are sometimes substituted for potatoes in South American dishes.

Red Banana

Not usually curved, they tend to turn a purplish color when ripe, They are very sweet tasting.

REPORTED HEALTH BENEFITS

Historically, bananas have been reported used to improve conditions such as stomach ulcers, colitis, diarrhea, hemorrhoids, and even to increase energy levels. The inner surface of banana skins were used on burns and boils.

<u>BERRIES</u>

All berries should be firm and their color bright. berries should be refrigerated and should not be allowed to dry-out. They should be used within 2-3 days after they are purchased for the best flavor and nutritional value. Berries do not ripen after being picked.

Choose only bright red strawberries and plump firm blueberries that are light to dark blue.

Always check the bottoms of berry containers to be sure they are not stained from rotting or moldy berries. Mold on berries spreads quickly and you never want to leave a moldy one next to a good one. This actually goes for all fruits.

Never hull strawberries until after they are washed or they will absorb too much water and become mushy and waterlogged.

Berries can be defrosted by placing them in a plastic bag and immersing them in cold water for about 10-12 minutes.

"BOTTOMS UP"

If your making a dish with berries, make sure the batter or consistency is thick enough to hold the berries in suspension. Berries placed into thin batters just go to the bottom.

Blueberries are higher in vitamin A than most berries. Fresh cranberries have 86% more vitamin C than canned cranberries.

One cup of strawberries contains only 55 calories and considerably more calcium, phosphorus, vitamin C, and potassium than blueberries and raspberries.

Blueberries and blackberries are better if cooked, since cooking will deactivate an enzyme that effects absorption of vitamin B_1.

Berry juice stains can usually be removed from your hands with lemon juice.

REPORTED HEALTH BENEFITS

Blackberries have been used for relieving symptoms of arthritis, weak kidneys, anemia, gout and minor skin irritations.

Blueberries have been used as a blood cleanser, anti-diarrheal, reduce inflammations and menstrual disorders.

Strawberries have been used effectively as a skin cleanser and blood cleanser as well as relieving the symptoms of asthma, gout, arthritis, and lowering blood pressure.

BREADFRUIT

Has the appearance of a large melon and may weigh up to 5 pounds. Very starchy and a staple food for the Pacific Islanders. Has a high carbohydrate content and is an excellent source of vitamins. The outside is a greenish color with a scaly covering with pale-yellow flesh. When ripe it is very sweet. Choose a relatively hard breadfruit and allow to ripen at room temperature until it has a degree of give.

CANTALOUPE

They are best if purchased between June and September. They should be round, smooth, and have a depressed scar at the stem end. If the scar appears rough or the stem is still attached, the melon will not ripen well. Cantaloupes are best if the netting is an even yellow color with little or no green. Melons can be left at room temperature to ripen. The aroma will usually indicate if it is ripe and sweet. Refrigerate as soon as it is ripe. Whole melons will last for a week if kept refrigerated. Cut melons, wrapped in plastic with seeds in and refrigerated, are best eaten in 2-3 days.

If cantaloupe is ripe, you should be able to hear the seeds rattle inside. It should also give off a sweet fragrance. The "belly button" should be somewhat soft, but if the melon is soft all over, its probably overripe.

REPORTED HEALTH BENEFITS

has been used in cases of high fever, to reduce blood pressure, arthritis, bladder problems, and constipation.

CARAMBOLA

The color when ripe should be golden-yellow and when sliced will yield perfect star-shaped sections. It has a sweet but somewhat tart flavor and may be purchased green and allowed to ripen at room temperature. Excellent natural source of vitamin C.

CHERRIES

Cherries are one of the most popular fruits and are grown in 20 countries worldwide. The United States grows 150,000 tons of cherries annually. 50% of the sweet cherries and 90% of the sour cherries are canned or frozen.

Cherries were a favorite fruit of the Roman's, Greek's and Chinese thousands of years ago. Cherries originated in Asia Minor and were named for a Turkish town Cerasus, which is presently called Giresun, and is located on the Black Sea. it is believed that birds brought the cherry pits to Europe. Europeans enjoy a chilled cherry soup as a summertime treat.

French colonists from Normandy brought pits that they planted along the Saint Lawrence River and throughout the Great Lakes areas. Sweet cherries are primarily grown on the West Coast, while tart cherries are grown in the Grand Traverse Region of Michigan.

CHERRY VARIETIES

TART

MONTMORENCY

Usually round but slightly compressed. Very juicy and a clear medium-red color. Excellent for pies. tarts and jams. This is the most widely grown tart cherry in the United States.

EARLY RICHMOND

Round; medium-red color with tender flesh and a tough, thin skin. Not generally grown in the United States.

ENGLISH MORELLO

A round shaped cherry, very deep red in color becoming almost black. The flesh is red, tender, and somewhat tart. It is not grown commercially in large quantities in the United States.

SWEET

REPUBLICAN (Lewellan)

It is small to medium-sized, heart-shaped with crisp flesh ranging from very red to purplish-black. The juice is very dark and sweet.

ROYAL ANN (Napoleon or Emperor Francis)

These are heart-shaped and a light golden color. The flesh may be pink to light red; usually firm and juicy with an excellent flavor. The light flesh variety is used commercially in canning.

BING

These are usually very large, heart-shaped with flesh that ranges in color from deep red to almost black. The skin is usually smooth and glossy.

SCHMIDT

Similar to Bing Cherry.

TARTARIAN

Very large, heart-shaped with purplish to black flesh. Very tender and sweet. The skin is thin and one of the most popular cherries of the mid-season.

CHAPMAN

Large round, purplish-black flesh. Produced from a seedling of the Black Tartarian variety. The fruit usually matures early in the season.

LAMBERT

A very large, usually round cherry with a dark to very dark red flesh. Very firm and meaty.

REPORTED HEALTH BENEFITS

Very high in magnesium, iron, and silicon making them valuable in arthritis, as a blood cleanser, worms, asthma and high blood pressure. They tend to stimulate the secretion of digestive enzymes. Numerous people have reported that consuming 8-10 Bing cherries per day relieved symptoms of arthritis. This claim has not been substantiated.

COCONUT

Coconuts are always available. When choosing one be sure that its heavy for its size and you can hear the sound of liquid when you shake it. If the eyes are damp it would be best not to buy it. Coconuts can be stored at room temperature for 6-8 months depending on how fresh it was when it was purchased.

To remove the coconut milk just piece two of the eyes with a strong ice pick then wrap it in a towel large enough to tie a knot in the end and crack it open with a hammer.

Coconut meat is very high in saturated fat, however, the milk is low in fat.

CRANBERRIES

Cranberries are usually too tart to eat raw and are therefore made into sauces, relishes, and preserves. Only 10% of the commercial crop in the United States is sold in supermarkets, the balance is made into cranberry sauce or juice.

Canned cranberries have only 14% of the vitamin C content than that of fresh and 3 times the calories. Cranberries contain ellagic acid which is discussed further in chapter 9 as a phytochemical.

When choosing a fresh cranberry in the supermarket, make sure it bounces. Another name for cranberries is "bounceberries." Buy berries that are hard, bright, light to dark-red and sealed in plastic bags. When frozen they will keep for up to one year.

Cook cranberries only until they "pop." Further cooking will make them sour and bitter. When cooking cranberries, always add one teaspoon of unsalted butter to each pound, that will eliminate overboiling and reduce the foam that develops.

REPORTED HEALTH BENEFITS

Cranberries have been used for numerous skin disorders, reducing high blood pressure, and for liver and kidney disorders. It has been extensively used as a urinary tract cleanser for hundreds of years.

DATES

These are one of the sweetest fruits and may contain up to 70% sugar. California and Arizona are the major suppliers for the United States, however, Africa and the Middle East have been cultivating them for 4,000 years.

Dates are classified as either soft, semi-soft, or dry. Semi-soft dates are the most common sold in the United States and Deglet Noor is the most common variety. Two of the other popular varieties are Zahidi and Medjool.

A date cluster may weigh up to 25 pounds. They supply 250% more potassium than an orange and 64% more than a banana ounce for ounce. Dates are a concentrated source of calories and not a diet food.

REPORTED HEALTH BENEFITS

Used in cases of anemia, raising low blood pressure, colitis, and improving sexual potency. Crushed dates have been made into syrup for coughs and sore throats.

FIGS

Figs are one of the oldest know fruits. Almost all of the figs grown are sold dried, less than 10% reach markets in their original form. They were brought to California by the Spaniards and most are still grown in California.
The most popular fig is the Calimyrna. They are pollinated by a small fig wasp. Dried figs have 17% more calcium than milk but are very high in calories fir their size.

Varieties include; Black Mission, Kadota, Calimyrna, Brown Turkey, and Smyrna.

REPORTED HEALTH BENEFITS

Beneficial for constipation, anemia, asthma, gout, and a number of skin irritations. Fig juice makes an excellent natural laxative as well as in a poltice on boils.

GRAPEFRUIT

As with all citrus, the heavier the fruit, the juicier. Florida grapefruit are juicier than those from California and Arizona. However, Western fruit has a thicker skin which is easier to peel. If refrigerated, grapefruit will last for 2-3 weeks. Grapefruit should be firm and not discolored. Fruit that is pointed at the end tend to be thick-skinned and have less meat and juice. White fruit has a stronger flavor than the pink variety. They are available year round, but are best January through May.

Grapefruits were developed from crossing an orange with a shaddock. Shaddock's are rarely found in markets since they have almost no juice, a thick skin, a sour taste, and many seeds.

Pectin derived from the skin of grapefruit has shown in recent studies to be more effective in lowering cholesterol levels than any other source of pectin.

Always rinse citrus fruit in case there are still traces of pesticides on them, especially before cutting. Also, allowing grapefruit to stand in boiling water for a few minutes will make it easier to peel.

A small amount of salt will make a grapefruit taste sweeter.

REPORTED HEALTH BENEFITS

Used in the dissolution of inorganic calcium found in the cartilage of the joints of arthritics. Fresh grapefruit contains organic "salicylic acid" which is the active agent.

GRAPES

All varieties of grapes are really berries and are native to Asia Minor where they were cultivated for 6,000 years. Grapes are presently grown on six continents. The growing of grapes is known as "viticulture." California produces 97% and Arizona produces 3% of all European varieties grown in the United States.

Grapes should be plump and firm, and attached to a green stem. They should have goof color, showing no fading. Grapes do not ripen off the vine, so be sure that they are sweet and ripe when purchased. It is always best to try and taste a grape from the bunch you are buying before you buy them. If this is not possible then only purchase a small quantity then taste. Grapes will stay fresh for 5-7 days if refrigerated.

Raisins will not stick to food choppers if they are soaked in cold water for 10 minutes.

COMMON VARIETIES

BLACK BEAUTY
The only seedless black grape.

CALMERIA
Large dark red grape with a light gray finish with very few seeds.

CHAMPAGNE
Used to make currents or sold through gourmet markets.

CONCORD
Major variety of American grape. The color is blue-black with a sweet but somewhat tart flavor.

DELAWARE
Small pink-colored grape with a tender skin.

EMPEROR
One of the most popular small grapes. Reddish-purple color and seedless.

EXOTIC
Blue-black in color with seeds.

FLAME SEEDLESS
Deep red and seedless, about the same size as the Emperor, but somewhat more tart.

ITALIA
Also called Muscat and used mainly for winemaking. Green-gold grape with seeds.

NIAGARA
Large amber-colored grape, may be somewhat egg-shaped and not as sweet as most other varieties.

PERLETTE SEEDLESS
Green grape imported from Mexico.

QUEEN
Large red grape that has a mild sweet flavor.

RED GLOBE
Very large grape with seeds and a delicate flavor.

RED MALAGA
Thick-skinned reddish somewhat sweet grape.

RIBIER
Large blue-black grape with tender skin.

RUBY SEEDLESS
A very sweet deep red grape.

STEUBEN
A blue-black grape similar to the Concord.

THOMPSON SEEDLESS
Everybody's favorite and the most common grape sold in the United States. They are small green grapes with a sweet flavor. Common raisin grape.

TOKAY
A sweeter version of the Flame Seedless.

HONEYDEW MELONS

The best are creamy white or pale yellow with a silky finish. They are best if purchased between June and October. A faint smell indicates ripeness. Blossom end (opposite from the stem) should be slightly soft. Like most melons, honeydews taste better if left unrefrigerated for a few days. Whole ones keep fresh for up to one week when refrigerated. Store cut melons with seeds in plastic bags and eat within 2 days.

REPORTED HEALTH BENEFITS

Used for kidney problems, a diuretic and to improve a person's completion.

KIWI

originated in China and was brought to New Zealand in 1906. The original name was "Chinese gooseberry." It was renamed for the New Zealand bird and has been known as "Kiwi." It is a commercial crop in California and with the reverse growing seasons between California and New Zealand they are available year round. They store for up to 10 months in cold storage.

Kiwi fruit is an excellent meat tenderizer, containing the substance "actinidin." If the raw Kiwi is rubbed over meat before cooking it will provide a tenderizing effect. The Kiwi flavor will not permeate the meat. Never add Kiwi to gelatin as it may not gel due to the action of actinidin.

Firm Kiwis, left at room temperature, soften and sweeten in 3-5 days. Ripe Kiwi feel like ripe peaches. Refrigerated, they stay fresh for weeks with their average size approximately 2-3 inches long. They have a furry brown skin which is peeled off before eating. The inside should be lime green.

Two Kiwis = the fiber in 1 cup of bran flakes and is an excellent source of vitamin C. Best to peel with a sharp vegetable peeler for less waste.

Kiwi will ripen faster if placed next to an apple or a banana in a brown paper bag.

LEMONS AND LIMES

Lemons and limes were probably brought to this country by one of the early explorers and were grown in Florida around during the sixteenth century. The commercial industry was started around 1880 for lemons and around 1912 for limes. California is now the largest producer of lemons.

There are two types of lemons, the very tart and the sweet. We are more used to the tart, however, the sweet are grown mostly by home gardeners. Limes originated on Tahiti. Key limes are a smaller variety with a higher acid content. The California variety of limes are known as the "Bears" and is a seedless lime.

If sprinkled with water and refrigerated in plastic bags, lemons and limes will last for 1-2 months. If frozen, both their juices and grated peels will last about 4 months. Look for lemons and limes with the smoothest skin and the smallest points on each end. They have more juice and a better flavor. Also, submerging a lemon or lime in hot water for 15 minutes before squeezing, will produce almost twice the amount of juice. Also, warming the lemon in the oven for a few minutes will work.

If you only need a few drops of juice, slightly puncture one end with a skewer before squeezing out the desired amount. Return the lemon to the refrigerator and the hole will seal up and the balance of the fruit will still be usable.

Lemons and limes will keep longer in the refrigerator if you place them in a clean jar, cover them with cold water and seal the jar well. After using 1/2 of the fruit, store the other half in the freezer in a plastic bag. This reduces the loss of moisture and retards bacterial growth.

When lemon is used as a flavoring, it tends to mask the craving for the addition of salt. Lemon and lime peelings may cause skin irritation on susceptible people. They contain the oil "limonene."

REPORTED HEALTH BENEFITS

Used as a natural antiseptic to destroy harmful bacteria that may cause infections and as a topical agent for relief of acne and other skin irritations (peelings are not used).

MAMEY

Resembles a small coconut and is the national fruit of Cuba. It has a brown, suede-like skin and the inside is salmon-colored or bright red. The pulp is scooped out and eaten or added to milk and made into a shake.

MANGOES

Mangoes originates in India and that country is still the primary producer. Mangoes come in hundreds of varieties and a number of shapes and sizes. The majority of the mangoes sold in the United States are imported from Mexico, Central America and Hawaii. Only about 10% of the commercially sold fruit is grown in Florida. The most popular variety is the Tommy Atkins, which is an oval-shaped fruit with a bland taste.

They are available in late December through August. Mangoes are an excellent source of vitamins A and C and should be eaten when soft. They ripen easily at room temperature. Recently, they have been found to contain traces of a carcinogenic fumigant, ethylene dibromide (EDB). Purchase only mangoes and papayas grown in Hawaii or Florida.

Mangoes are one of the best sources of beta-carotene, they contain 20% more than cantaloupe and 50% more than apricots.

Mangoes will last for about 5 days if refrigerated in a plastic bag.

Green, hard mangoes may never ripen, try to purchase them ripe and ready to eat.

REPORTED HEALTH BENEFITS

May be beneficial for kidney diseases and to reduce acidity and aide digestion. Also, used for reducing fevers and asthma. When crushes and used as a paste it helps to cleanse the skin pores.

NECTARINES

Nectarines have been around for hundreds of years and are not a new fruit as many people think. The Greek gave them the name of "nektar" which is where the present name was derived from. California grows 98% of all nectarines sold in the United States. Basically they are just a peach without fuzz. There are over 150 varieties of nectarines.

Their peak season is in July and August. They combine a peach and a plum characteristics. Color should be rich and bright. If they are too hard, allow them to ripen at room temperature for a few days. Avoid the very hard dull-looking nectarines.

REPORTED HEALTH BENEFITS

Used as a digestive aid and to relieve flatulence. It has also been used to lower high blood pressure and arthritis.

ORANGES

Commercially oranges were first grown in St. Augustine, Florida in 1820. Florida grows more citrus than any other state. When frozen orange juice was invented in the 1940's oranges became the chief crop of the United States. Florida still produces 70% of the Unites States crop.

The color of an orange is no indication of its quality because oranges are usually dyed to improve their appearance. Brown spots on the skin indicates a good quality orange. Pick a sweet orange by examining the navel. Choose ones with the largest openings. If you place an orange into a hot oven for 2-3 minutes before peeling it, no white fibers will be visible and the pectin content will be higher in the flesh.

Oranges that look green have undergone a natural process called "regreening." This is due to a ripe orange absorbing chlorophyll pigment from the leaves. They are excellent eating and usually very sweet. Mandarins are a very close relative to the orange, are more easily peeled and the sections are more pronounced. They come in a number of varieties.

The rinds of oranges and grapefruits should be stored in a tightly sealed jar and refrigerated. They may be grated and used for flavoring cakes, frostings and cookies.

VARIETIES

BLOOD
The flesh is a blood-red color, and they are sweet and juicy. They are imported from the Mediterranean countries. The reddish color of the flesh comes from anthocyanin pigments.

HAMLIN
Grown primarily in Florida, best for juicing. Averages 46 mg. of vitamin C per 3 1/2 oz serving.

JAFFA
Imported from Israel and similar to Valencia, but are sweeter.

NAVEL
A large thick-skinned orange that is easily identified by its "belly-button" located at the blossom end. It is seedless and sweet, easily peeled and one of the favorites in the United States.

PARSON BROWN
Good juice orange from Florida. Averages 50mg. of vitamin C per 3 1/2 oz. serving.

PINEAPPLE
They have been named for their aroma which is similar to a pineapple. Very flavorful and juicy. Averages 55mg. of vitamin C per 3 1/2 oz. serving.

TEMPLE
Sweet-tasting juice orange. Averages 50mg. of vitamin C per 3 1/2 oz. serving.

VALENCIA
Most widely grown of any orange used mostly for juice. Averages 50mg. of vitamin C per 3 1/2 oz. serving.

REPORTED HEALTH BENEFITS

Recommended for asthma, bronchitis, arthritis, and to reduce high blood pressure. The desire for alcohol is reduced by drinking orange juice.

PAPAYAS

The papaya is also known as the "pawpaw", however, this is a different fruit. They originated in South America and are now extensively grown in Hawaii, the United States and Mexico. The fruit can weigh from 1/2 pound up to 20 pounds and can be in any number of shapes, from pear to oblong.

The papaya seeds are edible and can be used as a garnish similar to capers. They may also be dried and ground, then used like pepper. The Hawaiian papayas are the sweetest and the most common in the markets. The Mexican papayas are much larger and not as sweet.

It is an excellent meat tenderizer utilizing an enzyme called "papain." Only papaya that are not fully ripe have sufficient papain to be useful as a meat tenderizer. The more ripe a papaya the less papain content. The papaya leaves also contain the tenderizer and meat is commonly wrapped in these leaves while it is cooked in Hawaii.

When ripe they will be completely yellow. They will take 3-5 days to ripen at room temperature.

REPORTED HEALTH BENEFITS

Used as a digestive aid, because of the papain content also, as an intestinal cleanser. The juice has been used to relieve infections in the colon and has a tendency to break down mucous.

PEACHES

Peaches are a native of China and was brought to the United States in the 1600's and planted along the eastern seaboard. It has been a commercial crop since the 1800's with Georgia actually being known as the Peach State.

In recent years peaches have had their fuzz removed before being shipped to market by mechanical "defuzzers." They are an excellent source of vitamin C and are available in many varieties, the favorite being Elberta's.

Peaches ripen quickly by placing them in a box covered with newspaper. Gasses are sealed in and it only takes 2-3 days to complete the ripening. The skins may be removed with a potato peeler. Peaches will not get sweeter after being picked, they will just become softer and more edible.

REPORTED HEALTH BENEFITS

Valuable for anemia due to its high vitamin and mineral content. Has also been used for reducing high blood pressure, bronchitis, asthma, bladder and kidney stones and de-worming.

PEARS

Pear trees will live and produce for approximately 90 years and were brought to the Americas by early European settlers. The skins of pears are an excellent source of fiber and a member of the rose family. The majority of the vitamin C in a pear is concentrated in the skin which is why canned pears are not a good source.

VARIETIES

ANJOU
A winter pear with a smooth yellow-green skin that has a taste which is not as sweet as most pears.

BARTLETT
A summer pear and one of the most popular in the United States, accounting for 65% of all commercial production. It is a large, juicy pear and is best when purchased golden yellow or allowed to ripen to that stage.

BOSC
Has a long tapering neck and is excellent for baking.

COMICE
This is the sweetest pear and a favorite among chef's when preparing pears for dessert recipes. it is usually found in gift baskets.

Other pear varieties include; Red Bartlett, Seckel, Asian Pear, and Clapp.

Ripen pears at room temperature for 2-3 days by placing them in a brown paper bag along with a ripe apple. Punch a few holes in the bag and store in a cool, dry location. Apples give off ethylene gas which will help speed the ripening on most fruits. As pears ripen their starch content turns to sugar and they may become somewhat mealy.

REPORTED HEALTH BENEFITS

Excellent for constipation and as a digestive aid. Has also been used for skin irritations.

PERSIMMONS

The persimmon is a native of Japan, and is widely grown there. Persimmons are high in vitamins and minerals but have never really caught on as a popular fruit in the United States. The Japanese persimmon variety sold in the United States is the Hachiya and the Fuyu. The Fuyu is the smaller of the two and shaped like a tomato.

They are available October through January. Persimmons have a smooth, shiny, bright-orange skin, which should be removed before eating or they will taste very sour. They may be ripened overnight by wrapping them in tin foil and placing them into the freezer. Cold temperature will cause a persimmon to become sweeter. Thaw at room temperature and should be eaten the next day.

REPORTED HEALTH BENEFITS

Used to increase energy levels, and treat stomach ulcers and colitis. Have also been used for pleurisy and sore throats.

PINEAPPLE

Pineapples originated in South America and was brought to the Hawaiian Islands in the 1700's for cultivation. It became the main crop of Hawaii and was canned there for the first time. Pineapples are similar to melons in that the starch which converts to sugar as a fruit ripens is found only in the stem until just before the fruit reaches maturity. The starch then converts to sugar and enters the fruit. The fruit will not become any sweeter after it is picked.

It is available year round, but is best March through June. Buy as large and heavy as possible and be sure the leaves are deep green. Do not purchase if soft spots are present and refrigerate as soon as possible.

Fresh pineapple contains the enzyme "bromelain" that will prevent gelatin from setting up. This enzyme may also be used as a meat tenderizer. Studies in the future may also show that bromelain may be effective in reducing the plaque in arterial walls.

To ripen pineapple, cut off the top, remove the skin and slice. Place the pineapple in a pot and cover with water, sweeten to taste if it is not naturally sweet and boil for 5 minutes, cool and refrigerate.

REPORTED HEALTH BENEFITS

Found to assist in gland regulation, as an aid to digestion, and to relive arthritis symptoms.

PLUMS

There are over 140 varieties of plums and they are found growing worldwide. The majority of the United States crop is the Santa Rosa variety which was developed by Luther Burbank in 1907. Plums are used for making prunes and their flavor vary from sweet to tart.

They are available June through September. Buy only firm to slightly soft plums, hard plums will not ripen well. To ripen, allow to stand at room temperature until fairly soft. Do not place in a window where they will be in direct sunlight, as this will eliminate their vitamin C content. They should be refrigerated after ripening and only last for 2-3 days.

The traditional "English Plum Pudding" never contained plums, only currents and raisins. The California French plum is the most common variety for prunes.

REPORTED HEALTH BENEFITS

Used for liver disorders, constipation, to relieve flatulence, and bronchitis.

POMEGRANATES

This has always been a difficult fruit to eat and has never gained popularity. The seeds and pulp are edible, however, it is best to just juice the fruit to obtain its vitamins and minerals. The pulp-like membrane is bitter and not usually eaten. Pomegranate juice is used to make grenadine syrup. Excellent source of potassium.

They are available September through December.

REPORTED HEALTH BENEFITS

Used as a blood purifier and for worm problems, especially tapeworm. Possible benefit in cases of arthritis.

PRICKLY PEARS

A type of cactus fruit that has a yellowish skin, is covered with spines and has a purple-red inside. It has a sweet taste similar to watermelon. Other names it may go by are Indian fig, and Barberry fig.

SAPOTES

Also, called custard apples. They have green skins and creamy, white pulp. They are a good source of vitamin A and potassium.

STAR APPLES

The skin is usually dull purple or light green. A cross section reveals a star-like shape. Used in jellies and eaten like an apple.

UGLI FRUIT

Produced by cross-breeding a grapefruit with an orange or tangerine. It has pinkish-orange flesh, nearly seedless and sweeter than a grapefruit. The fruit originated in Jamaica and is mostly grown in Florida.

Choose the heavier fruit. It has a yellow, pebbly skin with green blotches that will turn orange when the fruit is ripe. makes excellent eating and is high in vitamin C. Looks Ugli!

WATERMELON

The ground-based side of a perfect watermelon is yellow with the stem intact, dried out and brown. The rest of the exterior is smooth, waxy-green color with or without stripes. If cut, choose one with a bright, crisp even-colored flesh. Whole melons will stay fresh if refrigerated for 2-3 days. Once cut, they should be kept refrigerated and covered.

To test for ripeness, snap your thumb and third finger against the melon. If it says "pink" in a high shrill tone, the melon is not ripe. If you hear "punk" in a deep low tone, the melon is ready to eat and should be sweet.

VEGETABLES

Sea vegetables are becoming a new food experience. They may be called "wakame" or "kombu" and are derived from seaweed which is high in minerals.

"BEST TO GET A 4.0"
There are three grades of canned, frozen and dried fruits and vegetables; U.S. Grade A Fancy, U.S.Grade B Choice or Extra Standard, and U.S. Grade C Standard. Grades B and C are just as nutritious but have more blemishes.

"FANCY THAT"
Most fresh fruits and vegetables also have three grades; U.S. Fancy, U.S. Fancy #1, and U.S. Fancy #2. These grades are determined by the product's size, color, shape, maturity and the number of visible defects.

A new category of fruits and vegetables has recently arrived on the scene called "fruit-vegetables." These include; new varieties of eggplant, squash, peppers and tomatoes and are the seed-bearing bodies of these plants. Cross-breeding has also produced new vegetables such as the cross between broccoli and cauliflower.

"SAY GOODBYE TO SOGGY SALADS"
To prevent soggy salads, place an inverted saucer in the bottom of the salad bowl. The excess liquids will drain off under the saucer and leave the salad greens high and dry.

Never add salt to the water when cooking any fruit or vegetable. The salt will draw the liquid out and they may not cook evenly.

The chemical solanine has been associated with arthritis pain in a study by Rutgers University. Foods high in solanine are; green potatoes, tomatoes, red and green bell peppers, eggplant, and paprika.

Never eat home-canned vegetables before cooking them. Bacterial contamination is very common.

Try placing a few sponges in your vegetable drawer to absorb moisture.

Cabbage, turnips, kale, watercress, and rapeseed (Canola oil) contain a harmful chemical called a thioglucoside, which may adversely affect the thyroid gland. However, this chemical is destroyed by cooking. Olive oil is a better choice for a salad dressing oil than Canola.

Parsnips contain a chemical group called psoralens, which cause cancer readily in laboratory animals. They should be peeled and cooked to eliminate these toxins.

Plants high in oxalic acid should be avoided as you approach middle-age and beyond. These include; spinach, rhubarb, and cocoa bean (chocolate). Oxalic acid may interfere with calcium absorption.

Parsley make your skin sensitive to sunlight.

"SCRUB 'EM OR PEEL 'EM"
The FDA during a routine sampling of domestic and imported produce found pesticide residues in 31% of the 3,699 vegetables. The FDA, however, is only able to test 1% of all vegetables sold in the U.S.

Keep all produce wrapped loosely, especially if wrapped in plastic. Air must be allowed to circulate around them to reduce spoilage.

"MAD SCIENTIST"
Avoid using baking soda around fruits and vegetables. Baking soda is a base and many fruits and vegetables are somewhat acidic. When you mix a base and an acid you may end up with a salt and significant loss of taste.

Since the 1950's, we have reduced our purchase of fresh vegetables by 12%, and increased our purchase of frozen and canned by 50%. This is causing an enzyme deficiency and more fresh produce should be consumed.

If cut-up greens need to be crisped, dry them and place them in the freezer in a metal bowl for 5-10 minutes.

"GREAT CAESARS SALAD"
Caesars Salad was named after a restaurant owner in Tijuana, Mexico named Caesar Cardini. He ran out of food one day, took a large bowl and placed everything he had leftover in the restaurant in the bowl and served it as "Caesar Salad."

Egg substitutes may be used to replace raw eggs in a Caesar salad. This will be a lot safer.

"THE NOSE KNOWS"

Try placing a few unshelled pecans in your saucepan when cooking greens, kale, or collards to reduce the odor.

When cooking onions or cabbage, boil a small amount of vinegar in a pan to remove the odor.

The easiest way to cut parsley is with a scissors.

When washing your vegetables place a small amount of salt in the cold water to draw out any sand and insects.

To caramelize vegetables and make the flavors and colors more intense, toss them in extra virgin olive oil and roast them in a 500^0 F. oven for 30-40 minutes or until dark brown.

Adding a small amount of sugar to vegetables when they are cooking will bring out the flavor.

When boiling greens, either stir constantly or add a pat of butter to the water to prevent boiling over. The butter stops the buildup of air bubbles.

"PERKER UPPER"
If you cook with a small amount of milk or vinegar, it will help to retain the color of the vegetable.

Wilted or limp vegetables can be freshened by soaking them in a bowl of cold ice water with the juice of one lemon for 1 hour.

Always line your refrigerator drawers with paper towel to absorb excess moisture which will reduce the growth of mold.

Most vegetable stains can be removed with a slice of wet potato or white vinegar.

Tomatoes, cucumbers, and carrots rank as the most popular salad fixings, The least popular are Lima beans and peas.

"SHAPE UP!"
Use a well-greased muffin tin to bake tomatoes, apples or bell peppers, this will keep them in shape.

CHOOSING THE MOST NUTRITIOUS GREENS

1. Dandelion - Young leaves are the best.
2. Arugula   - Has a slight mustard green flavor.
3. Kale   - Young leaves are the best.
4. Parsley   - Helps bring out the flavor of others.
5. Romaine   - One of the best lettuces.
6. Spinach   - High in nutrients, but contains oxalates.
7. Beet   - Small young leaves are best.
8. Butter   - Lettuce leaves.
9. Endive   - Contains oxalates, use in moderation.
10. Iceberg   - Most popular green and the least nutritious.

By the end of 1996, a new plastic wrap may be released for sale that was developed by the USDA to extend the life of wrapped vegetables.

Fruits and vegetables should be cooked as fast as possible to retain their nutrients.

If salads are served dry, the dressing will adhere better.

Parsley will cure bad breath

THE TOP 10 FRUITS AND VEGETABLES

1. Broccoli
2. Cantaloupe
3. Carrots
4. Kale
5. Mango

6. Papaya
7. Pumpkin
8. Red Bell Pepper
9. Spinach
10. Sweet Potato

The nutrition "buzzwords" these days is pectin. Studies are reporting that pectin has the ability to lower LDL (bad cholesterol) levels and is being used to treat bowel diseases. There may be good validity to these studies and pectin supplement sales are on the rise. There are, however, many natural sources for pectin. The following are a few of the better ones.

FOOD	GRAMS OF PECTIN
Soybeans - 1 cup cooked	2.6
Figs - 5 fruit, dried	2.3
Orange - 1 medium	2.2
Chestnuts - 1 ounce, dried	2.1
Pear - 1 medium	1.8
Potato - 1 medium	1.8
Sweet Potato - 1/2 cup mashed	1.3
Brussels Sprouts - 1/2 cup, frozen	1.1
Apple - 1 medium	1.1
Papaya - 1/2 fruit	1.1
Broccoli - 1/2 cup	1.0
Banana - 1 medium	1.0

```
Strawberries - 1 cup...................... .9
Tomato - 1 medium......................... .9
Lima beans - 1/2 cup boiled.............. .9
Hazelnuts - 1 ounce, raw................. .9
Carrot - 1 medium........................ .8
Pistachio Nuts - 1 ounce, dried.......... .8
Peach - 1 medium......................... .7
Peas - 1/2 cup, boiled................... .6
Almonds - 1 ounce, dried................. .6
Walnuts - 1 ounce, dried................. .6
Green Beans - 1/2 cup, boiled............ .5
Lemon - 1 medium......................... .5
Summer Squash - 1/2 cup, boiled.......... .5
Grapefruit - 1/2 medium.................. .3
Spinach - 1/2 cup, raw................... .2
```

ARTICHOKES

Originated in Italy and was brought to the Unites States by the Europeans in the 1800's. Almost all artichokes sold in the Unites States are grown in California. The artichoke is an unopened flower bud from a thistlelike plant. The most tender and edible part is that of the "heart" or center of the plant. They tend to vary in size and produce a sweet aftertaste caused by the chemical "cynarin."

There are 50 varieties and it is best to purchase them March through may. Choose from compact, tightly closed heads with green, clean-looking leaves. Their size is not related to quality. Avoid ones that have brown leaves or show signs of mold. Leaves that are separated, show that it is too old and will be tough and bitter.

Best to wear rubber gloves when working with artichokes. Artichokes should never be cooked in aluminum pots as they tend to turn the pots a gray color. They are easily burned and should be kept covered by water while they are cooking, however, they are also easy to overcook.

Stainless steel knives should be used to cut artichokes. Carbon blades tend to react with the chemicals and darken the flesh.

When cooking artichokes you can obtain a better flavor if you add a small amount of sugar and salt to the water. They will be sweeter and retain their color better.

If your artichokes are too bland tasting, try adding a small amount of fennel to the cooking water, about 1/8 - 1/4 teaspoon.

Artichokes can be stored in a plastic bag in the refrigerator, <u>unwashed</u>, for 5-6 days.

REPORTED HEALTH BENEFITS

The juice of the leaves have been used as a powerful diuretic and in liver disorders and to relieve bad breathe. Other uses include arthritis, neuritis, and glandular disorders.

ASPARAGUS

Asparagus can be traced back to ancient Greece and has been referred to as the "aristocrat of vegetables." It is a member of the lily family and related to onions and garlic. It is an excellent source of vitamins and minerals. There are two types of asparagus, white and green. Canned asparagus contains less vitamin C due to losses into the water it is canned in. It is recommended to use the water in other dishes.

White asparagus is the result of planting under a layer of soil which does not allow the sun to reach the asparagus. Fresh asparagus stalks are more fibrous and need to be tenderized by removing a single layer with a potato peeler. Asparagus loses approximately 50% of its vitamin C content within 2 days after picking as well as some of its sugars. Fresh asparagus should be eaten within a day of purchase.

When choosing asparagus the stalks should be green with compact, closed tips and tender. Avoid flat stalks or stalks that contain white streaks. Never purchase them if they are being stored in water. The best time of year to purchase asparagus is March through June. Refrigeration will help to retain the nutrients providing you cut a small piece off the ends wrap the ends in moist paper towel and seal them in a plastic bag.

"WHOOPS"
Always open an asparagus can from the bottom or you may break the tips. However, some asparagus is canned upside down and it is best to read the top of the can before opening.

"ALMOST AS BAD AS PEPE LE PEW"
Asparagus contains a sulfur compound that may cause a strange odor in a persons urine. This happens in only 40% of the population and is harmless.

If the asparagus is overcooked, try cutting the asparagus into small pieces and adding the asparagus to a can of creamed soup.

"THIS WILL STRAIGHTEN THEM OUT"
Asparagus that has become limp can be revived by placing them in ice cold water with ice cubes for 30-45 minutes.

To improve the taste of asparagus, try adding a bouillon cube or a small amount of soy sauce to the cooking water.

REPORTED HEALTH BENEFITS

The juice has been used to break up oxalic acid crystals in the kidneys. It has also been used for arthritis.

BEANS (Edible Pods)

This type of bean is picked before they are fully ripe and as the inner seed (bean) is just starting to form. These immature seeds contain a higher level of beta-carotene and vitamin C. The dried seeds are high in protein and carbohydrate.

These beans may be green, purple or yellow and should have no scars or discolorizations. When broken they should have a crisp snap. They are available all year round, but are best May through August. Refrigerate whole and unprocessed in any way to retain their vitamin content. Never leave them soaking in water.

To prevent beans from becoming mushy, try adding a pinch of baking soda to the water while they are cooking. Never use salt until the beans are tender, salt will toughen them.

VARIETIES

CHINESE LONG BEANS

Mild-tasting, long, thin beans. These can be as long as 18" and have been called the "yard-long" bean. Best when young and tender.

HARICOTS VERTS

A slender variety of a snap bean developed originally in France.

ITALIAN GREEN BEANS

Also known as Romano beans. Have a broad, flat, bright green pod and are a popular frozen bean.

PURPLE WAX BEAN

Has a dark purple pod that changes color to green when cooked. Looks similar to a small yellow wax bean.

SCARLET RUNNER BEAN

Pods are broad and flat, the pod is green and the seeds are a reddish color. The blossom is also edible.

SNAP BEANS

Have tender, crisp pods that will easily snap in half. The ends are usually just "snapped off" instead of cutting them. These are the familiar green beans or yellow wax beans. Formerly known as "string beans." The string has been bred out from the inside and their name has been changed.

Cooked beans have a refrigerator life of approximately 5 days. If you boil the beans whole without even removing the ends you will retain 50% more of the nutrients.

If you place a very small amount of sugar in the cooking water of beans it will bring out the flavor.

Baking soda should never be added to green beans while they are being cooked as it will reduce the nutrient content of the beans.

Acidic foods such as tomatoes will cause the color of green beans to be lightened.

"IT'S ALL IN THE BREEDING"
String beans gained that name because originally they were very stringy, however, in recent years the stringiness has been bred out of the bean.

REPORTED HEALTH BENEFITS

Have been used for hemorrhoids and anemia.

BEANS (Shell)

These are actually mature fresh seeds that are between the fresh seeds and dried seeds. Shell beans have a higher level of vitamins and dried beans are high in protein, potassium and iron.

VARIETIES

CRANBERRY BEAN

Identified by their red markings on the white pods as well as the actual bean.

FAVA BEAN

Similar to Lima beans in taste and texture. Has been called "broad bean" and the pods are longer than Lima. A popular favorite in salads.

LIMA BEAN

The most common shell bean in the United States. Originated in Peru. Almost all of the domestic crop goes for canning or freezing. They are very perishable and should be used as soon as purchased.

If you add a small amount of sugar to the cooking water it will help bring out the flavor.

SOYBEANS

Usually sold as a dried bean, however, they are more popular in the orient as a fresh bean. They have a high protein content and a mild flavor. Soybeans contain a complete protein which makes it equivalent to animal products in relation to the quality of the protein.

The following are a few of the more common soy products:

TOFU

> Made from soy milk by using a coagulating agent to separate the milk into curds and whey. The curds are compressed into blocks then stored in water under refrigeration or vacuum-packed. If you purchase unpackaged tofu be sure and change the water it is stored in daily. Low-fat tofu is now being sold.

TEMPEH

> Made from whole cooked soybeans that is infused with a starter bacteria then allowed to ferment. This produces a product that is very dense and chewy with a nutty flavor. Can be fried, grilled, or used for veggie burgers. Because of the fermentation process, it contains one of the only vegetable sources of vitamin B_{12}.

MISO

> This is a fermented soybean paste. It is high in protein, isoflavones, and antioxidants. Has a high sodium content. Used more as a condiment and flavoring agent.

SOY MILK

> Extracted from soybeans and consumed by
> people who have an allergy to cow's milk. Usually,
> found supplemented with vitamin D and B$_{12}$.
> Commonly found flavored with chocolate.

TEXTURED SOY PROTEIN (TSP)

> Made from compressing soy flour. Excellent source
> of calcium and because of its consistency is used
> as a replacement for hamburger meat in many
> recipes. Try replacing 30-50% of your ground beef
> with TSP next time you make a meatloaf.

Shell beans should have a bulge and a tightly closed pod. If
the pods are sealed, they should last for 2-3 days. When
they are cooked, if you add a small amount of baking soda to
the cooking water it will help retain their color.

Gas-free Lima beans are now being grown, They will contain
less of the hard-to-digest complex sugar that causes the
problem.

REPORTED HEALTH BENEFITS

Lima beans are very rich in iron and have been used to treat
anemia. Soybeans have been given to athletes because of
their high quality protein.

BEANS (Pinto)

Pinto beans are a dried bean that is an excellent source of
protein. They should have a bright uniform color, fading is
a sign of aging or long storage periods. When preparing
pinto beans, try and purchase ones of uniform size, the
smaller ones may become mushy before the larger ones are
cooked. If you feel that this may be a problem, try adding a
small amount of baking soda to the water while they are
cooking.

Beans can be stored in an airtight container for up to 1
year while retaining a high nutrient level.

"BEAN OVERBOARD"
When you are cooking dried beans, make sure you add 3
teaspoons of a pure vegetable oil to the water, this will
help prevent boilovers.

Beans contain 22% protein, beef has only 18%, and eggs has
13%.

To tell whether a bean is fully cooked squeeze the bean, you should never feel a hard core.

If you are cooking the beans in an acid medium, such as with tomatoes, this will slow down the cooking time and testing the tenderness of the beans is a must.

Cooked beans will store for only 6 months in the freezer, but only 4-6 days in the refrigerator.

If beans taste too salty, try adding a small amount of brown sugar.

"OH, WHAT A RELIEF IT IS"
Pinto beans are noted for their gas-giving properties that are a result of complex sugars. This problem can be eliminated and the sugars removed or neutralized by adding a teaspoon or two of fennel seed to the water the beans are soaking in. The fennel seed tends to neutralize the complex sugars.

"NUTRITIONALLY SPEAKING"
Beans are one of the best vegetable sources of protein. The following evaluates their protein quality on a scale of 1-10:

Kidney Beans.... 10   Lentils.... 7.0
Navy Beans...... 9.5   Chickpeas.. 6.5
Lima Beans...... 8.5   Split Peas. 5.5

If beans seem too salty, try adding a small amount of brown sugar to the pot. Cooked beans will store for up to 6 months in the freezer, but only 4-6 days in the refrigerator.

BEAN COOKING CHART

BEAN	PRE-SOAK	COOKING TIME
ADZUKA BEANS	YES	1 HOUR
BLACK BEANS	YES	1-2 HOURS
BLACK-EYED PEAS	NO	1-1.5 HOURS
CHICK PEAS(GARBANZOS)	YES	2.5-3 HOURS
GREAT WHITE BEANS	YES	1.5-2 HOURS
KIDNEY BEANS	YES	1.5-2 HOURS
LENTILS	NO	30-45 MIN.
LIMA BEANS	YES	1 HOUR
MUNG BEANS	NO	45 MIN.-1 HOUR
NAVY BEANS	YES	1-1.5 HOURS
SPLIT PEAS	NO	1-1.5 HOURS
PINTO BEANS	YES	1.5-2 HOURS
SOY BEANS	YES	3+ HOURS

BEETS

Beets have the highest sugar content of any vegetable, yet low in calories. They are an excellent source of vitamins and minerals. Both the roots and the leaves are edible. Beets are a relative of spinach. it is best to buy only small or medium-sized beets, the larger beets are not very tender and may have a stronger flavor. Do not purchase if they look shriveled or flabby, they should be firm.

Greens should be used as soon as purchased and the roots within 5-7 days. Beets should be cooked whole and unpeeled to retain their nutrients. Beets contain the chemical pigment "betacyanin" which gives the beets their red color. Some people cannot metabolize this pigment and it turns their feces and urine red for a few days, however, it is harmless.

"BETTER BEETWARE"
Betacyanin "beet red" is difficult to remove from your hands and disposable rubber gloves are recommended when working with beets.

Sugar beets are 20% sucrose by weight and have twice the sugar content of standard beets. It takes 100 pounds of sugar beets to produce 5 pounds of sugar.

Beets should be cooked whole to retain their red color and nutrients.

When preparing any dish that contains beets, be sure and add the beets last. Beets will lose some of their color and color the other foods red.

"OFF WITH THEIR TOPS"
As with any vegetable with a leaf top, the leaf top should be removed when they are purchased and stored. The leaf top will leach moisture from the root or bulb and shorten their shelf life.

REPORTED HEALTH BENEFITS

Used to relieve headaches and toothaches. Two pounds of raw mashed beets consumed daily have been used for tumors and leukemia. Beet greens have a higher iron content than spinach and have been used to treat anemia.

BROCCOLI

A member of the "cruciferous" family of vegetables which also include cabbage and Brussels sprouts. it was first grown in United States in the 1920's and is one of the nutritious vegetables. They will have a higher nutrient content if eaten fresh.

Broccoli is available year round and is best from October through may. The stem should not be too thick and the leaves should not be wilted. If the buds are open or yellow the broccoli is old and will have a significant loss of nutrients. The florets should be closed and a good solid green color, they contain 8 times the beta-carotene as the stalks. Use as soon as purchased, refrigeration will help retain the vitamin A and C content.

One cup of broccoli contains 90% of the USRDA of vitamin A, 200% of vitamin C, 6% of niacin, 10% of calcium, 10% of thiamin, 10% of phosphorus, and 8% of iron. It also provide 25% of your fiber needs and even has 5 grams of protein.

Broccoli should be washed in good organic cleaner. The EPA has registered more than 50 pesticides that can be used on broccoli. 70% of these cannot be detected by the FDA after picking. 13% of broccoli, in a study showed that pesticide residues were still present even after initial processing. Organic broccoli would be an excellent choice or eat in moderation.

Broccoli consumption has risen over 50% since 1983 to 21 servings per person in 1995. Broccoli that has been cooked still has 15% more vitamin C than an orange.

Cruciferous vegetables such as broccoli and cabbage tend to release strong-smelling chemical compounds when cooked. These ammonia and hydrogen sulfide compounds will smell up the kitchen. Steaming or cooking in a small amount of water and as fast as possible will lessen the odor. Also, if you place a fresh piece of white bread over the vegetables while they are cooking, the bread will absorb much of the odor.

Broccoli stems will cook in the same amount of time if you slice an "X" all the way down the stem before cooking.

Broccoli should be cooked as quickly as possible to retain its green color. Broccoli's color is also very sensitive to acidic foods.

If you are only using the broccoli floret tops and wish to save the stems, you need to blanch in boiling water for 2-3 minutes before freezing them in an airtight plastic freezer bag. They will last for about 3-4 months and still retain most of their nutrients.

REPORTED HEALTH BENEFITS

Used for constipation, to reduce high blood pressure and as a digestive aid.

BROCCOFLOWER

A cross between broccoli and cauliflower and looks more like a cauliflower with a light green color. It has a milder flavor than either of its relatives. Make sure that the florets are tightly closed for maximum nutritional content.

BRUSSELS SPROUTS

This vegetable was named after the capital of Belgium, where it originated. A relative of the cabbage family, it even resembles small heads of cabbage. They were brought America in the 1800's from England and were first grown in Louisiana. They are an excellent source of protein, but not a complete protein unless you eat them with a grain.

They are easily overcooked and will become mushy. Best to store them in the refrigerator to keep the leaves a green color instead of yellow.

REPORTED HEALTH BENEFITS

Used as a general tonic for blood cleansing, constipation and to reduce hardening of the arteries.

CABBAGE

Originated in the eastern Mediterranean region and was popular among the ancient Greeks. it is available year round in three main varieties; red, green, and savoy which has crankily leaves. Avoid cabbage with worm holes and be sure to smell the core for sweetness. Green and red cabbage should have firm tight leaves with good color, Cabbage should be refrigerated in plastic bags and used within 7-14 days.

Cabbage along with its other cruciferous family members are being studied in cancer prevention due to its "indole" content. Studies indicate that if you consume 1/2 of a standard cabbage daily you may prevent a number of cancers.

When you need cabbage leaves for stuffed cabbage, try freezing the whole cabbage first, then let it thaw, and the leaves will come apart without tearing.

Cabbage odor can be reduced by placing a slice of fresh white bread on top of the cabbage while it cooks. Another method is to add a 1/4 of a fresh lemon to the cooking water.

Cabbage will last longer if stored in the refrigerator sealed tightly in a plastic bag. It should stay for about 2 weeks.

Flatulence problems from cabbage can be eliminated by boiling the cabbage for about 5-6 minutes then draining the water and continuing to boil it in fresh water. The chemical that causes the problem is released during the first few minutes of cooking.

If you are preparing a recipe that calls for cabbage wedges, try steaming them instead of boiling them, they will retain their shape better.

VARIETIES

BOK CHOY

Looks like a cross between celery and Swiss chard. When cooked bok choy will have slightly sharp flavor, but the stalks are rarely bitter. They contain an excellent amount of calcium and vitamin A.

GREEN

Has smooth, dark to pale outer leaves, while the inner leaves are pale green or white.

NAPA

Has a more delicate flavor than most cabbages. Is high in vitamins and minerals.

RED

Has a solid red to purple outer leaf, usually with white veins or streaks on the inside leaves.

SAVOY

Has a crinkled, ruffled yellow-green leaf and is less compact than most cabbage.

REPORTED HEALTH BENEFITS

Used for asthma, blood cleansing, healthier hair and nails, bladder disorders and skin irritations. Present research shows that 1/2 head of cabbage a day may help to prevent certain types of cancer (contains indoles).

CARROTS

Carrots are the best source of beta-carotene in the diet. Studies show that carrots may lower blood cholesterol levels. Drinking an excessive amount of carrot juice may turn your skin orange due to high level of carotenoid pigment. Reducing the intake will alleviate this color problem.

They are available year round and should have smooth skins, a solid orange color and be well-formed. Should be stored in the refrigerator and never placed in water for any period of time, especially if peeled.

The tops of carrots should be removed before storing. The tops will drain the carrots of moisture, making them limp and dry. Carrots should be kept away from apples and tomatoes since these fruits give off ethylene gas and will turn them bitter.

If carrots are to used in a stir-fry, try boiling them first, them place them in cold water until needed. It takes longer to cook the carrots since they are so hard. They should not be left in the water for more than 30 minutes or nutrients will be lost.

To slip the skin off carrots, drop them in boiling water, let stand for 5 minutes, then place them into cold water for a few seconds.

To curl carrots, peel slices with a potato peeler and drop them into a bowl of ice water.

When grating carrots, leave a portion of the green top on to use as a handle. This will keep your fingers from becoming shorter.

"THE YOUNGER, THE BETTER"
If you wish to freeze vegetables, try to purchase "young ones." Their nutrient content will be higher and they will contain less starch. Freeze as soon as purchased. Fresh produce has stronger cell walls and will handle freezing better.

"CARROT TOP"
Carrot greens are high in vitamin K and E which are lacking in the carrot.

Carrot skins only contain 10% of all nutrients found in the carrot.

The USDA has completed studies showing that 7 ounces of carrots consumed every day for 3 weeks lowered cholesterol levels by 11%. This was probably due to calcium pectate, a type of fiber found in carrots and usually lost during the juicing process.

REPORTED HEALTH BENEFITS

Carrot juice has been used for the treatment of asthma, insomnia, colitis, improved eyesight, and healthy hair and nails. It is also an excellent antioxidant. The levels of beta carotene in carrots has increased by 50% over carrots grown in 1950 due to improved new varieties.

CAULIFLOWER

Another member of the cruciferous family, it has a very compact head and grows on a single stalk. It is surrounded by green leaves which protect it from the sun and cause the cauliflower to remain white instead of producing chlorophyll.

It is best purchased September through January, but is available year round. Do not purchase if the clusters are open. If there is a speckled surface, this is a sign of insect injury, mold or rot. Should be stored in the refrigerator.

To keep cauliflower white during cooking, add lemon to the water. Overcooking tends to darken cauliflower and make it tough. Prior to cooking, you should soak it head down for about 30 minutes in salted water to remove any grit and insects.

To reduce the odor when cooking cauliflower, replace the water after it has cooked for 5-7 minutes.

Due to certain minerals found in cauliflower it is best not to cook it in an aluminum or iron pot, Contact with these metals will turn cauliflower yellow, brown or blue-green.

REPORTED HEALTH BENEFITS

Used as a blood cleanser and for kidney and bladder disorders. Also, in some cases of asthma, gout, and high blood pressure.

CELERY

Arrived in United States from Europe in the 1800's. Celery has a very high water content and is low in calories. it is available year round, Stalks should be slid, with no softness along any of the stalks which will denote a pithiness. If even one stalk is wilted, do not purchase. Celery will store in the refrigerator for 7-10 day at the most and should not be placed in water.

Don't discard the celery leaves; dry them, then rub the leaves through a sieve turning them into a powder that can be used to flavor soups, stews, salad dressings, etc. It can also be made into celery salt.

Celery, carrots and lettuce will crisp up quickly if placed into a pan of cold water with a few slices of raw potato. To prevent celery from turning brown, soak in lemon juice and cold water before refrigerating for only a few minutes.

REPORTED HEALTH BENEFITS

The juice has been used as a tonic to reduce stress. Other used include; asthma, diabetes, as a diuretic and to reduce the incidence of gall stones.

CELERIAC

A root vegetable that looks like a turnip and is prepared like any other root vegetable. It has an ivory interior and has a strong celery taste with a dash of parsley. Celeriac should be firm and have a minimum of rootlets and knobs. Excellent in salad, shredded like carrots.

CELTUCE

A combination of celery and lettuce, does not have a high nutritional content and is prepared similar to cabbage.

CORN

Corn was first grown in Mexico or Central America and was an early staple of the American Indian. Corn is a good source of protein and can be part of a complete protein by serving it with rice. When ground for tortillas, an excellent amount of niacin is released. Corn contains 5-6% sugar making it a taste favorite. Americans consume about 25 pounds of corn per person annually.

It is available May through September and the kernels should be a good yellow color. Do not purchase if the husks are a straw color, they should be green. The straw color indicates decay or worm infestation. Yellow corn usually has a more appealing flavor than white and is higher in vitamin A content.

The best way to remove kernels from an ear of corn is to use a shoehorn or a spoon. The best tasting corn is grown in Florida and is known as "Florida Sweet."

There are 200 varieties of sweet corn.

Corn is one of the least nutritionally complete grains.

"WELL FANCY THAT"
When wrapping corn in tin foil for barbecuing, try placing a sprig of marjoram next to each ear of corn.

"PILED HIGHER AND DEEPER"
When storing corn, keep it cool. When corn gets warm the sugar tends to convert into starch. In fact, hen corn is piled high in the markets and is allowed to stay for days, the bottom ones will be less sweet due to the heat generated by the weight of the ones on top.

The kernels at the tip of an ear of corn should be small, large kernels are usually a sign of over maturity. If the kernels are shrunken away from the tip, the corn may be older and not as sweet. When a kernel is popped or broken, the juice should be milky, not clear.

Never salt the water that corn is cooking in, it tends to toughen the corn. Steaming corn for 6-10 minutes is one of the preferred cooking methods. To store corn longer, cut a small piece off the stalk end, leave the leaves on, then store the ears in a pot with about an inch of water, stems down.

Corn chips in all colors have the same amount of fat and calories, unless they are labeled "reduced-fat" or "baked." Blue corn chips are made from blue corn.

Cornmeal may be purchased in two varieties; steel-ground which has the husk and germ almost all removed, and stone or water-ground which retains a portion of the hull and germ and is usually only available in health food stores.

Cornstarch is a thick, powdery flour that is made from the corn's endosperm. It is an excellent thickener for sauces but tends to form lumps easily unless it is mixed slowly into a cold liquid and then added to a hot liquid. Stir the cornmeal until it mixes thoroughly then boil it for a few minutes to thicken the sauce or stew.

POPCORN FACTS

"WEAR YOUR GOGGLES"
Corn used for popcorn needs to contain enough moisture to puff up the starches when it is heated. The hull is thick enough to contain the steam, yet is easily able to explode.

"BETCHA CAN'T EAT JUST ONE"
Two quarts of plain popcorn = the calories in 15 potato chips.

"WISING UP"
Every man, woman and child in the United States consumes approximately 47 quarts of popcorn each year. After the fat content information was released in 1994, consumption was down 15%.

"A SLIPPERY SUBJECT"
Movies switched to Canola oil and by 1995 consumption was back to its original level. Canola did not change the fat content at all, just the use of a healthier fat.

"THE FIRST REAL POPPERS"
The Aztecs were the first to pop corn and use it as a decoration.

Air poppers make the popcorn pop into larger blossoms, but they are usually tougher and less crisp.

"SAVING AN OLD MAID"
To restore moisture to an "old maid" (stubborn kernels that refuse to pop), fill a one-quart jar 3/4 full of unpopped kernels, add one tablespoon of water, cover the jar and shake for 2-3 minutes or until all the water is absorbed. Store the jar in a cool location (not the refrigerator) for 2-3 days before trying to pop.

"TOO BAD, YUPPIES"
There is no nutritional difference in regular popcorn and gourmet popcorn, only a slight difference in the size. The gourmet pops into larger blossoms.

REPORTED HEALTH BENEFITS

Used for anemia and constipation.

CUCUMBERS

Originated in Asia, cucumber were brought to the Americas by Columbus. They come in all sizes from the smallest gherkins to as large as 20" long. They have a very high water content and are an excellent source of fiber. The Greenhouse or English cucumber is becoming more and more popular, however, the price of this thin-skinned skinny "cuke" is considerably higher than the standard market cucumber.

Cucumbers should be firm and a good green color, either dark or light, but not yellow. Purchase only firm cucumbers and refrigerate. Large thick ones tend to pithy and give when squeezed. Cucumbers only have 13 calories per 3 1/2 ounce serving.

"PICKLED CALORIES"
Pickled dill cucumbers have 3 calories per ounce compared to sweet pickles at 30 calories per ounce.

"GETTING PICKLED"
When making pickles, remove 1/4 inch from each end. The ends contain an enzyme that may cause the pickles to soften prematurely.

Pickle juice should be saved and used for making coleslaw, potato salad, etc.

If you add a small piece of horseradish to the pickle jar, it will keep the vinegar active while keeping the pickles from becoming soft.

REPORTED HEALTH BENEFITS

Used as a natural diuretic and to help lower high blood pressure. Cucumber contain the enzyme "erepsin" which aids in the digestion of proteins.

EGGPLANT

Eggplant is a member of the "nightshade" family of vegetables which also include potatoes, tomatoes and peppers. it is not very high on the nutrient scale. varieties include; Chinese purple eggplant, Globular eggplant, Japanese eggplant and Italian eggplant.

"THE FAT SPONGE"
Eggplants in a recent study absorbed more fat when fried than any other vegetable; 83 grams in 70 seconds - four times more than and equal portion of french fries adding 700 calories to the low-calorie eggplant.

They are available all year but are best during August and September. Their outer purple-black skin should be smooth and glossy, free of scars and they should be firm. Soft eggplants are usually bitter. Keep them cool after purchase and use in 2-3 days.

Never eat raw eggplant, since it may contain the toxin solanine which is destroyed by cooking.

REPORTED HEALTH BENEFITS

Used for constipation, colitis and various nervous disorders.

FENNEL

Fennel is a member of the parsley family and looks like a very plump bunch of celery. Fennel tastes like "anise" and has a sweet flavor. It is very low in calories, can easily be substituted for celery and is high in vitamin A, calcium and potassium.

The bulbs should be firm and clean with fresh-looking leaves. If any brown spots are seen, avoid the fennel. It tends to dry out quickly and should be wrapped and used within 3-4 days.

HORSERADISH

Horseradish is usually available year round and stores very well. Make sure that you purchase only firm roots with no signs of soft spots or withering. If tightly wrapped in a plastic bag it should last up to 3 weeks in the refrigerator. If not used in 3-4 weeks it may turn bitter and lose its hot bite.

Try mixing a small amount of horseradish with applesauce as a unique condiment when serving pork.

JERUSALEM ARTICHOKES

These are members of the sunflower family and also known as the "sunchoke." Do not buy them if they are tinged with green or have any soft spots. They should be firm and look fresh. They will stay fresh under refrigeration for about a week. They may be peeled with a vegetable peeler, however, they do contain a fair amount of nutrition in the skin.

It has a somewhat nutty, sweet flavor and should be crunchy. it can be boiled, sauteed, or even breaded and fried.

JICAMA

Originated in Mexico and is becoming very popular in the United States. It is a root vegetable that can weigh up to 5 pounds or more. The skin is brown and the flesh is white. It can be used in salads either diced or in small sticks. Choose only unblemished jicama with no soft spots. Excellent for stir-fries. Excellent source of vitamin C.

It has a slightly sweet flavor and has been substituted for potatoes. One pound equals about 3 cups. The texture is similar to a water chestnut.

LEEKS

Leeks are a close relative of the onion family, but are milder and sweeter. They are more nutritious, having a wide variety of vitamins and minerals. They are best purchased between September and November. The tops should be green with white necks 2-3 inches from the roots. Do not purchase if tops are wilted or if there appears to be signs of aging. Refrigerate and use within 5-7 days after purchase.

LETTUCE

Lettuce can be traced back to Roman days and was originally named for the Romans (Romaine). Lettuce is second only to potatoes in popularity in the United States. They are mainly used in salads and as garnish.

It is available year round and most should be heavy and solid, depending on the variety. The greener the leaves the higher the nutrient content. Never add salt to lettuce prior to serving as this may cause the lettuce to wilt.

Lettuce will not rust as quickly if you line the bottom of the refrigerator vegetable compartment with a paper towel. The paper towel will absorb the excess moisture. it is also best to remove the core before storage.

American consume approximately 11 pounds of lettuce per person, per year. Romaine lettuce has 6 times as much vitamin C and 8 times as much vitamin A as iceberg lettuce.

Over 60 chemical agents can be applied to lettuce. Most can be removed by washing with a good organic cleaner or by placing the head stem side up in a sink with 6-8 inches of cold, lightly salted water for a minute while shaking and swirling around.

Before you store your lettuce you should remove the core by hitting the core once against a hard surface, them twist the core out.

BUTTERHEAD

Has a soft "buttery" texture and a is a "loose" head lettuce. Also, known as Boston or Bibb lettuce. The leaves are a dark green to grass-colored green.

ICEBERG

This is the most popular and extensively sold in the United States. It is the least nutritious lettuce of all the greens except Belgium endive due to a very high water content. Best to choose any other lettuce.

LOOSELEAF

The leaves are loosely packed and joined at the stem. The leaves are usually green with a tinge of red near the edges. They are a crisp lettuce with a mild and delicate flavor.

ROMAINE

Has long green leaves and is usually very crisp. It is mainly used in Caesar salads.

Romaine lettuce has 6 times as much vitamin C and 8 times as much vitamin A as iceberg lettuce.

STEM

Has a thick edible stem, approximately 6-8 inches long. Widely grown in China. The U.S. variety has been called Celtuce. It has a mild flavor.

ARUGULA

A solid green lettuce with a high beta-carotene and vitamin C content. Has small flat leaves on long stems and resembles dandelion greens with a somewhat peppery flavor. A cruciferous vegetable which may be studied regarding cancer prevention.

BELGIUM ENDIVE

Related to chicory and escarole. Has a bullet-like head with tightly closed creamy white or somewhat yellow leaves. Low in vitamins and minerals, even lower than iceberg lettuce.

CHICORY

Has loosely bunched ragged leaves on a long stem. The outer leaves are dark green and it has a somewhat bitter taste. The center leaves, however, are yellow and have a mild taste.

ESCAROLE

Has broad wavy leaves with smooth edges and a bitter flavor.

MACHE

Has a delicate green colored leaf, very perishable and more expensive than most lettuce. The leaves have a fingerlike shape with a mild taste and only sold in small bunches.

RADICCHIO

A chicory-family member that looks like a small head of red cabbage with leaves in a variety of colors.

WATERCRESS

Another member of the cruciferous family with dark green leaves and a mustardlike flavor. More popular as a garnish than in salad use.

REPORTED HEALTH BENEFITS

The cruciferous lettuce's are being studied in cancer prevention. Endive has been used in cases of asthma, gout, high blood pressure, arthritis and liver ailments.

MUSHROOMS

Mushrooms can be traced back to the Egyptian pharaohs. They are an excellent source of nutrients and are a fungus without any roots or leaves. There are approximately 38,000 varieties of mushrooms, many toxic and a few varieties that are edible. It is best never to pick and eat a wild mushroom unless it is in the supermarket.

Mushrooms contain the chemical substance hydrazine, which are found mainly in the stems. Cooking tends to neutralize this chemical and therefore if you consume mushrooms they should be cooked. However, most of the hydrazine is found in the stems. Studies from the University of Nebraska showed that mice developed malignant tumors from ingesting large quantities of mushrooms.

They are available year round but are best November through march. The caps should be closed around the stems. Refrigerate after purchase and use as soon as possible. Never immerse mushrooms in a pan of cold water when cleaning, since they will absorb too much water. This will make it more difficult to cook them without losing flavor.

The same flavor enhancer found in MSG is found naturally in mushrooms, glutamic acid. To keep mushrooms white and firm when sauteeing them, add a teaspoon of lemon juice to each quarter pound of butter.

VARIETIES

BUTTON

The standard mushroom that is widely cultivated throughout the world. A large majority of the production goes into jars and is canned and dried. They are a short, stubby mushroom with a round cap and gills on the underneath side. Sizes can vary from 1-10 inches.

CEPE

Has a stout stem and a spongy surface, instead of gills on the underneath side and a brown cap. It is also known as bolete, cep and porcino mushrooms. They can range in size from 1-10 inches and one of the best tasting of all mushrooms.

CHANTERELLE

These are shaped like trumpets. They are large with frilly caps and range in color from gold to yellow-orange.

ENOKI

These are sproutlike and have very small caps on a long thin stem. Their color is a creamy white and they have a mild flavor. Best served raw in salads or soups. Have also been known as enokitake.

ITALIAN BROWN

These are less expensive mushrooms and are similar in appearance to the standard button mushroom. They have a good flavor and are not as tender as button mushrooms.

KOMBUCHA

Also know as Japanese tea fungus. Claims have been made recently that it is a cure-all for numerous diseases and recommended for the prevention of hair-loss, arthritis, psoriasis, and cancer. According to recent information from the FDA, scientific evidence is lacking. Cornell University is studying the mushroom and has found it to have properties that may have an anti-tumor effect.

A West African study showed that the tea caused organ damage in rats. A report from the Iowa Department of Public Health stated that two women who drank the tea for several weeks suffered from acidosis. Never use ceramic or lead crystal for storing then tea, its high acidic nature may leach the lead out.

MOREL

These are one of the more high-priced mushrooms, They are a dark brown mushroom with conical shaped, spongy caps. They also have a honey-combed surface.

OYSTER

A wild variety, ranging in color from off-white to a gray-brown, they grow in clusters and have a very dense chewy texture. More flavorful when cooked.

PORTOBELLO

Also known as Roma mushrooms, they have a hearty flavor, circular caps and long, thick stems.

SHIITAKE

At one time these were only grown in Japan, but are now available in the United States. They are grown on artificial logs and are umbrella-shaped, and brown-black in color. They have a rich flavor and are excellent in salads. They may also be called; golden oak, forest, oriental black, or Chinese black mushrooms.

WOOD EAR

May have anti-coagulant properties and health claims are presently are showing up in the literature. There are no conclusive studies at present in relation to the avoidance of heart attacks. They are mostly sold dried and have flattened caps that tend to vary in size with a crunchy texture. They have also been known as tree ear, and black tree fungus.

"SNIFF, SNIFF, SNIFF"

TRUFFLES

These are fungi that grow underground, and are only found by pigs and trained truffle-seeking dogs. They have excellent flavor, are a very expensive delicacy. There are two types, the black truffles from France and Italy and the white truffles from Northern Italy.

REPORTED HEALTH BENEFITS

In Japan a chemical compound extracted from shiitake mushrooms has been approved as an anticancer drug. Studies showed that it repressed cancer cell growth.

OKRA

Originated in Ethiopia or North Africa and brought to the United States in the 1700's. has been a southern favorite and used in many Creole dishes. The taste is a cross between eggplant and asparagus and because of its sticky juice has been mainly used in soups and stews. It is a good source of vitamins and minerals

The pods should be green and tender, Do not buy if the pods look dry or shriveled, since they will lack flavor and be tough. Okra spoils quickly and should be refrigerated as soon as purchased. It is usually best between may and October. Never wash okra until you are ready to use it or the protective coating will be removed that keeps the pods from becoming slimy.

Try grilling okra with a small amount of olive oil brushed on.

REPORTED HEALTH BENEFITS

Dye to its mucilaginous nature it has been used as a treatment for stomach ulcers.

ONIONS

Probably originated in prehistoric times and was a popular favorite in ancient Egypt and Rome. They are a member of a family that has over 500 varieties. They are low in calories and some are an excellent source of vitamin A.

Onions should be purchased hard and dry, avoid onions with wet necks, this indicates decay. Also, avoid onions that have sprouted. Onions can be stored either at room temperature or refrigerated.

If you only need half an onion, use the top half. The root will stay fresh longer in the refrigerator.

To shed fewer tears when slicing onions, cut the root off last, refrigerate before slicing and peel them under cold water. Other tricks that have worked is to ball up a piece of white bread and place it on the tip of the knife to absorb the fumes. Chewing gum may help and placing them into the freezer for 10 minutes before slicing has been used with excellent success.

Salt or vinegar will remove the smell of onions from your hands.

Chives need to be refrigerated and used within 3-4 days after purchase for the best flavor. If frozen they can be added to any dish while still frozen.

Chives can be stored in the refrigerator wrapped in paper towels in a plastic bag. They should last for about 1 week.

Vidalia onions are a variety of sweet onion, grown in Georgia and one of the best tasting onions. Sweet onions brown better in the microwave. Place 1 cup of sliced onions in an uncovered dish with 2 tablespoons of butter for approximately 15 minutes on high. No need to cover there should be no splattering and they will not brown if covered.

When preparing onion rings, make sure you place the onions in the dish as evenly as you can to assure even cooking.

REPORTED HEALTH BENEFITS

Used to increase the flow of urine as a diuretic, has laxative effects and has been used as an antiseptic.

PARSNIPS

Looks like a top heavy ivory-colored carrot. It has a celerylike nutty flavor. Waterhemlock is occasionally confused with parsnips but is a poisonous root. Parsnips are best cooked since they are very fibrous.

REPORTED HEALTH BENEFITS

Used for gout and as a diuretic.

PEAS

Peas are actually legumes, plants that are pod-bearing with inner seeds. Green peas are one of the highest vegetable sources of protein and have been used as a food since ancient times. Only 5% of all green peas arrive at the market fresh, almost all are frozen or canned.

The pods should be selected that are well-filled without bulging. Do not purchase flabby, spotted or yellow pods, Refrigerate and use within 1 week. When you cook fresh peas, add a few washed pods to the water to improve the flavor and give the peas a better green color.

If peas are cooked in their pods the pods will open allowing the peas to rise to the surface. Either method is acceptable. When dried peas are placed in water, the good ones will sink to the bottom and the bad ones will float to the top for removal. Snow peas, however, can be served fresh in salads or cooked without removing the pea.

REPORTED HEALTH BENEFITS

Peas contain nicotinic acid and may lower cholesterol levels.

PEPPERS

When purchasing peppers, be sure the sides of the pepper is firm. Do not purchase if the colors are dull. Refrigerate and use within 3 days. High in vitamin A and C. Studies have shown that eating hot peppers does not cause stomach ulcers.

Sweet red peppers contain more vitamin C than an orange. When making stuffed bell peppers, coat the outside of the pepper with vegetable oil and it will retain its color.

"EYE CHIHUAHUA"
When cutting hot peppers it is best to wear rubber gloves so that your hands will not be burned and you won't rub your eyes. If you do get hot pepper juice in your eyes you will never forget the experience.

New Mexico has one of the lowest incidence of heart disease. Researchers say that it is due to the high consumption of chili peppers, which are grown there. Over 55,000 tons are eaten annually in New Mexico. They may also lower blood fat levels and increase blood coagulation time.

Chilies are probably the oldest known spice having been found in archaeological digs in Mexico that have been dated to 7,000 B.C.

"ANCIENT TEAR GAS"
Chili peppers were burned by the American Indians when they were fighting off the invading English. The fumes kept the English at bay.

The hottest part of the chili is the inner membrane that holds the seeds. it is almost 100 times hotter.

SWEET VARIETIES

Sweet peppers contain more vitamin C than an orange

BELL

Sweet bell peppers are available in four colors, green, red, orange or yellow. They are all relatively sweet but each has its own distinctive flavor difference. When the four are mixed in a salad it is a real taste treat. Bell peppers contain a recessive gene which neutralizes capsaicin, which is why they are not spicy.

Bell peppers should be stored in the refrigerator in a plastic bag, they will stay fresh about a week. They can be frozen for 6 months and retain a good amount of their nutrients.

To seed a bell pepper is to hold on to it tight and hit the stem end on the counter hard. This will loosen the seed core and it should pull out easily.

"WELL EXCUSE ME"
If you find that you "burp" too much after eating bell peppers, try peeling the skin off before you use them.

BANANA

Mild yellow peppers resembling bananas and available fresh or pickled.

CUBANELLE

Long tapered pepper about 4 inches long. Sold in either green or yellow.

PIMENTO

Heart-shaped peppers which are generally sold in jars. Usually found in gourmet markets.

HOT VARIETIES

ANAHEIM

One of the most common chili with a mild to moderately hot bite. Consumed in either the green or red stages of growth. Often found in long string of red peppers. Used for chili rellanos.

ANCHO

Dried peppers that are flat, wrinkled and usually heart-shaped. Mild to moderately hot and usually ground and used in sauces and salsa.

CASCABEL

Moderately hot red chili with seeds that tend to rattle. When dried their skin turns a brownish-red.

CAYENNE

These are one of the hottest chilies, They are long with sharply pointed, curled tips. usually dried and made into a spice for chili and salsa.

CHERRY

Shaped like a cherry and range from mid to moderately hot, Either sold fresh or commonly found in jars.

HABANERO

Lantern-shaped peppers which grow to about 2-3 inches. Their color is yellow-orange and one of the hottest peppers. They are known for extending their bite for some time, best to have milk handy for this one.

HUNGARIAN WAX

Moderately hot yellow-orange pepper. May be purchased fresh or pickled.

JALAPENO

One of the most common peppers. They are usually moderately hot to very hot and are sold at their green stage. The red stage which is full maturity is super hot. Canned jalapenos are usually milder because the seeds are removed and they are packed in liquid.

SERRANO

A popular chili in Mexico. They look like a small torpedo and are very hot.

RADISHES

Originated in China thousands of years ago. They are a cruciferous vegetable and contain phytochemicals that are under investigation relating to cancer prevention. Their green tops are edible and tend to have a peppery flavor. Radishes are a good source of vitamin C.

They are available year round. Larger radishes tend to be pithy and smaller ones are usually a better choice. Squeeze to be sure they are not mushy and don't buy if the tops are yellow or if there is any sign of decay.

Varieties include; California Mammoth Whites, Daikons, Red Globe, and White Icicles.

Radish leaves can be added to salads or stir-fried vegetables to add a little zest to the flavor. They are not as spicy as radishes.

REPORTED HEALTH BENEFITS

Used as an appetite stimulant, relieve nervousness, constipation, and to dissolve gallstones.

SALISIFY

Also called "oyster plant." Their appearance is similar to parsley but tastes like an oyster. Blossoms on the plant always close at high noon and thus it was also called the "Johnny go to bed at noon" plant.

SPINACH

Was first grown in the United States in the 1700's. it is high in vitamins and minerals as well as being one of the best vegetable sources of protein. Spinach, however, contains the chemical, oxalate which tends to bind with certain minerals such as calcium and limits their usefulness by the body.

To retain the nutrient level in spinach, boil it in as little water as possible and for the shortest period of time. Boiling in one cup of water rather than two cups will help the spinach retain 50% more of its nutrients.

REPORTED HEALTH BENEFITS

Used for anemia, tumors, arthritis, high blood pressure, and bronchitis.

SPROUTS

When seeds are moistened they change into edible sprouts or shoots. When this occurs the seed utilizes its carbohydrates and fat and leaves a good percentage of its vitamins intact, making sprouts a healthy food. Their nutrient content, while preserved is not appreciably high compared to most mature vegetables, however, they are healthy a pleasant departure from the standard vegetables.

Sprouts should be refrigerated in their original containers.

COMMON VARIETIES

ADZUKI BEAN

Very sweet, small-bean shaped with grasslike sprouts. has a nutty taste.

ALFALFA

Threadlike white sprouts that have small green tops and a mild nutty flavor.

CLOVER

Looks similar to the alfalfa sprout, their tiny seeds look like poppy seeds.

DAIKON RADISH

Have a silky stem and leafy top. The taste is somewhat peppery and spicy hot.

MUNG BEAN

These are larger than the alfalfa sprouts and have a blander taste. They are thick white sprouts and used in many oriental dishes.

SOYBEAN

Sprouts have a somewhat strong flavor but a good source of protein. They contain a small amount of a toxin and large amounts should be avoided. Cooking for at least 5 minutes tends to neutralize the toxin.

SUNFLOWER

Crunchier than alfalfa and has a milder flavor.

SQUASH

Squash is a fleshy vegetable with a solid protective rind. It has been a staple vegetable for thousands of years. They are a low calorie food and contain an excellent level of vitamins and minerals which vary depending on the variety. It is available all year round. The soft-skinned types should be smooth and glossy. The hard-shelled type should have a firm rind. Refrigerate all soft-skinned varieties and use within a few days.

Varieties of summer squash are; chayote, patty pan, yellow crookneck, yellow straightneck and zucchini. Winter squash varieties include; acorn, banana, buttercup, butternut, calabaza, delicata, golden nugget, Hubbard, spaghetti, sweet dumpling, turan and pumpkin. Winter squash develops more beta-carotene after being stored than it has immediately after being picked.

Squash blossoms are edible and have an excellent flavor. They make a great garnish for many dishes and can even be battered and fried. Try stuffing then with cream cheese for a real treat.

The smallest squash are usually the tastiest.

" "A" WINNER"
Canned pumpkin is one of the best sources of beta-carotene, it contains approximately 27,000IU in a 40 calorie 8oz. serving.

"MEDICAL MIRACLE?"
Pumpkins may be preserved for a few extra days after they are cut for a jack-o-lantern by spraying the areas that are exposed to the air with an antiseptic spray. This will retard the bacterial growth. Do not use for eating after it has been sprayed.

REPORTED HEALTH BENEFITS

Zucchini has been used in cases of high blood pressure.

TOMATILLOS

These look like small green tomatoes but with a thin parchmentlike skin. They are also called Mexican green tomatoes and they have a somewhat lemon-apple flavor. They are popular in salads and salsas. Purchase only firm tomatillos. They are usually available year round.

TOMATOES

The question of whether the tomato is a fruit or a vegetable was settled by the Supreme Court in 1893 when it was officially declared a vegetable. Botanically, it is still a fruit, actually a berry. it is a member of the nightshade family relating it to potatoes, bell peppers, and eggplant. It is available year round and should be well formed and free of blemishes. Green tomatoes will eventually turn red, but will not have a good flavor. A vine-ripened tomato is best. Refrigerate, but do not allow to freeze.

To peel tomatoes easily, place them in boiling water and remove from heat, allow to stand for 1 minute then plunge them into cold water. Tomatoes will store longer if you store them stem down. Never allow tomatoes to ripen in direct sunlight, they will lose most of their vitamin C.

Americans consume approximately 24 pounds of tomatoes per person, per year. If you are expecting a frost and have tomatoes on the vine, pull them up by the roots and hang them upside down in a cool basement until the fruit ripens. Green tomatoes will ripen faster if you store them with apples.

"AYE CHIHUAHUA"
Salsa has replaced ketchup as the top selling condiment in the United States. A new product due out in 1996 will be a salsa/ketchup combination.

"PUREE CONCENTRATE"
One ounce of tomato puree has twice the vitamin C and 20% more beta-carotene than one ounce of fresh tomato.

"KA BOOM, KA BOOM"
Never place a whole tomato in the microwave, it will explode.

REPORTED HEALTH BENEFITS

Tomatoes have been used as a natural antiseptic and protects against infection. Has been used to improve skin tone and as a blood cleanser.

TURNIPS

Turnips are related to cabbage, it grows easily, even in poor soil conditions and is a good source of complex carbohydrates. It is a cruciferous vegetable and can weigh up to 50 pounds. One-half cup of turnips have more fiber than an apple.

WATER CHESTNUTS

Chestnuts are actually the underground swollen tip of a tuber, and stores carbohydrates for the plants growth. Unless they are kept cool they will sprout. They are an excellent source of potassium.

THE 900 CALORIE SALAD

FOOD   CALORIES

1 cup of lettuce...................... 9
1/2 medium tomato..................... 16
1/2 cup cottage cheese................120
4 cucumber slices..................... 5
1/2 cup mixed beans...................160
1/4 cup macaroni salad................ 90
2 small ladles of salad dressing.....230
1/4 cup cheddar cheese................116
2 black olives....................... 40
2 hot peppers........................ 15
1/10 cup sunflower seeds.............. 75
1/10 cup croutons.................... 50

FRUITS AND VEGETABLES

CARBOHYDRATE CONTENT ANALYSIS

VERY LOW	LOW	MEDIUM
Asparagus	Beets	Artichokes
Bean Sprouts	Brussels Sprouts	Kidney Beans
Beet Greens	Carrots	Parsnips
Broccoli	Chives	Peas (green)
Cabbage	Collards	Apples
Cauliflower	Dandelion Greens	Cherries
Celery	Eggplant	Grapes
Chard, Swiss	Kale	Olives
Chicory	Kohlrabi	Pears
Cucumber	Leeks	Pineapple
Endive	Okra	Mango
Escarole	Onions	Blueberries
Lettuce	Parsley	
Mushrooms	Peppers (green)	
Mustard Greens	Pumpkin	
Radishes	String Beans	
Spinach	Rutabagas	
Tomatoes	Turnips	
Cantaloupe	Apricots	
Strawberries	Cranberries	
Watermelon	Oranges	

HIGH	VERY HIGH
Corn	Rice
Dried Beans	Potato (sweet)
Lima Beans	Yams
Pickles (sweet)	
Avocado	
Bananas	
Figs	
Prunes	
Raisins	

EDIBLE PLANTS FOR LANDSCAPING

NAME	LANDSCAPE USE	EXPOSURE
Asparagus	Tall, fine texured	Full sun perenial
Beans/Legumes	Herb	Full sun to partial shade
Bitter Melon	Bush or climbing variety	Full sun
Cabbage	Colorful foliage	Full sun to partial shade
Chard	Decorative, very large foliage	Full sun to partial shade
Chinese Cabbage	Compact, glossy green foliage	Full sun to partial shade
Chives	Very low-growing herb	Full sun
Cucumber	Bush or as a vine	Full sun
Eggplant	Compact, very ornamental bush	Full sun
Kale	Highly decorative foliage	Full sun to partial shade
Lettuce	Fancy-leaf type	Full sun to partial shade
Mint	Lush herb/repels rodents	Shade or part sun
Nasturtium	Edible flowering vine	Full sun or partial shade
Parsley	Decorative herb	Full sun or partial shade
Peppers	Ornamental bush with red or yellow fruit	Full sun or partial shade
Sage	Colorful accent herb	Full sun
Snow Pea	Sprawling bush or vine	Full sun or partial shade

Chapter 8

Spud Facts

POTATOES (SWEET)

They are available year round. The skins should be uniformly copper or a light tan color and should not be purchased if they have and soft spots, visible mold or white areas. Sweet potatoes tend to decay faster than white potatoes due to their higher sugar content.

Yams originated in Asia and are a close relative to the sweet potato but are less sweet and contain 10-20% less nutrients. Sweet potatoes have 10 calories per ounce less than yams.

"YAM-A-DABA-DO"
The best way to tell the difference between sweet potatoes and yams is to look at the flesh which should be orange in a sweet potato and reddish in a yam. Supermarkets commonly label yams as sweet potatoes.

Sweet potatoes contain the same number of calories as white potatoes, however, they contain more vitamin C and 3 times the beta-carotene.

The best sweet potato is called a "boniato" or "Cuban Sweet Potato" and has a very light yellow flesh.

To peel a sweet potato easily, take them from the boiling water and immediately immerse them in a bowl of ice cold water for about 20-30 seconds. The skins should almost fall off by themselves.

POTATOES (WHITE)

Potatoes originated in South America and were introduced to Europe in the 16th century. They are one of the most nutritious vegetables and a member of the "nightshade" family. The potato is actually a "stem" not a root and stores carbohydrates for the leafy parts above ground. The potato plant actually bears fruit that looks like a cherry tomato.

They are available all year and should be purchased unbruised and without any green tint to the skin which may indicate the presence of the chemical "solanine" produced from a chlorophyll buildup. Solanine has been implicated in poor nerve impulse transmission, vomiting, diarrhea, and abdominal discomfort. Americans consume approximately 125 pounds of potatoes per person annually with the United States producing 35 billion pounds per year. In the last 30 years Americans have reduced their consumption of fresh potatoes by 40%.

"I KNOW WHERE THE YELLOW WENT...."
If you would like a richer color to your potato salad, try adding a small amount of yellow food coloring when you are mixing it.

"HIDE AND SEEK"
Potatoes should be stored at room temperature in a dark area and not refrigerated. Refrigeration tends to turn potato starch to sugar. However, if the potato is removed from the refrigerator and left at room temperature the sugar will convert back to starch.

There are many varieties of potatoes such as the Russets, White Rose, Red Pontiac, Katahdin, and Finish Yellow. The most popular is the Russet which is mainly grown in Idaho and may weigh up to a pound or more.

SPUD FACTS

It is best to purchase potatoes in bulk bins and not in bags. It is too difficult to determine which ones are bruised. If ginger root is stored with potatoes it will help them stay fresh longer. If half an apple is stored with potatoes it will stop the sprouting by absorbing any moisture before the potato.

To boil potatoes in less time, remove a small strip of skin from one side. After they are cooked the balance of the skin will be more easily removed. To keep peeled potatoes white, place them in a bowl of cold water, add a few drops of white vinegar then refrigerate.

Baked potatoes should be pierced with a fork to release the steam as soon as they are baked to keep them from becoming soggy. Old potatoes should have a small amount of sugar added to the cooking water to revive some of the lost flavor.

"THAT'S ALL FOLKS"
If you store a boiled or baked potato in the refrigerator for 3-4 days it will lose approximately 90% of its nutrient value. Potatoes should only be stored for 1-2 days.

To reharden potatoes, try placing soft raw potatoes in ice water for 1/2 hour or until they become hard. Brown areas on potatoes are the result of oxidation and vitamin C losses.

The digestive time for a medium potato is approximately 2 hours. Cooking a potato with its skin will result in the retention of most of its nutrients. Recommendation is not to eat potato skins. They are one of the only vegetable skin that tends to hold pesticide and fertilizer residues even after washing and cooking. The EPA has registered 90 different pesticides for use on potatoes. The FDA laboratories can only detect 55% of these. Some of the problem pesticides are Chlordane, Aldicarb, and Dieldrin.

"A FRENCH FRY FIT FOR A KING"
For the greatest gourmet french fries, try allowing crinkle-cut potatoes stand in ice cold water, refrigerated for 1 hour before frying. This will harden them so that they will not absorb as much fat. Dry them thoroughly before frying and then fry them twice. The first time for only a few minutes, dry them well, sprinkle a small amount of flour on them and fry them until they are a golden brown.

A potato will bake faster and the skin will not crack if the skin is oiled or rubbed with butter rather than being wrapped in tin foil. Inserting an aluminum nail will also speed the cooking time by 15 minutes. To really speed them up just boil them for 10 minutes before placing them into the oven.

When boiling potatoes, place them into a mesh frying basket to make them easier to remove and drain since they may get somewhat mushy.

Potatoes and onions tend to give off natural gases and for this reason should never be stored together. The potatoes will become soft and rot.

Potatoes prefer to be stored in pantyhose. Just cut a leg off and drop the potatoes in, then hang it up in a cool, dry location.

"DO THE MASHED POTATO"
The best mashed potatoes are made from Russet potatoes.
Always cook them with their skins on and use very warm
buttermilk, never cold milk. Add a pinch or two of baking
powder (not baking soda) to fluff them up and a small amount
of whipped butter and chopped onions to taste.

To keep peeled potatoes white during cooking add a small
amount of white vinegar to the water.

Instead of adding liquid milk to the potatoes when making
mashed, try adding powdered milk or instant potato flakes
for extra fluffy mashed potatoes.

"UP, UP AND AWAY, ON A BUFFET"
If you go to a buffet and take a serving of mashed potatoes,
the chances are that they will contain little if any
nutrients. After 45 minutes almost all nutrients have been
lost to the air, light, and heat.

"I WONDER WHERE THE YELLOW WENT"
When a potato salad is yellowish, try to find out whether
the color is from mustard or an artificial coloring agent.

"NEVER COOK A NAKED POTATO"
Baking or boiling a potato without its skin causes a 10-30%
nutrient loss. If you have problems peeling the potato, drop
it into a bowl of ice water for a few seconds to loosen the
skin.

"HOT POTATO, COLD POTATO"
Vichyssoise, a cold potato soup was invented when King Louis
XV of France was so worried about being poisoned that he had
a number of his servants taste his food before he ate it. As
they passed the soup around, it got cold by the time it
reached him. He liked the cold soup and had it served that
way thereafter.

"ONE POTATO, TWO POTATO, WHOOPS, FAKE POTATO?"
Flaked, frozen, and powdered potato product sales have risen
500% in the last 30 years. The more a potato is processed,
the higher the nutrient losses that occur.

"THREE CHEERS FOR THE CHIPPER"
Potato chips were invented at Saratoga Springs, New York in
1853 when Commodore Vanderbilt complained to his steward
that he had made his french fries too thick. The steward was
unhappy about the complaint, went back to the kitchen and
sliced some potatoes as thin as he could, fried them and
served them. The Commodore instead of getting upset was
delighted and so the potato chip was invented.

"BAKE EM, DANO"
Commercial potato chips are cooked in long vats of oil (75 feet long) with the oil being filtered and rarely changed. Production is about 200 pounds an hour. Reusing the oil which is continually kept at 375^0 F. causes the oil contain mostly trans-fatty acid oil, a potentially harmful oil and may produce free-radicals.

Potato, corn, or tortilla chips contain 10 times more fat than pretzels or air-popped popcorn. Most potato chips are 61% fat. Presently, there are 30 flavors of potato chips sold in supermarkets nationally.

"THE REAL THING"
To make a quality potato chip, cut potatoes in half crosswise, exposing two flat surfaces. Then use a potato peeler cut paper thin slices and place the slices on a vegetable oil sprayed cookie sheet. Brush the tops of the potatoes with a very small amount of fresh pure vegetable oil, preferably corn oil, then bake at 450^0 F. for about 10-12 minutes or until a light golden brown. Finally, place the chips in a brown paper bag with a small amount of sea salt (1/4 teaspoon per potato) and shake.

Chapter 9

Supplements and Retaining Nutrients

WHY WE NEED SUPPLEMENTS

How often have we heard that if we eat a balanced diet with all the food groups in the right proportions, we will be able to obtain all the necessary nutrients our bodies need. We are all tired of listening to this statement from professionals who have a limited education in the field of nutrition or have been brainwashed to really believe this is possible.

The above statement was, however, true 70 years ago before we were bombarded with more environmental insults than our bodies know how to cope with. The following information will alert you to the all the reasons why we cannot possibly remain in optimum health without taking supplements.

Every week on television there seems to be another show telling of another problem with our food supply. We are not inspecting our foods properly due to lack of inspectors, our fruits and vegetables are grown in soils that are nutrient-deficient due to the depletion of trace minerals from over-farming.

Our products are stored too long before sale and many of the natural nutrients are processed out before they reach us. No one will ever convince me that they are enriching our foods sufficiently to provide us with anywhere near the original levels.

We use preservatives and coloring agents that are borderline chemical agents and many have been proven to cause cancer in laboratory animals. We don't have time to eat a balanced diet and we kill off all the enzymes with heat before we eat the food.

Then we take a supplement that has probably lost a percentage of its potency and has a low level of "biologic activity" to save a few dollars. Many supplement products are just not active enough and cannot provide you with the level of nutrients you buy them for.

The following information will give you some insight into the "real" world of nutrition and the many factors that relate to your obtaining the level of nutrients from the foods you purchase. It will also provide some additional information regarding the need for supplementation in relation to a variety of lifestyle factors.

LOSS OF NUTRIENT AVAILABILITY IN FOODS

CAUSES

Food Processing

Depleted Soil Minerals

Artificial Ingredients

Smoking

Cooking Methods

Aging Process

Dieting

Medications

Sickness

Birth Conrol Pills

Storage

Fertilizers

Unbalanced Diets

Sugar Intake

Smog

Stress

Alcohol

Restaurants

Lack of Enzymes

Bioavailability

THE REASONS FOR NUTRIENT LOSSES

PROCESSING OF FOODS

EXPOSURE TO HEAT

FRIED FOODS

The longer a food is fried and the higher the temperature, the more vitamin and mineral potency loss. Frying temperatures usually reach 375^0 F. Canola oil is best for frying since it has the highest smoke point (500^0 F.) of any oil, allowing it to be used for a longer period of time before breaking down.

CANNED FOODS

Vitamin and mineral potency losses occur from blanching, and the sterilization process, which involve temperatures of 240^0 F. or higher for 25-40 minutes.

FROZEN FOODS - Many are cooked before freezing. Higher quality foods are sold fresh, lower quality ones are used in frozen foods.

DEHYDRATED FOODS - Very dependent on the quality of the product processed. Certain methods of commercial dehydration use temperatures of 300^0 F.

DAIRY PRODUCTS

Many vitamins lose their potency or are totally destroyed by the pasteurization process. The homogenization process breaks down the normal-sized fat particles, thus allowing the formation of an enzyme called "xanthane oxidase." This enzyme then enters the bloodstream and may destroy vital body chemicals that would ordinarily provide protection for the coronary arteries.

NOTE:
Various nutrients have different degrees of stability under the condition of processing and preparation. Vitamin A is easily destroyed by heat and light. Vitamin C is not only affected by heat but is also affected by contact with certain metals, such as bronze, brass, copper, cold rolled steel, and black iron processing equipment. Studies conducted on the canning of foods found that peas and beans lose 75% of certain B vitamins, and tomatoes lose 80% of their naturally occurring zinc content.

EXPOSURE TO COLD

FROZEN FOODS - Freezing may have only minimal effect on the vitamin and mineral potency, depending on the method used and whether they are frozen shortly after being harvested. Remember, in most instances the higher quality foods are sold fresh.

FRESH FRUITS AND VEGETABLES - These are occasionally harvested before they are ripe, then allowed to ripen on the way to market. This may cause a reduction of some trace minerals.

METHODS OF FREEZING

There are four major methods of freezing foods commercially:

AIR BLAST FREEZING

Products are frozen by high velocity cold air. This is the most widely used freezing technique in the prepared food industry, and is used on all kinds of products.

PLATE FREEZING

The product is placed in contact with cold metal surfaces.

CRYOGENIC FREEZING

Freezing at very low temperatures (below -100^0 F.) in contact with liquid nitrogen or carbon dioxide. Used for freezing meat patties and other meat products.

FREON IMMERSION FREEZING

Utilizes freon to freeze the product instantaneously, thus allowing the product to retain its total weight. Presently, being used to freeze hard-boiled eggs, scrambled egg patties, and shrimp. Some foods may retain a higher level of nutrients since they are frozen shortly after being harvested. A Stanford University study showed that frozen spinach had 212% more vitamin C and frozen Brussels sprouts had 27% more vitamin C when this method of freezing was used.

Freon methods have recently come under fire and may be discontinued due the potential of environmental damage from this chemical.

QUALITY OF THE FOODS PROCESSED

FRUITS AND VEGETABLES

May be affected by genetic differences, climatic conditions, maturity at harvest or soil differences. Many fruits and vegetables are purchased from out of the country and nutrient levels will vary significantly.

MEAT AND POULTRY

The lowest quality is usually used for canned goods and frozen foods, especially TV dinners.

ENRICHMENT AND FORTIFICATION

REFINING OUT AND REPLACING NUTRIENTS

Bread is a good example, many nutrients are processed out and only a few replaced.

FORTIFICATION

Vitamin D is added to milk and almost all breakfast cereals are fortified unless they contain the whole grain. Vitamin C and calcium are added to numerous products.

NOTE:
During processing more vitamin E is lost than any other vitamin. Wheat flour (not the 100% or whole grain type) loses up to 90% of its vitamin E potency. Rice cereal products may lose up to 70% of their vitamin E.

When purchasing any whole wheat product, make sure the first ingredient on the list is "100% whole grain." If the first ingredient says; "whole wheat flour" most of the bran has been removed and there is very little difference in that bread and white bread.

STORAGE OF FOODS

SUPERMARKETS

CANNED AND PACKAGED PRODUCTS

Length of time on the shelf as well as warehouse time results in reduced potencies of vitamins and minerals.

FRUITS AND VEGETABLES

Harvested before fully ripened then allowed to ripen on the way to market or at the market. When cut into smaller halves or pieces the surfaces are exposed to the effects of air and light causing oxidation to takes place thus reducing their nutrient content.

AT HOME

ROTATION OF FOODS

Canned, frozen, and packaged products are rarely dated and rotated properly. Dehydrated foods as well as leftovers do lose a percentage of their nutrients over a period of time and should be eaten within a reasonable period of time.

COMMERCIAL FOOD PRODUCERS

WAREHOUSING

Storage times and temperature changes affect retention of nutrient potencies.

GOVERNMENT WAREHOUSES

CANNED AND PACKAGED FOODS

Storage times usually exceed all other types of storage facilities. Temperature changes are always a possible cause for concern.

RESTAURANTS

PURCHASING

Restaurants purchase large quantities, possibly resulting in long storage times, especially if the restaurant is not one of the busier ones. Fast food restaurants avoid this problem due to frequent food turnover.

Excess storage times may result in the purchase of foods thought to contain adequate amounts of certain nutrients which end up with little or none. Oranges from supermarkets have been tested and found to contain no vitamin C content, while a fresh picked one contains approximately 80mg. Vitamin and mineral potency losses may occur before the product receives its expiration cods date.

A potato in storage for a period of 6 months may lose up to 50% of its vitamin C content. Most food charts will deduct 25% of the nutrient value of foods to allow for storage, packaging, transportation, processing, preservation, and cooking. In some cases this is not nearly enough.

NUTRIENT DEPLETED SOILS

SOIL PROBLEM

FERTILIZERS

Farmers normally only replace the minerals that are crucial to crop growth, such as phosphorus, potassium, and the nitrates.

TRACE MINERALS

The selenium content in soils may vary by a factor of 200 in the United States depending on the years that particular field has been used. A kilogram of wheat may contain from 50mcg. to 800mcg. of selenium depending on where it is grown.

Chromium and zinc are also critically deficient in the soil. This problem is presently under extensive study by the Department of Agriculture.

Studies performed at Rutgers University by Dr. Firman E. Bear showed that some carrots tested for nutrient potency were almost completely without nutrients, This reduction in nutrient potency occurred in carrots from different farms all over the United States.

Dr. William Albrecht of the University of Missouri has shown that over a 10 year period the protein content of grains in the Midwest has declined 11%. The use of nitrogenous fertilizers is causing copper deficiencies, and the overuse of potash fertilizers is creating magnesium deficiencies.

FOOD ADDITIVES

FLAVORINGS

There are approximately 1400 natural and synthetic flavorings available. Scientists are most concerned regarding the toxicity of many of these flavorings. Flavorings make food taste better, restore flavors lost in processing, and can improve natural flavors.

STABILIZERS/JELLING AGENTS/THICKENERS

These are used to keep products such as jellies, jams, and baby foods in a "set state." They are also used to keep ice cream creamy, and improve the consistency, as well as affecting the appearance and texture of foods. The more common ones are modified food starch and vegetable gums.

COLORINGS

Ninety percent are artificial and have no nutritional value. Some foods have a tendency to lose their natural color when processed and must be dyed back to make them more appealing to the consumer. An example of this is banana ice cream which is dyed yellow and cherries which usually turn white when heat processed.

SWEETENERS

The United States consumption of artificial sweeteners is estimated at approximately 8 pounds per person, annually. Since Nutrasweet (Equal) came on the market this has raised significantly in the 90's. Sweeteners are designed to make the food more palatable.

AROMA ENHANCERS

An example is the yellowish-green liquid "diacetyl" which is used in some cottage cheeses to produce an artificial butter aroma.

PRESERVATIVES

They help maintain freshness and prevent spoilage that is caused by fungi, yeast, molds, and bacteria. Extend shelf life or protect the natural color or flavors.

ACIDS/BASES

Provide a tart flavor for many fruit products, is used for pickling and makes beverages "fizz." Two main carbonating agents are used; phosphoric acid and carbonic acid. Phosphoric acid beverages should be kept to a minimum for post-menopausal women due to an upset in the calcium\phosphorus ratio and osteoporosis.

ANTIOXIDANTS

Reduces the possibility of rancidity in fats and oils. Common natural ones are vitamins C, E and flower pollen. Artificial antioxidants are BHA and BHT which are used extensively.

TASTE ENHANCERS

Brings out the flavor of certain foods. Monosodium glutamate (MSG) is a good example and is not only used in food preparation in restaurants but in numerous soup and stew products.

IMPROVING AGENTS

Examples include: humectants, which control the humidity of a food. Anti-caking agents, which keep salt and powders free-flowing. Firming and crisping agents used for processed fruits and vegetables. Foaming agents for whipped toppings and root beer and anti-foaming agents which keep pineapple juice from bubbling over when you pour it.

EMULSIFIERS

These help evenly mix small particles of one liquid with another, such as water and oil products. Lecithin is a natural emulsifier, just place the contents of one ampoule in your oil and vinegar salad dressing and the oil will not separate.

Keep in mind that you are rarely aware of the quantity of additives you are consuming. Almost all of these additives require work by the liver and vitamins and minerals to assist in their breakdown.

POORLY BALANCED MEALS

MEAL PLANNING

Too few people plan their meals in advance. This results in poor combinations of foods, leading to inadequate vitamin and mineral intake. Lack of nutritional education also plays an important role.

RESTAURANTS

The majority of these meals are lacking in fruits and vegetables, especially those from fast food restaurants.

SUGAR INTAKE

MULTIFACETED PROBLEM

Sugar requires B vitamins and minerals to enable the body to metabolize it into glucose, yet it contains none of these. Therefore, it must take the nutrients away from other body functions that may need them.

Sugar may also increase the rate at which we excrete the mineral calcium, making bones more fragile and weakening the heartbeat. Oxalates contained in chocolate unites with calcium, carrying it through the intestine as an insoluble compound.

Theobromine in chocolate may reduce the absorption of protein through the intestinal wall. Bodybuilders should avoid chocolate snacks.

High sugar intake reduces the effectiveness of the body's healing mechanism, causing a prolongation in the healing time for injuries.

SMOKING

EFFECTS ON VITAMINS

VITAMIN C

Studies have shown that smoker's require approximately 40% more vitamin C than non-smokers to achieve the adequate blood levels. Every cigarette reduces bodily stores by about 30mg., which means that a pack of cigarettes requires at least a 600mg. increase in vitamin C intake.

VITAMIN B_{12}

Cigarette smoking reduces the blood levels.

COOKING/FOOD PREPARATION

PREPARATION

WASHING/SOAKING

Many vitamins are water-soluble and will be lost or forced to bind with other chemicals causing them not to be absorbed. This will occur through washing, scrubbing or long periods of soaking. Soaking carrots or allowing them to sit in a glass of water in the refrigerator causes the loss of the natural sugar, all the B vitamins, vitamins C and D, and all minerals except calcium.

DICING/SLICING/PEELING/SHREDDING

The smaller you cut fruit and vegetables the more surface you expose to temperature changes, air (oxidation), and light. Prepare these foods as close to serving time as possible. Shredding for salads causes a 20% loss of vitamin C and an additional 20% loss if the salad stands for an hour before eating it.

The skin of fruits and vegetables contains only 10% of the nutrient value of the food.

METHODS OF COOKING

CHARCOAL

Pyrobenzines may be produced by the fat dripping down on the charcoal. The smoke carries the chemical and deposits it in the black coating on the food. These chemical substances are known carcinogens (cancer forming agents) and should, at least, be scrapped off before eating the food. Artificial charcoal does not cause the problem.

CROCK-POT

Vegetables left in all day or for a long period of time lose a high percentage of all vitamins and minerals, as well as absorbing the fat from the meats. Steam vegetables first, then add them to the pot just before serving the dish.

BOILING

Stewing and boiling fruits and vegetables results in heavy nutrient losses.

STEAMING

This is by far the best method for preparing fruits and vegetables. They are subjected to high temperatures for only a short period of time.

MICROWAVE

This a good method, since it cooks the foods in a short period of time allowing less nutrient loss.

FRYING

The high temperature of frying and the soaking in the oil, not only cause a high loss in fruits and vegetables but meats will lose vitamin B_1 and pantothenic acid.

NOTE:
Refrigerate all foods as soon as possible, this will help retain the potencies of the nutrients. Whole boiled carrots will retain 90% of the vitamin C content and most of the minerals. If sliced before cooking they will lose almost all the vitamin C and niacin content.

AIR POLLUTION

TYPES

SMOG

All major cities in the United States have some form of chemical air pollution. This pollution will effect your lungs' capacity to deliver oxygen efficiently to the cells of the body. The antioxidant vitamins A, C, E, selenium, the mineral OptiZinc, and proanthocyanidin have proved to be effective in combating some of the effects of chemical pollution.

SMOKE

The smoke from cigarettes, cigars, and pipes all effect the oxygen-carrying efficiency of your red blood cells. Smoke contains carbon monoxide which may compete for the site on the red blood cell that should be always carrying oxygen. This is one reason why smokers are short-winded, a percentage of their red blood cells are carrying carbon monoxide instead of the needed oxygen.

THE AGING PROCESS

REQUIREMENTS CHANGE WITH AGING

DAIRY PRODUCT INTOLERANCE

The mechanism to produce the enzyme to break-down lactase loses it efficiency over time in many people. This may lead to a reduction of available calcium by not eating dairy products. Dark green leafy vegetables will help supply calcium and a new product "Lactaid" will assist the body in breaking down lactase.

HORMONAL CHANGES

This problem exists more in the changes with aging in the production of female hormones, post-menapausal. This may lead to an increased loss of calcium, and supplementation or a diet somewhat higher in calcium should be considered.

LACK OF EXERCISE

Reduces the bodies efficiency to expel inner-pollutants, and increase the need for supplementation of the antioxidants.

DIETARY PATTERNS

Poor dietary habits sometimes lead to increased phosphorus intake, altering the normal ratios of calcium to phosphorus. A few of the guilty items are crackers, processed meat products, and soft drinks that contain phosphoric acid as the carbonating agent.

SENILITY

Some symptoms may be caused by a lack of vitamin B_6.

CIRCULATION PROBLEMS

Tissues receive a reduced level of oxygen and the group of antioxidant supplements should help improve the utilization of available oxygen.

IMMUNE SYSTEM

Antioxidants may reduce cellular degeneration, thus increasing the effectiveness of the system. Prostate problems may respond to OptiZinc supplementation or the herb Saw Palmetto.

NOTE:
Vitamin E prolongs the life of red blood cells by reducing the formation of toxic peroxides, which some scientists feel may speed up the aging process.

STRESS

VITAMIN B

The health of nerves and especially their protective sheath depends on an adequate supply of vitamin B's.

SUGAR AND ALCOHOL - Both require B vitamins for their breakdown and absorption. Excesses of either in the system will cause a shortage of the B vitamins and may reduce the bodies ability to cope with stressful situations

VITAMIN C

The bodies need for vitamin C increases as much as 100 times when we are under stress.

ILLNESS/DISEASE

ASTHMA

The degree of exercise induced bronchospasm may be reduced if the person takes approximately 500mg. of vitamin C six hours or less before exercising.

HYPERACTIVITY

The cause may be linked to vitamin B deficiency, due to the overconsumption of refined carbohydrates, mainly sugars.

CIRCULATORY PROBLEMS

Responds well to vitamin E supplementation of approximately 400 IU/day.

VARICOSE VEINS

Responds well to vitamin E therapy in a high percentage of cases.

UNEXPLAINED BRUISES

Vitamin C therapy has proved effective in many cases. The vitamin C should include the bioflavenoids for maximum effectiveness.

DIETING

GENERAL INFORMATION

Weight programs should contain the following nutritional components:

A variety of appealing meal replacement foods

No less than 900 calories per day

Behavior modification program

one balanced self-prepared meal per day

a quality supplement program

Due to the multitude of weight programs available to the public, it is impossible to list the nutritional inadequacies found in many of these programs. Many do not take into consideration the individual's lifestyle differences and provide the same information and products for all their clients.

ALCOHOL ABUSE

NUTRIENT RELATIONSHIP

VITAMIN AND MINERAL NEEDS

Alcohol requires a number of vitamins and minerals in order to be broken down by the body and removed before being allowed to accumulate and damage vital organs. Specific vitamins need to break-down alcohol are; thiamin, riboflavin, niacin, pantothenic acid, and biotin. Minerals include; iron, zinc, manganese, magnesium, phosphorus, and copper.

NOTE:
Alcohol causes the excessive excretion of the mineral zinc, possibly contributing to the early onset of prostate problems. It also cause excretion of magnesium which may lead to extreme nervousness. Prostate problems are appearing at an earlier stage in life than we have normally seen it, alcohol may be the culprit.

EXERCISE

OXYGEN REQUIREMENTS

ANTIOXIDANTS

Exercise tends to increase free radical production. Antioxidant supplements, especially vitamins C and E assist the body to fight the free radicals as well as allowing the body to utilize oxygen more efficiently.

BIRTH CONTROL PILLS

EFFECTS ON VITAMINS

HORMONAL EFFECTS

Because of the estrogen content in oral contraceptives, studies have shown that women on "the pill" have lower than normal blood serum levels of vitamin C and B_6. Supplementation is recommended by most nutritionists. Vitamin B_6 should be 50-75mg. and vitamin C should be 1,000-2,000mg. daily.

RESTAURANTS

One of the more significant losses of nutrient content in foods is through the continual heating of foods to keep them ready for instant serving. Oriental restaurants tend to do this more than any other. Buffet's that keep food hot for prolonged periods are also poor sources of nutrients. Mashed potatoes after 45 minutes on a buffet loses almost 100% of all nutrients.

SUPPLEMENT FACTS

Both red meat and sugar tend to cause a loss of calcium in the urine.

The nitrites in processed meats, such as; hot dogs, bacon, lunch meats, and sausage may turn into a carcinogen when coming in contact with stomach acid. They can be neutralized by chewing a vitamin C tablet 5-10 minutes before consuming these foods.

Vitamin B_6 absorption is effected by the hydrazines in mushrooms. If you are taking birth control pills, it may be best to only consume mushrooms occasionally.

Chocolate contains oxalates and theobromine which effects calcium metabolism and reduces the body's utilization of protein.

Boiling any food for more than 5-10 minutes will destroy 100% of the vitamin B and C content.

Chlorine reduce the effectiveness of vitamin C.

One years supply of folic acid can fit into 1/6th teaspoon.

Raw fish, shellfish, Brussels sprouts, and red cabbage contain thiaminase, a chemical which may destroy the B vitamins. Cooking inactivates the thiaminase, however, that will also kill the B vitamins.

The FDA has removed isolated amino acids from the list of safe substances (GRAS) stating that they may cause an imbalance of other amino acids, as well as affecting their absorption.

The tannins in teas and red wines may interfere with the utilization of iron, thiamin and B_{12}.

MINERAL INFORMATION, JUST THE FACTS

IODINE
      Stimulates the thyroid
      A deficiency may cause obesity
      Is needed to metabolize fat

ZINC
      A constituent of insulin
      A constituent of male reproductive fluid
      Combines in phosphorus to aid in respiration
      Assists in the absorption of foods through intestines
      Essential to nucleic acid metabolism
      Metabolized very fast in burn patients
      Deficiency may relate to atherosclerosis

MAGNESIUM
      Activates specific chemical reactions
      Sleep aid
      Allows you to stay cool and collected
      Relaxes nerves

MANGANESE
      Assists with the digestion process
      A factor in healthy nerves
      Deficient in alcoholism
      A co-factor with B vitamins

SODIUM
      Assists in maintaining a normal fluid balance
      Provides muscle strength
      A deficiency may cause flatulence
      Works with B vitamins to provide energy

MOLYBDENUM
      Has a role in iron metabolism
      Is found to be deficient in dental caries

CHROMIUM
      Necessary for normal glucose metabolism
      Deficiency related to adult diabetes
      Deficiency may be caused by excessive sugar intake
      Deficiencies noted in pregnancies and malnutrition

COPPER
      Needed to convert iron into hemoglobin
      May prevent general weakness
      Deficiencies seen in pregnancies
      May prevent impaired respiration

POTASSIUM
        Works with sodium to regulate heartbeat
        Joins with phosphorus to provide oxygen to the brain
        Stimulates the kidneys to dispose of body wastes
        Deficiency may cause constipation and insomnia

CALCIUM
        Needed for blood clotting
        Need to activate enzymes
        Relaxes heart muscle
        May help to prevent osteoporosis
        Need to assist with nerve impulse transmission

IRON
        Need to prevent anemia
        Assists in oxygen transport
        Deficiency may be implicated in poor memory

A new soft drink that advertises that it contains 25% of your daily vitamin needs, only provides the more common vitamins that would ordinarily easily be obtained even in a mediocre diet.

Coffee interferes with iron absorption and may leach magnesium out of the body.

Chocolate, cashews, collard greens, beet greens, Swiss chard, spinach, rhubarb, and beets contain the chemical oxalate which may interfere with the ability of the body to absorb calcium.

Vitamin C is required to assist in the metabolism of iron. If it is not present in adequate amounts, less than 30% of the ingested iron will be utilized by the body.

When taking a vitamin C supplement, remember that if it isn't time release your body is only able to metabolize approximately 250 mg. per hour. A 500 mg. in a non-time release is all that should be taken.

Studies have shown that PABA may retard or even aid in returning original hair color.

Vitamins A, D, E and K are best absorbed in the intestines when a small amount of fat is present. If you are taking a vitamin E supplement as a single supplement it would be best to take it with a small amount of 2% milk.

Americans are spending 4.2 billion on nutritional supplements annually.

A report in the Journal of the American Medical Society cited studies that revealed eating excessive amounts of foods high in vitamin A, such as, liver, carrots, cantaloupe, etc. may result in headaches and nausea.

Taking one teaspoon of crystalline vitamin C when you awake with 8oz. of water will usually result in a bowel movement within 30 minutes.

Studies show that Caucasian men and African-American women lose calcium stores at a faster pace than the rest of the population after age 30. For Caucasian women it begins at age 18. African-American men do not seem to have the problem.

Calcium is best absorbed with meals, since it tends to absorb best in an acid environment. Calcium is also best utilized by the bones when boron is present. The better sources of boron may be found in prunes, raisins, almonds, peanuts, dates, and honey.

Vitamin supplements will maintain their freshness longer if stored in the refrigerator.

Aspirin tends to reduce the effectiveness of vitamin C.

Vitamin A is important for a healthy immune system as well as assisting the body in the retention of vitamin C and zinc metabolism.

Studies have shown that if you consume a small amount of sugar with your calcium supplement, the absorption rate will improve.

"HIGH PROTEIN INTAKE = DANGER"
Can shorten life expectancy, increase the risk of cancer, deplete calcium from bones, can cause fluid imbalances, may stress and damage the liver and kidneys, cause a hazard to premature infants, one cause of obesity, and will increase the need for vitamin B_6.

"SOUNDS FISHY, BUT ISN'T"
Sardines are an excellent source of calcium. Three sardines supplies 370mg. of calcium, more than 8oz. of milk.

"CHOP, CHOP, SLICE, SLICE, NO, NO"
Cutting or chopping any fruit or vegetable high in vitamin C releases an enzyme that may destroy the vitamin C. Leave all fresh fruits and vegetables whole until ready to eat if possible.

Studies are being done relating low vitamin D levels to breast cancer. Areas of the country with low sunlight levels seem to have a higher incidence of breast cancer.

Beta-carotene is only available from plants, vitamin A is available from animal sources.

VITAMIN ROBBERS

The following information will provide information regarding some of the environmental factors, drugs, and everyday product use that can significantly affect the potency and availability of many nutrients. The awareness of these factors should assist you in making choices regarding your supplement program.

VITAMIN/MINERAL	ROBBER
Vitamin A	Mineral oil, air pollution/smog, fertilizer nitrates, antacids, corticosteroids.
Vitamin D	Anti-convulsive drugs (dilantin), consumption, alcohol, stressful situations, oral contraceptives. mineral oil, antacids, oral contraceptives, alcohol.
Thiamin B_1	Antibiotics, excess heat/cooking, sugar
Riboflavin B_2	Antibiotics, exposure to light, diuretics, reserpine.
Niacin	Excessive heat, alcohol, most illnesses reduce intestinal absorption, nitrites and nitrates, penicillin.
PABA	Sulfa drugs.
Pantothenic Acid	Methyl bromide insecticide (fumigant for foods).
Pyradoxine B_6	Aging causes levels to decline after 50, steroids, hormones, hydralazine (hypertension drug), excessive heat, food processing, corticosteroids, hydralazine.
Folic Acid	Oral contraceptives, stress situations, vitamin C deficiency.
Vitamin B_{12}	Prolonged iron deficiency, stress, oral contraceptives.

Biotin	Excess heat, antibiotics, sulfa drugs, avidin in raw egg white, oral contraceptives.
Calcium	Antacids, aspirin, corticosteroids, diuretics, lidocaine.
Choline	Sugar consumption, alcohol.
Inositol	Antibiotics.
Magnesium	Thiazides, alcohol, diuretics.
Vitamin C	Overexertion, fatigue, stress, aspirin, smoking, alcohol, corticosteroids, antihistamines, fluoride, oral contraceptives, barbituates.
Vitamin E	Oral contraceptives, food processing, rancid fats, mineral oil.
Vitamin K	Antibiotics, mineral oil, radiation, anticoagulants, phenobarbital, alcohol.

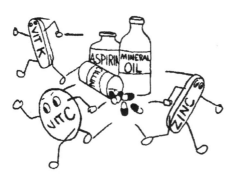
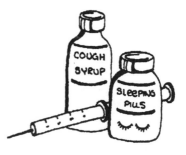

NEW SUPPLEMENTS OF THE 90'S

PHYTOCHEMICALS

These chemical extracts from fruits and vegetables are becoming the latest fad in prevention. basically, they ar the biologically active, non-nutritive substances found in plants that give them their color, flavor, odor, and provides them with their natural defense system against diseases. Simply put, these are not nutrients, nor vitamins or minerals, just chemical compounds that exist in fruits and vegetables. Their new name in many publications is "Nutraceuticals." They have been known to exist for years, but never received much press or attention until recent studies started linking then to cancer prevention in laboratory animals.

Studies on phytochemicals are presently being conducted by numerous agencies and universities including The National Cancer Society and The National Academy of Science. The phytochemicals already are showing results in animals arresting cancer in all stages of cellular development. Exactly which phytochemicals will be beneficial to humans and in what types of cancer, are questions that will take years to answer.

We have always known that whole grains, fruits and vegetables should be consumed in adequate amounts on a daily basis for optimum health, and that cancer was not as prevalent in the early part of the century as it is today. The possible explanation is that our grandparents ate a healthier diet with more unprocessed foods and more fruits and vegetables. The naturally occurring compounds in these foods provided a degree of "natural" protection.

Cancer has only become more prevalent since the 1940's when we learned how to process foods, can them, use chemicals more efficiently in our foods and heat them until almost all the nutrients were either lost or biochemically altered. Phytochemicals may, however, be one answer to reducing the incidence of cancer.

One very important factor is that phytochemicals are not destroyed by cooking or processing to any great degree. The problem is that we just don't eat enough of them. If that is the case then we should consider taking a "Nutraceutical" supplement or any supplement that contains these phytochemicals or phytoextracts.

There are over 100,000 phytochemicals and the more sophisticated our analysis equipment becomes over time, we will probably identify even more. The following list, provides the most current information obtainable on the more potent and important of these extractions. All information has been taken from laboratory animal testing only.

PHYTOCHEMICALS IN FRUITS, VEGETABLES AND HERBS

FOOD	PHYTOCHEMICAL
Broccoli, cauliflower, Brussels sprouts, kale, turnips.	**SULFORAPHANE** Activates enzyme that aids in removing carcinogens from the body.
	DITHIOLTHIONES Triggers production of enzymes that may block carcinogens from damaging DNA.

The phytochemicals have shown special cancer fighting benefits by inhibiting cancer of the breast tumors in laboratory animals. Cooking methods such as; microwaving and steaming increases the availability of the phytochemical.

Broccoli has 40 phytochemicals.

Sweet potatoes, yams, artichokes, red grapes, red wine, strawberries.	**FLAVONOIDS/POLYPHENOLS** Attaches to cancer cells and stops hormones from attaching.

may reduce the risk of cancer by attaching to free radicals and flushing them out of the body, this may also reduce the risk of cardiovascular diseases. This phytochemical is a part of the red wine/lower heart disease factor in France. however, it would be wise to avoid the red wine and consume the foods until additional studies are more conclusive. Recommendations are 1/3 cup per day.

Cabbage, turnips, dark green leafy vegetables.	**INDOLES** Studies show that they reduce the risk of breast cancer.

Tends to improve immune system function and may protect against cancer by allowing the body to eliminate toxins more easily. Stimulates the production of an enzyme that may make estrogen less effective which may give a degree of protection against breast and ovarian cancers.

Soybeans, dried beans,   **GENISTEIN**
mung bean sprouts.   Cuts off the blood supply to
                                  tumors cells by retarding
                                  their capillary growth.

This phytochemical is called a "phytoestrogen" and may offer protection against breast cancer, osteoporosis, heart disease, and most female hormone associated problems. Additional phytochemicals found in soybeans may help reduce blood cholesterol levels and slow replication of cancer cells.

Three four-ounce servings of "tofu" or three cups of soy milk daily is recommended.

Chili peppers   **CAPSAICIN**
                                  Stops toxic molecules from
                                  attaching to DNA.

An anti-inflammatory substance that prevents carcinogens from attaching to DNA and discourages the growth and replication of cancer cells. Other potential uses are killing bacteria that may cause stomach ulcers and as a treatment for bronchitis and colds.

Eat in moderation as red chili peppers tend to stimulate gastric acid causing indigestion and general stomach irritation. Recommendations are no more than 2-4 small peppers per day if tolerated well.

Citrus fruit   **LIMONENE**
                                  Activates enzyme that disposes
                                  of carcinogens.

The active substance d-limonene, has shown to offer protection against breast cancer in laboratory animals. It also increases the production of additional enzymes that may assist the immune system in disposing of carcinogens. Future studies may also show that this phytochemical will actually reduce plaque in arteries. The pulpier the product, the better. Recommendations are 16-24 ounces of pulpy orange juice daily or 3-4 pieces of citrus fruit.

Orange juice has 59 known phytochemicals.

Apples/fruits   **CAFFEIC ACID**
                                 Increases the solubility of
                                 toxins so they can be flushed
                                 from the body.

                                 FERULIC ACID
                                 Binds to nitrates in stomach.

Grapes, strawberries,   **ELLAGIC ACID**
raspberries.   may prevent carcinogens from
                                 entering DNA.

Garlic, onions, leeks.   **ALLYLIC SULFIDE**
                                 Detoxifies carcinogens.

Chives   **ALLIUM COMPOUNDS**
                                 Slows reproduction of
                                 carcinogens, allows more time
                                 for then to be destroyed.

Recent studies show that these vegetables may lower HDL (bad
cholesterol) and detoxify the body by increasing the
production of glutathione S-transferase, which may cause
carcinogens to be excreted more easily. When combined with
the mineral selenium it may have an effect on breast cancer.
May reduce incidence of heart disease by having a mild blood
thinning effect and may decrease the risk of stomach
cancers.

Garlic and onions have 50 phytochemicals.

When garlic is processed, it releases the sulfur compound
which can stimulate immune responses. Too much garlic powder
may interfere with anticoagulants and cause stomach upsets.

Recommendations are 2-4 fresh cloves of garlic or 1/2 cup of
raw onion daily. Keep mints handy!

Grains, especially rye,   **PHYTIC ACID**
wheat, rice, sesame seeds,   Binds to iron, thus reducing a
and peanuts.   free radical production
                                 mechanism.

Studies are being conducted relating to the prevention of colon cancer and to reduce the severity of intestinal cancers.

Tomatoes, green peppers

P-COUMARIC & CHLORGENIC ACIDS
Kills cancer-forming substances in their formation stages. This group contains over 10,000 phytochemicals.

Carrots, seaweed, squash, peaches, red, yellow, dark green vegetables.

ALPHA-CAROTENE/BETA-CAROTENE
Fights free radicals which may invade the DNA causing an abnormal cell to be produced.

Tends to improve vitamin A effectiveness and improves immune system responses as well as decreasing the risk of lung cancer in laboratory mice. Carrots should cleaned thoroughly and left unpeeled to preserve the phytochemicals. Recommendation is 1-2 carrots or one cup of seaweed daily.

Licorice root

GLYCYRRHIZIN AND TRITERPENOIDS
Has disease-fighting properties. Still under investigation.

Increases the effectiveness of the immune system and tends to slow the rate at which cancer cells replicate. Also, useful in treating gastrointestinal problems and ulcers. Contains antibacterial properties and helps fight tooth decay and gingivitis. Prevents breast cancer in laboratory animals by activating the production of liver enzymes, reducing the level of tumor-promoting estrogens.

Person's with high blood pressure should not eat licorice. Anise, a licorice flavoring does not contain the phytochemical, only licorice root.

Green tea/black tea
(Not herbal teas)

POLYPHENOL CATECHINS AND THEAFLAVIN
Studies are ongoing regarding cancer fighting abilities.

May have a tendency to increase fat metabolism as well as increasing the effectiveness of the immune system and lowering cholesterol. The phenols have been found in recent studies to protect tissues from oxidation.

Tea must be brewed for at least 5-10 minutes to get maximum catechin content. Excessive consumption may cause stomach upsets and provide a large dose of caffeine. Moderation is the key.

Rosemary   **CARNOSOL**
                            An antioxidant.

Tends to reduce the development of certain types of tumors and may protect fats in the body from oxidizing. May be used freely on salads or other foods.

Flaxseed   **LIGANS**
                            Antioxidant of which flaxseed
                            is the pre-cursor.

Flaxseed contains elements that are capable of producing "ligans" a potent antioxidant, it also contains Omega-3 fatty acids which may have anti-cancer properties. Recommendations are to use ground, fortified flaxseed with B_6 and zinc added. Daily dose in 1 tablespoon of grain or 1 teaspoon of oil.

Red grapefruit, tomatoes,   **LYCOPENE**
watermelon, apricots.   An antioxidant.

May decrease the risk of colon and bladder cancer in laboratory mice as well as reducing the risk of heart disease. Protects DNA and cells against damage from free radicals. Fruits should uncooked and as fresh as possible. One cup daily is recommended.

Yellow squash, spinach,   **LUTEIN/ZEAXANTHIN**
collard, mustard and   Slows growth of cancer
turnip greens.   cells.

Reduces the risk of lung cancer, strengthens the immune system and may have a role in the prevention of colon, prostate, and esophageal cancers. Steam the greens in a small amount of water for a short period of time. Two-thirds of a cup daily is recommended.

Cranberry juice   **ANTHOCYANINS**
                                   May prevent and cure urinary
                                   tract problems.

Best to use unsweetened cranberry juice to water or tea. Two
8 ounce glasses per day is the recommendation.

Ginger root   **GINGEROL**
                                   Relieves motion sickness.

Has anti-inflammatory properties and may relieve symptoms of
headaches. One-half teaspoon of powdered root or 1 teaspoon
of fresh ginger daily. Tea can be made by simmering several
slices in 2-3 cups of water for 8-10 minutes then strain.

Horseradish, cabbage,   **PHENETHYL ISOTHIOCYANATES**
turnips.   Tends to reduce tumor growth.

Activates enzymes that block carcinogens from damaging the
DNA. May inhibit cancer of the lungs.

Kidney beans, chickpeas,   **SAPONINS**
soybeans, lentils.   Slows the growth of cancer
                                   cells and may even prevent
                                   them from replicating.

Basil, carrots, parsley,   **MONOTERPENES**
mint, caraway seeds,   may interfere with the
citrus fruits, cabbage.   replication of cancer cells.

Nutraceuticals, at present, are regulated by the FDA as
dietary supplements only and are not classified as drugs.
They are extractions from natural foods, to date have had no
definitive extensive studies completed, and all claims made
for them as mentioned above are still speculative. Studies
that have been reported have all been on laboratory animals.
Hopefully, more human studies will be forthcoming in the
very near future.

Claims made for products that offer cancer protection and
cure should be viewed with caution. Products that contain
herbal or botanical ingredients should indicate the part of
the plant the product was produced from. Be sure labels list
all the ingredients that are present in significant amounts.

A future statement that may appear on these products may read; **"This food product is not intended to diagnose, treat, cure or prevent any disease."** Phytochemicals in the future will be transferred to different foods and produce foods that will be called **"functional foods."** The Functional Foods For Health project is presently underway at the University of Illinois.

Phyto-Fortified Foods (FFH) will be the new wave of the future.

PROANTHOCYANIDIN (PAC)

A relatively new antioxidant that may be purchased under a brand name (Pycnogenol) or by its generic name (proanthocyanidin) has only recently appeared in many products. it is a natural plant product originally extracted from the bark of pine trees. However, it is now being extracted from grape seeds as well as pine bark. The substance is found in many natural foods, however, it is relatively expensive to extract it from most of them.

Proanthocyanidin, is stated to be 20 times more powerful than vitamin C and 50 times more powerful than vitamin E. It also, may have the ability to protect a number of antioxidants from being destroyed before they are able to perform their functions or be utilized by the cell.

PAC is water soluble and has the ability to be absorbed and utilized by the cell very shortly after ingestion. PAC remains in the body for three days circulating in body fluids and is gradually eliminated. If taken regularly cells will acquire a saturation level which provides a continuum of beneficial antioxidant activity.

PAC is one of the most efficient free radical scavengers known. It has the unique ability to actually adhere to collagen (connective tissue) fibers and ward off the potential damage that might be done by circulating free radicals. This function may be the emphasis of future studies that relate to aging of the skin and joint diseases, such as arthritis.

CAROTENOIDS

Fruits and vegetables contain over 500 carotenoids. Carotenoids are a pigment that give these foods their colors. About 10% of the carotenoids will convert to vitamin A and provide 25% of the bodies usable vitamin A. Studies are continuing and the future may show that carotenoids are more effective when taken together as a potent antioxidant.

Beta-carotene may not be the "magic bullet" to slow down or stop a cancer cell from replicating, however, a combination of carotenoids may provide the protection we are hoping for. One of the more interesting findings is that carotenoids improve communications between premalignant cells and normal cells. Tumor growth is slowed when they receive regulating signals from the normal cells.

Animal studies have shown that when a combination of carotenoids were given there was a decrease in the number of cancer cells.

MAJOR CAROTENOIDS

CAROTENOID	FOOD SOURCE	POSSIBLE BENEFIT
Alpha carotene	Carrots	Activity of vitamin A decreased the risk of lung cancer and slowed the growth of cancerous cells in mice as well as increasing immune system response.
Beta-carotene	Broccoli, cantaloupe, carrots	Same response as alpha-carotene, with the additional decrease of colon, bladder, and skin cancers in mice.
Beta-cryptoxanthin	Mangos, oranges, papayas, tangerines	Vitamin A activity.
Canthaxanthin	Natural food color added to jellies, jams, soft drinks, and tomato sauce	Found to slow skin cancer in mice as well as slowing the growth of cancer cells and improving immune response in mice.
Lutein	Broccoli, dark green leafy vegetables	Decreased the risk of lung cancer in mice.

| Lycopene | Tomatoes, tomato products | Decreased the risk of colon and bladder cancer and slowed the replication of cancer cells in mice. |
| Zeaxanthin | Cress leaf, Swiss chard, okra, beet greens. | May prevent macular degeneration. Blocks peroxide free radicals. |

CO-ENZYME Q_{10} (ubiquinone)

Ubiquinone$_{10}$ is not a vitamin and can be produced by the body from two proteins tyrosine and mevalonate. Ubiquinone$_{10}$ is necessary for the cell to produce energy and has proved to be an active antioxidant in reducing free radical production. A number of factors may reduce the available Ubiquinone$_{10}$ in the body causing lower energy levels. Dietary sources of the nutrients needed to produce Ubiquinone$_{10}$ are lean meats, nuts, vegetables, and grains.

Studies have shown that if levels of Ubiquinone$_{10}$ are low (below 25% of normal levels) cells cannot produce enough energy to live and cells will start to die until the level increases. The elderly, malnourished, and chronically ill have lower levels of Ubiquinone$_{10}$ and may need to be supplemented. However, if a sufficient supply is always available energy levels are maintained.

Ubiquinone$_{10}$ may also be active in keeping the immune system healthy and at optimum efficiency.

SHARK CARTILAGE

Studies are continuing in all major countries regarding the use of shark cartilage and the prevention or treatment of cancer. Most studies are finding that there is an ingredient that seems to reduce the growth of tumors. The following results have been taken from a small study of only 21 patients and should be viewed in that context:

    61% Had a reduction in tumor size
    87% Stated that they had improved their quality of life
    100% of prostate cancer patients had a lower PSA level
When claims are made it is best to obtain a copy of the study and review it before taking this or any new product for an extended period of time.

DHEA (dehydroepiandrosterone)

This a naturally occurring hormone which may enhance the efficiency of the immune system. It is normally produced by the adrenal gland and is a component of a number of hormones, such as; testosterone, progesterone, estrogen, and corticosterone.

As we age the blood levels of DHEA decline and studies are being done to determine if this decline may speed up the aging process. It has been used successfully to increase libido in persons that have experienced a lowering of their sex drive as related to aging. Many of the degenerative effects of aging may be slowed with the supplementation of this as we age.

Studies, however, are not conclusive at this time to actually prescribe a dosage that would be beneficial for a specific problem. DHEA has been banned by the government until more studies are done. However, herbal products are being sold that companies claim to be the precursor of DHEA. These herbal products are for the most part derived from the Mexican Yam (Dioscorea villosa) roots. Also called diosgenin it can be converted to DHEA in the body.

High dosages when given to rats have caused liver damage.

ANTIOXIDANT ENZYMES

Superoxide Dismutase (SOD)

One of the first lines of defense the body has from free radicals is from a substance called SOD. SOD is a natural antioxidant that keeps the free radicals under control and eliminates them. SOD always has a partner called "catalase" which helps carry away some of the debris when SOD reacts with a free radical. The most dangerous element of the debris is hydrogen peroxide which if left alone will create additional more destructive free radicals.

This partnership is one of the most effective free radical eliminators in our bodies. A deficiency of SOD can reduce the body's effectiveness in fighting free radicals and increases the risk and severity of a number of diseases such as arthritis, bursitis, and gout.

Glutathione Peroxidase (GP)

The main constituents of this antioxidant enzyme is the amino acid glutathione and the mineral selenium. One of selenium's main function in the body is to become a component of the glutathione peroxidase enzyme.

The key role of GP in the body is to protect the lipids in the cells walls from being destroyed by a group of free radicals known as lipid peroxides. Studies are being done to determine the significance of the cell damage by peroxides (when adequate GP is not present) in relation to diseases such as; heart disease, premature aging, cancer, liver and pancreas damage, and skin disorders.

Methionine Reductase (MR)

This antioxidant enzyme has been effective in neutralizing another free radical called a hydroxyl radical. These are formed by the reactions involving heavy metals and other free radicals. Hydroxy radicals are also formed by the exposure of the body to x-rays and radiation. MR plays a significant role in the destruction and neutralization of these free radicals, especially the ones formed by athletes or during strenuous exercise periods.

Hydroxy radicals are a by product of fat metabolism which occurs after the depletion of our carbohydrate stores. An athlete that can keep a high level of MR during a strenuous exercise period or sport may be able to improve their performance.

CHLORELLA

Chlorella is derived from freshwater algae and is one of the newest green algae products. It has 50 times the chlorophyll content of alfalfa and scientists estimate it has survived for approximately 2.5 billion years. Studies have concluded that the longevity of chlorella is due to the strength of its hard cell wall and unique DNA repair mechanism.

Only recently has science discovered a method of breaking down the hard cell wall and be able to produce it as a health food. At present, chlorella is the fastest-selling health food product in Japan and is used as both a dietary supplement and for medicinal purposes. Chlorella has a high protein content, approximately 60% compared to soybean's 30% making it an excellent non-meat protein source.

Chlorella contains over 20 vitamins and minerals and is an excellent source of vitamin B_{12}, especially for vegetarians. Chlorella is far superior than spirulina in all categories. Studies are surfacing showing that chlorophyll has been related to improved metabolism, tissue growth (wound healing), and lowering cholesterol levels. Additional studies are ongoing relating to cancer prevention since chlorella may stimulate the immune system to produce macrophages which kill abnormal cells. At present, all studies regarding cancer and chlorella are all being conducted in Japan.

Chapter 10

Eggs Cheeses and Other Dairy Products

DAIRY PRODUCTS

EGG KNOWLEDGE

The egg is still one of the best and most complete sources
of protein, regardless of all the negative publicity it has
received. Most of this publicity revolves around cholesterol
and the high levels found in the egg yolk (approximately 200
mg.).

New major studies have recently shown that consuming egg
yolks do not appreciably elevate blood cholesterol levels.
One of these studies related the substance lecithin found
naturally in eggs as a factor which may help the body clear
the cholesterol. Recommendations are still to limit egg
consumption to no more than 4-5 eggs per week.

WEIGHT OF EGGS

```
Jumbo.......................30 ounces
Extra Large.................27 ounces
Large.......................24 ounces
Medium......................21 ounces
Small.......................18 ounces
Pee Wee.....................15 ounces
```

CALORIES

```
1 Large egg = 80 calories
1 Egg white = 20 calories
1 Egg yolk  = 60 calories
```

MEASURING EGGS

```
1 Large egg (2 oz)    = 1/4 cup
1 Med. egg(1 3/4 oz) = 1/5 cup
1 Small egg(1 1/2oz) = 1/6 cup
```

EGG FACTS

If an egg cracks when being
boiled, just remove it from
the water and while it is
still wet, pour a generous
amount of salt over it, let it
stand for 20 seconds, wrap it
in tin foil, twirl the ends
and replace it in the boiling
water.

There are three grades for eggs: U.S. Grade AA, U.S. Grade A, and U.S. Grade B. The Grade B are usually used by bakeries and commercial food processors.

When using eggs and solid shortening, break the egg into the measuring cup before measuring the shortening, the shortening will come out easier.

If you want your deviled to have greater stability, cut a slice off the end and they will stand up for easy filling.

Egg whites should be beaten in a bowl with a small rounded bottom to reduce the work area and increase the volume.

The refrigerator shelf life of an egg is approximately 10-14 days.

Always store eggs in a closed container or the original carton for longer life and to avoid the egg absorbing refrigerator odors. If they are stored with the large end up they will last longer, the yolk will stay centered.

"SEE, SAW?"
Never separate eggs by passing the yolk back and forth from one half of the shell to the other. Bacterial contamination may be present on the shell. A funnel over a bowl works really well.

Yolks will last longer if covered with water.

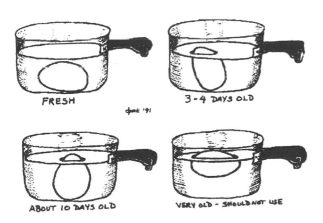

FRESH   3-4 DAYS OLD

ABOUT 10 DAYS OLD   VERY OLD - SHOULD NOT USE

To tell how old an egg is, place the egg in a pan of cold water, if it lies on its side, it's fresh, if it tilts on an angle it's 3-5 days old, if the egg stands upright, it's 10-14 days old, if it floats to the top, don't crack it open in the house, bury it in the backyard and use it for fertilizer. It may even grow an eggplant!

Hard boiled eggs should never be frozen. Egg white changes texture and becomes tough. When freezing fresh eggs always break the yolk, The whites can be frozen alone and the yolks can be frozen alone unless you plan on using them at the same time.

You can prevent boiled eggs from cracking by rubbing a cut lemon on the shell before cooking. Boiled eggs should be cooled at room temperature before refrigerating them in an open bowl.

When whipping eggs for omelets, they should be three days old and allowed to stand for 30 minutes at room temperature before using. This will result in a greater volume. For baking projects eggs should be as fresh as possible.

When poaching eggs, add a small amount of butter to the tin cup before placing the egg in to prevent them from sticking and the yolks from breaking.

When making meringue, try adding a teaspoon of cold water to the egg white to create more volume when you are beating them.

You should never pour raw eggs or yolks into any hot mixture. If you need to add them, add them gradually for the best results. Adding the eggs too quickly may cause the dish to curdle.

If you are having trouble with omelets collapsing, try adding a pinch of cornstarch and a pinch of confectioners sugar to the yolks before folding in the whites.

To guarantee a white film over the eggs when cooking, place a few drops of water in the pan just before the eggs are done and cover the pan.

To make eggs easier to peel when boiling them, just add a small amount of salt to the water to toughen the shell.

To tell if an egg is hard-boiled or raw, just spin it, if it wobbles it's raw.

If you wish to store eggs for 2-3 weeks, just rub a small amount of vegetable oil on it to seal the shell.

Egg whites contain more than 1/2 the protein of the egg and only 25% of the calories.

When making scrambled eggs, use a small amount of water instead of milk. Milk makes the eggs watery and doesn't blend well. Water will make the eggs fluffy and light.

When frying an egg, try adding a small amount of flour to the pan to prevent splattering.

If you store your hard boiled eggs with your fresh eggs, try adding a small amount of vegetable coloring to the boiling water and it will be easier to tell them apart.

If you allow eggs to sit out for 30 minutes and go to room temperature before you beat them, you will get more volume. Chef's rarely take an egg directly from the refrigerator and use it in a recipe.

If you add a teaspoon of white vinegar to the water eggs are being boiled in they may not crack. The vinegar tends to soften the shell allowing more expansion. However, they may not be as easy to peel.

If you come up one egg short when baking a cake, substitute 2 tablespoons of mayonnaise. Thus will only work for one egg.

Commercial eggnog has a very short shelf life. Make sure that you check the date carefully, it will only stay fresh for about 5 days.

If you want to reduce the calories in homemade eggnog, try separating the eggs, beat the whites until stiff, then gently fold them into the balance of the mixture just before serving.

Eggnog can be substituted in many recipes that call for whole milk for a great taste. However, it may add lots of cholesterol and calories.

If you freeze eggnog and find that it separates, place it in a blender before using it.

"NOT SLIPPERY WHEN WET"
When handling eggs or removing them from the carton, try wetting your hands first and they won't slip away.

There is no difference in white or brown eggs in either nutritional quality of taste.

The FDA regulations state that eggs should be refrigerated at all times during shipping and in supermarkets. Many times they will be left on pallets in markets without refrigeration. The internal temperature of eggs should never fall below 45^0 F. and in a controlled humidity of 75%.

A soft-boiled egg should be cooked at least 3 1/2 minutes to kill bacteria if it is present. Fried eggs should have the white hard and the yolk may be soft. The internal temperature will be approximately 140^0 F. Some eggs have been found to contain "micro-cracks" which allow harmful bacteria to enter.

Egg shells should be dull not shiny if the egg is really fresh. In very fresh eggs the yolk will hardly be visible through the white.

"EGG KNOWLEDGE"
All egg cartons that are marked "A" or "AA" are not officially graded. Egg cartons must have the USDA shield as well as the letter grade.

If you purchase eggs and find a cracked one, throw it out it is probably contaminated.

The average hen produces about 200 eggs per year, the laying begins 5 months after they are hatched.

It is best not to taste cookie or cake batter that contain raw eggs. Approximately 3,000 people became ill in 1995 from raw eggs. The problem was that a number of chicken ovaries had salmonella which was carried into the sealed fresh eggs. Some eggs also have almost invisible "micro-cracks."

The total digestive time for an egg is four hours due to it's high fat content.

To keep yolks centered when boiling eggs for deviled eggs, just stir the water while they are cooking. When storing deviled eggs, place the halves with the filling together and wrap tightly with tin foil, twirl the ends and refrigerate.

Hard boiled eggs will slice easier if you dip the knife in water first.

Egg will clean off utensils easier if you use cold water.

To remove an unbroken egg that has stuck to the carton, just wet the carton.

"PEEK-A-BOO"
To separate egg yolks from the whites, try poking a small hole in one end and drain the white out. If you want the yolk just break it open. Another method of separating the whites from the yolks is to use a small funnel placed over a measuring cup. This will work very well as long as the yolk doesn't break.

Aluminum bowls and cookware tend to darken an egg due to the aluminum reacting with the egg protein.

"NEW PRODUCT"
An excellent new product called "Just Whites" is a powdered egg white only product that will assist you in reducing the fat in a whole egg. It may be used in recipes that call for the whites only such as a meringue.

Egg whites become firm at 145^0 F., yolks at 155^0 F. Eggs should be cooked at a low temperature to guarantee a tender white and smooth yolk.

When preparing any dish that calls for egg whites only such as a meringue, remove all traces of egg yolk with a Q-tip or edge of a paper towel, before trying to beat. The slightest trace of yolk will effect the results. Vegetable oil on your beater blades will also effect the results.

"A LITTLE DIP WILL DO YA"
If you are preparing a number of omelets or batches of scrambled eggs, try wiping the pan with a piece of paper towel dipped in table salt after three batches. This will eliminate the eggs sticking to the pan.

To prepare an fluffy omelet or scrambled egg dish, try adding a small amount of water instead of milk while you are beating the eggs. Milk tends to harden the yolk, water tends to slow down the coagulation of the yolk.

To remove the shell from a hard boiled egg, crack the egg and roll it around in your hands with gentle pressure. Insert a teaspoon between the shell and the egg white then rotate the spoon.

Always cool a hard boiled egg before you try and slice it, it will slice easier and not fall apart.

When microwaving eggs, remember that the yolk will cook first. Microwaves are attracted to the fat in the yolk.

The fresher the egg the better it will be for poaching. The white will be more firm and prevent the yolk from breaking. Make sure you bring the water to a boil and then to a simmer before adding the egg.

If you stir the water rapidly before placing an egg in for poaching the egg won't spread as much and will stay centered.

For the best scrambled eggs, you need to cook them slowly over a medium-low heat starting them in a cool pan.

When purchasing an egg substitute, make sure you read the label. Some contain MSG.

If you want to cool and egg and not have a grayish coating on the yolk, try placing the egg in ice cold water after cooking.

If you are using eggs for an Easter egg hunt, write down the location of every egg. Many children have become ill from finding eggs after they have been removed from refrigeration for more than 3 hours.

"SUBSTITUTIONS"
You can substitute 2 egg yolks for 1 whole egg when making custards, cream pie filling, and salad dressings. You can also substitute 2 egg yolks plus 1 teaspoon of water for 1 whole egg in yeast dough or cookie batter.

The twisted strands of egg white are called "chalazae cords." These hold the yolk in place and are more prominent in very fresh eggs.

"QUACK, QUACK, QUACK"
Duck eggs develop harmful bacteria as they age. The bacteria can only be destroyed by boiling the eggs for 10-12 minutes.

An excellent plant fertilizer may be made by drying eggshells and pulverizing them in a blender.

The difference in the quality of eggs can be determined by the amount of spread when they are broken. U.S. Grade AA eggs will have a small spread, be thick, very white and have a firm high yolk. U.S. Grade A eggs will have more spread with a less thick white. U.S. Grade B eggs will have a wide spread, little thick white and probably a flat enlarged looking yolk.

"THE EGG HULK"

When eggs are overcooked the yolks may turn a greenish color as a result of the leaching out of an iron compound. This occurs more frequently in older eggs and is harmless.

Eggs with blood spots are twice as likely to contain salmonella according to the USDA. However, they can still be eaten if the whites are cooked hard and the yolk begins to harden, about 160^0 F. Blood spots usually occur from a blood vessel rupturing of the yolk's surface. They do not necessarily mean that the egg was fertile. Best to remove the spot with the tip of a knife.

If you have a problem with fried eggs splattering, try adding a small powdering of cornstarch to the pan before adding the eggs. The butter should be very hot before adding the eggs. Reduce the heat once the eggs are in the frying pan.

HEALTH HINT:

After you make hard-boiled eggs, never place them in cool water after they are peeled. Eggs have a thin protective membrane that if removed or damaged and placed in water or a sealed container may allow for bacteria to grow.

MILK

While milk has been described in numerous nutrition publications as a "near-perfect" food, there are a number of facts that should be taken into consideration:

Milk quality is dependent on the feeding habits of the cows. Poor feeding habits with insufficient green feed produces a lower nutrient milk.

Many cows will receive large doses of antibiotics, traces of which may show up in the milk.

If a recipe calls for buttermilk and you don't have any, try using slightly soured milk. Soured milk may be used in many baking recipes.

If you allow milk to sit at room temperature for more than 30-40 minutes it will reduce it's fresh lifespan.

The homogenization process may allow an enzyme "xanthane oxidase" to be released into the bloodstream and reduce the effectiveness of important body chemicals that protect the small coronary arteries.

The pasteurization process has also been implicated in a number of other health problems.

> *Milk allergies in children and adults*
> *Destroys 50% of the vitamin C content*
> *Destroys 25% of the vitamin B_1 content*
> *Destroys 9-15% of the vitamin B_2 content*

The fat content in milk has deceived us for years due to advertising the does not take into consideration the water content of the milk which should be removed before giving us the actual fat content of the milk.

The following figures are the actual amount of fat in milk after the water weight is removed:

Whole Milk	49% Fat
2% "Low-Fat" Milk	34% Fat
1% Low-Fat Milk	17% Fat
.5% Low-Fat Milk	9% Fat
Buttermilk	1-2% Fat
Skim/Non-Fat Milk	0-1% Fat

MILK FACTS

Milk processed at high temperatures that has been sold in Europe for years will be available soon in the United States. Ultra-High-Temperature (UHT) milk is a process whereby milk is sterilized while preserving its nutritional value. The process allows milk to be stored unopened without refrigeration for up to 6 months.

California produces the most milk, 3 billion gallons per year.

Overall milk consumption in the United States is down 17% in the 1990's. One reason is the number of meals we eat out substituting soft drinks and other beverages for the milk.

Milk is always thought of as the best source of calcium. It is one good source, others are cheeses and dark green leafy vegetables.

If milk is getting close to the curdling stage, try adding a teaspoon or two of baking soda to the milk. It will give you a few more good days.

Cream is easy to whip into whipped cream, yet milk won't whip up at all. The reason is that even whole milk is only 3.3% fat (50% fat without the water) while heavy cream is low in water content and 38% fat.

Fresh milk will stay longer if you add a pinch of salt   to each quart.

Sour cream can be made by adding 3-4 drops of pure lemon juice to every 3/4 cup of whipping cream. Let stand at room temperature for 30-40 minutes.

Powdered milk should always be kept on hand in case you run out of milk. It is also excellent for thickening skim milk without adding fat.

To avoid freezer burn on ice cream, cover the top of the container with a plastic bag.

The average American consumes 15 quarts of ice cream annually. A high quality ice cream has a butterfat content of 15%. Non-fat yogurt is recommended.

Buttermilk is produced from a culture of skim milk, making it low-fat.

Buttermilk may be substituted for whole milk in most recipes, but you will need to add 1/2 teaspoon of baking soda to the dry ingredients for each cup of buttermilk you use.

Dry milk comes in three forms; whole milk, non-fat and buttermilk. Buttermilk powder is presently becoming available in most markets. The powdered whole milk requires refrigeration because of its high fat content of 49-50%. Other powdered milks can last for about 6 months without refrigeration.

Once powdered milk is reconstituted it will last for about 3 days under refrigeration.

Milk can retain its freshness for up to 1 week after the expiration date on the carton.

Whole milk is the highest source of saturated fat in the American diet.

Calcium in milk stimulates the secretion of stomach acids that may irritate ulcers. Antacids with high buffering qualities are better. Food will also act as a buffer.

Milk is better purchased in paper cartons which block 98% of the harmful effect of the lights in supermarkets. The clear plastic containers in just four hours of store light, can destroy 44% of the vitamin A content in low-fat and non-fat milk containers. Some markets have already installed light shields to avoid the problem. Recently, yellow plastic containers have been appearing in some markets. Whole milk contains 65% saturated fatty acids.

Bovine Growth Hormone (BGH) is used to help cows increase milk production, it is not banned by the FDA and according to the latest studies and tests, traces have not been found in milk. However, our advise is to still not use any milk from cow's that has been given this hormone.

Light cream can be whipped by adding 1 tablespoon of unflavored gelatin that has been dissolved in 1 tablespoon of hot water. If you add this to 2 cups of light cream, it will whip up similar to heavy cream and will keep refrigerated for up to 4 hours.

Milk that has been pasteurized and homogenized may be frozen for up to 2 weeks, however, make sure you pour a small amount off to allow for expansion.

After you open a can of evaporated milk, place a small piece of wadded-up wax paper in the holes to keep it fresh longer and stop the crusting in the holes.

Sour cream contains approximately 18% fat, light sour cream has 10-12% fat. Low-fat or non-fat are your best choices.

Frozen yogurt should be purchased only if the label reads non-fat and sugar-free if you ar looking for a healthier substitute for ice cream.

Imitation milk contains no dairy products. It is made from water, sugar, and vegetable fat and is usually low in protein.

Evaporated milk is now available in whole, low-fat and nonfat and is only sold in cans. It is heat-sterilized and will store at room temperature for 5-6 months.

Partially frozen evaporated low-fat milk can be whipped and will make a low-fat whipped topping. If you need higher peaks, try adding a small amount of gelatin.

Sweetened condensed milk is not the same as evaporated milk. The sugar content is about 40%.

Filled milk is a combination of skim milk and vegetable oil to replace the milk-fat. It tends to replace some of the consistency of the milk, making it more appealing, taste-wise. However, the vegetable oil used is sometimes the high saturated fat oil, coconut oil.

The consumption of whole milk has dropped from 26 gallons per person in 1970 to only 9 gallons per person in 1995. Non-fat milk has risen from only 6 gallons per person in 1970 to the present level of 17 gallons per person.

Goat's milk is actually healthier than cow's milk for humans and especially infants. The protein and mineral ratio is closer to mother's milk and the milk contains a higher level of niacin and thiamin. The protein is even of a better quality and it less apt to cause an allergic reaction. It is also not mucous-forming.

Throw out any milk product that has mold on it.

ACIDOPHILUS (Lactobacillus Acidophilus)

Acidophilus is a soured milk product that contains a high degree of friendly bacteria. These bacteria enter the intestinal tract and multiply producing "friendly bacteria" that assist in the production of B vitamins. Acidophilus also may provide an antibiotic effect. Other products that can produce the similar bacteria building effect are yogurt, buttermilk, and kefir. To obtain the best result, acidophilus should be consumed one hour before breakfast.

If you have an allergy to milk or milk products, health food stores have a number of non-dairy products that can achieve the same results.

FOODS CONTAINING MILK

CHEESE

Cheeses come in a wide variety of colors and flavors, few of which are natural. Most cheeses are naturally white, not yellow, pink, green or burgundy.

The cheese industry has perfected methods of changing a good quality nutritious product into a chemical smorgasbord. The following is just a partial list of chemicals used by the cheese industry: Malic acid, tartaric acid, phosphoric acid, alginic acid, aluminum potassium phosphate, diacetyl sodium, carboxymethyl cellulose, benzyl peroxide and an unbelievable number of dyes and coloring agents.

These chemical are used to give cheeses their sharp taste, color them, make them smell more appealing or just to change their texture. All of the chemicals have been approved by the FDA and are supposed to be harmless, however, a number of the dyes and coloring agents especially are being studied and are related to cancer in laboratory animals.

Many of these same chemicals are also being used in other industries for making cement, bleaching clothes, producing cosmetics, printing, and even rust-proofing metals.

Be more aware of the type of cheese you buy and try to buy cheeses without the added chemicals, especially cheeses that are low-fat or even non-fat. If the label says **"all-natural"** you still need to see the wording **"no preservatives or coloring agents."** Consumers need to read the labels more than ever these days.

RIPENING CLASSIFICATIONS

Unripened — These are consumed shortly after manufacture. One of the most common is cottage cheese, a high moisture soft cheese, Unripened low-moisture cheeses are gjetost and mysost.

Soft — Curing will progress from the outside or rind of the cheeses, toward the center. Specific molds or cultures of bacteria which grow on the surface of the cheese assist in the specific characteristic flavors, body and texture. These cheeses contain a higher amount of moisture than the semi-soft ripened cheeses.

Semi-soft — These cheeses ripen from the inside as well as the surface. Curing will continue as long as the temperature is favorable. These are higher in moisture than firm-ripened cheeses.

Firm — Ripened utilizing a bacterial culture. Ripening occurs as long as the temperature is favorable. Lower moisture than the softer varieties and usually requires a long curing time.

Very hard — Cured with the aide of a bacterial culture and specialized enzymes. Slow-cured and very low moisture and contains a higher salt content.

Blue-vein — Curing is with the aide of mold bacteria and a specific mold culture that will grow throughout the inside of the cheese and produces the familiar appearance and unique flavor.

MOST POPULAR CHEESES

Blue (Bleu) — Noted for its white and blue-streaked appearance, blue cheese has a soft and often crumbly texture. Available in various shapes. 1 ounce = 40 calories.

Brick
A softer, yellow cheese available in a slightly soft-medium firm texture. Commonly available in sliced and brick forms.

Brie
Has an outer edible white coating and a mild-strong creamy outside. Originally, produced in France, Brie was only available in wedge and round forms.

Camembert
Reputed to be the favorite cheese of Napoleon. Camembert has a soft, yellow inside. Its outer coating is also edible and is usually a grayish-white color. This cheese takes 4-8 weeks to ripen.

Cheddar
The normal color is white to medium-yellow. Mild to very sharp taste. Firm smooth texture and comes in numerous shapes. Originated in England. One ounce = 105 calories. Artificial color is usually added to produce a very yellow or orange color.

Colby
A white to medium yellow-orange cheese with a mild to mellow flavor, and also has a soft texture similar to that of cheddar. It is available in cylindrical, pie-shaped wedges and originated in the United States.

Coldpack
Fresh and aged cheeses with whey cheese food solids added._Mild flavor and is very spreadable. Numerous flavorings and colorings are added.

Cottage cheese
Made from cow's skimmed milk, plain-cured or plain-cured with cream. Soft texture with a variety of sizes. Originated in the United States. If you see "curd by acidification" on the label, this will be a synthetic product. Look for a more natural one.

Cream cheese
Made with cream or concentrated milk. Very soft and spreadable. Never buy a cream cheese if it contains the suspect chemical, propylene glycol alginate. This cheese does not provide a good source of protein and is 90% fat.

Edam

A creamy-yellow or medium yellow-orange cheese with a surface coating of red wax. Has a mellow nut-like flavor. Semi-soft to firm texture with small irregular shaped round holes. Milk-fat content is lower than Gouda cheese. Usually available in a cannonball shape. Imported cheeses will usually be free of additives, domestic varieties are not. Originated in the Netherlands.

Feta

A curd cheese which is set in a very concentrated salt solution. Made from either goat's or sheep's milk. A sharp, salty cheese usually found chemical-free.

Farmers cheese

Similar to cottage cheese and pot cheese, but is pressed into a block form. Usually free of preservatives if purchased in bulk from a delicatessen.

Gjetost

A golden brown colored cheese with a sweet caramel flavor. Made from whey or goat's milk. Has a firm buttery consistency. Available in cubes or rectangular pieces. Originated in Norway.

Gorgonzola

Has a creamy white inside, mottled or streaked with blue-green ribbons of mold and a clay-colored surface. Has a tangy peppery flavor and a semi-soft crumbly texture, similar to blue cheese. Best when made with goat's milk.

Gouda

A creamy yellow or medium-yellow cheese that usually has a red wax coating and a nut-like flavor. Semi-soft to firm texture with a higher fat content than Edam cheese. Contains small irregular shaped or round holes. Sold in a bell shape with a flat bottom and top.

Gruyere

A variation of Swiss cheese, but usually without the use of bleached milk making it higher in vitamin content. If mold inhibitors are added, the information will appear on the label.

Limburger

Has a creamy white interior and a reddish-yellow surface, It is a highly pungent cheese with a very strong flavor. Ripens in 4-8 weeks and has a soft smooth texture. Originated in Belgium.

<u>Mozzarella</u>	A creamy white cheese made from whole or part-skim milk with a firm texture. Available in small rounds, shredded, or in slices. Preservatives may be added in "low-moisture" varieties. Originated in Italy.
<u>Muenster</u>	Has a creamy white inside and a yellow-tan surface. Mild to mellow flavor with a semi-soft texture. Contains more moisture than brick cheese. Available in wedges, blocks and
<u>Myost</u>	A light brown cheese with a sweet caramel flavor and a buttery consistency. Available in cubes, cylinders, and pie shaped wedges. Originated in Norway.
<u>Neutchatel</u>	A white cheese with a mild acidic flavor. Has a smooth texture similar to cream cheese but has a lower milkfat content. Originated in France.
<u>Parmesan</u>	A creamy white cheese with a hard granular texture and sharp piquant taste. It has less of a moisture content and a lower milkfat level than Romano. May be made from partially skimmed milk and may be bleached. Best to buy ungrated and grate yourself for a much better flavor. Originated in Italy.
<u>Pasteurized processed cheese</u>	A blend of fresh and aged cheese which has a consistent flavor after it has been processes. They melt easily and are used for cheeseburgers, etc.
<u>Pasteurized processed cheese food</u>	A blend of cheeses to which milk or whey have been added. Has a lower cheese and fat content, Soft texture and a milder flavor than regular processed cheeses due to a higher moisture content. One ounce = 90 calories.
<u>Port du Salut</u>	A creamy yellow cheese with a mellow to robust flavor. Has a buttery texture with small holes. Comes in wedges or wheels. Originated in France.
<u>Pot Cheese</u>	This is a similar cheese to cottage cheese but is drier and never creamed. It is usually made without salt and additives.

Provolone

Has a light creamy interior with a light golden brown or golden yellow surface. The flavor is mellow and has a smooth texture. May have coloring added and is usually salted or smoked. It may also be produced from bleached milk which will reduce the vitamin potencies. Originated in Italy.

Quark

This is a soft unripened cheese which has the texture of sour cream. The flavor is richer than yogurt.

Ricotta

A normally white cheese with a somewhat sweet, nutlike flavor. Usually made from cow's milk, whole or partially skimmed milk, with or without whey. Resembles cottage cheese.

Romano

A yellow-white cheese with a greenish-black surface and a sharp flavor, It has a hard granular texture and is available in wedges or grated. Similar to Parmesan, but made with whole milk, giving it a higher fat content. May contain a number of preservatives. The best is made from sheep's milk. Originated in Italy.

Roquefort

Has a creamy white interior and may be marbled or streaked with bluish veins of mold. Usually made of sheep's milk and has a peppery flavor with a semi-soft crumbly texture. It is available in wedges and is usually free of additives. Originated in France.

Stilton

Has a creamy white interior with streaks of blue-green mold. Made with cow's milk and milder than Gorgonzola or Roquefort. The texture is semi-soft and is more crumbly than blue cheese. Available in wedges and oblongs. Originated in England.

Swiss   A light yellow cheese that has a sweet nut-like flavor and a smooth texture with a variety of different size holes. It has a good firm texture and is available in rectangular forms and slices. Originated in Switzerland. May use bleached milk to give it the yellow color. This will reduce the vitamin content. One ounce = 105 calories.

The holes in Swiss cheese are caused by gas-forming bacteria. As the organisms grow they produce carbon dioxide gas bubbles during the early stage of ripening while the cheese is still soft. The cheese then "sets" around the gas bubbles.

Tilsit   Has an ivory to yellow interior and is semi-soft. Made from raw milk and ripened for about five months. Contains 30-50% fat. Originated in Germany.

CHEESE FACTS

Cottage cheese will last longer if you store it upside down. When you open cottage cheese spores enter from the air and live on the oxygen layer. When you turn it upside down and allow it to fall to the top, you eliminate a percentage of the oxygen layer, the spores can't grow as fast and the cottage cheese will last 7-10 days longer.

Cottage cheese only retains 25-50% of the calcium from the milk it is made from.

TYPES OF COTTAGE CHEESE

Creamed Contains 4.2% fat or 9.5 grams per cup. Not recommended for diets.

Low-Fat Made with either 1% or 2% milk. Recently .5% milk has become available. The 1% or .5% or non-fat is recommended. The 2% is not that low in fat.

Uncreamed Similar to low-fat and is often sold salt-free. may be used in recipes calling for cottage cheese, however, it may need to be seasoned more than standard cottage cheese.

Cottage cheese only retains 25-50% of the calcium from the milk it is produced from.

Sour cream should only be added to recipes just before serving if added hot. If it is necessary to reheat a dish containing sour cream, reheat it slowly or the sour cream will separate.

An ounce of cream cheese may contain as much as 110 calories. As advertised, it does have fewer calories than butter for a comparable weight, but we tend to use more and more frequently.

Try to choose from low-sodium, low-fat, or reduced-fat cheeses. New varieties are appearing weekly in the supermarkets and health food stores.

Moldy cheeses may contain a harmful toxin, especially Gorgonzola, blue cheese and Roquefort.

If a cheese is "natural" the name of the cheese will be preceded by the word "natural."

One cup of grated cheese is made from 1/4 pound of cheese.

When grating cheese, try spraying a liquid vegetable oil on the grater before grating and cleanup will be much easier.

Cheese making is fast becoming a popular pastime. For information call the hot line at 1 (800)542-7290.

When too much fat is removed from cheese, it may become rubbery. The fat content of cheese gives it the smooth texture we prefer. Exceptions are ricotta, Camembert and Brie which have a higher water content and lower fat content.

Cheese can also become rubbery when heated to too high a temperature. Best to cut the cheese into smaller pieces to avoid the problem.

Remember, different cheeses cook and melt at different temperatures. Best to check the cheeses you are using if they are different types before starting the recipe. Cook one or two small pieces for 1 minute. If the cheese is very soft and melts easily, adjust the cooking time for the different cheeses.

Most cheese substitutes are produced from soybean vegetable fats.

The higher the water content of cheeses such as cottage cheese the sooner they will go bad. Cottage cheese will only last for 3 weeks after it is produced. Cheddar cheese, however, is so low in moisture that it will last for years with the taste becoming stronger with aging.

Many low-fat cheeses substitute water for the fat reducing their shelf life.

It requires 8 pounds of milk to produce 1 pound of cheese. One average slice of cheese = 8oz. of milk.

The wax coating on cheeses will protect it. If there is an exposed edge try covering it with butter to keep the area moist and fresh.

To keep cheese longer without mold forming, place a piece of paper towel that has been dampened with white vinegar in the bottom of a plastic container that has a good seal before adding the cheese.

Mold may also be prevented from forming if the cheese is stored in a sealed container with two sugar cubes.

Soft cheeses can be grated using a metal colander and a potato masher.

Dishes containing cheese should be cooked slowly to avoid curdling and stringiness.

A dull knife works better to cut cheese, especially if you warm the blade first.

Yellow cheddar cheeses contain 71% fat, of which 39% is saturated.

Dried out cheese, without mold, should be saved and used for grating.

The United States is the leading producer of cheese in the world. Wisconsin is the leading state, producing over 2 billion pounds annually.

There are approximately 800 varieties of cheese in the world, The United States produces 200 of them.

ICE CREAM

The ingredients in most commercial ice cream contain chemical substitutes for just about everything good. Most ice creams that are available through supermarkets, ones that carry their own brand especially, are almost all produced using a standard "ice cream base" purchased from only a few manufacturers of the bases in each State. These bases are then flavored given a funny name and sold under the store brand.

When purchasing ice cream from an "ice cream shop", if you are curious regarding the ingredients, ask to see the list of ingredients on the original container. They must show you the list, you are entitled to see it by law. You may be surprised at the chemicals used, even in the best shops.

ICE CREAM INGREDIENT COMPARISON

HOMEMADE	MOST COMMERCIAL
Milk/low-fat	Dry milk solids
Eggs/egg substitute	Carrogeenan
Natural colors	Carboxymethyl cellulose
Natural fruit	Yellow dye #5
Weight 8 pounds	Ethyl acetate
per gallon	Weight 4-5 pounds
	per gallon/airated

ICE CREAM FACTS

Carrogeenan used to replace eggs has caused intestinal ulcers in test animals.

Yellow dye #5 has studies which show that it causes rashes and allergic reactions in susceptible people.

Ethyl acetate vapors have been known to cause damage to lungs, heart, and livers in laboratory animals. It is also used as a cleaner and solvent for leather and plastics.

Carboxymethyl cellulose is used in the printing industry as an ingredient in inks, in resin paints and produces tumors in laboratory animals.

Piperinol which is used as a vanilla substitute may also be used as a chemical to kill lice.

Ethyl vanillin, another flavoring agent should be avoided and has caused multiple organ damage in laboratory animals.

Butyraldehyde provides ice cream with a nutlike flavor and is also used as an ingredient in rubber cement.

Ice cream made from whole milk contains 10-15% fat.

Imitation ice milk contains only 4% fat.

Imitation ice creams must contain at least 6% fat and may be made using vegetable oils high in saturated fat (tropical oils).

Dietetic ice creams contain sugar substitutes, however, the fat content is the same as regular ice cream at 10-15%. Sherbet has very little fat but is high in sugar.

If the chemical "torutein" is listed on the ingredient list, don't buy the product. This chemical has been linked to cancer in humans and is banned in several states and Japan.

The first known recipe for ice cream was brought to Venice, Italy by Marco Polo after a journey to Japan. The Italians then introduced "cream-ice" to Europe and it was later renamed "ice cream" by our own Dolly Madison for a White House function.

Ice cream sales in the United States in 1995 were $2.5 billion dollars.

We average almost 15 quarts of ice cream per person in the United States per year.

If you place a small marshmallow on the bottom of an ice cream cone, the ice cream will not leak through.

If ice cream thaws, it should not be refrozen.

Ice cream can be frozen for 2-4 weeks.

A high quality ice cream has a butterfat content of 15%.

TAPIOCA

Tapioca is usually sold as a pudding mix and is actually a starch that has been extracted from the cassava root. It is found in three forms:

PEARL TAPIOCA
This is the type that the puddings are made from and usually has to be soaked for a number of hours before it is soft enough to be prepared.

QUICK-COOKING TAPIOCA
This is normally sold in granular form, needs no presoaking, and is popular for use as a thickening agent.

TAPIOCA FLOUR

Normally only found in health food stores and is also very popular as a thickening agent for soups and stews.

Tapioca should be mixed with water until it is a thin paste and then added to the food that needs to be thickened. Never add tapioca directly to the food, it tends to become lumpy.

Try not to overstir tapioca when it is cooking or it may become a thick paste and not be very palatable.

Chapter 11

Food Storage and Freezer Facts

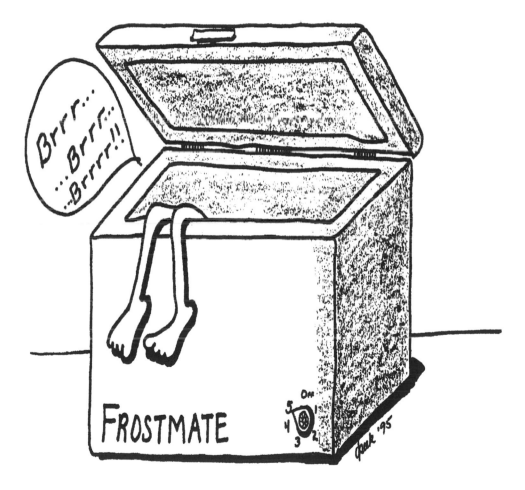

COLD AND FREEZING FACTS

There is always an uncertainty in the public's mind regarding whether or not to freeze or refreeze a food and if it is frozen, how long it will retain its nutrient value, as well as its flavor and consistency. Many foods do not do well when frozen, some get tough, some develop ice crystals shortly after being place in the freezer, while others get mushy when defrosted.

Refreezing foods will lower their quality. When foods are frozen, the cellular fluid expands into crystals and causes a break in the cell membrane, disrupting other structures, thus changing the texture of the food. This may alter the taste of the food but does not affect the food safety factor regarding spoilage. Meats are an exception as well as dairy products, since bacterial growth starts when they warm-up and refreezing may just place the bacteria in a state of suspended animation until the food is thawed out.

The longer a food is frozen the more the chances for nutrient loss. Seal all freezer stored foods as well as possible to avoid freezer burn and the formation of ice crystals. While ice crystals are not a serious problem they can affect the food as it is being thawed and make the food mushy.

A good trick when you go away on vacation is to place a baggie with a few ice cubes in the freezer. If a power failure occurs while you are gone and the foods thaw and refreeze, you will be aware of this fact and discard the food.

Always remove meat from store packaging materials and re-wrap using special freezer paper if you are planning to freeze the meats for more than 2 weeks. Chops, cutlets, and hamburger should be freezer-wrapped individually. This will assure maximum freshness and convenience.

Never freeze foods in aluminum foil. Almost invisible holes are created when the foil is crinkled.

Brown sugar won't harden if stored in the freezer. Freeze raw eggs whole or separated. However, foods with cooked egg whites do not freeze well and their consistency changes.

Fish can be frozen in clean milk cartons full of water. When thawing, use the water as a fertilizer for your house plants.

Frozen sandwiches will thaw by lunchtime. If the bread is buttered prior to freezing, the bread will not become soggy and absorb any filling.

"BRRRRRRRRRRRRRR"

If you are going to try and freeze any dish that has alcohol in it, remember alcohol will not freeze like water and may need to be frozen at a lower temperature.

If frozen produce are processed at the site they are picked at, they may have a higher nutritional value than some fresh produce.

If ice cream thaws it should not be re-frozen. Jelly, salad dressing, and mayonnaise do not freeze well on bread products. The freezer in your refrigerator is not the same as a supermarket food freezer. It is best used for storing foods for short periods only. Foods should be frozen as quickly as possible and temperatures should be 0^0 F. or below.

Potatoes become mushy when frozen in stews or casseroles. Their cells have a high water content and break easily when frozen. However, mashed potatoes freeze well. Any bakery item with a cream filling should not be frozen. They will become soggy. Custard and meringue pies do not freeze well. The custard tends to separate and the meringue becomes tough. Waffles and pancakes may be frozen, thawed and placed in the toaster.

FREEZER TEMPERATURE AND FOODS

FREEZER TEMPERATURE	QUALITY CHANGES AFTER
30^0 F.	5 DAYS
25^0 F.	10 DAYS
20^0 F.	3 WEEKS
15^0 F.	6 WEEKS
10^0 F.	4 MONTHS
5^0 F.	6 MONTHS
0^0 F.	1 YEAR

FREEZER STORAGE TIMES AT ZERO DEGREES FAHENHEIT

FOOD   MONTHS

MEATS

Beef, Lamb..............................6-12
Chops, Cutlets, Beef Hamburger......3-5
Ground Pork.........................1-3
Sausage.............................1-2
Bacon (unsliced)....................3-5
Bacon (sliced)...................... <1
Fish................................3-6
Ham.................................3-4
Liver...............................3-4
Poultry.............................4-6
Giblets............................. 3
Duck, Goose.........................5-6
Rabbit..............................9-12
Shrimp or Shellfish (cooked)........2-3
Turkey..............................6-8
Hot Dogs............................2-3
Luncheon Meats (ready-to-eat)....... 0

DAIRY PRODUCTS

Milk................................ <2 weeks
Ice Cream...........................2-4 weeks
Cream (40%).........................3-4
Eggs (not in shell).................7-10
Margarine...........................2-4
Butter..............................2-4
Cheddar Cheese......................5-6

FRUITS

Apples (sliced).....................10-12
Apricots............................10-12
Berries.............................11-12
Cherries (sour)..................... 12

FOOD PRESERVATION

The preservation of food is possible only if some method is used to destroy or control the growth of microorganisms that cause spoilage. There are a number of methods which include: drying, dehydrating, salting, smoking, radiation, heating, freezing, and the use of chemical agents (preservatives, etc.).

The microorganisms that cause food spoilage can be found everywhere. They are in the water, air, counter surfaces, brought home on foods, and even in the product. In many case the foods are contaminated as a natural occurrence, such as salmonella being present in the chickens ovary. Microorganisms can exist in two forms, either visible to the naked eye, such as in colonies or in small spores which are for the most part invisible to the naked eye and are carried by the air.

The destruction of these spores or retarding their growth is the important factor in food preservation. Turning cottage cheese upside down eliminates a percentage of the oxygen the spores need to grow and retards their growth. The early methods used salting and dehydrating. When foods are frozen it retards the spore growth.

There are three divisions of microorganisms, molds, yeast, and bacteria.

MOLDS, YEAST, AND BACTERIA

Molds, are usually airborne "spores" or "seeds" that may light on a food product and start to multiply. They tend to send out feelers or "filaments" and grow in colonies which may be seen in many colors depending on their food source. Mold spores will move from one food to another, especially fruits, so it would be wise to check your foods to be sure one is not moldy.

Yeasts are small one-celled fungus cells that produce enzymes which convert sugars to alcohol and carbon dioxide in a process called fermentation. It is also an excellent dietary source of folic acid.

Bacteria needs only a small amount of organic material and some moisture to grow and multiply. They grow by splitting their cells and may develop either acid or alkaline properties.

When there is no moisture or the available moisture is used up growth in all of these microorganisms ceases and they dry up and become dormant until moisture is again introduced.

FRESH FOOD, IS IT REALLY FRESH?

The freshness and quality of food depends on may factors such as:

>Transportation times
>Storage conditions and times
>Methods of packaging
>Type of fertilizers used
>Time of harvesting
>Number of supermarket washings
>Length of exposure to air and light

Canned Foods

The majority of canned foods are flavor poor with a "canned taste." Shelf life, however, is excellent and is usually between 2-4 years, depending on the food item.

Many of the vitamins and minerals tend to wash out over time from the liquid, usually resulting in a chemical breakdown of the nutrient. Enzymes are non-existent.

The cost of canned foods are generally twice the cost of dehydrated foods since the consumer pays for the water weight as well as the food. Up to 1/2 the weight of a canned product may be water.

Frozen Foods

The flavor varies from excellent to poor depending on the product. If the foods are frozen at the time they are picked, the nutritional quality may be equal to, or even better than fresh, at the time of purchase.

Shelf life and quality is very dependent on maintaining the proper freezer chest temperature levels. Foods are extremely vulnerable to spoilage. The cost of frozen foods is higher than dehydrated or canned, but nutritional quality will drop depending on the length of time the food is kept in the freezer.

Dried Foods

Flavor varies depending on the age. These foods should not be stored for a long period of time, since the moisture content is only 25-30% water.

Freeze Dried Foods

Excellent flavor, but they yield considerably less servings per can, due to retention of their cellular structure, and have less shrinkage than dehydrated foods. Their shelf life is generally considered to be 4-7 years, if properly packed. Once opened they will spoil within 5-7 days. The cost is considerably more than dehydrated foods and it has a moisture content of approximately 25-30%

Dehydrated Foods

Many are vine-ripened with excellent flavor. In some instances it was found that dehydration actually enhanced the flavor of foods.

The following is an example of dehydration reduction:

        12 pounds of fresh beans = 1 pound of dehydrated
        14 pounds of carrots   = 1 pound of dehydrated
         6 pounds of cheese   = 1 pound of dehydrated

Most dehydrated foods are nitrogen vacuum packaged and if unopened may last indefinitely. They would be capable of sustaining life even after many years of storage. However, the nutritive life-span is probably is only 5-7 years.

For best results, foods should be rotated and used allowing a shelf life of 2-3 years. Once the cans are opened they should be kept covered with a good sealing lid. The nitrogen in the can will leak out if the cans are tipped after opening and the product should be then used up soon after. They should be stored in a cool, dry location.

Dehydrated foods are processed under a very high vacuum and very low drying temperature, making it possible to remove all but 2-3% of the moisture in the food. These foods also retain their nutritional value since they are not cooked to death in a canning process.

Purchasing and using dehydrated foods may reduce your grocery bill by as much as 40%, if they incorporated into the diet properly and frequently. Generally, as a rule of thumb, dehydrated foods will reconstitute 2-3 times their weight. This will call for conservative measure when using these foods.

Chapter 12

Fat Facts

FATS (Lipids)

Fats are substances such as oils, waxes, lard, butter and other compounds that are insoluble (unable to mix with) in water. Some fats are readily visible, such as fat on meats, butter, cream cheese, bacon and salad dressings. Other fats are less visible, such as fat in egg yoke, nuts, avocado and milk.

Fats are a combination of "fatty acids" which are their "building blocks" or basic sub-units. The type of fat depends on the specific mixture of these fatty acids. The body uses fat as its energy storage reserves, padding to protect organs, as a constituent in hormones, an important building block of a healthy cell wall and insulation.

Fats fall into three main categories

1. Simple Fats
    These are basic fats called a triglyceride and are composed of a glycerol base with three fatty acids.

2. Compound Fats
    These are a combination of fats and other components. One of the more important being the lipoproteins, which are fats that combine with proteins. Lipoproteins are the main transport system for fats. They may contain cholesterol, triglycerides, neutral fats, and fatty acids. Since fat is insoluble (unable to mix with water) it needs a vehicle to carry it around the body.

3. Derived Fats
    Produced from fatty substances through digestive breakdown.

The fats you eat are composed of three chemical elements:

Carbon	C
Hydrogen	H
Oxygen	O

The carbon atoms are like a skeleton and can be compared to the framework on a house. In a saturated fat, all the carbons are completely surrounded by hydrogen and oxygen atoms. Since the carbons are totally saturated this type of fat is solid at room temperature.

In a polyunsaturated fat some of the carbons have a free space where an atom of hydrogen could be attached. It is because of these openings that a saturated fat is liquid at room temperature. A few exceptions to this rule do exist, such as coconut oil, which is highly saturated and yet it is liquid at room temperature.

There is also a middle of the road fat called a monounsaturated fat.

```
 H      O H H H H H H H H H H H H H H H
 H-C—O—C-C-C-C-C-C-C-C-C-C-C-C-C-C-C-C-H      SATURATED
 |      H H H H H H H H H H H H H H H H
 |      O H H H H H H H H H H H H H H H H H
 H-C—O—C-C-C-C-C-C-C-C-C=C-C-C-C-C-C-C-C-C-C-H  MONOUNSATURATED
 |      H H H H H H H        H H H H H H H H
 |      O H H H H H H H H H H H H H H H H H H
 H-C—O—C-C-C-C-C-C-C-C-C=C-C-C=C-C-C-C-C-C-H    POLYUNSATURATED
        H H H H H H H      H      H H H H
```

THE THREE MAJOR TYPES OF FATS

POLYUNSATURATED FATS (PUFA)

This type remains liquid at room temperature. Safflower, corn, and sunflower are examples of PUFA fats. Studies have shown that some PUFA fats have a tendency to lower cholesterol levels.

MONOUNSATURATED FATS (MUFA)

These are still liquid at room temperature but thicken when refrigerated. Examples are olive oil, avocados, Canola oil, and many nuts. Recent studies show that MUFA oils may have more effective cholesterol lowering quality than the PUFA oils.

SATURATED FATS (SFA)

These are either solid or semi-solid at room temperature. Examples are butter, lard, shortening, and hard margarine. Exception to the rule are coconut oil and palm oil which are now listed on products as "tropical oils." SFA's have the tendency to raise cholesterol levels and should be used in moderation.

HYDROGENATION

Many vegetable products will say that they are hydrogenated on the label. This simply means that the manufacture is adding hydrogen atoms from water to harden the fat in the product and make it more "saturated" thus adding a different texture to the food to make it more palatable and possibly last longer.

A liquid fat can be turned into a solid in this manner, however, you can turn a good fat into a bad saturated fat. Remember, the more hydrogenated a product the higher the saturated fat level it contains.

THE BAD PARTS OF A GOOD FAT

We have now covered a number of important points regarding fats and their relationship to the foods we eat, however, we now need to discuss the fact that those "good guys", the polyunsaturated fats and the monounsaturated fats may have a bad side to them.

It is important to remember that when any fat is heated a percentage of that fat converts to what is called a "trans-fatty acid." The more the fat is heated, and especially at a high temperature for a long period of time, the higher the percentage of trans-fatty acids.

An example of this is eating at a fast food restaurant and ordering a potato patty for breakfast. Since it is early morning and the frying vat has just been filled with a good vegetable oil, the majority of the fat will probably be related to a good polyunsaturated fat.

However, when you go back to that same restaurant for lunch, they have now fried in that oil for four hours and the majority of the oil has converted to a bad oil called a trans-fatty acid. Studies have implicated this oil in the acceleration of the aging process, raising the bad cholesterol and lowering the good cholesterol.

When you purchase the oil from the supermarket for the most part your buying good oil or the "cis" form. The "trans " form should be avoided as much as possible. Never place a raw potato in your frying oil to clean it and place it in the freezer. If you reuse the oil it will be almost 100% trans oil.

Cis-Form Fatty Acids - A horseshoe shaped molecule of polyunsaturated fat that occurs naturally in nature and is normally incorporated into a healthy cell wall. The health of the cell wall depends on a supply of "cis" form fatty acids. When these acids are not available the cell wall is constructed with abnormal openings (ports of entry) that may allow foreign substances to enter and cause a disease process to start.

Trans-Form Fatty Acid - Instead of the normal horseshoe form, the trans-fatty acid are found in a straight line shape. This form of the fat is difficult for the cell to utilize in the construction of a healthy wall. The blueprint calls for a horseshoe shape, not a straight line. Margarines may contain up to 54% trans-fatty acids and shortenings as much as 58%. heating and storage of these fats increase the percentages.

Fast food restaurants may deep-fat, par-fry, french fries before the arrive at the restaurant to save time. This may cause a higher level of trans-fatty acids in the fries. As much as 10 grams of fat may come from the par-frying.

High-fat diets may reduce the efficiency of the immune system.

Soy oil changes in flavor due to the changes in the linolenic acid it contains.

Canola oil has a high smoke point and is best for high temperature cooking. Heating fats too quickly accelerates the breakdown of fats. When an oil starts to smoke it is best to dispose of it since it will be high in "trans-fatty acids" which are not good for the body.

Olive oil is best for low temperature cooking and is high in monounsaturated fat. Oils that are high in monounsaturates such as Canola and olive oil should be stored in the refrigerator unless they will be used within 1 month. They tend to go bad more quickly.

If oil is refrigerated it may tend to become cloudy. Allow to stand at room temperature or place in a bowl of warm water for a few minutes and it will clear up.

Oils will become rancid over time. Before you use an oil that you have not used recently, open it and smell it.

If you really want to get all the shortening out of a can, try pouring 2 cups of boiling water into the container and swish it around until all the fat melts. Place the container into the refrigerator until it sets up and the fat is on the top. Then just skim off the fat.

Used oil should never be poured down the drain. It may solidify and clog the drain. Save the oil in a metal can and dispose of it in the garbage.

Always purchase oils in dark containers or tins to lessen the rancidity risk.

Crisco is improved and contains an equal amount of saturated to polyunsaturated fats, instead of being high in saturated fats.

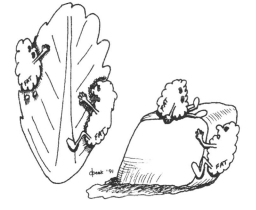

To eliminate fat from soups and stews, place ice cubes in a piece of cheesecloth and move it around in the food, Fat will adhere to the ice cubes. Lettuce leaves will also work as well as refrigerating the food for one hour.

If your recipe requires that you cream shortening with a sugary substance, try adding a few drops of water to the mixture. This will make it easier to stir. When creaming butter in the blender, cut the butter in small pieces.

The highest quality butter is U.S. Grade AA which is produced from fresh sweet cream. U.S. Grade A is almost as good but has a lower flavor rating. U.S. Grade B is usually produced from sour cream. The milk-fat content of butter must be at least 80%.

If you would like to have your butter ready and spreadable at all times, go to a kitchen store and purchase a "British butter dish." It is a butter dish made from terra cotta, the top of which needs to be soaked in cold water every day.

Cooking wine will stay fresher longer if you add a tablespoon of very fresh vegetable oil to the bottle.

"THE FAT SPONGE"
When broiling meats, place a few pieces of dried bread in the bottom of the broiler pan to absorb the fat drippings. This should eliminate the smoking fat and reduce the fire hazard.

Studies have shown that dieters miss fat more than sweets.

FAT CALORIES IN COMMON FOODS

The following is information regarding fat in relation to total calories in a person's diet:

FOODS	PERCENT OF FATS
Bacon, butter, margarine, lard, mayonnaise, solid shortenings, cooking oils, olives, baking chocolate, cream cheese.	90-100
Macadamias, salad dressings, pecans, walnuts, avocados, sausages, corned beef, coconut.	80-90
Hot dogs, peanuts, most chips, bleu cheese, cashews, lunch meats, peanut butter, prime rib, tuna in oil, Swiss cheese, sunflower seeds.	65-80
Hamburger, rib steak, chicken with skin, canned ham, salmon, trout, bass, veal cutlet, eggs, ice cream.	50-65
Most baked goods, lean hamburger, ground turkey, Canadian bacon, ham, steak, whole milk, round steak.	35-50
Low-fat yogurt, 2% milk, veal chop, loin and rump cuts of beef, sweet breads.	20-35
Crab, baked chicken without skin, most shellfish, tuna in water, low-fat cottage cheese, low-fat broiled fish.	10-20
Buttermilk, skim milk, beans, rice, cereals, potatoes. pasta, fruits, vegetables, egg whites,	Very small amount

SOURCE: Nutritive Values of Foods, USDA 1994.

PERCENT SATURATION OF COMMONLY USED FATS

	PUFA	MUFA	SFA
VEGETABLE OILS & SHORTENINGS			
Safflower Oil	75%	12%	9%
Sunflower Oil	66%	20%	10%
Corn Oil	59%	24%	13%
Soybean Oil	58%	23%	14%
Cottonseed Oil	52%	18%	26%
Canola Oil	33%	55%	7%
Olive Oil	8%	74%	13%
Peanut Oil	32%	46%	17%
Soft Tub Margarine	31%	47%	18%
Stick Margarine	18%	59%	19%
Vegetable Shortening	14%	51%	31%
Palm Oil	9%	37%	49%
Coconut Oil	2%	6%	86%
Palm Kernal Oil	2%	11%	81%
ANIMAL FATS			
Tuna Fat	37%	26%	27%
Chicken Fat	21%	45%	30%
Lard	11%	45%	40%
Mutton Fat	8%	41%	47%
Beef Fat	4%	42%	50%
Butter Fat	4%	29%	62%

PUFA - POLYUNSATURATED FATTY ACIDS
MUFA - MONOUNSATURATED FATTY ACIDS
SFA - SATURATED FATTY ACIDS

SOURCE: National Heart, Lung, and Blood Institute

HIGH FAT Vs LOW FAT LUNCHEON FOODS

HIGH FAT

FOOD	CALORIES	FAT(g.)
Cheddar Cheese (1oz.)	110	9
Swiss Cheese (1oz.)	110	8
American Cheese (1oz.)	110	9
Provolone (1oz.)	100	7
Bologna (4oz.)	360	32
Sausage (2oz.)	140	11
Hot Dog (1 med.)	160	12
Cream Cheese (1oz.)	100	10
Potato Chips (1oz.)	150	10
Cream of Mushroom Soup (1 cup)	100	7
Cola Drink (12oz.)	145	0
Double Burger w/Cheese	695	45
Vanilla Shake (12oz.)	290	11
Onion Rings (reg. order)	270	16
Butter/Margarine (1 Tbl.)	85	9
Mayonnaise (1 Tbl.)	100	11
Tartar Sauce (1 Tbl.)	70	8
Avocado (1/2 Haas)	150	14
Croissant Roll (1 small)	170	9

LOW FAT

FOOD	CALORIES	FAT(g.)
Danish Ham (4oz.)	100	4
Turkey (3oz.)	110	3
Turkey Pastrami (3oz.)	100	4
Mustard (1 Tbl.)	12	0
Mayo Lite (1 Tbl.)	45	5
Ketchup (1 Tbl.)	16	0
Pickle Relish (1 Tbl.)	30	0
Pretzels (1oz.)	110	1
Diet Soda (12oz.)	1	0
Vegetable Soup (1 cup)	60	2
Lettuce (1 cup)	12	.2
Tomato (1 small)	15	.1
Mozarella Cheese (1oz. skim)	80	5
Lite-Line American Cheese (1oz.)	50	2
Lit-Line Swiss Cheese (1oz.)	50	2
Hamburger (reg.)	275	12
Chicken Hot Dog (1 reg.)	125	8
Pita Bread (1 pocket)	75	.7

234

The best quality oil is "cold-pressed" extra virgin olive oil. It is made from the plumpest, "Grade A" olives, has the best flavor, and is processed by pressing the oil out from the olives with as little heat and friction as possible. The next best is virgin olive oil then pure olive oil which is a blend of both. Many companies are using "cold-processed" instead of "cold-pressed." Cold-processed may mean the olive oil is produced by using a chemical solvent to extract the oil. Chemical residues are not uncommon. Read the labels and watch for this intentional use of a similar phrase which does not denote a quality processing.

Olive oil is one of the healthiest oils to use in salads or for low temperature cooking. It has a low smoke point, however, which means that it will break down easily and start smoking. You can extend the usable life of olive oil and slow its breakdown by adding a small amount of Canola oil to the olive oil. Canola has a very high smoke point. This will also work well with butter.

To test whether a hot oil is still usable, drop a piece of white bread into the pan. If the bread develops dark specs, the oil is deteriorating. Never allow oil to heat to the smoke point, as it may ignite. It will also make the food taste bitter and may even irritate your eyes. The oils with the highest smoke points are Canola, safflower, and corn oil.

"REMEMBER WHEN"
Remember when grandmother fried foods, cleaned the oil out with a few slices of raw potato and stored the oil in the freezer for future use. When oil is reused the level of trans-fatty acid rises until it is 100%, which doesn't take too long. Oil should never be reused.

When you deep-fat fry, try adding 1/2 teaspoon of baking powder per 1/2 cup of flour in your batter to produce a lighter coating and fewer calories.

"FATS IN THE FIRE"
If the frying fat is not hot enough food will absorb more fat. However, if you get it too hot it will smoke and burn and produce trans-fatty acids. Use a thermometer, the temperature should be 360^0 to 375^0 F..

"PIG ABS"
Lard is derived from the abdomen of pigs and is used in chewing gum bases, shaving creams, soaps, and cosmetics. Future studies may implicate lard in shortened life-spans as well as a factor in osteoporosis. Leaf lard is derived from the kidney area of the pig and is a higher quality than all other types of lard (best for pie crust).

"FATTY PATE"
Pates are bordered with pork fat from the flank of the pig.

Dietary fats are being implicated as a key factor in over 300,000 cases of skin cancer reported annually.

"PUTTING ON THE RITZ"
Some of the highest fat content crackers are Ritz, Town House, and Goldfish which contain about 6 grams of fat per ounce.

Lard can be stored at room temperature for 6-8 months. If you substitute lard for butter or shortening, reduce the amount you use by 25%.

"CAN'T WIN"
Mayonnaise must contain at least 65% oil by weight, any less and it must be called salad dressing. Most fat-free mayonnaise contains more sodium than the "real" mayonnaise. A tablespoon of mayonnaise contains only 5-10mg. of cholesterol since very little egg yolk is really used.

When you are greasing a pan, make sure you don't use too much grease or you may cause the food to overbrown.

"PIGS IN A BLANKET"
Pancakes wrapped around sausages deliver 60% of its calories as fat, mostly saturated.

Every ounce of fat contains 250% more calories than an ounce of carbohydrate or protein.

Any product or margarine listing tropical oil, hydrogenated fat, coconut, or palm oil on the list of ingredients will be higher in saturated fat than a comparable product.

Buttermilk can be substituted for 2% or whole milk in most recipes. Buttermilk is less than 1% fat, almost equal to skim milk, however, it has a thicker consistency.

"AND AWAY IT GOES"
A high fat intake has been related to calcium losses through the urine.

"BEAT ME, BEAT ME"
Butter will go farther and have fewer calories per serving if you beat it well, thereby increasing the volume with air.

"YOLKS AWAY"
When preparing any recipe or omelet, try replacing the egg yolks with an equal amount of egg substitute or just reduce the number of yolks.

"LONGEVITY"
The most popular oil is olive oil with soy oil coming in second. Olive oil will stay fresh longer than most oils while soy oil tends to lose its flavor, the longer it is stored due to the nature of the linolenic acid it contains.

"YUMMY, YUMMY"
8 ounces of potato chips are the equivalent to eating 16-20 teaspoons of fat.

"NEEDS SHADES"
Only purchase oils in containers if you cannot see the oil. Oil is very sensitive to light and will become rancid. All oils with the exception of cold-pressed olive oil starts oxidizing as soon as it is heat processed and breaks down very quickly.

"WHY CAROB?"
When carob is made into candy products, fat is usually added to improve the texture. This usually brings the fat content close to real chocolate. In fact, cocoa butter used in real chocolate is 60% saturated fat while the fat used in a carob candy is 85% saturated fat.

Most margarines contain over 90% fat. Diet margarines usually contain 80% fat, 16% water, 2% salt, and 2% non-fat milk solids. Margarines are naturally white, colorings and additives are added to all margarines. A liquid duet margarine, however, may contain as low as 40% fat.

"THE DEBATE"
The margarine, butter controversy is still going on with neither side really winning. Margarines have the bad fat, trans-fatty acids due the method of heat processing they must go through and butter contains cholesterol, since it is an animal product. My preferred choice would be whipped, unsalted butter in moderation.

The harder the margarine, the higher the percentage of saturated fat it contains. Even though it does not contain any cholesterol, saturated fats may assist in the production of cholesterol.

Refined corn oil is a chemical extraction, a triglyceride, with no relationship to the nutrients in a "real" ear of corn. The vitamins that would normally assist with the digestion of corn oil are absent, even the vitamin E is lost.

A burrito topped with sour cream and guacamole may contain up to 1,000 calories and 59% fat.

Diets high in total fat and especially trans-fatty acids (from heated fats) have been related to cancer of the colon, the prostate and breast. Studies are also showing that the efficiency of the immune system may be depressed by high fat diets. Recommended dietary fat levels are 20-25% of your total daily calories, however, a person can actually survive on only 5% dietary fat if the fat is of the essential fatty acid type.

Recent studies have shown that stearic acid, one of the saturated fats has little effect on raising cholesterol levels. As our laboratory tests become more sophisticated more information about which fats will actually raise your cholesterol will be forthcoming. We can then avoid only those foods that may be harmful.

SALAD AND COOKING OIL USE

```
1909 - 1.5 pounds per person
1972 - 18   pounds per person
1990 - 29   pounds per person
1995 - 33   pounds per person
```

MARGARINE USE

```
1950 -  6   pounds per person
1972 - 11   pounds per person
1990 - 16   pounds per person
1995 - 18   pounds per person
```

Approximately 10 grams of fat is cleared from the stomach per hour. Two scrambled eggs, bread and butter, coffee and milk = 50 grams of fat. Assimilation time is 5-6 hours. An example of high fat foods are bacon and cheddar cheese. The percent of fat to calories in each is 75% fat. Americans spend $3 billion per year on bacon.

Most non-dairy creamers are made from coconut oil, which is high in saturated fat. Mocha Mix is your best bet.

Studies now show that dieters miss fats more than sweets.

There are 312 fats that are available for use in frying.

"EDUCATION A MUST"
Americans consumed 53 pounds of hard fats and oils per person in 1972. In 1995 the consumption has risen to 65 pounds, not a good direction. Poor nutrition education and the increased eating out at fast food restaurants is to blame.

Rapeseed (Canola oil) for years has been grown as a forage crop for animals in the United States and Canada. Originally, it was banned in the U.S. when imports from Canada showed high levels of "erucic acid." However, new varieties have shown to contain lower levels and is now being produced and sold in large quantities. It is high in monounsaturated fat and has a high smoke point, making it the preferred oil for frying.

Current studies show that if your body is higher in "brown fat" rather than "white fat" your fat is of the more active type, which may relate to some people being able to control their weight easier than others. Studies are being conducted at Harvard University regarding these fats and their effect on human metabolism.

Most fat should be consumed either at breakfast or lunch, few, if any for dinner. High fat meals late in the day may cause the digestive system to overwork while you ar sleeping, causing restless sleep patterns.

Butter left open in the refrigerator will absorb refrigerator odors. Butter only stores well under refrigeration for two weeks. If a longer time is needed it should be frozen. One pound of butter = 2 cups.

Reduced fat Oreo cookies contains 47 calories and 1.67 grams of fat. The original Oreo has 53 calories and 2.33 grams of fat. Not a big savings. It is still necessary to read past the reduced-fat, low-fat, and lite to see if there is really a good savings. Many of these products cost more because they are lower in fat content.

The new reduced-fat peanut butter has the same number of calories per serving as the regular peanut butter, about 190 per serving, sweeteners were added in place of the fat.

To make a creamy salad dressing, try pouring cold-pressed olive oil very slowly into a running blender containing the other ingredients and spices.

Purchase empty plastic ketchup bottles to use for your oils. The narrow spout makes it easy to pour oils when cooking. Label them with a permanent felt-tip marker.

"IT'S MAGIC"
If you wish to keep your oil and vinegar salad dressing in suspension and not have them separate, try placing the contents of 2 lecithin ampoules in the dressing and shake.

When oils are refrigerated and become cloudy, it is due to the buildup of harmless crystals. Manufacturers will sometimes pre-chill the oils and remove the crystals in a process known as "winterization." These oils will remain clear when refrigerated. Lard has larger fat crystals than butter which has a lot to do with the texture of these fats and is controlled during processing. The large fat crystals in lard will make it the choice for a number of baked goods where a flakier crust is preferred, especially pies. Moderation in eating these lard products, however, is the key word.

The average American diet is about 44% fat. Dietary guidelines suggest no more than 30% of total calories. My recommendation is no more than 20% or less with the type of fats leaning toward the PUFA and MUFA types.

Medium-chain triglycerdides (MCT) are sold in health food stores for people who have trouble absorbing fats. They are for the most part produced from coconut oil, have a very low smoke pointy and can't be cooked with without producing trans-fatty acids very quickly. Body builders tend to use this fat to increase caloric intake, but there are no good studies to date to justify it.

There are 312 fats and oils that can be used for frying.

One 8 ounce bag of potato chips contains 6 tablespoons of oil amounting to 80 grams of fat.

FAT SUBSTITUTES

The new "fat substitutes" are now appearing in our foods. These are synthetically produced and not natural products. They should be viewed with caution and used in moderation only.

OLESTRA

Olestra is a large synthetic fat molecule, so large that it passes through the intestinal tract undigested. This increase of undigested material may cause diarrhea. Olestra as it goes through the system, however, tends to attract the fat-soluble vitamins A, D, E, and K and binds with them. Proctor and Gamble the inventor of the product is familiar with the problem and may have to fortify the products with vitamins, however, this may not solve the problem.

A more significant problem may be that the carotenoid family are also fat soluble and the over 500 carotenoids may also be in trouble. A percentage of carotenoids may be washed out of the body. These include beta-carotene, alpha-carotene, lutein, lycopene, and the rest of the family. Since these are not considered to be essential nutrients P & G does not feel that they have to add them through fortification. The carotenoids are a nutrient that is under investigation as a possible cancer preventive nutrient.

The official name that will appear on products with olestra is Olean. Olean has only been approved for snack foods. It is being added to snack chips, crackers, tortilla chips, cheese puffs, and potato chips initially. The FDA is requiring that a warning label be added which reads:

> *This product contains Olestra. Olestra may cause abdominal cramping and loose stools. Olestra inhibits the absorption of some vitamins and other nutrients. Vitamins A, D, E, and K have been added.*

The "fake-fat chip" will only have a caloric reduction of 50% fat. The downside to all of this is that people may consume more junk foods and still end up with the same number of total calories. P & G will probably be licensing Olean to other companies.

HYDROLYZED OAT FLOUR

This fat substitute may even be good for you. It is oat flour that has been treated with water to break down the starches into individual sugars. This causes a change in the texture and provides that fat texture that people like in their foods. The flour is high in beta-glucan which may have a cholesterol sopping up ability. The product was developed by the USDA. It contains only 1 calorie per gram instead of the 9 calories per gram in fat.

Studies have shown a definite cholesterol lowering in the 24 volunteers that took part in the study. Over 40 new products are being developed and it will be necessary to read the label to find it. It may also be called "hydrated oat flour" or "Oatrim." Currently, it may be found in cookies, cheeses, low-fat hot dogs, and low-fat lunch meats. It is a safer alternative than Olean products.

"WHERE'S THE FAT?".....''HERE'S THE FAT"

Most of us never realize how much fat we really do eat. The following information will help you become more aware of the higher fat foods. We rarely think of fat in "teaspoons," but you may find it easier to comprehend when presented in this form.

MEATS/FISH

Hot Dog/All Beef	1 medium	2 ½ teaspoons
Bologna	1 slice	2 teaspoons
Big Mac	1	7-9 teaspoons
Turkey Pot Pie	12 oz	6 teaspoons
Sirloin TV Dinner	1 medium	7 teaspoons
Ham TV Dinner	1 medium	3 teaspoons
Chicken TV Dinner	1 medium	7 teaspoons
Lean Beef	3 oz	2 teaspoons
Medium-Fat Beef	3 oz	4 ½ teaspoons
Chicken Breast/No Skin	4 oz	1 teaspoon
Chicken Breast/Skin	4 oz	2 ½ teaspoons
Fried Oysters	1 serving	3 ½ teaspoons
Trout/Raw	3 ½ oz	3 teaspoons
Bacon	1 strip	1 1/4 teaspoons
Canadian Bacon	1 strip	1 teaspoon
Hamburger	1/4 pound	3 ½ teaspoons
Frog Legs	2 large	2 ½ teaspoons
Ham/Lean	2 slices	1 1/4 teaspoons
Pork Chop	3 ½ oz	6 ½ teaspoons
Veal Cutlet	3 ½ oz	4 teaspoons
Duck/Roasted	3 ½ oz	7 teaspoons
Goose	3 ½ oz	5 ½ teaspoons
Rabbit	3 ½ oz	1 ½ teaspoons
Squab	3 ½ oz	5 ½ teaspoons
Turkey	3 ½ oz	2 teaspoons
Lobster Newburg	3 ½ oz	2 ½ teaspoons
Salmon/Canned	3 ½ oz	3 ½ teaspoons

Chapter 13

Meats Fowl and Fish

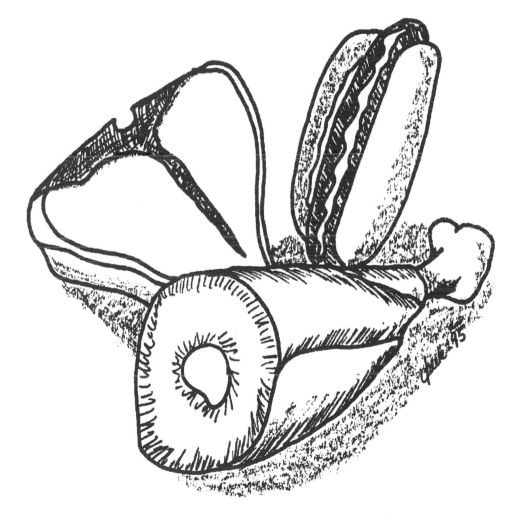

GENERAL INFORMATION

Americans have always been a society that consumed large amounts of meats and poultry as far back as colonial days. The cattle industry during the 1800's thrived and methods were improved as to transportation and preservation of meats so that the entire country could have their beef. Meat and poultry were the most important main dish and this has stayed with us until recent years when we discovered that excessive meat intake may increase the blood fat levels of fat and cholesterol to such a degree as to cause serious health problems.

Recently, other factors have brought meat and poultry into the media in a negative light. The fact that the inspection procedures may be lacking the tools and manpower to do an efficient job, mad cow disease, E. coli contaminated meats, salmonella in chickens and even sealed eggs, and hormone residues in meats.

Education is the key factor if you are to continue to consume meat and poultry. The public must learn what types of meats are the healthiest and the safest, how to prepare the meats, what signs to be aware of, and even how to clean up after you work with meat and poultry.

Americans consume 34% of all meat products in the world even though we are only 7% of the world population. We presently eat 180 pounds of meat and poultry per person, per year. Red meat consumption, however, has declined since the 1970's and poultry has increased significantly to a 50/50 level in the mid-1990's. 1995 statistics show that 91% of all Americans eat beef on a regular basis. The beef industry spends $42 million each year on advertising to maintain this level.

Numerous medical studies have surfaced in recent years that leave no doubt that a high red meat diet, high in saturated fat is one of the significant factors that may be the cause of a number of cancers, especially colon cancer. Meat does provide a number of significant nutrients and in moderation should still be considered a healthy food.

Meats should be treated more of a side dish and not the main course. Meat and poultry are composed mainly of muscle, which is approximately 73% water, 21% protein and 6% fat in beef and 3% fat in poultry.

The following facts are meant to be usable in the choosing and preparation of meat and poultry as well as providing some general information that might be of interest.

MEATS

GOVERNMENT MEAT GRADING

    USDA PRIME - Most tender cut, highest fat content.
    USDA CHOICE - Very tender cut, most common grade sold.
    USDA GOOD   - Less fat, needs tenderizing.
    USDA COMMERCIAL - From older animals, usually tougher.
    USDA UTILITY, CUTTER AND CANNER - Lowest grades usually
                         used in processed meat products.

-------   ----------------------------

The Skinniest Six Cuts Of Meat

Eye Of The Round	Top Round	Round Tip
143 Calories	153 Calories	157 Calories
4.2gr. of Fat	4.2gr. of Fat	5.9gr. of Fat
1.5gr. Sat. Fat	1.4gr. Sat Fat	2.1gr.Sat. Fat
59mg. Chol.	72mg. Chol	69mg. Chol

Top Sirloin	Top Loin	Tenderloin
165 Calories	176 Calories	179 Calories
6.1gr. of Fat	8.0gr. of Fat	8.5gr. of Fat
2.4gr. Sat. Fat	3.1gr. Sat. Fat	3.2gr. Sat. Fat
76mg. Chol.	65mg. Chol.	72mg. Chol

"BUYER BEWARE"
Special wording is used by supermarkets to make you believe
that the grade you are purchasing is of a higher quality
than it really is. Many markets purchase "good" grade beef
and call it "Premium Beef", "Quality Cut", "Select" "Market
Choice", "Prime Cut", etc. They do this because they do not
sell USDA Choice or Prime beef, if they did they would brag
about it.

SECRETS OF THE INNER COW

There are eight main cuts of beef; shank, flank, brisket,
chuck, round, rib, plate and loin. These eight cuts are then
given secondary names which will be closer to the names you
are more familiar with such as; sirloin, porterhouse, top
round, etc. These explain the way the eight main cuts are
actually cut up. The tenderness of beef will depend on the
method of cutting.

The toughest cuts of beef are pot roasts, which are cut from
the neck of the cow, these are also the least expensive.

CHUCK CUTS
These usually need to be cooked for long periods of time and
in a liquid for tenderizing.

RIB CUTS
These include rib steaks, rib roasts or back ribs and should
be cooked slowly in an oven or grilled for about 20-30
minutes per pound. Best to use a marinade or sauce.

LOIN CUTS
These come from behind the ribs and are the most tender
cuts. Examples of these are; tenderloin roasts and the
better quality steaks such as, porterhouse and New York.

ROUND CUTS
These are top round, eye of the round, and bottom round.
They should be braised and roasted similar to pot roasts.

FLANK AND PLATE CUTS
These include flank steaks and skirt steaks. They are long,
thin cuts and are recommended for stir-frying.

BRISKET CUTS
Cut from behind the cow's front leg or from the leg itself.
This cut is usually tough and needs extensive cooking in a
liquid for a considerable period of time. For best results
when cooking a roast, rotate it 1/4 turn every 20-25
minutes.

In the last few years the bacteria E. coli has been associated with the risks of eating beef. However, more of an explanation is needed regarding the actual risk and how it can be eliminated if it is present at all. The bacteria E. coli is an intestinal bacteria that may not be washed off after processing. It is capable of causing severe illness or even death.

The bacteria, if present, would normally be found on the surface of the meat and searing or cooking a piece of meat on both sides would easily kill the bacteria. When you cook a steak or roast all sides are normally cooked and the risk is eliminated. This means that if you wish to eat a medium or medium-rare steak it should not place you at risk if the meat is cooked on both sides, even for a short period of time.

The problem occurs mainly with hamburger or raw meat dishes, such as steak tartar. Since hamburgers are ground beef, if the bacteria is present on the surface, it will move to the inside during grinding and if the hamburger is not cooked through, the bacteria may still be present when ingested.

Never eat raw meat of any type, since cooking destroys many toxins that may be present.

The approximate percentage of calories from the fat in beef:

        USDA PRIME.........................50%
        USDA CHOICE........................39%
        USDA GOOD..........................30%

Small cuts of meat will spoil more rapidly and should not be kept in the refrigerator without freezing for more than 2-3 days. Liver, sweetbreads, cubed meats and marinated meats should be used within 1 day or frozen.

Meats that have been cooked (the more well done the better) will be more easily broken down and digested. If meats are cooked to medium-well (170^0 F.) it will increase the availability of vitamin B_1 by 15% over well done beef (185^0 F.).

Never pierce meats with a fork while it is cooking, it allows the juices to run out and the meat may dry out.

Adding beer to meats will give them an excellent flavor.

Beware of the wording on meat packages. If the steak packaging reads "lean" the steak cannot have more than 10% fat. "extra lean" cannot have more than 5% fat. The only time I have seen this low a fat content in a steak was a Buffalo steak. Ground beef when labeled "lean" is allowed to have as much as 22% fat.

In a roast, the juices tend to shift to the center when it is cooking. If you allow the roast to rest for about 10-15 minutes after it is finished cooking, the juices will redistribute and the roast will be juicier throughout.

Ribs should always be marinated in the refrigerator before cooking. A ready-made barbecue sauce is fine and the ribs may be placed in the broiler for a few minutes if desired.

Amino acids, the building blocks of protein are best absorbed and utilized if they come from beef. They have an absorption rate of approximately 90% compared to grains at 80% and legumes at about 60-85%.

Another common problem is not cooking a piece of meat through at the original time of cooking. Partially cooked meats of any type allow the uncooked areas to grow bacteria.

Roasts will take about 12-14 minutes per pound for rare and 13-15 minutes for medium at 325^0 F.

The USDA normally monitors only 1-2% of all beef carcasses for illegal drug residues, or in about 1.5 pounds out of the 89 pounds each person consumes each year. There are over 1.6 million beef producers. They are for the most part on the **"honor system"** regarding hormonizing cattle. By the time a problem is found it is too late to recall the beef since it has been sold. The biggest problem is in the retired (older) cattle that are being used for hamburger meat, soups, stews, pot pies and TV dinners.

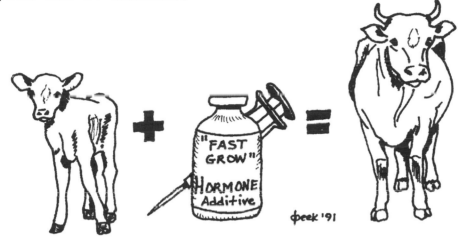

All meat should be thawed as quickly as possible, preferably under refrigeration, then cook immediately. Fresh beef is cherry-red in color. The darker the beef, the older the animal. Fat should be white not yellow.

There are 1.3 billion cattle worldwide, which consume a third of the world's grain.

Sweetbreads are a calf's thymus gland which helps the animal fight disease. It disappears six months after they are born, Three ounces of sweetbread contains 21 grams of fat.

"CHOLESTEROL HAS A FIELD DAY"
Father's day is the biggest beef eating day of the year, with over 80 million pounds consumed.

When tenderizing your meat, try spreading a small amount of flour on the surface to help retain the juices. If you want cooked meat to remain tender, store it in its own cooking juices.

"LOVE MEAT TENDER...."
Placing meats in white vinegar for 5 minutes will make them more tender. When reheating meats, try placing the slices in a casserole dish with lettuce leaves between the slices. They will come out tender and moist.

MARINADES

Most marinades contain an acid which will break down the meat protein, thereby tenderizing it. Marinades may be a product that contains papain, bromelin, tomato juice, lemon juice, white vinegar, etc.

Foods should always be marinated in a glass container for the best results. The acidic nature of the marinades may react with metals and give the food a poor flavor.

Never baste the food with marinade that the food was in. Bacteria from the food may contaminate the cooking food and the food may not cook long enough to kill the new bacteria.

Always cover the food that is marinating, and keep it refrigerated. Also, make sure the food that is in the marinade is fully covered with the marinade.

"COTTERED CATTLE"
The Japanese are producing the world's most expensive beef. Kobe beef cattle are fed a diet of soybeans and beer and given a daily massage. Kobe beef has 2-3 times the fat of USDA Prime beef.

"PREMATURE AGING"
If you are troubled by meats turning gray when they are cooked, try cooking a smaller quantity the next time in the same pot. Excess steam generated by overcrowding is the problem.

RATING OF NON-VEGETABLE PROTEINS

1.	FISH	6.	VENISON
2.	TURKEY	7.	LAMB
3.	CHICKEN	8.	PORK
4.	VEAL	9.	GOAT
5.	BUFFALO	10.	BEEF

A beef brisket is done when the fat starts to roll off, but will be overcooked if you can pull the fat off with your fingers.

"IN THE DOG HOUSE"
Hot dogs contain less protein in 3 1/2 ounces than any other meat source. They may also contain up to 56% water and 3% powdered bone if listed on the list of ingredients. Sugar in the form of corn syrup may be found in a number of hot dogs.

Beef should not be seasoned with any type of salt until it is 3/4 cooked. This will aid in retaining the flavor and make it juicier. Salt tends to draw the liquid from the beef.

Beef and veal kidneys have more than one lobe while lamb and pigs have only one lobe. They should be firm, not mushy, and should have a pale color. Before you cook them, be sure to remove the excess skin and fat.

Ready-to-eat meat products will usually contain a higher amount of fat than fresh meat. The manufacturer can get away with leaving more fat in the product which is not as noticeable.

"SAVE WEAR AND TEAR ON YOUR GOLF SHOES"
Flat beer and hard cider are excellent tenderizers for beef. The fermentation process has a breakdown effect on the meat.

The most tender chuck steak is the first cut, which may also be called the blade cut. If you can see a small piece of white cartilage near the top of the steak, you have found the first cut.

"SEEING IS BELIEVING"
The eye of the round steak is normally cut into two pieces. Best to buy the roast that has the same diameter ends, This will be the first cut and the most tender. Round steak should be purchased in uneven cuts or "oyster-cut" shapes. These will be the first cuts and be closed to the more tender sirloin.

Tomatoes or tomato sauce will act as a natural tenderizer for all types of beef. If you cut meats across the grain whenever possible, it will be more tender and have a better appearance.

"THE BOTTOM LINE"
When you figure the cost per meal of a meat portion, consider the weight of the fat and bone. It may account for up to 30% of the cost.

Never re-freeze meats, including all lunch meats and even hot dogs. The salt content may cause rancidity to develop in the fat.

"STALKING THE PREY"
To keep lamb chops, pork chops or even poultry from sticking to the bottom of the pan, try placing a few stalks of celery under the food to prevent it from sticking to the pan. This also works well with meatloaf.

It requires 16 pounds of grain to produce 1 pound of beef. Not a very efficient use of the grain.

"BIG DOGGIE"
In an average week Americans consume 350 million hot dogs. This amounts to a hot dog 60 feet thick and the length of a soccer field.

Leftover cooked meat can be kept refrigerated for 4-5 days.

"TENDER BUNS"
When boiling hot dogs, try using the top of the double boiler to warm your buns.

"OVEREXPOSURE"
Ground meats, such as hamburger and hot dogs are prone to "self-oxidation." This is a deterioration caused by exposure to oxygen, not only will the meats go bad very quickly, they tend to lose their nutrients due to exposure of the addition surface from the grinding and processing.

"BAA-WARE"
When purchasing a lamb shank, be sure that it weighs at least 4 pounds, any smaller and it will contain a higher percentage of bone and less meat.

15 billion pounds of beef were sold through retail outlets in 1994 compared to 19 billion pounds in 1976. During the same period, chicken sales increased from 43 pounds per person to 63 pounds per person.

"HOW DRY I AM"
If the hamburger is too dry due to reduced fat content, try adding one stiffly beaten egg white for each pound of hamburger. You can also add one large grated onion for each 1 1/2 pounds, or you could make the patties with a tablespoon of cottage cheese in the center. Instant potato flakes will also provide a great moist hamburger.

Hamburger is the most commonly purchased meat in the United States, however, It contains more saturated fat per ounce than any other salable meat.

"EASY MATH"
When buying meat, calculate the cost per pound realizing that a boneless cut usually cost less per serving even if the cost per pound is higher.

To make a fatty roast look better, try refrigerating the roast after it is cooked or at least until the fat solidifies, remove it from the oven, remove the fat, baste and cook until heated.

Hamburger will cook faster if you make a few punctures with a fork before cooking, thus allowing the heat to circulate more evenly.

Meats will be easier to slice if they are partially frozen. Especially if you need thin slices for sandwiches.

"L'IL DOGGIE"
Veal has less fat than any other meat and usually comes from young milk-fed calves. It is more costly, but has less hormones and is very tender. It also contains 1/10 the fat of lean beef, however, the cholesterol content is the same.

Game meats dry out quickly and should not be overcooked. Use ginger ale to cook in if you want to eliminate the gamy flavor.

Game meats are lower in fat than most of the beef we normally purchase, however, it is more difficult to find in the stores. Many game meats also contain appreciable amounts of an Omega-3 fatty acid. The following are two mail order sources for game meat:

> **Broken Arrow Ranch** **Swift International**
> P.O. Box 530   4110 Mississippi St.
> Ingram, TX 78025   San Diego, CA 92104
> 1 (800) 962-4263

Buffalo (bison) meat is also gaining in popularity throughout the United States. A meat that is low in fat, cholesterol and even calories compared to beef. Today's herds total about 135,000 head and growing steadily. The National Bison Association has 2,300 members.

A study performed by Dr. Martin Marchello, of North Dakota State University, Department of Animal and Range Sciences found that in 26 species of domestic game meat, bison meat was lower in fat than beef, pork or lamb. 3.5 ounces of bison contained only 138 calories, was low in sodium and high in iron. Bison does not have the gamy flavor of many of the game meat animals.

A BURGER BY ANY OTHER NAME

ARGENTINA
Burgers are broiled and served with a fried egg on top of a piece of pumpernickel bread.

GERMANY
The ground beef is mixed with pieces of wet bread, onions, mustard, and an egg is added.

SWITZERLAND
Burgers are served American style, but are always eaten with a knife and fork. Very civilized!

KOREA
Add a unique touch of their own, kimchee, a mixture of pickled beets and beef mixed in a brown sauce with fried onions and of all things ligonberry preserves. Try it, you might like it!

HOW TO COOK A SAFE BURGER

While undercooked burgers may pose a risk of E.coli, a well done burger may pose a risk of a potentially harmful carcinogen called a heterocyclic aromatic amine (HAA). This compound is formed when meat is cooked to high temperatures. If you microwave the meat for a few minutes before cooking, this will make the meat safer and remove a large percentage of the HAA's.

1.   Choose a lean cut of beef. Have the butcher remove all the visible fat from around the edges, and grind it through the meat grinder twice. That will break up the remaining fat.

2.   Place the hamburger in a microwave oven just before you are preparing to use it for 1-3 minutes on high power. Pour off the excess liquid which will contain additional fat and the creatine and creatinine that form the HAA's.

3.   Reduce the meat content of the burgers by adding mashed black beans or cooked rice and you will have a safer and great tasting medium-well burger.

To avoid meatloaf from cracking, try rubbing a small amount of cold water on the top and sides before placing it in the oven.

"SHAPING UP"
When you are going to make hamburger patties or meatballs, place the meat in the refrigerator for 30 minutes before forming the patties or meatballs and they will form better and stay in shape when cooking. If you place a small piece of ice inside your meatballs before browning, they will be moist.

Three ounces of hamburger will supply you with twice the fat as the same weight of top sirloin steak. The best hamburger is made by choosing the leanest piece of round steak you can find, having the butcher remove all visible fat, then asking to have it ground through the grinder twice. That will break the fat globules up even more and more fat will be eliminated during cooking. Always cook hamburgers on a small rack placed on the bottom of your frying pan, so that the fat will drip away from the meat.

"SMOKE A STEAK"
One pound of charcoaled barbecued steak contains as much carcinogens (cancer forming agents) as the inhaled smoke from 15 cigarettes. The fat dripping on the "real" charcoal causes a chemical reaction that places "pyrobenzines" on the outer black covering of the meat. Wrapping the meat in foil helps or just barbecuing with artificial briquettes solves the problem.

Beef consumed in large quantities can inhibit the absorption of the mineral manganese as well as causing an increased loss of calcium in the urine.

HERBS THAT ARE BEST SUITED FOR CERTAIN MEATS

BEEF.............Basil, thyme, sweet marjoram, summer savory and rosemary.

VEAL.............Summer savory rosemary, thyme, tarragon and basil.

LAMB.............Mint, summer basil.

PORK.............Sweet marjoram, thyme, sage, chives, and basil.

POULTRY..........Thyme, sage, tarragon, sweet marjoram, chervil, and summer savory.

FISH............Chervil, fennel, sage, parsley, dill, sweet marjoram, basil, and chives.

"OUCH!"
If you scorch meat, soak it in a towel, that has been dampened with hot water and wrung out well. Cover the meat for about 5 minutes, remove the towel and scrape off any burnt areas with a sharp knife.

"SETTING A SPEED RECORD"
When you need to barbecue for a large crowd and your grill isn't big enough, you can save time by using a cookie sheet and placing a few layers of hamburgers between layers of tin foil and baking the burgers at 350^0 F. for 25 minutes, them finish them on the grill in only 5-10 minutes. Hot dogs may be done the same way but only cook for 10 minutes.

"REAL PORKERS"
Pigs are not an efficient source of protein. They require almost 8 pounds of grain and soy to produce 1 pound of meat. Cow's require 7 pounds and chickens less than 3 pounds.

If your going to buy a canned ham, purchase the largest you can afford. Smaller canned hams are usually made from bits and pieces and glued together with gelatin.

The Italian name for ham is "prosciutto." Prosciutto is never smoked and is prepared by a salt-curing process, seasoned and then ar dried. Prosciutto cotta means that the ham has been cooked and is common terminology in a deli.

The flavor of a fully cooked ham can be improved by cooking. Cooking releases the juices.

If you want thin ham slices, place the ham in the freezer for 20 minutes before you begin slicing.

Only 1 in 1,000 pigs are now found to contain the trichinosis parasite. However, it is still recommended to cook pork to an internal temperature of 160^0 F. The parasite is killed at 137^0 F.

When cooking a pork loin roast, place the fat side down for the first 20 minutes. This will cause the fat to release juices, then turn the roast over for the balance of the cooking time to allow the fat to baste the roast.

To stop bacon from curling up when being fried, try soaking the bacon in cold water for 2 minutes first. Dry it well with paper towels. If they still curl, sprinkle with flour, if that doesn't work, poke some holes in them or use a heavy flat metal object.

If you want a moist ham, place the contents on a 12 ounce can of cola in your pan and wrap the ham in tin foil. About 30 minutes before the ham is done, remove the tin foil and allow the ham juices to mix with the cola.

Sliced bacon will only stay fresh for 1 week under refrigeration once the package is opened and the bacon is exposed to air.

If you allow bacon to sit at room temperature for 20-30 minutes before cooking it will separate more easily.

"BASIC CHEMISTRY"
Choose bacon with the most meat. The higher nitrite levels will be found in the fat. If you would like to reduce the amount of consumed nitrites, cook the bacon in the microwave on a piece of paper towel.

"SLIMMED"
Never buy bacon if it looks slimy, chances are that it's not fresh.

"FAKIR"
Most imitation bacon products including "Sizzalean" still contain nitrites. If you can find it, purchase only nitrite-free bacon.

"MINERAL BATH"
Cured hams are immersed in a solution of brine salts, sugar, and nitrites are injected into the ham. If the total weight goes up 8%, the label will read "ham, with natural juices." If the weight goes up more than 8% the label will read "water added."

Pork sausage and breakfast sausage may contain up to 50% fat. Ground pork products should be kept frozen for no longer than 2 months.

To stop sausages from splitting open when they are fried, try making a few small punctures in the skins while they are cooking. If you roll them in flour before cooking it will reduce shrinkage.

To bring out the flavor in a ham loaf, add a small amount of rosemary.

To remove a ham rind easily, slit the rind lengthwise before it is placed in the pan. As it bakes, the rind will pull away and can be removed.

"DESALTING YOUR BUTT"
When cooking pork buttes, rub the meaty side with table salt an hour before cooking to draw any water in the pork to the surface. This will help reduce the saltiness of the ham, and tenderize it. Draining it after half the cooking time and pouring a small bottle of ginger ale over it will also reduce the saltiness.

"POOR RUDOLPH"
Reindeer meat should be avoided if imported from Finland due to radiation contamination from the 1986 Chernobyl disaster.

VERY FRANK FURTER INFORMATION

1937 Frankfurter	1990's Frankfurter
Fat............19%	Fat..........28%
Protein.......20%	Protein.......12%

If hot dogs are labeled "All Meat" or "All Beef" they must contain at least 85% meat or beef. The "All Meat" variety can contain a blend of beef, pork, chicken or turkey meat. It can also contain bone, water, etc. Kosher hot dogs are only pure beef muscle meat and are the better source of protein. However, they all still contain nitrites.

Liver will be more tender if you soak it in milk or tomato juice then place it in the refrigerator for 1-2 hours before cooking.

There are 5 grades of lamb; prime, choice, good, utility, and cull. Prime never makes it to the markets and is only sold to restaurants.

"JOLLY GOOD SHOW"
The best lamb comes from New Zealand (spring lamb). It is against the law to use hormones and tenderizers. Their meats are safer than most countries.

FAT AND CALORIES IN MEAT

	FAT(gm.)	% FAT CALORIES	TOTAL CALORIES
BEEF			
Round Bone	4	19	152
Sirloin Roast	4	19	156
Round Steak	5	22	161
Sirloin (dbl bone)	5	22	162
Chuck Arm	6	25	164
Flank Steak	6	25	167
Porterhouse	6	24	168
T-Bone	6	25	170
Sirloin Steak	8	30	184
Rump Roast	8	30	184
Club Steak	11	36	208
Chuck Rib	12	37	212
Ground Beef (lean)	15	44	230
Ground Beef (reg.)	17	46	245
LAMB			
Foreshank	5	23	152
Sirloin of Leg	6	26	154
Loin Chop	8	32	176
Blade Chop	10	37	178
Arm Chop	12	35	230
PORK			
Loin, Tenderloin	5	20	142
Ham Leg (rump)	9	32	188
Ham Leg (shank)	9	33	183
Shoulder	11	38	194
Loin	12	38	209
VEAL			
Veal Cutlet	4	17	155
Sirloin Chop	5	20	167
Blade Steak	5	19	156
Rib Roast	5	24	136
Loin Chop	7	25	179

POULTRY

Most chickens in the United States are processed in a similar fashion. They are processed in long vats with a water temperature of 125^0 F. to 132^0 F. This is the temperature that bacterial growth is at a high level. Hot water opens the pores in chickens and may allow the entry of undesirable matter that is floating in the hot bloody water of this communal bath.

Commercial chickens must be cooked to an internal temperature of 185^0 F. to kill the bacteria that may be present. If the internal temperature shows that the chicken is fully cooked and you see traces of pink near the bone, it is not a sign of undercooking. It is only the bone pigment that has leached out during the cooking. This is more common in smaller birds or ones that have frozen and defrosted. The meat is perfectly safe to eat. This can be avoided by purchasing older birds.

Any kitchen item, whether it is a washcloth, sponge or the counter must be thoroughly cleaned after working with chicken to eliminate the possibility of contamination of other foods and utensils if any harmful bacteria is present.

The NAS (National Academy of Sciences) released a study in 1992 showing that toxic contamination of poultry poses a potential health risk. Most of the toxic chemicals and pathogens are largely undetected using present poultry inspection procedures. Studies by the National Academy of Science showed that 48% of food poisonings in the United States are caused by contaminated chickens. One person in every fifty who eat chicken regularly will receive some form of food poisoning from poultry.

USDA food inspectors have increased their inspections of chicken slaughtering plants by over 50% in the last 10 years. We still have a long way to go, since they have reduced the number of inspectors 30% in the last 10 years.

Americans consume 6 billion chickens per year and chicken farming is a $14 billion dollar industry.

THE PROCESSING OF KOSHER POULTRY

Kosher poultry is defeathered in cold water not warm or hot water. it is then soaked and submerged for 30 minutes in very cold water, then hand salted inside and out, and allowed to hang for 1 hour to remove any remaining blood.

After salting the birds are rinsed 3 separate times to remove the salt residue. The taste is clean and most people who eat chicken on a regular basis will immediately tell the difference.

"VERRRY FUSSSY"
Many Kosher processed chickens never make it to the marketplace even when passed by government inspectors. The quality control differs from most other processors and the standards are higher.

A 3 pound chicken will yield about 2-3 cups of chicken meat. A 5 ounce can of boned chicken will yield about 1/2 cup of chicken meat.

To tenderize chicken and give it a unique flavor, try basting it with a small amount of white wine as it cooks. Also, a low to moderate cooking temperature will produce a juicier chicken, since more fat and moisture are retained.

"FOWL CUBES"
Freeze leftover chicken broth in ice cube trays, then keep the cubes in a plastic bag in the freezer. When a recipe calls for chicken bouillon cubes, thaw them out in the microwave.

Chicken and hamburger meat should not be kept in the refrigerator for more than 2 days without being frozen.

"FOWL DEAL"
Ground poultry in supermarkets usually contain dark meat, and skin making them relatively high fat. Ground poultry should be labeled 98% fat-free.

"CLIP, CLIP"
To save money, purchase whole chickens, cut them with a poultry scissors and freeze the sections you want together. When you purchase whole birds, try not to buy the larger ones, these will be the older birds and usually tougher.

"RECYCLING"
Commercially purchased snail shells may be reused as long as they as boiled (as instructed) after each use and again before adding the new snails.

"GRANDMOTHER'S SECRET"
After breading a chicken part, place it in the refrigerator for 45 minutes before cooking and the breading will adhere to the food and not fall off.

Young chickens and turkeys have less fat.

Add a few slices of lemon to your stewing chicken and it will tenderize it. Chef's use another method and that is to submerge the chicken parts in buttermilk for 2-3 hours in the refrigerator before cooking it. This will tenderize it as well as imparting an excellent flavor to the meat.

If you wish your chicken or parts to be browned, try brushing them with a low-salt soy sauce.

"ONLY BUY 4.0 CHICKENS"
Chickens are grade Grade A, Grade B, or Grade C. Grades B and C are used in canned and frozen foods.

"DAMAGED GOODS"
Grade A chickens are sold in supermarkets. Grade B & C chickens are used for TV dinners and canned fowl products. These are usually blemished and would not sell well.

A 3 pound chicken will provide 1 pound 5 ounces of edible meat.

One large chicken slaughtering plant may use up to 100 million gallons of water daily. This is equal to the amount used by a city of 25,000 people.

All fowl should be cooked to an internal temperature of 185^0 F.

Poultry thaws at approximately 1 pound every 5 hours.

A farm raised duck will have more meat than a wild duck. Duck's are not a good candidate for stuffing. Their fat content is so high that the fat is absorbed into the stuffing when you are cooking them.

A yellow chicken doesn't necessarily mean a healthier and more nutritious chicken when compared to a pale one. Yellow skin is the result of yellow corn found in feed. Some suppliers of feed also may add substances that contain a yellow pigment or marigold petals to give the skin a healthier sheen.

"WHERE'S CHICKEY?"
Miniature chickens are called Cornish game hens. These are chickens that are only 4-6 weeks old and only weigh about 2 pounds.

"CHUBBY CHICKEN"
The USDA reports that chickens today are getting fatter. In fact, they actually may reach their market weight in 6-8 weeks. This is half the time it previously took. however, the body fat seems to be increasing. Turkeys reach maturity in 14-22 weeks, are more tender than chickens, have less fat and more white meat.

"NO CREATURE COMFORT HERE"
Most chickens in the U.S. are raised in giant coop farms holding more than 10,000 chickens each. Each bird is housed in a box and will have feed available with a light on so that they can eat 24 hours a day.

"CALL THE MASSEUR"
If you eat chicken in a foreign country, you will probably notice the difference in the flavor. Most foreign countries do not allow fowls to be raised under these poor conditions. If the odor of a fresh chicken is offensive, try giving the bird a massage with the juice of 1/2 lemon and 1/4 teaspoon of salt. The bird will enjoy this and it will totally remove the odor.

"GREAT CHICKEN RANCH"
One of the finest chicken ranches in the United States is Shelton's in Pomona, California (909) 623-4361. They raise only free range chickens, use no antibiotics, and hand process every chicken.

A significant number of fowl that is sold in markets labeled "fresh" have been frozen and defrosted which may affect the taste.

"REAL SICK BIRDS?"
In 1989 chicken farmers purchased $300 million dollars worth of antibiotics.

"MASS CHICKENDUCTION"
One of the largest chicken farms in the U.S. ships approximately 23 million chicken per week. 38 million chickens are processed in the U.S. every day according to the National Broiler Council.

"BUYER BEWARE"
It would be best to compare nutrition labels when purchasing ground turkey. You may be surprised that some brands have almost as much fat as lean beef.

"SKIP THE INJECTION"
Try cooking your next turkey upside down on a "V" rack for the first hour. The juices will flow to the breast and make the meat moist and tender. Turn the bird rightside up after the first hour, remove the "V" rack and you will never buy another fat-basted bird.

"SCRUB A-DUB-DUB"
To thaw a frozen chicken, place it in a pan of ice cold water with at least 1/4 cup of salt added. You will notice the difference in the flavor and have a cleaner chicken.

"LET'S TALK TURKEY"
The average American ate 20 pounds of turkey in 1991, 26 pounds in 1995 and only 2 pounds in 1930.

"SMART STUFF"
When stuffing your holiday bird, try placing a piece of cheesecloth inside the cavity before adding the stuffing. When you remove the cloth all the stuffing will be easily removed. Stuffing sacs are now available during the holiday season.

"RELAX!"
Turkey's should be left out of the oven after it is fully cooked for 20-30 minutes covered with tin foil before carving. Hot birds are difficult to cut and the white meat falls apart too easily.

"OUR TAX DOLLARS AT WORK?"
In a recent 1995 government study, (that I hope didn't cost us anything), 8 out of 10 people called the "stuff" inside a turkey "stuffing" and 20% called it "dressing." The 20% group were all over the age of 65.

"BACTERIA HAVEN"
Never stuff a turkey or other fowl and leave it overnight in the refrigerator thinking it is safe. Bacteria will grow and it is best to stuff the bird just before placing it in the oven.

When stuffing a bird the opening may be sealed with a piece of raw potato.

"GET A GRIP ON"
Use white gloves to remove fat from inside chickens and turkeys.

"NEWS YOU CAN NEVER USE"
There are 426 chickens per person in Arkansas.

American averaged 70 pounds of chicken annually in 1995. Almost 1/3 of the nations meat consumption is chicken with 5 billion pounds being sold by fast food restaurants.

"GETTING BUFFALOED"
an order of chicken wings (buffalo wings) may supply as much as 30 grams of fat, more than half the fat that a person should consume on an 1800 calorie daily intake.

Chicken will keep longer if rewrapped in wax paper instead of the plastic wrap used by the markets to cover it with.

A 3 1/2 ounce serving of white meat turkey without the skin contains only 115 calories and 1 gram of fat, which is about 10% less than white meat chicken.

"DITTO"
95% of all chickens sold in the United States are broilers or fryers, same chicken, different name.

"HOME, HOME ON THE RANGE"
A free range chicken has an average of 14% fat compared to a standard cooped chicken at 18% fat.

"RUBDOWN"
Rub the skin of your turkey with white vermouth about 15 minutes before you are ready to remove it from the oven. The skin will turn a nice brown color.

"GROUNDED"
The breast of migratory fowl are dark. The reason supermarket birds breast meat is white is that they never used their wings and had poor muscle development and blood supply to that area.

MEAT AND POULTRY HOTLINE 1-(800)535-4555

FISH

The popularity of fish has risen since the 1980's and more varieties of fish have become available. Consumption of fish presently averages 18 pounds per person, per year. More fish are now raised in aquaculture fish farms. The fats in fish are high in polyunsaturates and contain the omega-3 fatty acids that may protect us from heart attacks by keeping the blood from coagulating too easily.

Studies show that even canned or frozen fish contain most of their omega-3 fatty acids. Fish and shellfish may still harbors certain bacteria and parasites. Cooking is a must and fish and shellfish should not be eaten raw. Do not eat the skin or visible fat on fish. Most contaminants, if present will be found there.

Consumption of seafood in the United States has only risen from an annual level per person of 12 pounds in 1970 to the present level of 17 pounds per person. Never taste fish before it has been fully cooked, parasites may still be alive and you may acquire an unwanted intestinal guest.

HOW TO CHOOSE FRESH FISH

Skin	Should be firm and elastic. The skin should be shiny, show good color, and should spring back when finger pressure is exerted.
Eyes	Bright, clear and somewhat bulging. Stale fish eyes are usually cloudy and sunken into the head.
Scales	Should be tight to the skin, not falling off and should appear bright and shiny.
Gills	No slime, reddish pink and clean looking, not grayish.
Odor	Not overly strong. Fish should never smell "fishy." The smell is from the chemical compound "trimethylamine." It is produced from the deterioration of fish flesh.

Seafood should be as fresh as possible, usually no more than 2-3 days out of the water.

HOW TO CHOOSE FROZEN FISH

<u>Odor</u>   Should have little or no odor. Never buy if they have a strong fish odor.

<u>Skin</u>   Should be solidly frozen and have no discolorizations.

<u>Wrappings</u>   Moisture-proof with no air spaces or ice crystals between the fish and the wrapping.

Supermarkets offer up to 200 varieties of fish.

"SMELLS FISHY"
If you wash your hands in cold water before handling fish, your hands won't smell fishy. To eliminate the fish odor from a frying pan, try placing a small amount of white vinegar in the pan before washing it.

"FISHERMAN'S FACT"
Minnows will stay alive for a longer period of time if you drop 6-8 drops of iodine in the water they are residing in.

"THE REAL SKINNY"
Frozen fish will be easier to skin than a fresh one.

"FISH SHAKE"
The best method of thawing frozen fish is to place the fish in low-fat milk. The milk will draw out the frozen taste and return the fresh caught flavor. Try not to thaw frozen fish completely before cooking or the fish may become mushy and even dried out.

When cooking fish wrapped in tin foil, try adding a sprig of dill and a lemon slice for a great taste treat.

"EASIER THAN A CLIFF"
Scaling a fish will become easy if you rub white vinegar on the scales first. The mild acid tends to loosen the scales.

"SOUNDS FISHY"
Americans are consuming more fish than ever before, 18 pounds per person in 1990 and 22 pounds in 1995. Because of this fact aquaculture farms are becoming a major food industry raising mainly Trout, Catfish, Halibut, Turbot, Skipjack, Sole, and Pollack.

"POACHING"
When you are poaching fish, keep the fish in single layers and be sure that the poaching liquid reaches the top of the fish.

A small amount of grated onion added to the butter when cooking fish will add an excellent bit of flavor.

Depending on the species only 11-27% of the total fat in fish and shellfish is saturated, compared to 37-48% in pork and beef.

If fish is consumed 3-4 times per week it will keep the body supplied with essential nucleic acids (omega-3 oils) as well as reducing your risk of having a heart attack or stroke.

"GIFT WRAP?"
When baking fish it is best to place the fish in a piece of parchment paper or wrap it in tin foil. This will help to retain the moisture.

If you are going to broil or grill fish, be sure and purchase fish steaks that are at least 1 inch thick. Fish will dry out very quickly and the thicker the better, especially for barbecuing.

The skin should be left on fillets when grilling, then remove it after cooking.

When frying fish, make sure that the surface of the fish is dry.

Fish that feed on the bottom of lakes, such as Carp and Bass have a higher risk of becoming contaminated. However, cooking will neutralize most of the contaminants which tend to locate in the fat.

"HAVE YOUR ROD AND REEL READY"
If you are not sure if a fish is really fresh, place it in cold water, if it floats, its fresh.

"LOVE ME TENDER....."
When cooking fish, the concern should be more for retaining flavor than tenderness since fish is naturally tender.

Saltwater fish have thicker, more dense bones than freshwater fish, which have thin, minuscule bones. The reason for this is that saltwater has more buoyancy. If you hate fighting the bones, purchase saltwater fish, such as cod and flounder.

Fish tends to cool very quickly and should be served on warm plates or on a warmed server.

If you marinate fish, always do it in the refrigerator, never at room temperature. Fish deteriorates very rapidly at room temperature.

"SEAFOOD SAUNA"
To steam fish, place the fish wrapped in a piece of plain (no design) paper towel that has been moistened with water in the microwave for about 5 minutes.

"SKIP THE DETERGENT"
At the Montreal Expo '67, Eskimo women demonstrated how they cooked salmon in a dishwasher.

TOTAL FAT IN 3 1/2 OUNCES OF FISH

LEAN FISH

	GRAMS
Shrimp	1.1
Crab	1.3
Shark	1.9
Swordfish	2.2
Oyster	2.4
Bass	2.4
Grouper	2.8
Ocean Perch	2.8
Mullet	3.0
Sole	3.3
Flounder	3.9
Pollack	4.2
Halibut	4.3
Red Snapper	4.5
Cod	4.6
Haddock	4.9
Hake	5.2
Tuna (Bluefish)	6.5

FAT FISH

	GRAMS
Striped Bass	8.3
Butterfish	8.5
Salmon	8.6
Herring	9.0
Pompano	9.5
Porgie	10.4
Mackerel	13.8

If you are going fishing in the Caribbean, Florida, or Hawaii and plan on eating tropical fish, it would be best to call the fish safety hotline. This hotline will provide details on "ciguatera" poisoning and which fish not to eat.

FISH HOTLINE 1 (305)361-4619

MARKET FORMS OF FISH

WHOLE FISH	Marketed when caught.
DRAWN FISH	Only entrails are removed.
DRESSED FISH	Ready to party or cook.
FISH STEAKS	Slices cut crosswise.
FISH FILLETS	Boneless pieces cut from the sides.
BUTTERFLY FILLETS	Two sides cut away from backbone.
CURED FISH	Cured by smoking, drying, salting, or pickling.
COLD-SMOKED	Cured and partially dried. Won't keep long.
HOT-SMOKED	Partially or wholly cooked. Needs freezing.
DRIED FISH	Air or heat dried and salted.
SALTED FISH	Dry salted or brine cured. Can be pickled.

"A WORD TO THE WISE"
If you see a seafood product with *"USG INSPECTED"* on the label, report it to authorities, this is not a legal designation. The label should read "Packed Under Federal Inspection or (read "Packed Under Federal Inspection or (PUFI)" on the package. This means that the presence of a federal inspector.

SHELLFISH

ABALONE

The edible portion is the foot, which is very tough and needs to be pounded into tenderness. Has been so overfished that they are becoming rare. The price is very high and they are considered a delicacy.

Abalone needs to be cooked within 24 hours of purchase. It has a very short shelf-life.

"EXPENSIVE CHEWING GUM"
The method of tenderizing abalone, is to cut the abalone into the thinnest slices you can and then pound those slices even thinner using a special meat-tenderizing hammer. If this is not done properly the abalone is tough.

When abalone is cooked it should never be cooked for more than 30 seconds on each side. Overcooking makes it tough. Before cooking place small slashes about an inch apart across the whole piece to avoid curling.

When purchasing abalone, make sure that the exposed foot muscle moves when you touch it. Never buy shellfish if it dead.

CLAMS

Hard-shelled are the most sought after. Soft-shelled clams cannot close its shell because its neck sticks out too far. The largest soft-shelled clam is the geoduck, which may weigh up to 3 pounds. Sea clams are usually used for canning or in packaged soups.

If you dig your own clams, you must purge them of sand and debris before eating them. Allow the clams to stand 20-25 minutes in clear sea water. The water should be changed at least 3-4 times to be sure they are free of residues.

"CLAMMING UP"
Discard any clam that does not open when steamed or boiled, they are dead and possibly contaminated.

"RELAXATION TECHNIQUE"
To open clams they may be dropped into boiling water and let stand for a few minutes. This will relax their muscle and make them easier to open with a knife or beer can opener.

When making clam chowder, add the chopped clams during the last 15 minutes of cooking to avoid them becoming mushy and tough.

CRAB

Blue crab is from the Atlantic and Gulf areas. Dungeness is caught in the Pacific Ocean. King and snow crab are caught in the north off the coast of Canada and Alaska. Stone crab come from Florida.

Soft-sell crab comes in 4 sizes, "spiders" which are the bare legal size of 3 1/2 inches across, "hotel prime" at 4 1/2 inches across, "prime" at 5 1/2 inches across, and "jumbo" at 6-7 inches across.

Crabs should only be purchased if they are active and heavy for their size. Refrigerate them as soon as possible and cover them with a damp towel. Live crabs should be cooked the day they are purchased.

If canned crabmeat has a metallic taste, soak it in ice water for 5-8 minutes, then drain and blot dry with paper towels.

Cooked crab shells should be bright red and not orange, have little or no smell and should be displayed on a bed of ice.

CRAYFISH

Small freshwater crustaceans. Louisiana produces about 20 million pounds a year. Similar to shrimp, all the meat is in the tail. Also called, "crawdads."

LANGOSTINOS

A crustacean, sometimes sold as rock shrimp. Usually sold frozen and used in soups and salads.

LOBSTER

Two main lobsters are sold in the United States, they are; Maine and spiny. The most prized is the Maine lobster which is an excellent tasting lobster and sought after. The spiny lobster has most of the meat in the tail and has smaller claws.

"DO THE TWIST"
When purchasing live lobster, there should be movement in their legs and their tail should curl under when touched.

Lobsters should be cooked the day they are caught for the best taste. If this is not possible cook them as soon as possible.

If there is any doubt whether the lobster is alive, don't cook it, discard it. Bacteria grows very quickly in lobsters when they die.

Lobster roe (eggs) are a delicacy in many countries.

Before you start to tear a lobster apart, make sure you cover it with a towel so that the juices don't squirt out.

Lobster should be added to dishes just before serving in order to retain their flavor. Overcooking is the biggest problem in retaining the taste of lobster.

Newburg lobster is made using a cream and sherry mixture. Newburg pertains to an old Scottish fishing village.

MUSSELS

Mussel farming is becoming a popular business. They are raised on ropes, which keep them from the silty bottom, thus making them cleaner and thus more salable. When grown in this manner, they are also much larger.

Mussels, clams, and oysters should be alive when purchased. gaping shells should close when tapped. Discard the dead ones.

When you are cooking mussels, they will be cooked when their shell opens.

When mussels are shucked, the liquid that comes out should be clear.

Live mussels, covered with a damp towel may be stored for about 2-3 days on a tray in the refrigerator. Never place one on top of the other.

Mussels have a dark thread that protruded from their shell. These should be removed before cooking. However, this will kill them and they must be cooked immediately.

OYSTER

Over 90 million pounds are consumed worldwide. About 50% are now aquafarmed. The flavor and texture will vary depending on where they were harvested.

If you purchase an oyster and the shell is broken or cracked, discard it may be contaminated.

Store live oysters in the refrigerator in a single layer with the larger shell down and covered with a damp towel. They should be consumed within 3 days.

Shucked oysters will stay fresh frozen for up to 3 months if they are stored in their liquid and only 1-2 days under refrigeration.

Oysters should be scrubbed with a hard plastic bristle brush under cold water before shucking them.

If you are poaching oysters, only poach them until their edges start to curl. Oysters are easy to overcook and get tough.

"NEW BAR DRINK"
If you soak oysters in club soda for about 5 minutes, they are usually easier to remove from their shells.

SCALLOPS

A mollusk that dies very quickly when removed from the water. They should not be overcooked or they will become tough. They are usually shucked at the time they are caught and placed on ice. There are over 400 varieties of sea scallops.

SHRIMP

There are over 250 varieties of shrimp. They are classified as number of shrimp per pound. The jumbo shrimp should average 16 to 25 per pound, large shrimp average 20-32 per pound, medium shrimp average 28-40 per pound, while tiny ocean or bay shrimp can average over 70 per pound. One pound of raw shrimp will yield 1/2 to 3/4 pounds after cooking. Large shrimp are called prawns.

White shrimp are milder in flavor and more expensive than brown. Brown feed more on algae and have a stronger iodine taste.

"OFF WITH THEIR HEADS"
Shrimp with heads are more perishable than those without heads.

If shrimp has a slight ammonia smell, it is deteriorating. Since shrimp deteriorates very quickly, it should be used the same day it is purchased, or at least the next day. Never refreeze thawed shrimp, most of the shrimp you buy has been frozen. If you wish to keep it longer, buy it frozen solid.

"TALK ABOUT THINGS IN SMALL PACKAGES"
A shrimp head contains almost all its organs including most of the digestive system.

The dark-colored intestinal tube running down a shrimp's back is OK to eat as long as its cooked. However, it may be a little gritty due to the bacteria and other residues of digestion. The bacteria is killed by cooking. To de-vein shrimp, hold the shrimp under a slow stream of cold water and run the tip of an icepick down the back. This will remove the vein.

"NAUGHTY, NAUGHTY"
The FDA has taken action against some firms for overbreading shrimp to raise the weight and price.

Shrimp has more cholesterol than any other shellfish, but is low in saturated fat.

The flavor of canned shrimp can be greatly improved if you soak the can in ice water for at least an hour before opening it. To eliminate the canned flavor, try soaking the shrimp for 10-15 minutes in a mixture of 2 tablespoons of vinegar and 1 teaspoon of sherry.

Avoid making tough shrimp by first cooling the shrimp under very cold water for 1-2 minutes, then place them in a deep pot (not over heat) with a small amount of salt, then cover them with rapidly boiling water, tightly covered. Large shrimp take about 5-7 minutes, average size are done in about 4 minutes. The size of the shrimp will not affect their quality.

SQUID

Usually not thought of as a shellfish. Normally called "calamari." To keep it tender, don't cook it for more than 3 minutes. If stewing it, cook it for at least 15-20 minutes. The whole body and tentacles are edible. Squid has more cholesterol than shrimp.

"YUK"
Squid, shark, and snails (escargot) rate as the foods Americans hate the most. This is too bad, since shark is not only a lean fish but an excellent eating fish.

Mollusks, clams, and oysters are "filter feeders" and may build up concentrations of many toxins that may be present. Hepatitis has increased recently, resulting from shellfish caught in human sewage contaminated areas off the east coast. Shellfish live by filtering 15-20 gallons of water a day. Cook all shellfish. Most shellfish are never inspected.

Clams and oysters are easy to open, if first washed with cold water, then placed in a plastic bag and kept in the freezer for 1/2 hour. Cook shellfish in a heavily salted water to draw out the sea salt.

Never keep a shellfish in fresh water, it will kill them very quickly.

All shellfish are naturally high in sodium.

SALTWATER FISH

ANCHOVY

The majority of anchovies caught are from the waters around Southern California. Over 250 million pounds are caught and ground up as poultry feed. The average market size is 4-6 inches and are mainly used on pizza or Caesar salad. They may also be purchased canned in olive oil.

If anchovies are too salty, try soaking them in tap water for 10-15 minutes, then store them in the refrigerator for 30 minutes before using.

Anchovies will last about 2 months under refrigeration after the can is opened and up to 1 year without refrigeration in a sealed can. Opened ones should be kept covered with olive oil.

If you use anchovies in any dish, taste the dish before adding any further seasoning.

ANGLER

This category includes the monkfish, sea devil, bellyfish, lotte, and goosefish. They are for the most part all low-fat with a firm texture. They can weigh from 2-25 pounds and only the tapered tail section is edible. Tastes similar to lobster.

BARRACUDA

A moderate-fat fish that runs from 4-8 pounds. The only variety that is good for eating is the pacific barracuda which has an excellent taste. Great barracudas are known for their toxicity.

BLUE-FISH

Usually weighs in at 3-6 pounds. Does not freeze well. When cooking be sure to remove the strip of flesh running down its center. This fish may give a strong undesirable flavor.

COD

The three main types are; Atlantic cod, pacific cod, and scrod. They are all low-fat fishes with a firm texture. The Atlantic is the largest variety and the scrod is the smallest (a young cod). Available in many cuts, which include; fillets, steaks, whole and dressed.

CROAKER

Varieties include; Atlantic croaker, redfish, spot, kingfish, corvina, and black drum. All are low-fat except corvina. Size varies from 1/4 pound for the spot to 30 pounds for the large redfish, a popular chowder fish.

CUSK

A fish gaining popularity with a taste similar to cod. Low-fat and excellent for stews and soups. Weighs in at 1 1/2 to 5 pounds. Sold as fillets or whole.

EEL

A firm-textured fish that nay run up to 3 feet long and has a tough skin that is removed prior to cooking. More popular in Europe and Japan.

FLOUNDER

Also, called sole. The most popular fish in the United States. The varieties seem endless and all are low-fat with a fine texture. Most are found 1/2 to 3 pounds with some varieties weighing up to 10 pounds. One of the best eating fishes.

GROUPER

Can weigh in from 3-25 pounds and may be called a "sea bass." The skin is tough and should be removed. It has a firm texture and may be cooked in almost any manner.

HADDOCK

A close relation to cod and usually weighs in at 3-5 pounds. Smoked haddock is known as "Finnan Haddie."

HAKE

Usually caught in the Atlantic Ocean during summer and early fall. it is a low-fat, firm, textured fish. Usually weighs in at 1-8 pounds and has a very mild flavor.

HALIBUT

A flatfish that usually weighs in from 5-20 pounds. A low-fat fish with a firm texture.

HERRING

A small 1/4 to 1 pound fish with a fine soft texture and high-fat. Usually used for appetizers and sold pickled or smoked.

MACKEREL

Sold under a number of names, such as; wahoo, Atlantic mackerel, pacific jack, king mackerel, and Spanish mackerel. A high-fat fish with a firm texture, commonly sold canned.

MAHI MAHI

Also known as the "Dolphin Fish" or "Dorodo." However, it is no relation to a dolphin nor does it resemble a dolphin. May weigh up to 40 pounds and is an excellent eating fish.

MULLET

The fat content will vary, but is usually a moderate to high-fat fish with a firm texture. Has a mild nutlike flavor.

OCEAN PERCH

A low-fat fish with a firm texture. Most of the perch are imported from Iceland. Usually weighs in at 1/2 to 2 pounds and available fresh or frozen.

ORANGE ROUGHY

One of the most popular fish sold. Imported from New Zealand and is low-fat with a firm texture. Available in 2-5 pound weights. Very similar to sole but at a better price.

POLLACK

A close relative to cod with a firm texture. Fresh usually weighs in at 4-12 pounds. Best when sold as fillets.

POMPANO

Rated as one of the best eating fishes. It has a moderate fat level and a firm texture. One of the more expensive fishes.

PORGY

A firm textured low-fat fish that usually weigh in at 1/2 to 2 pounds. Primarily caught in New England waters.

RED SNAPPER

Has a rose-colored skin and red eyes. It is low-fat with a firm texture. Excellent for soups and stews.

ROCKFISH

Available in more than 50 varieties. Often sold under the name of pacific snapper. They have a firm texture and are low-fat.

SABLEFISH

Also, known as Alaskan cod or butterfish. A very high-fat fish with a soft texture due to its fat content. Makes an excellent smoking fish and is usually sold smoked.

SALMON

Blueback red salmon is the highest fat fish and is the most expensive in the higher quality. The lower quality are red or sockeye, Chinook or king, and pink salmon is the lowest grade.

Three ounces of salmon contains 120 calories. 1/2 cup of salmon contains more grams of protein than 2 lamb chops.

"GOOD NEWS FOR BAGEL AND LOX LOVERS"
Smoked salmon (lox) is usually heavily salted unless you purchase the "Nova" variety. Salmon used for smoking is usually raised on aquacultured farms and has never had a reported incident of parasitic contamination.

"SALMON (RUSSIAN) ROULETTE"
Salmon used for sushi gives you a 1 in 10 chance of consuming a roundworm from the "anisakis family" of parasites, according to the FDA in samples from 32 restaurants serving sushi.

If you see a label that reads "Norwegian Salmon" be aware that there is no such species.

SARDINES

These are actually soft-boned herring. They are descaled before being canned and the scales used to make artificial pearls and cosmetics. The Norwegian bristling sardine is the finest. Maine sardines are almost as good and cost considerably less. They are high-fat and best used for appetizers.

"HEALTHY LITTLE CRITTERS"
A single 3 1/2 ounce serving of sardines is higher in calcium and phosphorus than a glass of milk. Sardines also contain vitamin D to assist in the metabolism of the calcium. It also provides up to 53% of your minimum daily requirement of protein, more than the same weight of T-bone steak.

Norwegian sardines are the best source of Omega-3 oils, next is Chinook salmon.

SEA BASS

A moderate-fat fish with a firm texture. It has a mild flavor and is a popular seller.

SEA TROUT

A moderate-fat fish with a fine texture, excellent baked or broiled. Usually caught in the Southeastern United States waters.

SHAD

A high-fat fish with a fine texture. A difficult fish to bone and almost always sold as fillet. The eggs (roe) are considered a delicacy (caviar).

SHARK

Shark steaks are one of the most vitamin-rich foods in the sea, It is low-fat and has a firm, dense texture, and is occasionally sold in chunks. It is fast becoming a popular eating fish. There are 350 species of shark.

"MMMM GOOD"
In Asia, dried shark fins sell for $53 per pound and are used to make shark soup. In Hong Kong, a bowl of shark soup sells for $50 per bowl.

The 60 foot whale shark is the world's largest fish. In 1995 over 120 million sharks were caught.

SKATE
The wings are the only part that is edible. They have a flavor similar to scallops and are low-fat with a firm texture.

SWORDFISH

The flavor is not as strong as shark and is best served as steaks. It is somewhat higher in fat than shark but has a similar texture.

TUNA

White tuna is from albacore tuna and is the best grade of tuna. Light tuna comes from the other 5 species. It is nutritious and has an appealing taste.

The average American consumes more than 4 pounds of tuna per year. Tuna packed in oil has 50% more calories as water packed tuna. Recent studies show that mercury contamination in tuna is too low to be a concern.

Solid-pack tuna is tuna that is composed of the loins of the tuna with the addition of a few flakes. Chunk tuna will include pieces that will contain a portion of the muscle structure. Flake tuna has the muscle structure and a high concentration of the pieces all under 1/2 inch. Grated tuna is just above a paste.

"JUST CALL ME CHARLEY"
The best tuna is labeled "white" and is albacore. Three other types are sold, "light', "dark" and "blended." The darker the tuna the stronger the flavor and usually the oilier. These are mostly skipjack and bluefin. Bluefin tuna may weigh up to 1,000 pounds.

When tuna is packed in oil it is sometimes called "tonno tuna."

"SAVING FLIPPER"
Choosing tuna for tuna salad is more a matter of taste than the type of tuna. If you have noticed that tuna in cans is darker than it used to be, your right, the reason being is that smaller nets are being used so that the porpoises won't be netted. This means that the larger tuna won't be netted either. The smaller tuna has the darker meat.

"NUMERO UNO"
Tuna ranks as the number one fish or shellfish consumed in the United States in 1995. Shrimp came in second, cod third, and Alaskan pollack fourth due to its popularity in imitation crabmeat.

Watch the tuna label for the chemical "pyrophosphate." It is a preservative that should not be eaten.

TURBOT

A low-fat fish with a firm texture. A flatfish similar to flounder. Usually sold only as fillets.

WHITING

A relative of hake with a low-fat, firm texture. Best when broiled or steamed.

FRESHWATER FISH

BUFFALO FISH

A moderate-fat fish with a firm texture. Usually caught in the Mississippi and the Great Lakes. Weighs in fresh at 2-8 pounds.

CARP

The first fish to be aquacultured hundreds of years ago in China. A scavenger fish which is only recommended for eating, if labeled aquacultured.

CATFISH

Approximately 70% of all catfish sold are from aquacultured farms. There are over 20 varieties of catfish, They are low-fat with a firm texture. Another scavenger fish which is healthier if only purchased aquacultured.

PERCH

A small fish which is usually pan-fried whole. A low-fat fish that is excellent for eating.

PIKE

Has been fished out of existence. An excellent eating low-fat fish. The most popular being the walleyed pike.

SMELT

A very small fish that is usually pan-fried and eaten whole (head and all). Larger ones are usually cleaned and gutted in the usual manner. They are very high-fat with a firm texture.

STURGEON

The largest freshwater fish in the world weighing up to 1,500 pounds. They are high-fat with a very dense texture. Their eggs (roe) are a favorite for caviar.

64% of the calories in caviar are from fat.

TROUT

There are three main varieties; lake trout, rainbow trout, and steelhead trout. All contain moderate to high-fat contents, have a firm texture, and one of the best eating fishes. All commercially sold rainbow trout are from aquacultured farms.

WHITEFISH

Ranks as the best freshwater eating fish. It is high-fat with a firm texture and is best when broiled or baked.

All fish purchased in markets should be labeled Grade A.

CAVIAR

BELUGA

Comes from the beluga sturgeon from the Caspian Sea. The roe (eggs) range in size, but are usually pea size and silver-gray to black. This is the most popular in the United States.

OSETRA

Somewhat smaller than the beluga. The color is a gray to brownish-gray.

SEVRUGA

Even smaller than the osetra and gray in color.

WHITEFISH, LUMPFISH, AND SALMON

These are the less expensive caviars, sometimes called "red caviar."

If you see the Russian word "malossol" on the caviar container, it means that only a small amount of salt was used to process it. This caviar will not have a long shelf life.

Caviar loses much of its flavor and texture when cooked. Best to eat it cold.

Caviar should be stored in the refrigerator and will last for 1 month if the temperature is about 28^0 F.

In many European countries, caviar has been used to treat hangovers due to its acetylcholine content.

Always cook fish at a moderate temperature to retain the moisture and preserve the natural tenderness. Never cook fish at oven temperatures over 350^0 F.

"AND AWAY SHE GOES"
If you doubt the freshness of a fresh fish, place it in cold water, if it floats (or swims away) it has recently been caught.

To test a cooked fish to see if it is finished cooking, try pressing your finger on the side of the fish. No dent should remain, however, the fish may flake under the pressure.

When cooking fish in a microwave, many manufacturers suggest that the fish is cooked at 50% power for more even cooking. Check your instruction manual for your particular microwave oven.

The oils associated with fish are more beneficial than those associated with meats. Fish contains a high percentage of omega 3 fatty acids.

"MODERATION"
Due to the contamination problems with fish, pregnant women should not eat fish of any type more than twice a week. Bonita, a substitute for tuna and swordfish from the Pacific Ocean has been found to contain high levels of PCB's. White croakers are one of the most popular fish sold in markets on the west coast, however, They have been found to contain the highest levels of DDT and PCB's of any fish.

Since most people do not eat large amounts of fish on a daily basis, the levels of contaminants that are consumed is negligible, and therefore you should not give up eating fish. The safest fish to eat are halibut, sole, skipjack tuna, aquacultured trout and turbot.

"TO SUSHI OR NOT TO SUSHI"
Sushi may contain the larva of a parasite called Anisakis, a roundworm. Violent pain sets in about 12 hours after ingestion, however, some symptoms may not show up for at least a week. Fish used in sushi must be cooked to an internal temperature of 140^0 F. or frozen for 3 days at -5^0 F. to kill the larva. Suspect fish include; mackerel, herring, squid, sardines, bonita, salmon, sea trout and porgy.

"AH SO!"
A frequent trip to the sushi bar for a meal may leave you short of vitamins B_1 and B_2. Raw fish contain a substance that destroys these vitamins.

"BUYER BEWARE"
Approximately 60% of all fish eaten in the United States comes from 116 foreign countries, many have poor sanitary conditions when the fish are processed. Only 5% are actually inspected by U.S. inspectors.

"IT'S A BIRD, IT'S A PLANE, NO, IT'S A FISH INSPECTOR"
The U.S. has 2,500 fish processing plants, 70,000 fishing ships and less than 300 inspectors, who would have to be faster than a speeding bullet to do even a borderline job.

"HOW DRY I AM"
If you are planning a fish barbecue, use the high-fat fishes, they won't dry out as fast and be juicier and more tasty.

SNAILS

Snails are considered a fair source of protein and are cultivated in the United States and Europe on snail farms. Fresh snails have been a gourmet treat for hundreds of years in Europe. If you have a recipe calling for snails, fresh snails must be trimmed and cooked before they can be used in a recipe to replace canned snails.

"YUM, YUM?"
Fresh snails should always be cooked the day they are purchased and should be kept in the refrigerator until you prepare them.

"SNAIL STUFFING"
When purchasing snails in a gourmet shop, the shells will be separated from the snails. The shell should be cleaned before using them by boiling them for 30 minutes in a solution of 1 quart of water, 3 tablespoons of baking soda, and 1 tablespoon of sea salt. Make sure that you dry the insides of the shell before using them with a hair dryer if necessary.

Biologic Value Of Protein Foods

When amino acids are broken down, a percentage of the protein is lost in the process. Therefore, the quality and quantity of that protein that will remain useful to the body is called the "biologic value" of that protein. The following is a classification of the more common proteins we consume:

Protein Foods	Biologic Value %
Egg Yolk	95
Egg, Whole	94
Milk, Whole	90
Milk, Evaporated	88
Milk, Skim	84
Egg White	83
Pork Tenderloin	79
Corn, Germ	78
Beef Liver	77
Beef Muscle	76
Wheat Germ	75
Rice	75
Soybean Flour	75
Ham	74
Swiss cheese	73
Watermelon Seed	73
Red Salmon	72
Cashew	72
Sweet Potato	72
Coconut	71
Sesame Seed	71
Limburger Cheese	69
Potato	67
Whole Wheat	67
Brewer's Yeast	63
Pumpkin Seed	63
Pecan	60

Corn, Whole	60
Soybeans, Raw	59
Rye	58
Peanut, Roasted	56
Walnut	56
White Flour	52
Almond	51
Peas, Raw	48
Cocoa	37

SEAFOOD HOTLINE 1 (800)332-4010

Chapter 14

Beverage Facts

BEVERAGE FACTS

The average person consumes approximately 183 gallons of fluid each year. This includes; water, milk, colas, alcoholic beverages, juices, coffee, and tea.

If fruit juice is labeled "cold-pressed" it is a high quality product with most of its nutrient content in tact. Canned juices are usually an enriched product, since the heat processing destroys most of the vitamins and minerals. Watered down juices may go under a variety of names, such as; orange juice drink, orangeade, orange-flavored drink, or orange juice blend.

A "juice drink" may contain up to 50% juice. An "ade" drink may contain up to 25% juice and a "drink" can have as little as 10% juice. Fruit juices help to maintain a normal acid-base balance in the stomach.

When making lemonade, put the lemons through a meat grinder and you will be surprised at the additional juice you will have and the improved flavor.

To improve the taste of tomato juice, pour the juice into a glass bottle and add one green onion and a stalk of celery cut into small pieces.

Hot drinks will not raise your body temperature in cold weather.

To keep juice cold without watering it down, place a tightly sealed plastic bag of ice into the juice. Also, when serving fruit juices or punch, try making ice cubes from the drinks to avoid the drinks from becoming watered down.

MILK SHAKES Vs THICK SHAKES

The word "milk" in milkshakes use to mean that you were actually purchasing a relatively nutrient-rich food product. The product was high in fat and cholesterol and packed full of calories, but it was the "real thing."

These days, however, with the advent of the "new chemistry" you now receive a drink from some fast food restaurants that they would like you to believe is a "milkshake." Actually it is a chemical concoction made from fat-free milk solids, sweeteners, chemical thickeners, coloring and flavoring agents and saturated fat.

They are not called milkshakes because they are not milkshakes. However, in some cases they may display the "real milk" emblem since they do use parts of the milk. They are high-fat, high-saturated-fat, high calorie drinks that you would be better off without.

SOFT DRINK FACTS

Americans consumed 24 gallons of soft drinks per person in 1970 which has increased to 48 gallons in 1995 or approximately 500 bottles and cans each year. We have increased our soft drink consumption 200% since the 1950's and millions of Americans are now being called "colaholics." Soft drinks account for 25% of all sugar consumed by Americans and the Coca Cola Company purchases more sugar than any other company in the world. Sugar supplies 99% of the 144 calories in a 12 ounce soft drink.

Coca Cola is consumed 190 million times every 24 hours in more than 35 countries speaking 80 languages. The soft drink industry is a $40 billion dollar a year business. Colas have a higher physiological dependence than smoking and alcohol, and is harder to give up.

The carbonating agents carbonic acid and phosphoric acid used in soft drinks are now being implicated in a number of medical problem areas. According to an article in the Pennsylvania Medical Journal, a study showed that the increase carbonic acid use may lead to an increase in nearsightedness.

Excess dietary phosphorus is fast becoming a medical concern, The ideal calcium to phosphorus ratio is approximately 50:50 in adults. The concern is that soft drinks supply an excessive amount of phosphorus, which may upset this ratio. This may lead to a calcium deficiency, which should be of special concern to women who are post-menopausal and entering their "osteoporosis years."

Due to a quantity of refined sugar in soft drinks, they tend to cause a rise in blood sugar levels for a short period of time. The levels may then plummet down causing a severe drop in physical strength and mental alertness. Soft drinks are not recommended by students before taking exams.

The average intake of phosphorus in the United States is presently approximately 1500-1600mg. per day. The recommended daily allowance is 800mg. The following is the phosphorus content of a few of the more common soft drinks:

SOFT DRINK	MILLIGRAMS OF PHOSPHORUS
Coca Cola	69.9
Pepsi-Cola	57.2
Diet Cherry Coke	55.7
Diet Pepsi	49.3
Dr. Pepper	44.7
Tab	44.4
Kool-Aid (Lemonade Flavor)	31.6
Hires Root Beer	22.4
Hawaiian Punch (Lemonade Flavor)	16.7
7-Up	3.0
Canada Dry Ginger Ale	3.0
A & W Root Beer	3.0

A study in Florida showed that people who drank a large number of Dr. Pepper or Diet Coke had problems with recurrent kidney stones probably from the phosphoric acid used in the carbonation process. Person's with stone problems should avoid drinking these beverages.

Soft drinks are the beverage of choice over milk and juice in children across the United States. One of the reasons is the advertising that is run at certain times and days of the week and recently baby bottles are looking like soda cans. Fast food chains have their names and pictures or replicas of their products in every toy store in the United States.

A child who consumes 4 cola drinks a day takes in the equivalent caffeine of two cups of coffee. The carbonic and phosphoric acid content can affect the potencies of a number of vitamins. 40% of the nation's 1-2 years olds drink an average of 9 ounces of soft drinks per day.

Teenagers now prefer soft drinks over milk. 10% are drank before breakfast. Calcium levels are marginal in teenagers due to their soft drink consumption. The acid in soft drinks can also erode tooth enamel.

Americans in 1995 spent three times the dollars on soft drinks than they did on milk, and six times more on alcoholic beverages.

Soft drinks may react with certain antacids, leading to constipation, headaches, and even nausea.

The following is a breakdown of the typical adult consumption of the 183 gallons of beverages annually:

> *44.5 Gallons of Soft Drinks*
> *44.3 Gallons of Water*
> *26.3 Gallons of Coffee*
> *23.8 Gallons of Beer*
> *20.1 Gallons of Milk*
> *23.5 Gallons of Tea, Juice, and other*
> *Alcoholic Beverages*

TEA

Tea was originated in China and was originally used to flavor water that tasted flat after boiling for purification. It was introduced to Japan from China, however the Island of Ceylon is the world's leading producer of tea. Tea is still picked by hand and an experienced tea picker can pluck about 40 pounds of tea leaves a day. Iced tea was first created at the 1904 Louisiana Purchase Exposition in St. Louis, Missouri.

Black teas are the most popular in the United States. In 1996 our tea imports were approximately 140 million pounds with our annual consumption topping 35 billion servings. The United States imports 72% of its tea from India.

One pound of tea will brew 200 cups, which is the equivalent of 200 teabags. Brewed tea contains approximately half the quantity of caffeine as instant coffee.

Tea has diuretic effects and should not be relied upon for providing your daily intake of water.

CLASSIFICATION OF TEAS

Black Teas   Turns black due to oxidation. This is the best quality tea and includes Assam, Ceylon, Darjeeling, English Breakfast, Keemun, Lapsang, and Souchong. Black tea leaves are produced by being allowed to "ferment" for a few hours and then dried.

A new study from the Netherlands could find no link between drinking black tea and cancer cure or prevention. The study was done on 120,000 men and women ages 55-69 who had cancer.

In a Dutch study drinking black tea did show that drinking 4.7 cups of black tea per day reduced the risk of stroke compared to men who only drank 2.6 cups per day.

Green Teas   Oxidation is omitted, The natural color is green. Two main types are Basket Fired and Gunpowder. Green tea comes from an evergreen related to the camellia family. The leaves are steamed. rolled and dried.

Studies in Shanghai and Japan showed that drinking green tea was effective in protecting against stomach cancer and lowered cholesterol and triglyceride levels. However, the effective amount of tea may be 10 cups per day, which is unrealistic for most Americans. In the future the active ingredient may be isolated which will provide a more realistic preventive product.

Oolong Teas   Semi-processed, making the leaves partly green and brown. The two types are Formosa and a combined Oolong/Jasmine.

TEA FACTS

Iced tea and coffee can be greatly improved if the ice cubes are made of tea or coffee instead of water.

You can avoid cloudiness in iced tea by letting freshly brewed tea cool to room temperature before refrigerating it. If the tea does become cloudy, pour little boiling water into it until it becomes clear.

Salada and Bigelow English Teatime are two of the highest caffeine content teas. They average about 60mg. of caffeine per cup.

Tannin found in tea and red wine may interfere with the body's utilization of iron, thiamin, and vitamin B_2.

Current studies do not show any risk factors related to tea drinking and heart disease.

Styrofoam cups should not be used for hot tea if you add lemon. The combination of the two acids and the heat cause a chemical reaction to take place which will break-down the Styrofoam, actually make a hole through the cup and cause a carcinogen to enter the tea from the Styrofoam.

TOXIC TEAS

Buckthorn.......................May cause diarrhea
Burdock.............Blocks nerve impulses to organs
Comfrey....................Can cause liver problems
Foxglove................May cause heart arrythmias
Groundsel.................May cause liver problems
Hops....................can destroy red blood cells
Jimsonweed........Blurred vision and hallucination
Kava-Kava...May cause deafness and loss of balance
Lobelia....................May cause liver problems
Mandrake........May block nerve impulses to organs
Meliot............Can cause tendency to hemorrhage
Nutmeg.....................Can cause hallucinations
Oleander...................Can cause heart stoppage
Pokeweed.........May cause breathing difficulties
Sassafras....................May cause liver cancer
Senna.............................May cause diarrhea
Thorn Apple.................Blocks nerve impulses
Tonka Bean...........Causes tendency to hemorrhage
Woodruff.............Causes tendency to hemorrhage

SPECIAL NOTE:

In recent literature tea has been discussed as a possible protective beverage for cancer. Research is presently being performed but there have not been any definitive studies released that can provide information as to whether tea will act as a cancer preventive or cure.

The substance in iced or hot tea is polyphenol that is suspect to have possible benefits. Canned iced teas would be the worst source of polyphenols due to the high sugar content.

HERBAL WARNING

Historically, the blossoms of the germander plant (Teucrrium chamaedrys) were used for weight-loss. However, according to researchers in France they have been found to cause liver damage.

A number of cases were reported of hepatitis (liver inflammation) in people taking germander for 3-18 weeks. Dosages taken ranged from 600 to 1,620 mg. a day in capsule form. Teas were also used and may be just as harmful.

Most manufacturers have stopped producing the product for weight control, however, it is still available through herb shoppes without a prescription.

COFFEE

Coffee trees originally came from Africa. The first people who actually drink the beverage known as "coffee" were the Arabs, who would not allow the bean to be exported. The coffee beans were finally smuggled to Holland in 1660 and then to Brazil in 1727.

Coffee trees require 70 inches of rainfall annually and one coffee tree produces approximately one to twelve pounds of "coffee cherries" from a six year old tree. Approximately 2,000 coffee cherries are required to produce one pound of coffee.

The United States consumes about 50% of all coffee worldwide, approximately 400 million cups per day. Eight out of 10 adults drink at least one cup of coffee daily. On the average a person drinks 3 cups per day.

Coffee prices have risen dramatically over the last 2 years due to major frosts in Brazil which destroyed over 1 billion pounds of coffee, approximately 10% of the world's coffee supply.

The only coffee grown in the United States is Kona, which is grown on the Island of Hawaii. The coffee is grown in volcanic soil and has the richest coffee flavor in the world.

COFFEE AND CAFFEINE FACTS

The freshness of a cup of coffee only survives 10-30 minutes in a coffee warmer.

Beverages that contain caffeine may cause your skin to become dehydrated and promotes premature aging.

Caffeine takes 30 minutes to affect your brain and lasts for 2-6 hours.

Coffee reduces the healing time of stomach ulcers.

Caffeine may affect zinc absorption, which may adversely affect the prostate gland and possibly reduce sexual urges in some people.

Opened coffee cans should be stored in the refrigerator upside down, The coffee will retain its freshness and flavor for a longer period of time.

The U.S. consumes 3 billion pounds of coffee annually.

Caffeine reduces the bodies ability to handle stress.

Ground coffee oxidizes and loses flavor, it needs to be used within 2-3 days for the best results. Best to buy coffee vacuum packed. Fresh-roasted beans are usually packed in non-airtight bags to allow the carbon monoxide formed during the roasting process to escape. If the carbon monoxide doesn't escape, the coffee will have a poor taste.

A dash of salt added to coffee that has been overcooked or reheated will freshen the taste and revive it.

If you run out of coffee filters, try using a piece of white paper towel with no colored design.

Clean your coffee pot regularly. The slightest hint of soap or scum will alter the taste. Baking soda and hot water work well.

DECAFFEINATED COFFEE

1973	Trichloroethylene used. In 1975 it was implicated in liver cancer in mice.
1975	Methylene Chloride used. In 1981 it was found to cause cancer in laboratory animals. FDA said that the tests were not conclusive. Residues are low in coffee and may not harm humans.
1981	Ethyl Acetate. A number of coffee companies switched to ethyl acetate which is also found in bananas and pineapple. In concentrated form, its vapors have been known to cause damage to lungs, heart and livers in laboratory animals. It is also used as a cleaner and solvent for leather and plastics. Still in use in 1996.

1984	Water Process. Developed by Swiss and Belgium companies. A harmless method, but may cause some flavor loss. Presently, being used by a few U.S. companies.

When purchasing coffee, try to choose a coffee that states it has been decaffeinated using a "water process." Some U.S. companies are supposed to begin selling this type of coffee in the near future.

ESPRESSO BEVERAGES

Espresso	A dark roasted coffee, prepared by a rapid infusion of very hot water through the coffee grounds. The coffee is served in petit cups. Sometimes served with a twist of lemon. The strength of the coffee is controlled by the darkness of the beans after roasting, how dense they are packed and the amount of water that is forced through them.
Cappuccino	A combination of one shot of espresso, hot steamed milk, topped with a frothy head of milk, and to top it off a shake of cinnamon or cocoa. It will vary depending on the strength of the espresso.
Caffe Mocha	One shot of espresso, topped with the froth from hot chocolate.
Caffe Latte	One shot of espresso with a goodly amount of steamed milk. Some are served with a slightly higher amount of milk than espresso. Latte's are usually topped with a large amount of foam, while others have no foam at all.
Macchiato	One shot of espresso with a dollop of foam on top. Served in a petit cup.
Latte	Served in a large glass containing mostly steamed milk with a small amount of espresso on top. The espresso should remain on top but colors the milk a coffee color.
Cafe Au Lait	A mixture of strong coffee (not espresso) and steamed milk. Usually served in bowls.

Caffe Borgia   A frothy caffe mocha with orange and lemon peels.

Cafe L'Amore   A petit cup of espresso with a topping of gelato.

CAFFEINE IN FOODS AND DRUGS

Coffee   Per 8 oz. Serving

Perc...190-270 mg.
Drip...178-200 mg.
Instant.. 90-112 mg.
Decaf.. 3-7   mg.
Instant Decaf.................................... 3   mg.

Tea   Per 8 oz. Serving

Black 5 Minute Brew.............................. 32-78 mg.
Iced... 34-65 mg.
Oolong 5 Minute Brew.............................   45 mg.
Instant.. 20-34 mg.
Decaf.. 8-16 mg.

Chocolate

Cocoa (8 oz.).................................... 6-8 mg.
Milk Chocolate (1 oz.)........................... 5-6 mg.
Semi-Sweet Chocolate (1 oz.)..................... 20-35 mg.

Soft Drinks   Per 12 oz. Serving

Jolt Cola..   68 mg.
Diet Dr. Pepper..................................   65 mg.
Mountain Dew.....................................   49 mg.
Coca Cola..   45 mg.
Diet Coke..   44 mg.
Dr. Pepper.......................................   44 mg.
Pepsi Cola.......................................   35 mg.
Diet Pepsi.......................................   34 mg.
RC Cola..   34 mg.
Mr. Pibb...   33 mg.
7 Up...   0 mg.

Drugs   Per Tablet

Weight Control Aids..............................   250 mg.
Vivarin..   200 mg.
NoDoz..   100 mg.
Excedrin...   65 mg.
Vanquish...   38 mg.

```
Anacin.....................................    35 mg.
Darvon.....................................    33 mg.
Empirin....................................    32 mg.
Midol......................................    32 mg.
Soma.......................................    31 mg.
Aspirin....................................     0 mg.
Tylenol....................................     0 mg.
```

Caffeine is the most popular drug in the United States and can be derived from 60 different plants. It is found naturally in cocoa beans, cola nuts, tea leaves and coffee beans.

Caffeine is a stimulant to the central nervous system and is capable of warding off drowsiness and increasing alertness. It does, however, reduce reaction time to both visual and auditory stimuli.

Studies have shown that caffeine does not cause frequent urination, but does cause an acid increase in the stomach after just two cups. Chronic heartburn sufferers should avoid coffee completely. Caffeine intake should be restricted to 200 mg. per day.

The latest information on pregnancy and caffeine consumption is relating to studies performed at U.C. Berkeley recommending that pregnant women should try and limit their caffeine consumption to a maximum of 300 mg. per day.

ALCOHOLIC BEVERAGES

While alcohol is the most familiar of the multitude of available drugs, it has the distinction of being one of the least potent, ounce for ounce, of any of them. However, it is the most widely abused of all the drugs.

Since it is the least potent, large quantities are consumed which ultimately leads to the many alcohol related problems in todays society. Alcohol is one of the leading health problems in the United States today, surpassed only by heart disease and cancer.

The following is a brief description of the effects alcohol has on the various body systems after only 3 drinks of an 80 proof beverage:

MOUTH

The taste of most alcoholic beverages is not a pleasant experience for the taste buds, and unless the drink is "doctored up" (mixers, etc.). There is no permanent damage to the mouth, but the risk of oral cancer is increased four times.

STOMACH

As the alcohol comes in contact with the stomach lining, the lining may become inflamed and irritation occurs. A number of problems can result, such as small ulcers appear, tiny blood vessels burst, and the normally acid resistant coating losses a high degree of protection. Approximately 20% of the alcohol is absorbed directly into the bloodstream from the stomach.

INTESTINE

Soon the beer, whiskey, vodka or scotch finds its way into your small intestine and the remaining 80% is now absorbed into the bloodstream within 1 hour of consumption.

BLOODSTREAM

The bloodstream transports the alcohol to the processing site, the liver.

LIVER

The liver is assigned the task of breaking down the alcohol. This unique burden reduces the liver's efficiency and over a prolonged period of reduced efficiency may cause permanent liver damage. The liver may develop scar tissue and an increase of cellular fats, leading to the disease cirrhosis. Cirrhosis may cause the liver to stop functioning completely and thus become life threatening.

BRAIN

If you drink more alcohol than the liver can handle it spills over back into the bloodstream and a percentage of it goes to the brain. When alcohol reaches the brain it affects the frontal lobes first, which the are we use for reasoning. This affects our reasoning powers and our judgment.

Next the alcohol affects our speech and vision centers. Following that the effects tend to affect our large muscle control causing us to stagger and we lose our ability to walk a straight line. Eventually if you drink enough you will pass out due to an anesthetic effect on the brain. If you didn't pass out, which ends the drinking you would eventually kill yourself with a lethal dose.

VITAMIN/MINERAL RELATIONSHIP

Vitamins and minerals are required in order for alcohol to be metabolized (broken down) in the liver. If these nutrients are not available in the amounts needed, the liver will have difficulty breaking the alcohol down. The following list are the nutrients needed to break down alcohol:

<u>B VITAMINS</u>   <u>MINERALS</u>

Thiamin   *Iron*
Riboflavin   *Zinc*
Niacin   *Manganese*
Pantothenic Acid   *Phosphorus*
Biotin   *Copper*
                       Magnesium

It would probably be best to take a vitamin/mineral supplement if you plan on drinking more than 2 drinks of any kind.

ALCOHOL FACTS

Americans spend an average of $297 per person on alcoholic beverages annually.

Food slows down the absorption of alcohol, which means that you won't feel the effects as fast. Fatty foods will slow down the rate of absorption even more.

Alcohol has been linked to breast cancer in recent studies by Harvard University.

"BETTER WET YOUR WHISTLE"
The body uses 8 ounces of water to breakdown just 1 ounce of alcohol. Effects of dehydration may include dry mouth, hangovers, headaches, and queasy stomachs.

Scotch has been found to contain small amounts of nitrosamines (a carcinogen) as a result of the method of barley drying.

Food sensitivities may increase if you consume alcohol at the same time.

"A DRINK A DAY, KEEPS THE DOCTOR AWAY?"
Studies show that people who drink two alcoholic drinks per day are less likely to die of coronary heart disease than those who abstain. Helps to reduce stress levels.

A "lite" beer may not refer to the fact that the beer is lower in calories, but may pertain to the color of the beer.

Most alcoholic beverages sold in the United States contains 40% alcohol content or 80 proof. The "proof" figure will always be double the alcohol content.

"MEN BEWARE"
Alcohol causes excess excretion of the mineral zinc, possibly contributing to prostate problems as a man ages. It also causes excretion of magnesium, which may lead to extreme nervousness.

Some of the hangover problems related to alcohol are caused by cogeners (toxic substances produced by fermentation). Alcoholic beverages with the lowest levels of cogeners are vodka and gin. Some of the worst are bourbon, blended scotch, and brandy.

The expensive champagne Dom Perignon was invented by a seventeenth-century French monk. This discovery was instrumental in today's champagne production methods. True champagne only comes from the Champagne region of France.

Champagne should be served at 40^0 to 50^0 F. for most of the standard champagnes, especially the less expensive ones. Cold tends to mask the flavor somewhat.

Never refrigerate champagne for more than 1-2 hours before serving. If left in the refrigerator for long periods the flavor will be poor.

"DE-BUBBLER"
Soap film on a champagne glass or "flute" will ruin the effervescence.

Two glasses of white wine daily can supply you with half you daily requirement of chromium. Plain grape juice will work just as well.

Bourbon is too sweet to be used in most recipes that call for the addition of an alcoholic beverage.

An ounce of 80 proof whiskey, a 5 ounce glass of wine, and a 12 ounce can of beer, all have the same amount of alcohol.

Food sensitivities may increase if you consume alcohol during a meal.

Wine should be counted as part of the liquid in any recipe. As a rule of thumb for almost all sauce and soup recipes, use 1 tablespoon of wine per cup of sauce or soup.

Keep wine stored for cooking in small bottles. The less space between the wine and the top, the longer the wine will retain its flavor.

COOKING WITH WINES

SHERRY

Best when used in soups and sauces. The most popular dishes are those with seafood, chicken, and desserts.

WHITE WINE

Usually used in fish and chicken dishes.

RED WINE

Usually used in meat dishes, stews, gravies, and sauces. Also, used to marinate meats.

DESSERT WINES

These are the sweetest wines and are used in fruit compotes and sweet sauces.

BRANDY

Used in meat and chicken dishes as well as puddings and custards. Very popular in fruit compotes.

If you are having a problem igniting brandy, it is probably not hot enough. Some chef's warm the brandy before adding it to the food to assure that it will light. If you heat it too much, however, it may ignite.

RUM

Usually used in desserts containing pineapple or in sweet sauces.

TYPES OF WINES

BLUSH WINES

These are produced from red grapes from which the juice has had almost no contact with the grape skins. The color will vary depending on the type of grape and whether a small amount of white grape juice has been added. These wines are usually best if served chilled and not icy cold.

FORTIFIED WINES

This is a wine to which brandy or other alcoholic beverage has been added to increase the alcohol content. The most common wines to which this is done is port, sherry, and Marsala.

VINTAGE WINES

These are wines that are produced from grapes grown in a specific year. This information as to the year and even the particular vineyard are usually found on the label. A nonvintage wine may be made from grapes that were harvested in different years and never has a date on the label.

When heating wine, remember that wine reduces from 1 cup to 1/4 cup in about 10 minutes.

"CHEMISTRY 101"
Wine is composed of water, alcohol, various pigments, esters, some vitamins and minerals, acids, and tannins. It does not remain in a constant state, but is continually changing.

"DON'T WHINE ABOUT YOUR WINE"
If you wish to taste the wine in your recipe, don't add the wine until you are near completion since the alcohol content is lost to almost any heat.

To avoid curdling in recipes containing dairy products in which wine is added, try adding the wine before adding the dairy product, then keep the dish warm until served.

Brandy, sherry and whiskey will reduce the "fishiness" of a seafood recipe.

A "lite" beer may not refer to the fact that the beer is lower in calories, but may pertain to the actual color of the beer.

When heating wine, remember that wine will reduce from 1 cup to 1/4 cup in approximately 10 minutes of cooking.

"A GENTLE TOUCH"
Wine should be used in cooking with the utmost discretion, since it should not dominate the taste and should be use only to improve the flavor of the ingredients.

Alcohol may suppress the immune system increasing the risk of colds and infections.

Alcohol can cause adverse reactions with over 100 medications.

Only 5% of all alcoholics are on skid row, 20% are blue collar workers, 25% are white collar workers, and 50% work as managers or professionals.

Pregnant women should abstain from alcohol or they risk having a baby with fetal alcohol syndrome.

TRADITIONAL WINE/FOOD COMBINATIONS

SHERRY   Best when used in soups and sauces. The most popular dishes are those with seafood, chicken and in desserts.

WHITE WINE   Usually used in fish and chicken dishes.

RED WINE   Usually used in meat dishes, stews, gravies, and sauces. May also be used to marinate meats.

DESSERT WINES   These are sweet wines and are used in fruit compotes and sweet sauces.

BRANDY   Used in meat and chicken dishes as well as puddings and custards. Very popular in fruit compotes.

RUM   Usually used in desserts containing pineapple or in sweet sauces.

The best temperature for wine storage is 55^0 F.

White wine should be served at $50-55^0$ F. for the best flavor. Red wine should be served at 65^0 F.

Wine glasses should never be filled, there needs to be room to swirl the wine releasing its full flavor.

If bits of cork break off and fall into the wine, the wine must be strained into a decanter before pouring it.

Red wines that are over 8 years old tend to develop a sediment that accumulates on the bottom. This is harmless and the wine can be strained into a decanter.

The higher the temperature of wine the more rapid it will age. White wines are more susceptible to aging from the heat than red wines.

Always serve a dry wine before a sweet wine and a white wine before a red wine.

BEER FACTS

"BEER BELLY?"
The latest findings are that it is not the consumption of beer that causes the "beer belly." It is the fact that beer tends to slow down the rate at which the body burns fat, which is the real problem. It would be necessary to reduce your fat intake to reduce the problem bulge.

"TIS A SAD FACT"
More beer than milk is consumed in the United States. We average 34 gallons of beer per person opposed to 26 gallons of milk.

TYPES OF BEER

ALE

This may range in color from light to very dark amber with a slightly bitter flavor and is usually stronger than lager beer.

BOCK

A German beer that is usually dark and full-bodied with a slightly sweet flavor and twice as strong as the lager beers.

FRUIT BEER

These are the milder ales and usually flavored with a variety of fruit concentrates.

LAGER

This is a pale colored beer, light-bodied, and has a somewhat mellow flavor.

MALT LIQUOR

A hearty, dark beer that has a somewhat bitter flavor and a high alcohol content.

PORTER BEER

A relatively strong full-bodied beer that has a slightly bittersweet flavor and is usually found as a dark beer.

STOUT

A dark beer that is produced from a dark-roasted barley. It has a bitter flavor and is very hearty.

WHEAT BEER

Produced from a malted wheat. Has a pale color and a somewhat lager flavor.

"LIGHTEN UP!"
In Europe the term "light beer" denotes the difference between pale and dark beers. In the United States "lite beer" usually refers to a beer that is lower in calories.

"STRAIGHTEN UP"
Beer bottles should always be stored in an upright position. If they are on their side more of the beer is exposed to the oxygen in the bottle and oxidation will tend to affect the flavor of the beer.

If beer is moved from different locations in the refrigerator it can affect the flavor. Once a beer is used to a particular temperature it should remain there.

The amount of foam a beer produces is controlled by the temperature of the beer. A cold beer produces less froth than a room temperature beer.

"THE YOUNGER, THE BETTER"
Beer is not like wine and is best when consumed as soon as possible. Aging beer reduces the flavor and overall quality.

"SOONER THAN LATER"
If your beer is not pasteurized, it would be best to drink it within 1-2 weeks after it is produced. The ideal temperatures for "lite" and lager beer is 45^0-50^0 F., ales and porter beers should be at 50^0-60^0 F.

Make sure your beer mugs are soap-free. The slightest hint of soap may cause the beer to collapse the foam and affect the color.

If you like cooking with beer, try using a bock or ale for the best flavor. Light beers do not contribute much flavor to a dish.

Composition of Some Alcohol Beverages

Beverage	Approximate Measure	Weight gm.	Calories	Cho gm.	Alcohol gm.
Ale, mild	1 lg. glass; 8 oz.	230	98	8	8.9
Beer, avg.	1 lg. glass 8 oz.	240	114	10.6	8.9
Benedictine	1 cordial glass	20	69	7	7
Brandy California	1 brandy glass	30	73		10-5
Cider, fermented	6 oz. glass	180	71	2	9
Cognac	1 brandy pony	30	73		10.5
Cordial, Anisette	1 cordial glass	20	74	7	7
Apricot Brandy	1 cordial glass	20	64	6	6
Creme De Menthe	1 cordial glass	20	69	6.6	6.6
Curacoa	1 cordial glass	20	54	6	6
Eggnog, Christmas	1 punch cup; 4 oz.	123	335	18	15
Gin, dry	1 jigger; 1 1/2 oz.	43	105	18	15
Gin Rickey	4 oz. glass	120	150	1.3	21
Highball, avg.	8 oz. glass	240	166		24
Manhattan	1 cocktail glass 3 1/2 oz.	100	164	7.9	19.2
Martini	1 cocktail glass 3 1/2 oz.	100	140	.3	18.5
Mint Julep	1 tall glass; 10 oz.	300	212	2.7	29.2
Old Fashioned	4 oz. glass	100	179	3.5	24
Planter's Punch	3 1/2 oz. glass	100	175	7.9	21.5
Rum	1 jigger; 1 1/2 oz.	43	105		15.1
Tom Collins	1 tall glass; 10 oz.	300	180	9	21.5
Whiskey, Rye	1 jigger; 1 1/2 oz.	43	119		17.2
Scotch	1 jigger; 1 1/2 oz.	43	105		15.1
Wines					
Champagne, domestic	1 wine glass 4 oz.	120	84	3	11
Muscatel or Port	1 wine glass 3 1/2 oz.	100	158	14	15
Sauterne, California	1 wine glass; 3 1/2 oz.	100	84	4	10.5
Sherry, domestic	1 sherry glass; 2 oz,	60	84	4.8	9
Table type	1 wine glass; 3 1/2 oz.	100	85		10
Vermouth, French	1 wine glass; 3 1/2 oz,	100	105	1	15
Vermouth ,Italian	1 wine glass, 3 1/2 oz.	100	167	12	18

*Alcohol yields approximately 7 calories per gram. The percentage of alcohol varies widely in different preparations.

Compiled and calculated: Food Values of Portions Commonly used, 11th Ed., Bowes & Church, 1970.

THE PROBLEM WITH ALCOHOL

Alcohol is the major cause of accidents of all types. Examples of this are as follows:

69   Percent of Drownings
47   Percent of Industrial Injuries
83   Percent of Fatal Fire and Burn Injuries
50   Percent of Motor Vehicle Fatalities
50   Percent of All Divorces

Chapter 15

Grain and Nut Facts

GRAINS

Grains are one of the most important nutrients in our diets and one that is not eaten in anywhere near the levels recommended by nutritionists. They supply complex carbohydrates and are one of the major food sources worldwide. To obtain optimum health a person should consume 5-6 servings of products that contain grains, which include; whole grain cereals, pasta, rice, breads, baked chips, bran muffins, corn, etc.

Only 25% of the American diet contains these complex carbohydrates, compared to countries such as Japan at 65%. As we learn more about nutrition we are beginning to realize that a diet high in meat and meat products is not the healthiest way to go. In recent years the trend is improving as more and more information reaches the public regarding nutrition and health. Americans are taking more interest than ever before in their health, unfortunately it took an increase in cancer and cardiovascular diseases to bring this change about.

One example is the level of pasta consumed per person in the United States which has risen from 11 pounds per person in 1975 to 20 pounds in 1995. The nutrient content of whole grain products, if left in their natural form is excellent.

Consumption of grains in 1970 was 135 pounds per person and in 1994 increased to 189 pounds per person.

GRAIN COOKING CHART

GRAIN	QUANTITY UNCOOKED	AMOUNT OF WATER	COOKING TIME	QUANTITY OF COOKED GRAIN
AMARANTH	1 CUP	3 CUPS	25 MIN.	2 CUPS
BARLEY	1 CUP	4 CUPS	45 MIN.	4 CUPS
BROWN RICE	1 CUP	2.5 CUPS	45 MIN.	3 CUPS
BUCKWHEAT	1 CUP	4 CUPS	20 MIN.	3 CUPS
BULGHUR	1 CUP	2 CUPS	15 MIN.	2.5 CUPS
CORNMEAL	1 CUP	4 CUPS	40 MIN.	4 CUPS
MILLET	1 CUP	3 CUPS	40 MIN.	3 CUPS
OAT BRAN	1 CUP	3 CUPS	2 MIN.	3 CUPS
OAT GROATS	1 CUP	2 CUPS	30 MIN.	2.5 CUPS
ROLLED OATS	1 CUP	2 CUPS	5 MIN.	4 CUPS
QUINONA	1 CUP	2 CUPS	15 MIN.	2 CUPS
RYE	1 CUP	4 CUPS	1 HOUR	2.5 CUPS
WHEAT BERRIES	1 CUP	3 CUPS	1 HOUR	2.5 CUPS
WILD RICE	1 CUP	4 CUPS	40 MIN.	3.5 CUPS

Grains are composed of three parts; the bran, the endosperm, and the germ. The outer covering, or bran, contains the majority of the grains nutrients and almost all of the dietary fiber. This nutrient-rich portion of the kernel is removed during processing to make our refined foods that need to be enriched. The endosperm accounts for the majority of the grain's weight and contains the majority of the protein and carbohydrates. It is this portion that is used to make white flour. The germ portion of the grain contains polyunsaturated fat and is rich in vitamin E and B complex. It is usually removed to avoid rancidity.

GRAIN VARIETIES

AMARANTH

Amaranth has one of the highest levels of protein of any grain as well as being high in calcium, folacin, iron and magnesium, it even contains vitamin C. It was called the miracle grain of the Aztec's. The seeds can be popped like popcorn. It resembles golden poppy seeds and when cooked has a cornlike flavor. It is normally found in health food stores and is more expensive than most other grains. it requires 700,000 seeds to make up 1 pound of the grain.

"SUPER GRAIN"
Amaranth, unlike other grains in not deficient in the amino acid lysine. When this grain is eaten with rice, wheat, or barley it provides a complete protein food containing all the essential amino acids.

BARLEY

The United States is one of the world's major suppliers of barley. However, we prefer to use the barley for the production of beer or as cattle food. It is an excellent source of B vitamins and soluble fiber. One of the favorite forms of barley consumed in this country is as grits. Malted barley can be purchased in health food stores.

BUCKWHEAT

Buckwheat is actually the fruit of a leafy plant related to rhubarb. Has a strong nutlike flavor and is especially high in the amino acid lysine. Considered a minor crop in the United States, it is only found in health food stores and prepared as "kasha."

MILLET

The only grain which is higher in B vitamins than whole wheat or brown rice. It is also an excellent source of copper and iron. Person's with wheat allergies can usually tolerate millet without a problem. Millet is more popular in North Africa, China, India and Ethiopia where it is used to make flatbread.

Millet ranks as one of the highest nutritional quality grains.

OATS

Oats were first produced in the United States in the 1600's. By 1852 they were being packaged and sold with oatmeal becoming the popular breakfast food of that day. In 1995 the annual consumption of oats per person was approximately 14 pounds. Oat bran is being studied in relation to its cholesterol lowering qualities. It is high in a number of vitamins and minerals. Besides oatmeal, oats are used extensively in granola and muesli cereals.

Oats Have the highest fat content of any grain. If stored in an airtight container they will last for about 6-8 months.

TYPES OF OAT PRODUCTS

Instant Oats
Oats that have been sliced into very small pieces, then pre-cooked and dried. They require very little, if any, cooking. These type of oats cannot be used in recipes that call for rolled oats or quick-cooking oats. If you do try and use them your product will probably be a gooey mess.

Oat Bran
This is the ground outer casing of the grain. It is very high in soluble fiber, and may help to lower cholesterol levels.

Oat Flour
The oat grain is very finely ground, it must be mixed with gluten flour due to the lack of gluten or it will not be able to rise.

Quick-Cooking Oats
These are oats that are sliced into many pieces, then steamed and flattened. These oats take only 5 minutes to cook.

Rolled Oats
These are just steamed, flattened and made into flakes. These oats take about 15 minutes to cook. Both the Quick-cooking oats and the rolled oats can be exchanged in recipes with no problem.

Steel-Cut Oats
These are oats that are cut instead of rolled and take a longer amount of time to cook, usually 20-30 minutes. They have a chewy texture.

QUINOA

Related to Swiss chard and spinach, its leaves can be cooked in similar fashion for a nutritious green. It has a delicate flavor and can be a substitute for almost any grain. Quinoa is high in iron, potassium and riboflavin and has good levels of zinc, copper and manganese. Tends to increase 3-4 times in volume when cooked and is usually found only in health food stores. More expensive than most other grains.

RICE

Rice is the most common grain consumed in the United States at about 17 pounds per person, annually. This very low compared to the 300 pounds consumed per capita in Japan and China. Rice was first cultivated in Thailand in 3500 B.C., however, China produces more rice than any other country, almost 90 percent of all the rice grown worldwide. It is an excellent source of the B complex vitamins as well as a number of minerals. Brown rice is more nutritious and higher in the B vitamins and fiber than white rice. Vitamin E is only found in brown rice. Instant brown rice is now becoming available. When brown rice is cooked it looks similar to white rice, but retains a higher amount of nutrients.

Brown rice, rice with only the husk removed is available in small boxes because the bran portion is higher in fat which may cause the rice to go rancid if not used up in a short period of time.

Rice is the staple food of over 60% of the people of the world.

Enriched rice has a few of the vitamins that were lost in the milling process added back. As the rice is washed and cooked, however, it will be lost again, for the most part.

Minute and instant rice have the lowest nutritional content
of any rice. If you burn rice, the burnt taste can be
removed by placing a piece of fresh white bread on top of
the rice, cover the pot and allow to stand for a few
minutes.

"TOUGH STUFF"
Never add salt to rice until fully cooked, it will toughen
the rice. To keep the rice white while cooking, add a few
drops of lemon juice to the water.

Converted rice has been parboiled to remove the surface
starch.

To tenderize brown rice, allow the rice to soak for 1-2
hours before cooking.

Unopened packages of rice should be stored at a cool room
temperature.

Always wash rice before using to remove the hulls and other
debris.

A few minutes before the rice is finished cooking, try
placing a double paper towel just under the lid and allow to
finish cooking, the rice will come out more fluffy and dry.

"RICE 101"
To obtain the right amount of water to cook rice without
measuring, place a quantity of rice in a pot, shake the pot
to smooth out and settle the rice, then place your index
finger lightly on top of the rice....don't make a dent and
add water until your first knuckle is covered (about 1"
above the surface of the rice).

To cook rice, bring water to a boil, cover and simmer on low
heat for 35 minutes, turn off the heat and allow it to stand
covered for 10 minutes.

"FAUX CORN"
Jasmine rice has an aroma and flavor similar to popcorn or
roasted nuts. Makes a great side dish.

To make an excellent dessert from leftover rice, add stiffly
beaten whipped cream to the rice and fresh fruit.

Remember 1/2 cup of rice is only equivalent to 2-3 heaping
tablespoons.

Arkansas is the largest rice producer in the United States.

Long grain rice contains more protein and fewer minerals
than most standard rice.

"FLUFFIER BEATS MUSHIER"
Converted rice is actually parboiled rice, rice which has been soaked, steamed, and dried in such a way as to make it fluffier instead of mushier.

"DOWN THE DRAIN"
Never rinse packaged domestic rice before cooking, it is not necessary and tends to wash away a number of the nutrients that were added in the enrichment process. Cooking removes enough nutrients anyway.

RICE, WILD

This is not a grain, but actually a seed of a shallow water grass and not part of the grain family. It is more expensive than rice with the majority grown in wild rice paddies in Minnesota. The protein content is twice that of standard rice and it is high in the B vitamins as well. It has a more chewy texture and takes longer to cook.

Cooked wild rice will only keep in the refrigerator for 1 week.

RYE

Rye is higher in protein (86% higher than brown rice), iron and the B vitamins than whole wheat. Most breads and rye products are usually made from a combination of rye and whole wheat. It is unusual to find a rye product only rye as the single grain source. Only 25% of the rye crop goes into human food production, the balance being used for alcoholic beverage production and animal food.

TRITICALE

Triticale is a man-made hybrid grain. it is a cross between rye and wheat and has a higher biologic value than even soy beans. may be used as a bread flour due to its excellent gluten content. It has an excellent level of B vitamins. Most likely to only be found in a health food store.

WHEAT

Wheat is the number one grain crop in the world and used mainly in breads and pastas. Unfortunately the majority of the wheat is processed into white flour, reducing its nutrient content. Whole wheat is very high in the B vitamins and numerous minerals including iron. Wheat bran is presently being studied in relation to colon cancer. The hardest wheat is Durham, which is made into seminola and mainly used for pastas.

"DEFINITELY NOT SQUARE"
90% of all Durham wheat grown in the United States is grown in northeastern North Dakota. This area is known as the "Durham triangle."

When Durham wheat is cooked it is always tender and does not become mushy. Durham wheat when used for pasta does not need to be washed before being used.

Wheat berries (cracked wheat) is made from toasted grain keeping the bran and germ intact. It is usually prepared by grinding it into coarse, medium or fine granulations for faster cooking. Cracked wheat can replace rice in most recipes, but is a little more crunchier.

"NO GERMS HERE"
Many hot cereal products are "degerminated" reducing their nutritional quality to make them more palatable. These include Cream of Wheat and Farina.

Bulgar wheat is not as nutritious as 100% whole wheat products unless the granules have retained their dark brown coating. Bulgar wheat should be steamed, then dried and cracked into three different granulations. The coarsest is used for pilaf, medium is used for cereals, and the fine for tabboulch.

"TASTY DISH"
Tabbouleh is a Middle Eastern dish made from cracked wheat or bulgar, lemon juice, olive oil, parsley, dill or mint, plum tomatoes, scallions, minced garlic, salt and pepper, and other cold vegetables as desired.

Wheat bran contains 86% of the niacin, 73% of the pyridoxine, 50% of the pantothenic acid, 42% of the riboflavin, 33% of the thiamin, and 20% of the protein. This all discarded when we make white flour.

Wheat flour is not as good as 100% whole wheat flour or whole grain flour. Wheat flour should be used within 2 months of purchase to avoid rancidity. Refrigeration, however, will delay the rancidity for up to 4 months.

"SHAKE IT UP"
Before measuring a whole grain flour, sift it with a coarse sifter. Avoid the squeeze handle types. Sifting will make a difference of up to 2 tablespoons per cup.

"FINALLY, A GOOD GERM"

Wheat germ is an excellent food, high in nutrients and fiber. However, it is almost impossible to buy fresh wheat germ. Rancidity starts as soon as it is processed (exposed to air) and it should be eaten within 3-6 days of the original processing. If it leaves a bitter taste in your mouth it is not fresh and rancidity and oxidation has taken over. When fresh, wheat germ should have a sweet taste.

"OLYMPICS BOUND?"

A recent product produced from wheat germ or whole wheat is "octacosanol." The product is normally somewhat expensive since it takes 10 pounds of wheat to obtain 1,000 micrograms of octacosanol. Has been used by athletes to improve endurance and slow the buildup of lactic acid. It may also improve the glycogen storage capacity of muscles. Since wheat germ is a source, it would be wise to include _fresh_ wheat germ in an athletes diet.

"DO THE TWIST"

Pretzels are the fastest growing snack food in the United States and almost all products are fat-free.

"HIDE AND SEEK"

Cereals are now changing their names so that you won't see the word "sugar." Remember Post's Super Sugar Crisp which is now Super Golden Crisp and Kellogg's Sugar Frosted Flakes which changed their name to Frosted Flakes.

"A LITTLE OF THIS AND A LITTLE OF THAT = CEREAL"

Be aware that your favorite brand of cereal may contain so many additives that it may not be as healthy a product as you are made to believe.

Kasha (buckwheat groats) is the fruit of the buckwheat plant and is prepared the same as rice. It has a high nutritional value.

FOODS CONTAINING WHEAT

Beverages

Beer	Malt Liqueur	Malted Milk	Gin
Postum	Sanka	Whiskies	Home Brew

Breads

Crackers	Cookies	Biscuits	Rolls
Pretzels	Breads	Macaroni	Spaghetti
Noodles	Dumplings	Muffins	Vermicelli
Pie Crust	Cereals	Graham	Popovers

Pastries and Desserts

Pie   Cake   Doughnuts   Puddings
Candy Bars   Ice Cream   Cones   Waffles

Cereals

Corn Flakes   Crackles   Grapenuts   Wheatena
      Most cereals contain wheat..............

Flours

Buckwheat Flour   Corn Flour   Graham Flour
Rye Flour   White Flour   Gluten Flour
Whole Wheat Flour   Patent Flour   Lima Bean Flour

Miscellaneous

Bouillon Cubes Gravies   Griddle Cakes
Matzos   Sauces   Mayonnaise

The higher the percentage of sugar in cereals, the less room for nutrients. Some cereals have as much 56% sugar.

Quinona (keen-wa) is a grainlike product, related to Swiss chard and spinach. It contains high levels of iron.

NUTS AND SEEDS

The cultivation of nuts can be traced back to 10,000 B.C.. They are nutritious, are a good source of protein, potassium, vitamin E, B vitamins and iron. The only drawback to nuts is their fat content. Nuts are approximately 70-95% fat. Macadamia nuts contain the highest level of fat and join coconut, cashews and Brazil nuts as having their fat high in saturated fats. Peanuts contain the highest level of protein of any nut. Nuts are protected from oxidation of their oils by their shells, damaged nuts should never be purchased.

Seeds of many plants are edible and contain an excellent level of nutrients, especially trace minerals that may be deficient in many of our foods due to poor soil conditions. The most popular eating seeds are; pumpkin, sesame, and sunflower. Eating poppy seeds may cause you to have a positive urine test for drugs. Poppy seeds are a relative of morphine and codeine.

Sunflower seeds produce a similar reaction on the body as smoking a cigarette. It causes the body to produce adrenaline, which will go to the brain, resulting in a pleasant feeling. The seeds, however, must be raw, not roasted.

TYPES OF NUTS

ROASTED NUTS

Usually fried in oil and not always a healthy oil. Many are roasted in coconut oil, which is high in saturated fat.

DRY-ROASTED

Not cooked in an oil., but still contains a high fat content and is usually high in salt, sweeteners and possibly preservatives.

RAW NUTS

Usually sold in vacuum packed cans to retain freshness. May go bad and become rancid very quickly. Should be stored in the refrigerator to slow down the fat breakdown.

DEFATTED (LITE) PEANUTS

Some of the oils have been removed through processing, but their fat content does not really change that much.

GENERAL FACTS

Twice as much of our protein was coming from grains and cereals in the early 1900's compared to 1996.

"BONE FOOD"
One ounce of almonds contain as much calcium as 1/4 cup of milk.

"AH HA, A NUT, THAT'S REALLY NOT A NUT"
Peanuts are really not in the nut family but are actually a relative of the legume family of beans. The two varieties are the Spanish and the Virginia.

If you need to store peanuts, try wrapping them in a plastic bag and keeping them refrigerated. They should last for 6 months and be fresh.

If you are chopping nuts in a blender, add a small amount of sugar and the nut meat won't stick together.

Almond paste is used to make marzipan. It is made from almonds, glycerin, sugar (or substitute), and a liquid, usually almond extract.

"THE OLD SWITCHEROO"
If you run out of chopped nuts, try using a coarse bran, you'll hardly notice the difference. If you run out of coarse bran, use chopped nuts.

To shell nuts more easily, store them in the freezer.

Natural peanut butter will remain fresher longer if it is stored upside down in the refrigerator. If unopened it will stay fresh for 1 year. If refrigerated after opening it will last about 3-4 months.

The oil in natural peanut butter does not stay in suspension due to the lack of a stabilizer chemical.

Peanut butter was first introduced at the St. Louis World's Fair in 1904. It was labeled as a health food.

6 tortillas plus 1/4 cup of beans = 14 grams of top quality protein, has good fiber and is high in vitamins and minerals. Corn tortillas have less than flour ones.

"THE PERFECT PROTEIN"
1 1/2 cup of beans + 4 cups of rice = the protein in a 19 ounce steak.

Macadamia nuts have more fat (96%) and calories than any other nut.

"HEALTH THREAT ALERT"
Nuts, beans, whole grains, corn, and peanut butter should be discarded if there is even the slightest sign of mold or unusual odor. They may contain the dangerous "aflatoxin."

"A GRAIN-RAISING EXPERIENCE"
A good test for the nutritive quality of grains is to pour a small quantity into a pot of water, if the majority of the grain sinks to the bottom, they still contain most of their nutrients. If they float to the top they are no good.

Lentils are tiny seeds that need no soaking before cooking. They are a good source of protein and will cook slower if added to highly acidic foods such as tomatoes.

"HEAVVY"
One ounce of sunflower seeds contains 160 calories and is not a "diet" food as some would have you believe.

"X MARKS THE SPOT"
Chestnuts are the only nut that contains vitamin C, Before cooking or roasting chestnuts, cut an "X" on the pointed end. This will keep them from exploding and make them easier to peel.

"SUPERMAN TO THE RESCUE"
Black walnuts are very difficult to crack open. One of the best ways, if you have a trash compactor, is to place a wood platform on the bottom, raised up a few inches, make sure you have a clean bag and crush away.

FLOUR

Flour is ground from grains, fruits, vegetables, beans, nuts, herbs, and seeds. Primarily it is used in muffins, pies, cakes, cookies, and all other types of baked goods. It is also used as a thickener in soups, gravies, and stews. Many products are "floured" before they are breaded to help the breading adhere better.

The production of flour is mainly be the roller process in which the grain is sent through high speed roller and sifters which crack the grain, separate it from the bran and germ and then grind it into the consistency we are used to.

Wheat flours are more popular than all other types of flour because of its ability to produce "gluten." This protein gives wheat its strength and elasticity, which is important in the production of breads.

TYPES OF FLOURS

All-Purpose Flour (General-Purpose Flour)

A blend of hard and soft-wheat white flour. Has a balance protein/starch content which makes it excellent for breads, rolls, and pastries. It may be used for cakes when cake flour is not available. Pre-sifter all-purpose flour has been milled to a finer texture, is aerated and is best for biscuits, waffles and pancakes.

Bleached Flour

A white flour with a higher gluten-producing potential than other flours. Used mainly in bread-making.

Bran Flour

A whole wheat flour that is mixed with all-purpose white flour and tends to produce a dry effect on baked products.

Bread Flour

An all hard-wheat white flour with a high gluten content used for breads.

Bromated Flour

White flour in which bromate is added to the flour to increasing the usefulness of the gluten. This will make the dough knead more easily and may be used in commercial bread making plants.

Browned Flour

A heated all-purpose white flour that will add color to your recipe.

Cake Flour

A very fine white flour, made entirely of soft wheat flour and is best for baking cakes. Tends to produce a soft-textured, moist cake. Also excellent for soft cookies.

Corn Flour

Usually a very starchy flour used in sauces as a thickener.

Cottonseed Flour

A high protein flour used in baked goods to increase the protein content.

Durham Flour

A white flour that has the highest protein content of any flour and has the ability to produce the most gluten. Usually used in pastas.

Gluten Flour

A very strong white flour that has twice the strength of standard bread flour. Used as an additive flour to other flours.

Instant Flour

White flour that pours and blends easily with liquids and use mainly in sauces, gravies and stews. It is not used for baking due to its fine, powdery texture.

Pastry Flour

The gluten content is between cake flour and all-purpose white flour. Best for light pastries and biscuits.

Potato Flour

A thickener flour used mainly for soups and sauces.

Rice Flour

Excellent for making delicately textured cakes.

Self-Rising Flour

A soft-wheat white flour that should not be used in yeast-leavened baked goods. Contains a leavening agent that tends to cause deterioration and the flour should be used within 1-2 months of purchase.

Seminola

A white flour with a yellow tint made from Durham. Used mainly in commercial pasta and bread. Has a high protein content.

WHOLE WHEAT FLOURS

This a reconstituted flour made from the white flour with the addition of the bran and endosperm. It is sometimes sold as graham flour and has small specks of brown.

Whole wheat flour is more difficult to digest than white flour. It tends to cause flatulence and intestinal upsets in susceptible individuals.

PASTA

There are over 300 varieties of pasta. Pasta consumption in the United States averaged 20 pounds per person, which is low compared to the Italians at 60 pounds per person, per year.

Pasta should be cooked firm (al dente) and slightly chewy. Excessive cooking decreases the nutrient content. When cooking pasta, cover the pot after you place the pasta into boiling water. The water should be kept boiling and allowed to cool down to any great degree for the best results. When draining pasta make sure you warm the colander, a cold colander will cause the pasta to stick together. Adding a small amount of vegetable oil to the water as it is cooking will also help.

"GLUB, GLUB"
Spaghetti products that are advertised as "lite" are lower in calories due to their ability to absorb more water.

Avoid purchasing any pasta product that lists "disodium phosphate" on the list of ingredients. It is a chemical softening agent that helps the pasta cook faster.

The best quality pasta is made from amber durham wheat which is grown in Russia.

"YOU'R GETTING SLEEPY"
Serotonin, a chemical produced by the body helps you relax, levels of which can be increased naturally by consuming a complex carbohydrate (pasta) meal.

Pasta products are easily digested due to their low fiber content. This makes them an ideal food for young children, infants, and the elderly.

Most pasta is made with little or no salt and is excellent for a low sodium diet.

Noodles must contain 5-6% egg solids by law.

Use your frying basket or a pasta cooker, both have a large metal strainer basket. Makes it easy to drain pasta.

"PEEK-A-BOO"
Any pasta that is packaged in clear plastic wrappers is subject to nutrient losses from the lights in the supermarket. Pasta should only be purchased in boxes with only a small window.

One cup of uncooked pasta = two cups of cooked pasta.

Uncooked pasta has a protein content of about 12% which amounts to 3.4 grams per 3/4 cup serving.

If you eat pasta without a protein dish, you may feel somewhat sluggish 1-2 hours later. This is related to a blood sugar level change in some individuals.

Oriental noodle soups as well as many of the more popular soups in the market may contain MSG.

"I CAN MAKE A RAINBOW, MAKE A RAINBOW...."
Pasta made from Durham flour and whole eggs is naturally a golden yellow color. When spinach is added it will turn green, tomato paste will turn it salmon.

PASTA SHAPES

Anellini	Shaped like small rings.
Bavettine	A narrow linguine
Bucantini	Hollow thin strands
Cannaroni	Very wide tubes
Cannelloni	Hollow tubes up to 2 inches long.
Capelli d'Angelo	Angel hair, very thin strands
Capelveneri	Thin medium width noodles
Cappelletti	Shaped like small hats
Cavatappi	Short spiral macaroni shaped
Cavatelli	Short, shells with a rippled edge
Conchiglie	Shaped like a conch shell
Coralli	Tiny soup tubes
Cresti-di-gali	Looks like a roosters comb.
Ditali	Shaped like small thimbles
Ditalini	Small thimble shapes.
Farfalle	Shaped like a bowtie. The word means butterfly in Italian. Sold in two sizes, large and small.
Fedelini	Very fine spaghetti
Fettucce	Flat egg noodles
Fideo	Very thin, coiled strands
Funghini	These pasta are related to the mushroom family and are used in soups and stews.
Fusilli bucati	Corkscrew-shaped pasta.
Gemelli	Two stands of spaghetti twisted together.

Gnocchi	Very small rippled-edge stuffed shells.
Lasagna	Very long, broad noodles.
Linguine	Very narrow pasta ribbons.
Lumache	Pasta shaped like a snails shell.
Macaroni	Curved pasta, comes in many sizes with a hollow center.
Maccheroni	Italian for all types of macaroni.
Mafalde	Ripple-edged flat, broad noodles.
Magliette	Short, curved pasta tubes.
Manicotti	Very large stuffed tubes.
Margherite	Narrow, flat one-sided ripple edged noodles.
Maruzze	Pasta shaped like sea shells.
Mezzani	Short, curved tubes.
Mostaccioli	Tubes, about 2 inches long with a slight curve.
Occhi-di-lupo	Very large tubes of pasta, sometimes referred to as "wolf's eyes."
Orcchiette	Pasta shaped like ears.
Orzo	Pasta, the size and shape of rice.
Pappardelle	Wide noodles with rippled sides.
Pastina	A variety of pasta shapes, usually used in soups.
Penne	Tubes that are diagonally cut with ridged sides.
Perciatelli	Thin, hollow tubes, about twice as thick as spaghetti.
Pezzoccheri	Very thick buckwheat noodles.
Pulcini	Used mainly in soups and called "little chickens."

Quadrettini	Very small pasta squares.
Radiatore	Resemble small radiators.
Ravioli	Small squares of pasta stuffed with different ingredients.
Riccini	Pasta shaped like ringlet curls.
Rigatoni	Very large, grooved shaped pasta.
Riso	Another rice-shaped pasta
Rotelli	Small "wagon wheel" shaped pasta.
Rotini	Very small spiral-shaped pasta.
Ruoti	Round pasta with spokes, looks like a wagon wheel.
Semi de Melone	Small, melon seed-shaped pasta.
Spaghetti	Very long, thin strands of pasta.
Spaghettini	Very thin, spaghetti.
Tagliarini	Pasta shaped like ribbons, usually paper thin.
Tagliatelle	Very long, flat egg noodles.
Tortellini	Pasta that is supposed to resemble the Roman Goddess Venus' navel. "Little Twists."
Tripolini	Very small bow ties that have rounded edges.
Tubetti	Very tiny hollow tubes.
Vermicelli	Italian word for worms, which they resemble. Also known as spaghetti.
Ziti	A very short tubular-shaped pasta.

PASTA SAUCES

Genovese	A thick meat sauce, flavored with garlic, tomato, and herbs.
Marinara	A zesty tomato sauce flavored with garlic and herbs.
Neopolitan	A blend of tomato sauce, herbs, garlic, mushrooms, and bell pepper.
Alfredo	Made with fresh cream, garlic, and Parmesan cheese.
Alla panna	Combines fresh cream, garlic, Marsala wine, Parmesan cheese, mushrooms, and smoked ham.
Formaggi	Made with fresh cream, garlic, Parmesan, Romano, and Swiss cheeses.
Pesto	Made from cold-pressed, extra virgin olive oil, fresh basil, garlic, pine nuts, and fresh cream.
Clam sauce	Made with clam broth, tomatoes, and crushed red pepper. Red is spicy, green is mild.

Chapter 16

Baked Goods

BREAD & MUFFIN FACTS

Baking is a dry-heat method of cooking foods which surrounds the food with heated air. Baking for the most part dries the food and the need to control the amount of moisture lost is important.

Where to store bread will depend on the length of time it will take you to use a loaf of bread. For short period of up to 5-6 days a bread box works fine, it provides a closed compartment which will help keep the bread fresh. If the bread needs to last for more than 6-7 days then store it in the refrigerator to slow the growth of mold.

When thawing frozen bread, it would be best to consume it within 3 days since freezing causes the bread to dry out more quickly.

Bread labeled "cracked wheat" or "wheat bread" usually contains white flour.

For a different type of toast, try lightly buttering a piece of bread on both sides and placing it in the waffle iron.

"HEAVVVY"
Never expect whole wheat bread to rise as high as white bread or be as airy since it has more volume to it.

"SOUND THE ALARM"
If your using a dough mixer, try spraying the dough hook with a vegetable oil to keep the dough from climbing up and escaping.

Since bread tends to retain moisture, it freezes for weeks without losing most of its quality.

"BAGELLA CRAZE"
Bagel sales have increased 169% in the last 10 years and now ranks as one of the most popular breakfast foods. However, the size is increasing as well, turning a normally low-fat, low-calorie food into a high-calorie food.

"FRISBEE, ANYONE?"
French toast, waffles, and pancakes may be made and frozen. They can them be placed into the toaster for an easy breakfast.

"BUYER BEWARE"
When purchasing rye bread, it would be best to read the label. Most rye bread contains white flour and very little rye flour. The label should read "whole rye flour."

To purchase the highest quality white bread, make sure the list of ingredients reads "unbleacheed flour" instead of "white flour" or just "flour."

When baking anything you should always preheat any oven for 15 minutes before baking.

"NEED MY SPACE"
Airspace is important between pans, never place pans next to each other.

"PUCKER UP, DOUGH"
Whole wheat bread will rise faster if you add 1 tablespoon of lemon juice to the dough when you are mixing it.

"STARCH IT"
After you boil potatoes, try using the water in your bread recipe. The water contains a high level of starch which will keep your bread fresher for a longer period at room temperature.

"VITAMIN C TO THE RESCUE"
If you run out of yeast and need to make biscuits, try using a teaspoon of baking soda and an equal amount of vitamin C. The results will be the same, since a similar chemical reaction takes place. Vitamin C is just acidic enough to make it work.

"DON'T SETTLE FOR LESS"
When making pancakes or waffles, be sure to mix the batter between batches to avoid settling and keep it airated. You will be surprised at the difference it will make.

"EASY DOES IT"
100% whole wheat bread will be more moist if you add the flour to the water slowly, mixing thoroughly as you go along. Whole wheat grain tends to absorb water slower than standard refined flours and tends to dry out more as the dough rises.

Baking powder is made from a combination of baking soda, an acid, usually cream of tartar, and cornstarch which will absorb moisture. It is a leavener that is activated as soon as it is moistened. For this reason you combine the wet and dry ingredients separately.

Baking powder should always be stored in a cool, dry location. After it is opened it lasts about 6 months. Be sure to check the date on the box when you first purchase it to be sure it's fresh.

A wet measuring spoon should never be placed into a baking powder box.

Use 1 teaspoon of baking powder for each 1 cup of flour. If your mixing a batter for fried foods reduce to half the amount for each. This will give you a lighter coating.

Baking soda may go by the names of sodium bicarbonate or bicarbonate of soda. It produces carbon dioxide when added to a liquid acid medium (ie: buttermilk, yogurt, etc.).

When baking soda is added to a recipe, it has an immediate rising action with the release of the gas and you must be ready to have your oven already preheated or your pans greased before you even combine the ingredients. Baking soda should be added to dry ingredients first and the wet ingredients just before placing the food into the oven.

Baking soda will last for approximately 6 months if stored in an airtight container and in a cool, dry location.

If you are not sure of the activity level of baking soda, try placing 1/4 teaspoon in about 2 teaspoons of white vinegar, if carbon dioxide bubbles appear it's still has good activity.

Baking soda will not help vegetables to retain their color when added to the cooking water, milk or a small amount of white vinegar will.

"IT MAY BE A KILLER"
Add yeast to water, never water to yeast. The bacteria is easily damaged by the water, so be gentle with the little yeasties.

"WHAT A LITTLE SWEETNESS WILL DO"
Remember, yeast is a living organism with over 3,000 billion cells in a single pound. Their food supply is sugar and they produce alcohol and carbon dioxide (the riser we want). Enzymes in the wheat starch produce the sugar for the reaction to take place.

"SUSPENDED ANIMATION"
Dry yeast will stay fresh longer if refrigerated. The cold slows down the metabolic processes. This works for any product containing yeast. However, make sure you allow it to warm to room temperature before using it. The yeast needs to be woke up.

"ANCIENT YEAST TRAPPERS"
Sourdough bread is produced from a living bacterial culture called a "starter." The starter consists of water and flour which will ferment and trap "wild yeasties" from the air, thus giving it its distinctive "sour" taste.

"SAUNA"
Place a pan of water in the oven when baking bread to keep the crust from becoming too hard. The moisture and resulting steam work great.

"FOILED AGAIN"
Try placing a piece of tin foil under the towel in your bread basket to keep the bread and rolls warm.

"TRY CIRCULATING"
Freshly baked bread should be cooled on an open grill rack to allow air to circulate around the bread as it cools. This will keep the bread from becoming soggy in spots.

"LEVITATION?"
Use a heating pad on medium to assist your dough to rise perfectly for the occasion. Place the dough in a pan, then place the pan on the heating pad.

Bread sticks may contain up to 42% fat.

When making biscuits, never overwork the dough, be gentle if you want to have light biscuits. Overworking the dough makes them tough. Re-rolling also causes the biscuits to become tough.

"A LITTLE DIP WILL DO YA"
If you dip a biscuit cutter in flour it will keep the dough from sticking to it.

"UP, UP, AND AWAY"
Try substituting buttermilk for milk in a muffin recipe for the lightest muffins ever.

If you want your biscuits to be soft, try brushing them with milk or melted salt-free butter, they place them on the pan so that they touch each other.

"FILL'ER UP"
Pita bread pockets usually have no sugar or added fat and contains only 75 calories per ounce. A 7 inch pita pocket weighs only 2 ounces.

"BREAD BUYER BEWARE"
If white bread is your bread of choice, only purchase the bread if it clearly states "enriched", many do not.

When microwaving a sandwich, it would be best to use a firm textured bread such as French or sourdough rolls. Toasted white bread will not remain crisp. The filling may be heated separately. If the filling is heated in the sandwich, be sure and spread it evenly over the bread and very close to the edges. Wait a few minutes before serving as the filling may become very hot.

To increase the protein value of bread, remove 1-2 tablespoons of whole wheat flour and replace it with an equal amount of soy flour.

Most bread machines are timed for the use of dry yeast. Compressed fresh yeast should never be used in bread-baking machines.

THE FOUR MOST POPULAR TYPES OF BREAD

Batter Breads

These are yeast-leavened breads that are always beaten instead of kneaded.

Quick Breads

These use baking powder, baking soda, or eggs as leaveners and should be mixed gently.

Unleavened Breads

This would include matzo, which is flat due to the lack of a leavener.

Yeast Breads

These are leavened with yeast and are always kneaded to stretch the gluten in the flour.

If you use room-temperature ingredients in the yeast and quick-bread types it will accelerate the rising and baking times.

"JUST THE FACTS, MAMME"
Enriched white flour - The milling and bleaching process destroys 86% of the niacin, 73% of the vitamin B_6, 33% of the thiamin, 50% of the pantothenic acid, 42% of the vitamin B_2, and 19% of the protein.

"BE A SHARPIE"
To make cutouts from bread slices, try freezing the bread first. This will give your cutouts clean, sharp edges.

"CHEWY! FOOEY!"
Avoid any baked product made with hydrogenated fats or lard. Hydrogenation changes the texture of the product giving it added body. It allows provides more of a "feel" to the food in your mouth more as well as adding saturated fat.

If you are using raw or unpasteurized milk in your recipe, make sure you scald the milk before using. Raw milk contains an organism that tends to break down the protein structure of the gluten.

Always check baking bread at least 10-15 minutes before the baking time is completed to be sure your oven temperature is accurate.

Freshly baked bread will only stay fresh for about 5 days at room temperature and must be wrapped airtight.

"OVEN SPYING"
When reheating biscuits, place them in a well dampened paper bag, seal it tightly, then heat it in an oven at a very low temperature. To be safe keep an eye on the process, it only takes a 5-10 minutes.

"CIRCULATE"
Always bake biscuits on pans without sides, this allows the heat to circulate more evenly, then use an ice cube divider to cut the biscuits into smaller squares if desired.

"BREAD MAKING 101"
Bread pans should never be scoured to a shiny glean. Bread bakes better in a dull finish aluminum pan. A dark pan may cool too quickly and a shiny pan reflects heat to such a degree that you may not get even cooking.

"BREAD BIOCHEMISTRY"

If your bread is a "low-riser" it may mean that you used old yeast, too little water, or water that was too cold or hot. Remember hot kills yeast activity. Try again with fresh yeast and warm water.

"TIMMMMBER"
If your bread is a "high-riser" or has collapsed you may have added too much yeast or water. Use less next time. Remember a small amount of sugar is yeastie food and will feed the yeast and make the dough rise faster. If too much sugar is used then it will actually act to inhibit the rising.

Occasionally a dough rises too much before the bread starts to bake, thus causing the gluten strands to become weak and too thin leading to the escape of carbon dioxide gas. When this occurs the bread may rise then collapse and have a sunken top.

If your bread has a crumbly texture you might try adding a small amount of salt, which will give the bread a more even texture.

To keep bread fresh when freezing, tuck a paper towel into the bag with the bread or rolls. The paper towel will absorb the moisture that usually makes bread mushy when thawed.

Pumpernickel bread is usually made from white or rye flour, then colored with caramel.

"CUT UP"
To cut pizza more easily, try using a scissors.

Moldy bread should be disposed. The entire loaf should be discarded even if only one piece shows mold. Mold tends to send out feelers that are invisible to the naked eye.

Quick breads are leavened using baking powder or baking soda in place of yeast. No rising time is required since either one will react with water and the acid in the dough at oven temperatures to form carbon dioxide which causes the dough to rise.

If you burn bread, try removing the burned area with a grater.

"JOLLY POOR SHOW"
English muffins have no nutritional advantage over white bread.

Bagels are low-fat and a "normal size" one contains more protein than 2 slices of white bread.

"WHAT A LOSS"
Toasting bread reduces the protein efficiency ratio from 0.90 out of a possible 2.5 to about 0.32, a loss of almost a third of its protein.

"JUST A TEASPOON OF SUGAR...."
Biscuits will bake to a rich golden brown if you add a teaspoon of granulated sugar to the dry ingredients. Adds only 16 calories to the whole batch.

To reduce rising time approximately 1 hour, try adding one extra packet or cube of yeast to the recipe. It will not change the taste.

"OR USE A BELLOWS"
The secret to light dumplings is to puncture them when they are finished cooking, allowing air to circulate within.

"BE GENTLE"
Remember that salt and cold temperatures retard yeast growth, sweetness and warmth (up to a point) increases it. Oven temperatures will kill it.

To replace lost moisture in a stale loaf of bread, wrap it in a damp cloth or towel for about 1-2 minutes, then place it in a 350^0 F. oven for 20 minutes.

"SPRINKLES"
To replace the moisture in French or Italian bread and hard rolls, sprinkle the crust with cold water then place in a 350^0 F. oven for 10 minutes.

"VOILA"
To remove rolls or muffins from a sectioned pan more easily, try placing the pan directly from the oven on a wet towel for 20-30 seconds.

For a thick dough that is difficult to knead, try oiling your hands before you work it. Placing the dough in a plastic bag also may help.

Fresh bread will not get moldy as fast if you wrap it in waxed paper and place it in the refrigerator.

CAKE, PIE AND COOKIE FACTS

Pies and tarts are the most popular desserts with people whose dinner check is under $15.

"PIE PAINTING"
Try brushing the bottom crust of fruit pies with egg whites to prevent the fruit juices from soaking in.

Be sure that your oven has been pre-heated for at least 15-20 minutes before placing a cake in and always bake on the middle shelf of the oven to allow the heat to circulate more evenly.

"HOW DRY I AM?"
To keep a cake from drying out, attach slices of bread with toothpicks to any exposed cut edges. This will keep the area moist without altering the taste.

To ice a many layered cake, try attaching all the layers with a few pieces of spaghetti.

If your icing becomes too thick, try adding a few drops of lemon juice and mix well.

One teaspoon of butter should be added to chocolate when melting it for an icing recipe. This will improve the consistency.

When frosting cakes or pastries, dip your knife in cold water frequently.

If you have a problem whipping cream, try adding a small amount of lemon juice or salt to the cream.

Whipped cream will have an excellent flavor if you add a small amount of honey to it.

To glaze the top of rolls before baking or browning, beat one egg white lightly with one tablespoon of milk and brush on.

When cream cheese is used in any recipe, make sure you blend it well and its light and fluffy before adding any other ingredients to it, especially eggs.

To glaze cakes, try using one tablespoon of milk with a small amount of brown sugar dissolved in it.

If a cake gets hard and stale, throw it out, don't try and repair it.

When your baked food gets stuck to the bottom of the pan, try wrapping the cake pan in a towel when it is still hot or place the pan on a cold, wet towel for a few minutes.

If your having problems with bubbles in the batter, try holding the pan about 5 inches off the floor and drop it. It may take 2-3 times but the bubbles will be all gone.

When preparing a cheesecake, never make any substitutions, go exactly by the recipe. Cheesecakes will come out excellent if the recipe is followed to the letter.

When making cheesecake, be sure that the cheese is at room temperature before using it.

The slower you bake a cheesecake, the less chance there will be of shrinkage.

The oven should never be opened for the first 25-30 minutes when baking cheesecake, or you may cause the cheesecake to develop cracks or partially collapse. However, when cooling the cheesecake you can avoid cracking by leaving it in the oven and leaving the door ajar.

"GET OUT THE PUTTY KNIFE"
Cheesecake cracks can be repaired with creamed cream cheese or sweetened sour cream.

Never substitute a different size pan for a cheesecake recipe, use the exact size recommended.

To avoid your cheesecake cracking from the evaporation of moisture, it will be necessary to increase the humidity in the oven by placing a pan of hot water on the lower shelf before you preheat the oven.

To keep boiled icing from hardening, add 1/3 teaspoon of white vinegar while it is cooking.

A quick frosting can be made by mashing a small boiled potato, then beating in confectioners sugar and a small amount of vanilla.

To prevent icing from running over the tops of cakes, try sprinkling a small amount of corn starch or flour on top before you ice.

Before placing on pie filling be sure it is cool.

"HALF AND HALF"
To make a delicate cake, use half unbleached white cake flour and half whole wheat flour.

Remember cake flour will make a lighter cake due to its lower gluten content. If you don't have any cake flour, try using all-purpose flour, but reduce the amount 2 tablespoons for each cup of cake flour called for.

"BEAT ME, BEAT ME"
Butter or shortening when mixed with sugar needs to be beaten for the complete time the recipe calls for. If you shorten the time you may end up with a coarse-textured or heavy cake.

A richer cake will be produced by substituting 2 egg yolks for 1 whole egg as long as you don't worry about your cholesterol.

Remember never to fill the baking pan more than 3/4 full. The cake needs room to expand.

During the first 15-20 minutes of baking, never open the oven or the cake may fall from the sudden change in temperature.

"HEAVENLY FOOD"
An angel food cake may be left in the pan and covered tightly with tin foil for a day, or until you are ready to frost it.

"THE BLOB?"
The juices from pies will not spread when you dish it out if you blend 1 egg white which has been beaten until stiff with 2 tablespoons of sugar and add it to the filling before baking.

Never pour the pie filling into the shell until you are ready to place the pie in the oven. It will make the bottom crust soggy.

"BE THE FLAKIEST!"
There a number of ways to make a flakier pie crust, the following are just a few; (1) add a teaspoon of vinegar added to pie dough will make a flakier pie crust, (2) try substituting ice-cold sour cream or whipping cream for water, (3) replace your shortening or butter with lard, lard has larger fat crystals and 3 times the polyunsaturates as butter.

"CAKE SCENTS"
Try placing a rose germanium leaf on the bottom of the cake pan for a pleasant scent to a white or yellow cake.

"NEVER USE A SECOND STRINGER"
Never use low-fat margarine for baking. Cakes will collapse and cookies may flatten and lose their form. Low-fat margarine contains a higher air and water content which is released during cooking or baking and alters the consistency of the product. If you recipe calls for butter, use butter, the fat content of stick butter and margarine is the same, butter does have some cholesterol but margarine has trans-fatty acids.

All recipes call for large Grade A eggs unless specified otherwise.

"ABBRA-KA-DABBRA"
If you really want to add some pzazz to your lemon tarts or pies, try rubbing a sugar cube over the surface of a lemon, the sugar cube will extract oils from the lemon that will be released during the cooking process. Use the sugar cube as part of your sugar in the recipe. Also, works well with oranges.

Butter cakes should have an adequate amount of air bubbles in them. They can be produced by creaming the sugar with the fat. All fats for cakes should be at room temperature for the best results. If not they will not blend well with all the ingredients.

"CAKE TENDERIZER"
When making a chiffon cake, try using oil in place of butter to produce a more tender crumb.

"CONSISTENTLY DIFFERENT"
Sweeteners contribute to a cake's tender qualities, but remember that you cannot substitute granulated sugar for powdered sugar. Granulated is for baking, powdered is for frostings and glazes.

"ONLY GREASE YOUR BOTTOM"
If a recipe calls for you to grease or flour the pan, read the directions carefully. The recipe may only call for the bottom of the pan to be greased, not the sides. Some cakes need to be able to climb the sides.

"UP, UP, AND AWAY"
When mixing batter, spray the beaters with a vegetable oil spray before using them and the batter won't climb up the beaters.

"DON'T GIVE YOUR BUTTER A BREAKDOWN"
Butter used in recipes should be soft, not melted. Cakes will have a better texture if a creamy butter is used.

"SPLAT"
If you want to prevent a cake from falling after you place the batter in the pan, raise the pan and drop it suddenly to the counter to release the air bubbles.

"HARD BODY"
To keep a pie crust from becoming soft and soggy during baking, try warming the pan before placing in the undercrust. Another method is to coat the dough with egg white just before baking or spread a thin layer of butter on the pie plate bottom before placing the dough in.

When making a pie crust, be sure and have the kitchen cool. A hot kitchen will affect the results. All pie ingredients should be cold when preparing a crust.

When using a cream filling in a pie, coat the crust with granulated sugar before adding the cream. This may eliminate a soggy crust.

All-purpose flour is best for pie crusts, cake flour is soft and won't give the crust the body it needs, and bread flour contains too high a gluten content to make a tender crust.

Vegetable oil should never be used for a pie crust. Shortening or lard are best.

If you use some sugar in the pastry recipe it will tenderize the dough. Pastry dough should look like coarse-crumbs.

Never add water to pie dough unless it is ice water. Ice cold sour cream added to your recipe instead of ice water will result in a more flaky pie crust.

Never stretch pie dough when you are placing it in the pan. Stretched dough will usually shrink away from the sides.

To stop pie dough from becoming soggy, try refrigerating the crust for 15-20 minutes before using. Another method is to brush it with beaten egg white then refrigerate for 15-20 minutes. The egg white acts as a sealant.

Never place pie filling in a pie shell before it is fully defrosted.

"OUCH, A SCORCHED BOTTOM"
When baking a cake in a glass pan, always lower the oven temperature by 25^0 F. to avoid scorching the bottom of the cake. When reusing a cookie pan for numerous batches, try running the bottom of the pan under cold water without getting the cooking surface wet. This will greatly reduce the risk of "burned bottom" cookies.

"STAY IN SHAPE"
Cookies may also lose their shape when placed on a hot cookie pan. Another good idea is to keep rotating your pans.

Types Of Cookies

Bar Cookies - Soft dough is used and the batter is then placed into a shallow pan and cut into small bars after baking.

Drop Cookies - Made by dropping small amounts of dough onto a cookie sheet.

Hand-Formed Cookies - Made by shaping cookie dough into balls or other shapes by hand.

Pressed Cookies - Made by pressing the cookie dough through a cookie press or bag with a decorative top to make fancy designs or shapes.

Refrigerator Cookies - Made by shaping cookie dough into logs, then refrigerated until firm. They are then sliced and baked.

Rolled Cookies - The cookie dough is rolled out and made into thin layers. Cookie cutters are then used to make different shapes.

To avoid overbaking cookies, just remove them from the oven a few minutes before they are done, the heat from the pan will continue to bake them.

Whipped butter, margarine, or any other soft spread that is high in air and water should never be used in a cookie recipe.

When making cookies, sifting the flour is usually unnecessary.

"DOUBLE DECKER"
If you don't have a thick cookie pan, try baking the cookies on two pans, one on top of the other. It will eliminate burned bottoms.

Cookies should be cooled on an open rack not left in the pan. They should be fully cooled before you store them or they may become soggy.

When mixing the cookie dough, remember that if you over stir the cookies may be tough.

Unbaked cookie dough may be frozen for 10-12 months. Wrap as airtight as you can in freezer bags.

To keep cookies from becoming hard, try placing a slice of very fresh white bread in the cookie jar. Half an apple will work as well.

"THE PEAK OF PERFECTION"
For the highest meringue, add a small amount of baking powder to room temperature egg whites before beating them. Then as you beat them, add 2-3 tablespoons of granulated sugar for each egg used, beating continually. Perfect peaks should form and stand straight upright without keeling over. Another method is to add 1/4 teaspoon of white vinegar for each 3 egg whites, while beating. If you also add 4-5 drops of lemon juice per each cup of cream, the peaks will remain firmer for a longer period of time.

When you bake meringue kisses, line the baking sheet with a brown bag.

Fruit cakes will retain their moisture if wrapped in a damp towel.

"TO THE HEART OF THE MATTER"
To make a heart-shaped cake, bake a round cake and a square cake. Cut the round cake in half, then turn the square cake so that the corners face you in a diamond shape. Place each half of the round cake on the two uppermost sides of the diamond. You are now ready for Valentines Day.

If you bake an angel food cake on the bottom rack at 325^0 F. it will retain moisture better.

The best way to cut an angel food cake or a cake that has just been removed from the oven is with an electric knife or piece of unwaxed dental floss.

If you want to add a crunchy texture to oatmeal cookies, just lightly toast the oatmeal before mixing it into the batter. To toast, just sprinkle the flakes in a thin layer on a cookie sheet and heat at 185^0 F. for 10-15 minutes or until the flakes are brown.

Adding 1/4 teaspoon of almond extract to cherry or peach pies will give them a better flavor.

Sugar cookies will not get stiff or tough if you roll them out in sugar instead of flour.

"WATER RETENTION?"
When making frosting, try using a pinch of baking soda in the powdered sugar and the frosting won't crumble and dry out as quickly. The baking soda will help retain the liquid for a longer period of time.

"A SORROWFUL SITUATION"
To eliminate weeping meringue, try leaving the meringue pie or tart in the oven until it cools. Turn the oven off before it finishes cooking to stop the dish becoming overdone or burnt. Also, meringue tortes should be left in the oven to avoid cracking.

"A REACTOR"
When baking acidic fruit pies such as cherry or apple, try using ceramic or glass pie pans to avoid the pie from turning gray. Citric acid tends to react with a number of metals.

"THE INCREDIBLE SHRINKING PIE CRUST"
When using a pie dough for any pie or pastry product, always chill the dough before working it into a tin. The cold will firm up the fat and will relax the gluten in the flour which will cause it to retain its shape and reduce shrinkage.

If you need to use the same measuring cup for eggs and oil, try measuring the eggs first then the oil. The eggs will coat the cup allowing the oil to flow freely and not stick to the sides.

Baking powder will retain its potency for about 1 year.

Always use unsalted butter when greasing a pan. Salted butter tends to cause foods to stick to the pan.

When measuring flour for a pie crust, always sift the flour first for a more accurate measurement.

To maintain the shape of a souffle, serve immediately after it is steam-baked and always serve it on a warm plate to avoid a collapse.

The secret to keeping pancakes from sticking to a pan or griddle is to fill a small piece of cheesecloth with salt, then rub the bag over the surface of the pan or griddle just before pouring the batter in.

"TO CRUNCH OR NOT TO CRUNCH"
Wheat flour will give you crunchier cookies if butter is used as the shortening. If oil is used the cookies will turn out to be more tender and soft.

"RUNNY IS NOT FUNNY"
To keep the juices inside a pie crust when baking pies with juicy fillings, try adding a tablespoon of tapioca before baking to thicken the mixture. Another method is to insert a tube of macaroni in the center of the top to allow air to escape instead of causing bubbles.

To improve your pancake batter, try adding a tablespoon of maple syrup to the batter.

For the lightest pancakes ever, just use club soda in place of whatever liquid you normally use. They may be so light they will float around the house.

"SECOND DEGREE"
If you have problems with pie shells blistering, try placing a few slices of fresh white bread on the shell before baking. Bake as you normally would then remove the bread just before it is finished to brown the crust.

"RISING TO THE OCCASION"
For a real treat when making pumpkin pie, place a layer of marshmallows on the bottom. While the pie is baking they will rise to the top and form a great topping. The air in the marshmallows is expanded by the heat.

When you recipe calls for the flour to be sifted, add the leavening and the salt when sifting for a better blend.

If cookies are not browning properly, try baking them on a higher shelf.

An easy formula for a great cake flour is to mix together 2 tablespoons of cornstarch in 1 cup of all-purpose or cake flour, preferably cake flour.

If you wish to reduce the sugar needed for a cake, try using a small amount of vanilla extract to replace each 1/2 cup of sugar.

To create a better textured cake, add 2 tablespoons of boiling water to the butter and sugar while they are being mixed.

If you are having difficulty keeping your soft cookies moist, just add a teaspoon of jelly to the batter.

"THIN IS IN"
To make a thinner pie pastry, just coat the board or waxed paper lightly with olive oil. This will prevent the dough from crumbling when stretched.

Icing will remain where you place it if you sprinkle the cake first with powdered sugar.

Spray a small amount of vegetable oil on your knife before cutting a pie with a soft filling.

"WORLD'S GREATEST DOUGHNUT"
Allow freshly made doughnuts to stand for 15-20 minutes before frying. This will allow air to escape and make the doughnuts firmer. By doing this it will also absorb less fat when fried. Another method of reducing the fat that is absorbed is to place the doughnut into boiling water the instant it is removed from the fryer. The hot water will keep the excess grease from sticking to the doughnut and release it into the water. Remove the doughnuts after a few seconds and drain well on a metal rack.

Store cookies in a cookie jar that has a loose fitting lid. If you seal them too tightly they may lose their crispness.

When using plastic cookie cutters, they should be dipped in warm vegetable oil while you are working. You will get a cleaner, more defined edge on the patterns.

To make your cakes and pancakes more moist, try adding a teaspoon of honey to the batter.

To keep waxed paper down on the counter, try wetting the counter first.

The best way to cushion cookies for mailing is with popcorn.

"A CENTER CUT"
Always cut a cake from the center, then you can slide the remains next to each other to keep it fresher.

Cookie dough should be chilled for 15-30 minutes before rolling. This will eliminate the dough sticking to the rolling pin.

Make chocolate slivers by using a potato peeler on a candy bar.

When baking any pie with a graham cracker crust, dip the pan in warm water for 10 seconds and it will be easier to remove it in one piece.

"COOL IT"
Angel food cake should be cooled by turning the pan upside down over a tray of ice cubes.

"TOUGH DECISION"
If you increase the number of egg yolks in a doughnut it will absorb less fat. Egg yolks contain fat and cholesterol and the frying fat is probably high in trans-fatty acids.

"FOWL FACT"
Never taste cake or cookie batter. Over 3,000 people became ill in 1995 from eating batter, egg eggnog, and Caesar salad. Chicken ovaries may be contaminated with salmonella and even though eggs look OK and are not cracked they may still be contaminated.

Before placing a cake on a plate, sprinkle the plate with sugar to prevent the bottom of the cake from sticking.

"A REVIVAL"
If you want to revive a stale cake, just dip it quickly in cold low-fat 1% milk, then heat it in a 350^0 F. oven for 15 minutes or until soft.

Pastry should be rolled out between two pieces of waxed paper, then remove the top sheet to use the pastry for a pie.

"MAKING A WAFFLE HAPPY"
To prevent waffles from sticking to the waffle iron, add a teaspoon of wine to the batter.

"SHAME ON YOU"
If your custard pie shrinks away from the crust, you have baked it too long in too hot an oven.

"INCREASING THE HUMIDITY"
When a bread or cake browns too quickly, place a small pan of warm water above it in the oven.

"GOING UP?"
Try coating dried fruits and nuts with flour being used in the recipe to prevent them from falling to the bottom when baking.

Use a salt shaker filled with powdered or colored sugar for sprinkling candy or cookies. Make the holes larger if needed.

"FAT REDUCTION"
When using a packaged pastry mix for a pie crust, try substituting light cream or "lite" sour cream for the liquid in the recipe.

"DRYING OUT"
Cookies that have become soft can be crisped up by placing them into a low temperature oven for 5 minutes.

"DON'T GET YOUR BOTTOMS WET"
To cook dumplings so that the bottoms don't get soggy, place them on top of the chicken while it is bubbling hot. They will absorb less liquid, bake faster, and be lighter. This also works for fruit cobbler.

"NO GAS MASK NEEDED"
For a great taste, try burying a piece of vanilla bean in an airtight jar of granulated sugar for a few days before using the sugar for baking. The gasses given off by the bean will flavor the sugar.

Grind up a few black walnuts in a blender then add them to a pumpkin pie to improve the flavor.

Place at least 4 toothpicks around the top of a meringue pie and cover with waxed paper, if you are going to carry it any distance.

"IT'S PARTY TIME"
To eliminate a mess, freeze your unfrosted cake before cutting it into decorative party shapes. Your cake will also slice more evenly.

When storing a cake, place half an apple in the container along with the cake. This will help the cake retain moisture and freshness.

HIGH ALTITUDE BAKING

"A PIE IN THE SKY"
When baking at an altitude of over 3,500 feet it is
necessary to increase the temperature 25^0 and add 1
tablespoon of flour to the recipe. Then continue adding 1
tablespoon for every 1,500 feet increase in elevation. ie:
5,000 feet = 2 additional tablespoons of flour.

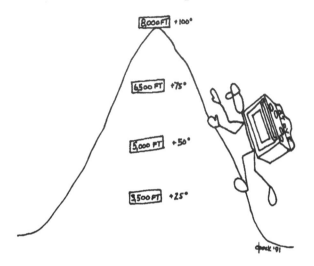

When using leavening, if 1 teaspoon is needed at sea level,
use 2/3 teaspoon at 3,500 feet and 1/2 teaspoon at 5,000
feet. Use 1/4 teaspoon at 6,500 or above.

Never use warped pans for cookies or cakes. The batter may
run and spoil the appearance of the food as well as the
product itself.

Use toothpicks to trace a design on the top of a cake before
adding colored toppings.

The top selling cookies in the United States in 1995

1.	OREO..............................	125 Million Pounds
2.	CHIPS AHOY........................	114 Million Pounds
3.	GENERIC BRAND ICING SANDWICH....	114 Million Pounds
4.	NABISCO NEWTONS, FIG AND APPLE..	77 Million Pounds

"DON'T CROWD ME"
Never overcrowd your oven, heat must circulate freely around
all the items that are baking or they will not bake evenly.

"TOO POOPED TO POP"
If you are having problems with your baking soda, powder, or cream of tartar, they may be too old. Date these products when they are purchased or you may ruin your product.

"ROCK AND ROLL"
To test the leavening ability of baking powder, place 1/2 teaspoon in 1/4 cup of hot water. If the powder is usable the water will bubble actively.

SOUFFLES

When preparing a souffle, be sure and use a souffle dish with straight sides which will force the expanding souffle upwards. Also, always use the exact size dish called for in the recipe.

A souffle dish should always be buttered unless the recipe says not to use any type of fat on the sides of the dish.

If more egg whites than yolks are used, the souffle will be lighter.

"CALL THE PARAMEDICS"
The egg whites should be beaten in such a way as to insure the highest amount of air be trapped. Never overbeat or they will become too dry and cause a collapse.

The oven door should never be opened when the souffle is cooking for at least 3/4 of the cooking time.

"WELL HAUTE DA"
European souffles are usually served a little underdone with a custard textured center. This is usually the preferred method in the finer restaurants.

"A ROYAL MISHAP"
A souffle must be served as soon as it is taken from the oven or the crown may collapse as it cools.

Chapter 17

Fast Food Facts

FAST FOODS, THE GOOD AND THE BAD

Fast food restaurants over the past 5 years have had to make a number of changes and are now offering a number of low-fat alternatives to their usual fare of high-calorie, high-fat foods. The level of education and media information that has been released has had an impact and raised the public's level of health consciousness.

Pizza parlors are now the number one fast food outlet in the United States. There are over 45,000 in operation compared to 37,000 burger stands, adding up to a grand total of 145,000 fast food outlets nationwide and rising everyday. According to National Restaurant Association, 46 million people are served at fast food restaurants every day of the year. fats food restaurants now have 45% of the dining out market.

The Roasted Chicken Invasion

BOSTON CHICKEN 1/2 chicken with skin contains 650 calories and 9.2 teaspoons of fat.

KENNY ROGERS ROASTERS 1/2 chicken with skin contains 750 calories and 8.7 teaspoons of fat.

KENTUCKY FRIED CHICKEN 1/2 chicken with skin contain 670 calories and 9.0 teaspoons of fat.

As you can see there isn't much difference. My personal choice, however, is Kenny Rogers Roasters. The chicken has a better flavor, even if you remove the skin and the assortment of healthy side dishes is excellent.

"LITE?????"
Kentucky Fried Chicken has a new entry into the market "Lite 'N Crispy" chicken, which is fried without the skin. If the public goes for this one, they will consume a product that contains 17 grams of fat which amounts to 52% fat by calories.

"IT'S THE REAL THING, OR IS IT?"
Arby's roast beef is not "real" roast beef, just a processed ground beef with added salt then formed into slices with added water and sodium phosphate. However, it is lower in cholesterol and fat than "real" roast beef or the average hamburger.

"IT'S ABOUT TIME"
Arby's now has an excellent roasted chicken sandwich.

Arby's spread that is used on their buns is made from a soy product that contains a number of artificial flavors and colors.

There is more sodium in most thick shakes than in an order of french fries, due to the additives.

The chocolate coating on soft ice creams is a blend of oils that have a low melting point. Tends to be a high-fat treat.

When the skin and special coatings are consumed on your fried chicken, the product ends up providing you with more fat and calories than a hamburger.

The "pure vegetable oils" now used by (and bragged about) fast food restaurants may be tropical oils containing coconut or palm oil, both high in saturated fat. Also, some chains are pre-frying their fries to reduce cooking time. The pre-frying may be done in high saturated fat oils.

"NUMERO UNO FRENCH FRIES"
The number one fast food restaurant french fry is made by In-N-Out Burger restaurant chain. They are never fried twice and always cut up fresh and fried immediately.

"THE GOOD IS OUT, THE BAD IS BACK"
McDonalds removed the Mclean hamburger which had only 350 calories and 12 grams of fat and replaced it with the Arch Deluxe hamburger which contains 570 calories and 31 grams of fat. Taco Bell removed the Border Light Taco from its menu which had only 140 calories and 5 grams of fat and replaced it with the Big Border Taco which has 290 calories and 17 grams of fat.

When a fish is coated and fried, 50% of its calories are from fat. In most cases this is higher than most burgers.

"HAR, HAR, HAR"
Baked fish is available at Long John Silvers, a reduction of over 200 calories over fried fish. Even the sodium content is in an acceptable range of 361mg. instead of the usual 1200mg.

A shrimp salad at Jack-In-The-Box has only 115 calories and less than 8% fat, providing you use the "lite" dressing.

Burger King's chicken sandwich contains about 42 grams of fat, the equivalent to a pint of ice cream.

"GREAT BUNS"
Multi-grain buns are showing up everywhere and are an excellent source of fiber.

"ALL OF ME, WHY NOT USE ALL OF ME"
When fast food restaurants advertise 100% pure beef and you find a large assortment of "gristle" material in your burger, you might inquire as to the percentage of edible offal they allow in their burger meat. Edible offal may be almost any part of the animal, including bone, it's all 100% beef.

"ADDITIVE ALERT"
Roy Rogers uses MSG as a flavor enhancer in their chicken and roast beef seasonings.

Carl's Jr. has a BBQ Chicken Sandwich that has been approved by the American Heart Association.

McDonald's Chicken McNuggets (6) have 21.3 grams of fat, of which 36.5% is saturated fat.

AVERAGE FAST FOOD MEAL

FOOD	CAL.	CHOL.	SODIUM	FAT
Hamburger on a bun	550	80MG.	800MG.	57%
Regular Fries	250	10mg.	115mg.	52%
Thick Shake	350	31mg.	210mg.	8%
Apple Pie	260	13mg.	427mg.	21%

"A WORD TO THE WISE"
When in a fast food restaurant, try ordering wisely. You can cut your fat and salt intake by 10-40% by smart ordering. Hold the special sauces, mayonnaise, ketchup, meat toppings, extra cheese, and pickles.

"NUMERO UNO?"
The most popular pizza topping is pepperoni. However, if you order extra cheese, you will add more fat than the pepperoni. In Japan the favorite pizza topping is tuna and scallops.

"STUFF IT?"
The new "stuffed pizza crusts" add 13-23 grams of fat to the pizza and an additional 400-500 calories.

"FAT CITY"
Carl's Jr Double Western Cheeseburger tops all charts with over 1,000 calories and a whooping 63 grams of fat, 32 grams of which is saturated. Then add a large fries and a Thickshake.

If you add one packet of ranch dressing to a McDonald's Chef's Salad, it will have more fat than a Big Mac.

When ordering pizza, be sure and ask for white cheese only, it may reduce the total fat content.

The quality of a pizza may depend on the type of flour used to make the crust. It may or may not contain "enriched flour."

"IT'S A HOLY CATASTROPHE"
Nine out of ten people consume doughnuts in a regular basis. Americans eat 10 billion annually.

The FDA has forced the fast food restaurants to provide nutritional information to their patron. Now we need to figure out how to get the patrons to read and understand the information.

"IDAHO'S STATE VEGETABLE"
McDonald's sells 2 million pounds of french fries daily, they contain approximately 1/2 million pounds of saturated fat and trans-fatty acids. 200 hamburgers are ordered every second, 24 hours a day.

"HIGH-FAT SALAD?"
One of the worst salads found at a fast food restaurant was the Taco Bell Taco Salad containing 838 calories and 55 grams of fat, 16 grams of which is saturated.

"THE UNINFORMED LEADING THE ADULT"
In over 83% of American families, kids make the decision as to which fast food restaurant to go to. The deciding factor is the toy promotion.

"LETS CLOG THE ARTERIES UP EARLY"
Over 1.7 million kids under the age of six eat in a fast food restaurant every day. The Vietnam Study on coronary heart disease in 20 year olds showed a significant closure of arteries.

Burger King leads the way with the adult population. Burger King's Weight Watchers Fettucini Broiled Chicken is 33% fat by calories.

A questionable food coloring FD&C Yellow Dye #5 can be found in McDonald's shakes, soft ice cream, Chicken McNuggets, hot cakes, and sundae toppings. MSG can be found in the bacon bits.

RATING THE FAST FOOD RESTAURANTS

FOOD	**BEST RESTAURANT**
1. Pizza (vegetarian)	Godfathers
2. Rotisserie Chicken	Kenny Rogers Roasters
3. Roast Beef Sandwich	Roy Rogers
4. Hamburger (single)	In and Out Burgers
5. Baked Fish Sandwich	Long John Silver's
6. Chicken Sandwich (grilled)	McDonalds

REASONABLE FAST FOOD CHOICES

FOOD	*CALORIES*	*TEASPOONS OF FAT*
BURGER KING		
Plain Bagel	270	1.0
Chef's Salad	178	1.9
Garden Salad	95	1.3
Side Salad	25	0.0
Tater Tenders	213	2.6
CARL'S JR.		
Chicken Salad	200	1.8
Hamburger, Plain	320	3.2
DOMINO'S PIZZA		
Cheese Pizza(2 lg. slices)	375	2.3
Ham Pizza (2 lg. slices)	417	2.5
HARDEE'S		
Chicken Fiesta Salad	280	3.4
Chicken Stix	210	2.0
Fried Chicken Leg(no skin)	120	1.1
Garden Salad	210	3.2
Grilled Chicken Sandwich	310	2.0
Roast Beef Sandwich (reg.)	310	2.7

JACK IN THE BOX

Chicken Fajita Pita	292	1.8
Hamburger, Plain	265	2.5
Hash Browns	115	1.6
Taco	190	2.5

KENTUCKY FRIED CHICKEN

Baked Beans	133	0.4
Chicken Little Sandwich	169	2.3
Cole Slaw	119	1.5
Corn on the Cob	175	0.7

LONG JOHN SILVER'S

Catfish Fillet (1 pc.)	180	2.5
Chicken Plank	110	1.4
Chicken, Baked	140	0.9
Clam Chowder Soup(w/cod)	140	1.4
Cod, Baked	130	0.0
Hushpuppies	70	0.5
Rice Pilaf	250	0.7
Seafood Salad	270	1.6
Vegetables	120	1.4

McDONALD'S

Apple Bran Muffin	190	0.0
Chunky Chicken Salad	140	0.8
Garden Salad	110	1.5
Hamburger, Plain	260	2.2
Hashbrown Potatoes	130	1.7

SUBWAY

Ham Sandwich	360	2.5
Roast Beef Sandwich	375	2.5
Turkey Sandwich	357	2.3

TACO BELL

Pintos and Cheese	190	2.0
Chicken Taco, Soft	210	2.3
Steak Taco, Soft	218	2.5
Taco	183	2.5
Tostada	243	2.5

WENDY'S

Chili	220	1.6
Garden Salad	102	1.1
Grilled Chicken Sandwich	340	3.0
Jr. Cheeseburger	310	3.0
Jr. Hamburger	260	2.1

Almost everyday fast food restaurants are changing their menus, many of these changes are low-calorie and low-fat. Send for their up-to-date nutritional information brochure or ask for one at any restaurant.

If you would like a copy of the list of ingredients in your favorite fast food, just write to the restaurant chain listed below:

Arby's
Ten Piedmont Ctr.
3495 Piedmont Rd. NE
Atlanta, GA 30305

Burger King
P.O. Box 520783
General Mail Facility
Miami, FL 33152

Burger Chef
College Park Pyramids
P.O. Box 927
Indianapolis, IN 46206

Church's Fried Chicken
P.O. Box BH001
San Antonio, TX 78284

Hardee's
1233 N. Church St.
Rocky Mount, NC 27801

Jack In The Box
Foodmaker Inc.
9330 Balboa Ave.
San Diego, CA 92123

Kentucky Fried Chicken
P.O. Box 32070
Louisville, KY 40232

Long John Silver's
P.O. Box 11988
Lexington, KY 40579

McDonald's
McDonald Plaza
Oak Brook, IL 60521

Pizza Hut
P.O. Box 428
Wichita, KS 67201

Roy Rogers
Marriot Corp.
Marriot Dr.
Washington, D.C. 20058

Wendy's
4288 W. Dublin Granville
Dublin, OH 43017

Kenny Rogers Roasters
899 West Cypress Creek Road, Ste #500
Fort Lauderdale, FL 33309
(305)938-0330

Chapter 18

Consumer Awareness Facts

CONSUMER AWARENESS

The safety of our foods is becoming more of a public concern than it has ever been. Our methods of inspection are lacking, the foods are not as nutritious, meats are suspect of disease, some chicken ovaries are contaminated with salmonella, our water supplies are going bad, we allow a degree of contaminants in our foods, and we use hundreds of chemicals in our foods.

Most of these statements were topics of TV expose shows during the 1995-96 season or could be found in newspapers nationwide. The public is becoming more aware that the food we eat may not be as good as we think it is or as nutritious as it should be.

Awareness is the key to eating healthy and knowledge is the key to awareness.

FOOD SAFETY FACTS

In a 1994 national survey 44% of the population, the public felt that the government was only doing a "fair" job of adequately inspecting fruits and vegetables regarding pesticide and fertilizer residues.

"THE BOARD OF CONTROVERSY"
It was determined in a 1994 study that wooden cutting boards may be a source of contamination and cleaning them with hot soapy water doesn't make a difference in the bacteria levels. Bleach will do the trick in most instances, but make sure you dilute it and rinse thoroughly. Plastic cutting boards were then thought to be the best. In 1996 new studies from Wisconsin's Food Research Institute showed that wooden cutting boards may be best and bacterial levels were low after only a few minutes.

"GERM SPREADERS"
Dish rags and sponges should be placed in the wash or dishwasher every day. Paper towels are safer to use in most instances.

"SALMONELLA A GO, GO"
A new study in 1995 completed by the federal government Center for Food Safety and Applied Nutrition showed that only one out of four people wash their cutting boards after cutting or preparing raw meats and poultry.

The bacteria E. coli may be responsible for 20,000+ cases of food poisoning each year. For your protection cook all meat to an internal temperature of 160^0 F. and poultry to 185^0 F.. Wash all fruits and vegetables grown in manure and drink only pasteurized milk and cider. Foodborne illness strikes 80 million Americans annually. Most are mild cases, however, 9,000 are fatal, most caused by meat and poultry.

Reported salmonella food poisoning cases have increased over 40% during the last 10 years. In 1995 almost 40,000 cases of salmonella poisonings were reported (how many were not?). A high percentage of these cases are caused by human error and many have been associated with fast food restaurants.

There are 1800 strains of salmonella, most of which will cause food poisoning.

A large majority of food poisonings are related to the "pot luck" type of event. These are usually a result of poor temperature controls of the foods containing egg or meat products.

Many bacteria are found on the surface of fruits and vegetables, even melons. Wash all surfaces before slicing any type of food, otherwise the knife may carry the bacteria to the inside.

Harmful bacteria do not stop multiplying unless they are refrigerated below 40^0 F. Most refrigerates rarely hold this temperature because of the door being opened too often. Freezing does not kill either, it only stops their growth. The only way to kill the bacteria is to cook the food.

Never store wine or spirits in a lead crystal decanter for a long period. They may leach out the lead. Vinegar dressing may also do the same due to its acidic nature.

Boil all kitchen sponges at least once per week to be sure they are contaminent-free. Use a fresh dish towel after you clean up from handling meats or poultry, then throw it in the wash and don't leave it sit out for further use.

Never reheat or save infant formula after a child has drunken from it. Bacteria will still remain alive.

"BACTERIAL SAUNA"
Never slow-cook a turkey overnight at 200^0 F., it gives the bacteria too long a period of time to multiply. A cooked or raw turkey should never be kept unrefrigerated for more than 45 minutes.

"SNIFF, SNIFF"
If the contents of a can or jar have a bulge, funny smell,
are moldy or have an off color, don't eat it! Never eat
foods directly from a jar or can, saliva may contaminate the
contents. Smelling a moldy food may trigger an allergic
reaction.

"UPSIDE DOWNER"
Never drink from a glass that has been stored upside down
over a bar. Smoke and other contaminants are able to get
into the glass and remain there.

If meats and poultry are being kept warm the temperature
should be no lower than 140^0 F.

Always keep eggs under refrigeration.

Refrigerate all foods as
soon as possible.
Bacterial growth starts
very quickly between 45^0
F. and 120^0 F.

"GIVE 'EM AN INCH...."
Small areas of mold on solid fruits or vegetables can
usually be removed leaving the food still edible. Cut away
an extra inch in case the mold has already sent out feelers.

"MED FACT"
Antibiotics should not be taken with food, it slows down the
absorption of the medication and may reduce its potency.

"CONTAMINATION"
Mayonnaise and salad dressing under normal conditions would
not have to be refrigerated after being opened. The reason
it is recommended is that when you are making a salad, you
tend to keep dipping the spoon in for more mayonnaise and
leaving residues of the salad in the jar. Saliva may also
cause a problem.

Never eat a salad dressing or mayonnaise-based dish unless
you are 100% sure it has been refrigerated and is still
cold. This is the cause of thousands of cases of food
poisoning in the U.S. annually.

Never eat food if it has been prepared by a smoker. Saliva from their hands, from continuously touching the cigarette may contaminate the food.

Never cover refrigerator shelves with tin foil. Air should be able to circulate around the foods.

Peanut butter should be stored in the refrigerator after opening to keep the fats from becoming rancid.

Leftover that have remained in the refrigerator for more than 36 hours should be recooked.

Never place cooked foods on the same surface that has fresh food on it.

Thaw frozen food in the refrigerator, not at room temperature. If this is not possible, use the microwave.

"HIDDEN DANGER"
Your can opener should be washed after each use. Food left behind may be contaminated after a few days and cause food poisoning. This is one of the most common sources of food poisoning.

Always strain soups that may contain pieces of bone through a strainer. Place a coarse strainer inside a fine one for best results.

Never stuff a turkey or other fowl with warm stuffing and leave it overnight in the refrigerator. Bacteria will grow and may not be destroyed by cooking.

To avoid fat from catching fire when broiling meats, place a few pieces of dried bread in the broiler pan to soak up the dripping fat.

Do not leave gravy, stuffing, or cooked fowl at room temperature for more than 30-40 minutes before refrigerating. If you do leave a fowl at room temperature, make sure it is fully cooked according to the thermometer. Salmonella thrive at temperatures of 60^0 to 125^0 F. All stuffing should be removed when the bird is ready for carving, never leave even a small amount of stuffing in the bird.

If turkey or chicken salad is made, wait until the meat is fully cooked before adding any type of salad dressing or mayonnaise.

When you marinate any meat or poultry, make sure you leave it in the refrigerator while it is marinating.

Never place barbecued meat of any type on the same plate that held the raw meat after it has been cooked. This is one of the most common causes of food poisoning when barbecuing. Also, never continue to use the same utensils that touched the raw meat.

"DON'T EAT CHILLY, CHILI"
If you make chili with beef, be sure and reheat it to a temperature of 160^0 F. before serving it.

"NO PICNIC"
Recently, a supermarket placed barbecued birds from the oven onto a pan that had held fresh chicken without washing the pan. Every barbecued chicken was contaminated with Salmonella typhimurium and caused food poisoning at a picnic.

Sulfites in foods for the most part are becoming a chemical of the past, especially after salad bars that were using the chemicals to retard the browning killed a number of people and brought on an untold number of asthmatic attacks. Occasionally, however, they seem to still appear in a few processed food products. The ones to watch out for are the following:

Sodium metabisulfite   Sodium sulfite   Sodium bisulfite
Potassium metabisulfite   Potassium bisulfite Sulfur dioxide

FOOD CANNING FACTS

When processing foods using the "open kettle" method, jars should still be sterilized.

When you cook the foods in the jars, the jars do not need sterilization, but should be thoroughly washed.

"STAY LOOSE!"
Peas, corn, and Lima beans and most meats should be packed loosely, since heat penetration of these foods is slow. Fruits and berries should be packed solidly due to shrinkage and the fact that their texture does not retard the heat penetration.

Never use preservatives or any other type of artificial chemical substance in the food being canned.

"THE DUNGEON?"
Canned foods should always be stored in a cool or cold dark location. The excessive heat of a hot summer may cause a location to develop enough heat to damage the canned foods. Dormant bacteria may become active and start growing.

When canned goods are frozen, then thawed, the texture may change, however, the food is still safe to eat providing the seal is intact.

"INFINITY?"
Canned foods will keep for an indefinite period of time as long as the seal is intact and they have been processed properly.

"ONE RINGY, DINGY......"
After canning the food, tap the top, you should hear a clear "ringing note." If the food is touching the top, this may not occur, but as long as the top does not move up and down, the food does not have to be reprocessed.

Black deposits that are occasionally found on the underneath side of the lid are usually nothing to worry about (as long as the jar is still sealed). These are usually caused by tannins in the food or by hydrogen sulfide released by the foods during their processing.

Corn, Lima beans, and peas or any starchy foods need to be packed loosely due to expansion when processed.

Cloudy liquid in the jar probably means that the food is spoiled. Be very cautious, these jars should be disposed of without being opened. Spores can be released that may be harmful.

The best vinegar to use when pickling is pure apple cider with a 4-5% acidity level.

The outside of jars should be wiped with vinegar before storing to reduce the risk of mold forming on any food that wasn't cleaned off well.

Pickles will become soft if you use a brine or not enough vinegar or if the vinegar acidity id too weak.

To avoid hard water deposits on sealers, add vinegar to the water bath when canning.

Jars of frozen fruits should be thawed in the refrigerator. This will allow the fruit to absorb the sugar as it thaws.

Jelly jars should have a small piece of string placed on top of the wax before sealing the jar. This will make it easier to remove the wax.

SUPERMARKET FACTS

One of the major problems in supermarkets are foods that are placed in a chest freezer in the center of an isle around the holidays and filled up over the freezer line. Chickens and turkeys that are over the line have probably thawed and defrosted a number of times. When you are ready to use them they may be bad.

The cleanliness of a market is important. This includes the floors, counters and even the employees. Check the bathrooms.

"BRRRRRRRRRRRR"
The meat freezer cases should have a thermometer in plain view and should read between 28^0 and 38^0 F.. The dairy products should be stored between 35^0 and 45^0 F.. The ice cream should be at -12^0 F. If you see ice crystals, don't buy the product, moisture has crept in.

Processed hams should be under refrigeration, because of the large volumes sold, they may not be around Easter time.

Never buy a jar if it is sticky or a can if its damaged.

"RING AROUND THE BOTTOM"
Check the bottoms of lettuce, to be sure that the ring in white not brown.

Don't buy frozen foods if there are ice crystals in the package. The food may have thawed and been refrozen.

"WHAT'S IN A NAME"

Many supermarkets have their own brand names to make you think that the product is of a higher grade than it really is. These names are usually similar to ones used by the USDA. They include "Premium," "Quality," "Select Cut," "Market Choice," "Prime Cut," etc.

Shop in a store when it is not crowded so that you can see the specials.

Remember, most weekend specials start mid-week.

Foods placed on the lower shelves are usually the least expensive. The most commonly purchased items are always found in the center of the shelf.

Tumble displays are more common than the old pyramid displays, since shoppers did not want to disturb a neat display.

Buy by the case whenever possible, if the market has a sale.

Check the weight of fruits and vegetables, the heaviest, not the biggest is usually the best value.

Don't be afraid to return poor quality goods.

LABEL TERMINOLOGY

Remember all food ingredients must be on the label.

All additives must be listed.

Symbols:

> "R" means that the trademark used on the label is registered with the U.S. Patent Office.

> "C" indicates that any literary and artistic content on the label is protected by copyright.

> "K" indicates that the food is Kosher.

DINING OUT

Be sure custards, whipped cream or cream-filled desserts are refrigerated or cool when served.

Make sure your dishes and silverware are clean.

If the server touches the top of your water glass, either ask for a new glass or ask for a straw with your water when you first order.

Is the cream for the coffee or tea being kept at room temperature or is it served cold.

If the menu or servers uniform is dirty, leave the restaurant.

If the cook is smoking, it would be best to leave.

If the bathrooms are dirty it is not a good sign.

COMMON FOOD POISONING BACTERIA/VIRUS

ORGANISM	SOURCE	SYMPTOMS APPEAR	TYPICAL DURATION
SALMONELLA	Undercooked, raw poultry, eggs, beef, pork, raw milk	12-48 hours	1-4 days
CAMPYLOBACTER JEJUNI	Raw poultry & milk	2-7 days	1-2 weeks
STAPHLOCOCCUS AUREUS	Improperly handled cooked food.	1-6 hours	12-24 hours
CLOSTRIDIUM PERFRINGENS	Improperly handled meats & foods only kept warm.	8-15 hours	6-24 hours
CLOSTRIDIUM BOTULINUM	Improperly canned foods, raw honey.	18-48 hours	1-7 months
BACILLUS CEREUS	Cooked grains & vegetables left at room temperature.	1-15 hours	6-24 hours
CAMPYLOBACTER	Undercooked chicken.	1-5 hour	12-24 hours
SHIGELLA	Contaminated food with feces from very young children.	36-72 hours	4-8 days

ESCHERICHIA COLI	Ground meat, raw milk, organic vegetables.	5-48 hours	3 days-2 wks
NORWALK VIRUS	Fecal contaminated food or hands.	35-40 hours	2 days
VIBRIO	Raw shellfish	12 hours	2-4 days
LISTERIA	Processed meat, deli-type salads, un-aged cheese.	3-12 hours	2-7 days

CAUTION

Symptoms of food poisoning will vary depending on the level of the germ or viruses ingested. Symptoms usually include chills, stomach ache, nausea, muscle aches, and diarrhea. If diarrhea occurs shortly after a meal it is usually a sign of food poisoning. If you experience any abnormal symptom or even feel that you have eaten a contaminated food, contact your doctor immediately.

Every day 20,000 people get sick from eating foods that are contaminated in the United States.

Radiation Exposed Foods

It is still the feeling by scientists and doctors that radiation exposed foods are not safe to eat. This view, of course, is not shared by the companies that plan to irradiate the foods. It is felt that exposure will destroy the nutritional quality of foods, especially vitamins A, C, E, K and some B's. Certain amino acids and enzymes will also be destroyed.

Studies have shown that radiation exposed foods can cause the following problems in lab animals:

Chromosomal damage   *Testicular tumors*
Reduced rate of offspring   *High infancy mortality*
Sperm-count reduction   *Mutagenicity*

The following symbol denotes radiated foods

CONSUMER NUTRITION SAFETY HOTLINE 1-(800)366-1655

CONSUMER AWARENESS FACTS

The "filth in food" guidelines are controlled by the FDA. The following levels of contamination (insects, etc) if found in food would be the cause for the FDA to take legal action to remove the food from the supermarket. However, the following is just a small sample of foods and contaminants, there is a complete manual listing all foods available from the government Consumer Affairs office in Washington.

Apricots   Canned, average of 2% insect infested or damaged.

Coffee Beans   If 10% by count are infested or insect damaged or show evidence of mold.

Citrus Juice   Canned, microscopic mold count average of 10%. Drosophila and other fly eggs: 5 per 250ml. Drosophila larva: 1 per 250ml.. If average of 5% by count contain larvae.

Peaches   Canned, average of 5% wormy or moldy fruit or 4% if a whole larva or equivalent is found in 20% of the cans.

Popcorn   One rodent pellet in one or more sub-samples or six 10 ounce consumer-size packages, and 1 rodent hair in other sub-samples; or 2 rodent hairs per pound and any rodent hairs in 50% of the sub-samples' 20 gnawed grains per pound and rodent hairs in 50% of the sub-samples.

Asparagus   Canned. 15% of the spears by count infested with 6 attached asparagus beetle eggs or egg sacs.

Broccoli   Frozen, average of 80 aphids or thrips per 100 grams.

Tomato Juice   10 fly eggs per 3 1/2 oz. or 5 fly eggs and 1 larva per 3 1/2 oz. or 2 larva per 3 1/2 oz.

Raisins   Average of 40mm. of sand and grit per 3 1/2 oz. or 10 insects and 35 fly eggs per 8 oz. of golden bleached raisins.

Wheat   One rodent pellet per pint. 1% by weight of insect-damaged kernels.

Brussels Sprouts	Average of 40 aphids per 3 1/2 oz.
Flour	The FDA allows wheat flour to contain approximately 50 insect parts per 2 ounces of flour. These are harmless and won't affect your health.

The government allows 350 pesticide ingredients to be used on crops. Approximately 70 of these have been classified as possible carcinogens.

LABEL TERMINOLOGY

Low Calorie	Allowed to contain only 40 calories per serving or a maximum of .4 calories per gram.
Reduced Calorie	Must have at least 1/3 fewer calories than the original product and should include a comparison of both versions.
Diet or Dietetic	The product may be lower in calories, sodium or sugar.
Lite or Light	This term can have any meaning the manufacture wants to use it for, such as a relation to taste, texture, color, or may have a lowered calorie, fat or sodium content.
No Cholesterol	Means that the item has no cholesterol, but still may be high in saturated fat.
Low Cholesterol	If the label states "low cholesterol" the food cannot contain more than 20mg. % of cholesterol per serving and 2 grams of fat.
Low Fat	When pertaining to dairy products, they must only contain between 0.45-2% fat by weight. By individual serving the food must not contain more than 3% fat per serving size.
Extra Lean	Usually pertains to meat and poultry. They must have no more than 5% fat by weight.

If a food is labeled "extra lean" it may contain more saturated fat than a "low saturated fat" food.

Lean	Usually pertains to meat and poultry. They must have no more than 5% fat by weight.
Leaner	Usually pertains to meat and poultry. Must have at least 25% less fat than the standard.
Sugar-Free or Sugarless	Should contain no table sugar, but still may contain some of the following; honey, corn syrup, sorbital, or fructose. Most of which are just other forms of sugar and still high in calories.
Sodium-Free	Should contain less than 5mg. per serving.
Very Low-Sodium	Contains 35mg. or less per serving.
Low-Sodium	Contain 140mg. or less per serving.
Reduced Sodium	The normal level of sodium in the product has been reduced by at least 75%.
No Salt Added	Salt has not been added during the unsalted processing. The food may still have other ingredients that contain sodium.
Imitation	A food which is a substitute for another food and is usually nutritionally inferior. May still contain the same number of calories and fat.
Organic	May pertain to almost anything. Usually, means a food that is grown without the use of artificial fertilizers.
Natural	May mean anything, no regulations apply and may be seen on foods that have no additives and preservatives.
Enriched	A degraded, processed product that is fortified with a percentage of the nutrients that were originally there.

97% of people who purchased processed foods never read the labels according to a 1988 survey. In 1994 the same survey showed that 84% still don't read the labels. In 1996 we hope that the survey continues to show improvement.

FOOD LABEL DECODING AND TERMINOLOGY

Food labels contain a large amount of important information. To make the information useful, you must first understand the labels. The following facts may make it somewhat easier:

Proteins contain.............4 calories per gram
Carbohydrates contain........4 calories per gram
Fats contain.................9 calories per gram
Alcohol contains.............7 calories per gram

If a label says that it is 80% fat free, it will be necessary to understand what that really means. As an example lets look at two hot dogs.

Hot Dog

Nutritional information per serving
8 links per package

Portion Size....................1 link (56g.)
Calories........................180
Protein......................... 6g.
Carbohydrate................... 2g.
Fat............................ 17g.
Cholesterol.................... 35mg.
Sodium.........................600mg.

    17 grams of fat
X   9 calories per gram
    equals 153 calories from fat

153 divided by 180 X 100 = 85% of calories from fat.

Light Hot Dog (80% fat free)

Nutritional information per serving
8 links per package

Portion size......................1 link (56g.)
Calories..........................130
Protein.......................... 7g.
Carbohydrate.................... 1g.
Fat............................ 11g.
Cholesterol.................... 25mg.
Sodium.........................600mg.

    11 grams of fat
X   9 calories per gram
    equals 99 calories from fat

99 divided by 130 X 100 = 76% of calories from fat

If this seems confusing, it is! This is just another way to fool the consumer into thinking they are getting a much better product, when there is only a minor difference. The reason for this is that a manufacture can list the percent of nutrients by weight (which includes water weight), not percent of fat by calories. The "light" hot dogs are 80% fat free by weight, which is determined by the total weight including the water content, not by the actual food value.

SUPERMARKET SAVVY

The loss of nutrients before you get products home are a real problem. Most of us believe that when we purchase a product from the market it will be fresh and have its full compliment of nutrients.....not so!

MILK - When milk is purchased in clear plastic containers and allowed to sit under the light for 4 hours you will have a 44% loss of vitamin A in low-fat and non-fat milks. The reduction in fat content, which protects the vitamin A is for the most part, absent.

Supermarkets in some areas of the country are now packaging milk in yellow containers to shield a percentage of the light, other markets have installed "light shields" or are storing the milk under the counters to protect them.

JUICES

Juices have a similar problem to milk in that the light may affect their nutrients, especially vitamin C. The juice containers should not be clear.

FRUITS AND VEGETABLES

Some vegetables will last for weeks in the market, under the lights, exposed to the air, and washed and rewashed continually. This reduce the nutrient content and recent studies have shown that frozen fruits and vegetables have more nutrients than fresh in many instances.

The latest fad is buying vegetables in bags already to open and eat. Studies were conducted as soon as these appeared on the market, and to everyone's surprise the nutrient content was excellent, even to the point of surpassing fresh in most cases.

Melons that have been sliced in half and fresh fruits that are sliced and packaged usually have a high nutrient loss, especially in vitamin C. This is caused by the effects of light and air (oxidation).

PASTA

Pasta is packages in thin see-through plastic bags. The effects of light reduces the nutrient content. Buy packages from the bottom of the stack or buy pasta in boxes without windows.

OILS

When an oil is processed the breakdown process is started and rancidity occurs at a slow pace, however, it can increase at a faster pace if the oil is left under the light in a market in a clear container. It is best to purchase oil in dark containers or tins and store in the refrigerator if the oil will not be used up within 30 days.

Cold-pressed extra-virgin olive oil does not need refrigeration for 60 days.

RESTAURANT EATING

Chinese

Soup Choices: Wonton or hot and sour soup

Main Courses: Vegetable dishes cooked in a Wok (stir fried), white rice, chow mien dishes and most vegetable-based dishes.

Stay Clear Of: Anything fried, especially egg rolls and breaded fried anything,. Sweet and sour dishes are high calorie and any dish sauteed in large amounts of oil such as Szechwan style foods.

Italian

Soup Choices: Minestrone.

Main Courses: Any grilled lean meats or seafoods, not creamed, vegetable dishes without creams, pasta with marinara sauce.

Stay Clear Of: Antipasto, garlic bread, dishes topped with cheeses, breaded and fried foods.

French

> Soup Choices: Broth or vegetable soups
>
> Main Courses: Any grilled lean meats or seafood, stews with a tomato base, vegetable dishes without cream sauces.
>
> Stay Clear Of: French onion soup unless they leave the cheese topping off, pate, anything in butter sauce, croissants, au fromage or au gratin dishes.

Mexican

> Soup Choices: Corn tortilla soup.
>
> Main Courses: Bean and rice dishes without cheese, chicken fajitas without cheese, corn tortilla or taco.
>
> Stay Clear Of: Flour tortilla and chips, cheese sauces, guacamole, beef dishes, fried tortilla dishes, enchiladas, burritos.

Fast Food Chains

> Breakfast: Recommended are scrambled eggs, English muffin with no butter, orange juice.
>
> Lunch: Smallest single burger with no cheese or sauce, Carl's Jr. or Roy Rogers roast beef sandwich, baked fish, rotisserie chicken with a salad at Kenny Rogers Roasters, salads with low-cal dressing, small single layer cheese pizza with vegetable toppings, Wendy's chili, Jack-In-The-Box Club Pita.
>
> Stay Clear Of: Everything else.

TRAVELERS FOOD FACTS

The best advise you can get where water is concerned in any foreign country is not to drink it, unless you are staying in a four or five star hotel. While water and food is relatively safe in Europe, Australia, New Zealand, and Japan, the rural areas of these countries still have a problem.

When staying in small hotels, it is recommended that you should not brush your teeth or eat any raw food that has been washed in the water. If you need water, then bring along an immersion heater to boil a small of water or use purifying tablets such as Halzone. If necessary Tincture of Iodine can be used, three drops per quart if the water is cloudy, six drops if the water is clear, then allow the water to stand for 30 minutes.

Water in Mexico and many other countries are still not safe to drink for the most part. Ice cubes have been the cause of many a case of "Montezuma's Revenge" or the "Tourists Two-Step."

Frozen water in test performed by the University of Texas, School of Medicine, showed that water contained bacteria even after being frozen at -20^0 F. for 1 week still contained 10% of the active bacteria that could cause disease. In fact, even after ice cubes were placed in 86 proof Tequila, one organism still survived that was capable of causing diarrhea.

Safe beverages are tea and coffee, providing you are sure that the water has been boiled first. Bottled wine, beer, and canned soft drinks are usually safe. Locally bottled waters are sometimes no safer than tap water. Never drink from a bottle or can, always use a straw or wrapped plastic cup.

Raw vegetables may be contaminated with a number of pesticides. Only eat cooked vegetables and never eat any fruit even after washing, especially if there are any breaks in the skin. If you must eat the fruit or vegetables, clean them under boiling water and skin them if possible before eating.

"A WORD TO THE WISE"
Fish should be thoroughly cooked and eaten within 2 hours of being caught, unless it is being kept under refrigeration in order to avoid bacterial contamination. Shellfish worldwide may carry the hepatitis virus and should be cooked and under no circumstances eaten raw.

Milk and dairy products have been known to cause many travelers a serious problem. If you have any doubts, don't eat them. Never eat custards, whipped cream, filled pastries, sliced meats, meat salads, or other perishables unless they are sold from a refrigerated case.

HEALTH HAZARDS IN OUR EVERYDAY PRODUCTS

ALUMINUM CONTAMINATION

This mineral can affect the absorption of calcium, magnesium, phosphorus, selenium, and fluoride. One of the problem products seems to be aluminum-containing antacids. Excessive intake can be harmful.

ENVIRONMENTAL CONTAMINANTS

Cooking Vessels	Antacids	Deodorants
Industrial Utensils	Lab Equipment	Aluminum Foil
Water Supplies	Aluminum Cans	Bronze Paint
Cables/Wiring	Air/Wastes	Beer
Alum	Nasal Sprays	Toothpaste
Cigarette Filters	Dental Amalgams	Smoke
Pesticides	Vanilla Powder	Baking Powder
Emulsifiers	Medicines	Foods
Coal Burning	Milk Equipment	Table Salt
Packaging Material	Soil	refining

OVEREXPOSURE SYMPTOMS

Skin Reactions	Fatigue	Gastric Upset
Heart Problems	Aching Muscles	Flatulence
Psychosis	Hyperactivity	Senility
Osteoporosis	Rickets	Kidney Problem
Memory Loss	Emphysema	Back Pain

LEAD CONTAMINATION

ENVIRONMENTAL CONTAMINANTS

Urban Atmosphere	Enamels	Batteries
Gasoline Additives	Newsprint	Foundries
Machine Shops	Paints	Printing
Ceramic Glazes	Solder	Insecticides
Cigarette Smoke	Plaster	Ammunitions
Hair Coloring	Putty	Lead Pipes
Wines (lead caps)	Plating	Glass
Old Paints	Mascara	toothpaste

OVEREXPOSURE SYMPTOMS

Headache	Depression	Dizziness
Confusion/Fatigue	Disorientation	Anxiety
Irritability	Nervousness	Insomnia
Drowsiness	Weak Muscles	Gout
Aching Muscles	Abdominal Pain	Ataxia
Memory Loss	Hypertension	Weight Loss
Constipation	Seizures	Hyperactivity
Loss of Appetite	Crying	Withdrawal

CADMIUM CONTAMINATION

ENVIRONMENTAL CONTAMINANTS

Cigarette Smoke	Cisterns	Silver Polish
Galvanized Pipes	Candles	Iron Roofs
Drinking Water	Batteries	Auto Tires
Instant Coffee	Motor Oils	Air Particles
Smelting of Zinc	Auto Exhaust	Incineration
Processed Meats	Shellfish	Cola Drinks
Process Engraving	Electroplating	Plastics
Paint Manufacturing	Rustproofing	Soldering
Fungicide Manuf.	Jewelry Making	Pigments
Welding Metal	Soil	Sewage Sludge
Rubber Carpet Backing	Plastic Tapes	Solders

OVEREXPOSURE SYMPTOMS

Fatigue	Liver Damage	Emphysema
Iron Deficiency Anemia	Loss of Smell	Renal Colic
Teeth Discolorization	Hypertension	Bone Softening
Pain in back and Legs	Arthritis	Cancer
Increased Mortality	Dyspnea	Glucosuria

MERCURY CONTAMINATION

ENVIRONMENTAL CONTAMINANTS

Water Based Paints	Thermometers	Floor Waxes
Dental Amalgams	Batteries	Camera Film
Fabric Softener	Ointments	Antiseptics
Pharmaceuticals	Cosmetics	Plastics
Florescent Lamps	Canvas	Pesticides
Chemical Fertilizers	Burning Coal	Adhesives
Fish/Shellfish	Body Powders	Talc

OVEREXPOSURE SYMPTOMS

Anxiety	Irritability	Drowsiness
Loss of Self Confidence	Nervousness	Shyness
Lack of Self Control	Depression	Weight Loss
Loss of Appetite	Insomnia	Tremors
Memory Losses	Ataxia	Dermatitis
Hearing Losses	Speech Problems	Renal Damage
Muscle Weakness	Paralysis	Vision Problem

Chapter 19

Cooking Facts

COOKING VEGETABLES

Baking Vegetables

Leave the skins on to preserve most of their nutrients. When baking, the vegetable must have a high enough water content not to dry out. Root vegetables are the best to bake as well as any type of potato, winter squash, or onion.

Steaming

Probably the best for all types of vegetables. They retain their nutrients by cooking in a short period of time.

Pressure Cooking

Will shorten cooking times, thus saving the nutrients. The problem is that if you overcook, even for a short period of time, the vegetables turn to mush. Since vegetables all have a different consistency this is a problem.

Pan Frying (Wok)

Using a small amount of oil is another fast method of cooking. Remember, however, that when cooking vegetables in oils, the fat soluble vitamins may end up in the oil. You may wish to keep the oil for the sauce. Wok's need very little oil.

Waterless Cookware

Works well for green leafy vegetables using only the water that adheres to their leaves after washing. This usually takes only 3-5 minutes.

Boiling

When boiling vegetables there are a few good rules to follow:

1. Never place vegetables in cold water and then bring them to a boil. If this is done some vegetables will lose up to 70% of their vitamin C content.

2. Allow the water to boil for at least 2 minutes, the water will lose a high percentage of its oxygen. It is the high oxygen content of the water that reduces the potency of the vitamin C.

3. Cook the vegetables in as large as pieces as possible, then cut them up after cooking.

Crock Pot

Should only be used for vegetables if they are precooked then added to the stew, etc. just before serving.

Microwave

Cooking times are fast allowing the nutrients to be retained. Cooking times will vary depending on the wattage of the unit. If food has a higher water content it will cook better in a microwave. Microwave ovens, however, that do not have a movable turntable may be guilty of leaving "cold spots." These result in undercooked areas of food.

If you wish to brown foods in the microwave, be sure and use a special dish for that purpose. The dish should always be preheated first for the best results. If you don't have a browning dish, try brushing the meat with soy or teriaki sauce.

Less liquid is required when microwaving than in conventional cooking methods.

A steak will continue cooking after it is removed from the microwave and it is best to slightly undercook them.

Measurement Facts

60 drops	= 1 teaspoon	3 teaspoons	= 1 tblsp.
2 tablespoons	= 1 fluid oz.	8 tablespoons	= 1/2 cup
Juice of 1 orange	= 5-6 tsp.	5 large eggs	= 1 cup
2 tblsp. butter	= 1 oz.		

COOKING TEMPERATURES

DEGREES FAHRENHEIT

Ground Beef, pork, lamb....................160
Beef, lamb, veal
     Rare......................................140
     Medium Rare..............................145
     Medium...................................160
     Medium-Well.............................165
     Well-Done...............................170

Pork
```
      Medium.................................160
      Well-Done.............................170
      Precooked.............................140
```

Poultry
```
      Ground Meat...........................165
      Whole Birds...........................185
      Parts.................................175
```

Stuffing (alone or in bird)..............170

Egg Dishes...............................165

Leftovers................................170

THERMOMETERS

DEEP-FAT/CANDY

The bulb should be fully immersed in the candy or food and should never be allowed to touch the bottom of the cooking container. To check the accuracy of the thermometer, place it in boiling water for 3-4 minutes. The temperature should read 212^0 F. or 100^0 C.

FREEZER/REFRIGERATOR

These thermometers read from -20^0 to 80^0 F. Frozen foods should always be stored at 0^0 F. or below to slow nutrient loss and maintain the quality of the food.

MEAT

Insert the thermometer into the center or thickest part of the meat, making sure that it is not resting on a bone.

OVEN

It is wise to check your oven temperature accuracy at least once a month. If the temperature is not accurate it can affect the results of the food being prepared, especially baked goods. The thermometer should be placed in the middle of the center rack.

Some microwave food packaging may now pollute your food. Popcorn and pizza are the two that are under investigation, and may leak hazardous chemicals into the foods.

To avoid damage to your microwave oven, keep a cup of water in it when it is not in use. If it turned on accidentally by a child, damage may occur.

Salt should be added after cooking. It ends to draw the liquids out of the foods.

"KA-BOOM, KA-BOOM"
Never microwave any food is a sealed container, it will probably explode.

"GIVE THE DOG THE BONE"
When microwaving meats with bones, remember the bone tends to attract more microwave energy than the meat, causing the meat not to cook evenly.

"USELESS FACT"
Microwave ovens are used most by people age 44 or younger.

It is just as safe to cook in a microwave oven than to cook on a range or in an oven.

"A FINE MESS YOU'VE GOT INTO"
Never place a whole egg in the shell in a microwave oven, it may explode. When cooking an egg in the microwave that is out of its shell, prick the yolk with a pin or it may pop.

When deep fat frying, use a pure vegetable oil, preferably one with a high smoke point such as Canola, oils can only be cooked to 400^0 F.

Cook all vegetables at the highest power setting in a microwave. The faster they cook the more nutrients they will retain.

"RAPESEED TO THE RESCUE"
Butter, margarine, or lard will burn before they reach a frying temperature. If you must cook with these oils add a small amount of Canola oil to them to raise the smoke point.

"KEEP YOUR SUNNY SIDE UP"
If you want to keep food wrapped in aluminum foil from overbrowning, keep the shiny side of the foil out.

If you need to place a thin layer of oil on food, try using a spray bottle with oil in it. Beats using a brush.

If you are having problems keeping a pot from boiling over, try placing a toothpick between the lid and the pot.

"LE PEW"
If odors are a problem with a particular dish, try placing a cloth that has been dampened with 1/2 water and 1/2 vinegar over the pot. Be sure and make sure that the edges are not near the flame or intense heat.

Unless you fry or cook in an oil, cooking will lower the fat content of any meat.

"WOK IT, WIPE IT"
After you cook in a Wok, wipe the inner surface with vegetable oil to retard the formation of rust.

When foods are cut they should be of uniform size to assure that they will be finished cooking at the same time.

Foods that are to be fried should be dried thoroughly before frying to avoid any splattering.

If you add 1 1/2 teaspoons of butter to a cooking pasta or soup it will not boil over. This doesn't work with vegetable oil.

Always use a shallow pot for cooking roasts, this will allow the air to circulate more efficiently.

Try not to fry too much food at once. The fat may overflow (bubble over) from the temperature difference of the cold food and the hot fat. Also, to avoid food from sticking together, try lifting the basket out of the fat several times before allowing it to remain in the fat.

Place all fried foods on a piece of paper towel for a few minutes before serving to allow the excess oil to drain off.

"PUNCTUATION"
When cooking potatoes, try piercing the skin with a fork to allow the steam to escape.

If you would like a crisp topping on your casserole, try leaving the lid off while it is cooking.

"SPEED COOKING"
When cooking complicated dishes that require long cooking times, try partially cooking them in a microwave first.

"NO SKINHEAD HERE"
When cooking custard, place a piece of waxed paper over the dish while it is still hot. This will avoid a "skin" forming.

Refrigerate all foods as soon as possible, this will help retain the potency of the nutrients. Whole boiled carrots will retain 90% of their vitamin C and most of their minerals, but if they are sliced before cooking, you will lose almost all of the vitamin C and niacin.

Baking soda should not be added to foods while they are cooking, it may destroy certain B vitamins.

"CURDLING UP"
Always cook recipes that contain eggs, sour cream or cream at a lower temperature setting to avoid curdling.

When cooking in a microwave, be sure to place the thicker, tougher areas of the food toward the outer edges of the cooking pan.

PREPARATION OF FOODS

Washing/Soaking

Many vitamins are water soluble and will be lost through washing, scrubbing, or long periods of soaking. Soaking carrots or storing them in glass of water in the refrigerator will cause the loss of the natural sugars, all the B vitamins, vitamin C and D, as well as all the minerals except calcium.

Dice/Slice/Peel/Shred

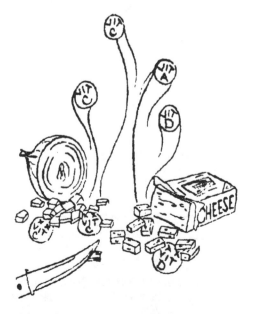

The smaller you cut fruits and vegetables, the more surface you expose to the effects of temperature, the air (oxidation), and light.

Prepare as close to serving time as possible. Shredding for salads cause a 20% loss of vitamin C and an additional 20% loss if the salad stands for an hour before serving.

The skins of fruits and vegetables contain less than 10% of the total nutrients and almost all of any pesticide and fertilizer residues.

COOKWARE, CURRENT 1996 FACTS

Aluminum

Almost 50% of all cookware sold in the United States is aluminum. Recent 1994 evidence shows that aluminum cookware does not pose any health risks, especially the risk of Alzheimer's Disease.

Iron

May supply a small amount of iron in elemental form to your diet, but not enough to be of that much use. Acidic foods such as tomatoes and applesauce when cooked for prolonged periods will absorb the most iron. After 25 minutes spaghetti sauce will have about 6mg. of iron per 3 1/2 ounce serving.

Stainless Steel

Not the best heat conductor unless they have a copper or aluminum bottom. When acidic foods are cooked in stainless steel it may leach a number of metals into the food. These may include chlorine and iron which may be useful, however, others such as nickel are not healthful.

Non-Stick Coating

These include Teflon and Silverstone and are made of a type of fluorocarbon resin that will not react with foods. If a small portion does flake off and get into the food it would pass harmlessly through the body.

"PAN ALERT, PAN ALERT"
Non-stick pans, including all of the best brands may be dangerous if you allow them to boil dry. At 400^0 F. the pans may release toxic fumes after about 20 minutes, enough to make a person sick. This could be even more serious for birds and other small pets.

Glass, Copper, and Enamelled

These do not react with foods and are safe to cook in. Copper conducts heat well and is preferred by many chefs. Copper pans should have a liner of tin or stainless steel to be safe._If you use glass or Corning Ware dishes in the oven you can reduce the heat by 25^0 F.

Clay-Pot Cookware

Remember to always immerse both the top and the bottom in lukewarm water for at least 15 minutes prior to using. Always start to cook in a cold oven and adjust the heat after the cookware is placed into the oven. If sudden changes occur, the cookware may be cracked. Never place a clay cooker on top of the range.

Convection Oven

This method provides a fan that continuously circulates the hot air and cooks the food more evenly and up to three times faster than conventional oven methods. It is great for baked goods and roasts. Make sure you follow the manufacturers recommendations as to temperature since you will be cooking at 20^0 to 75^0 F. less than you would normally. Baked goods, however, are easily overbrowned and need to be watched closely.

BARBECUING FOOD FACTS

Pour enough briquettes into a grocery bag for one barbecue and fold it down. When you have a quantity of bags filled, pile one on top of the other until you are ready to use them. Just place the bag into the old barbee, light the bag and voila, a perfect fire.

When barbecuing, place the herbs on the coals to enhance the flavor of meats and poultry. Try using stalks of savory, rosemary, or dried basil seed pods.

For a smaller fire, fill egg or milk cartons with briquettes, then light as needed.

Charcoal should always be stored in airtight bags. They absorb moisture very easily. Place it in a plastic trash bag and seal it.

When flareups occur from dripping fat, place lettuce leaves over the hot coals to cool them and eliminate the problem.

Flareups can be reduced if you trim all the excess fat from the meat.

"BYE, BYE, EYEBROWS"
Coat your grill with a spray vegetable oil before starting the fire, then clean it shortly after you are through. Never spray the oil on the grill after the fire has started, it may cause a flare-up.

Window cleaner sprayed on a warm grill will make it easier to clean.

HEALTH HINT

Charcoal cooking may release a chemical called a pyrobenzyne into the food. This is a known carcinogen and the black material that forms on top of the foods should be scrapped off. Best to use artificial charcoal or a gas grill. Eating a 12 oz. steal that has been cooked on a charcoal grill is the equivalent to smoking 15 cigarettes.

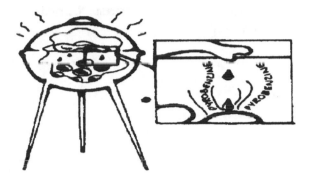

SAUTEING

When sauteing make sure that you only use a small amount of oil. If you wish to have the food turn out crisp you need to heat the oil to a high temperature before adding the food. To test the temperature of the oil, try dropping a small piece of food into the pan, if it sizzles it is ready for you to saute.

Remember to always have the food at room temperature if you wish the food to brown faster and more evenly.

Cold foods tend to stick to the pan.

Before sauteing carrots, potatoes or any dense food, try parboiling them first. This will assure that all the food will be done at the same time.

Foods that are to be sauteed should be dry.

Never salt any food that is to be sauteed, salt tends to retard the browning of foods.

During the sauteing process the pan should be moved gently back and forth a number of times to assure that the browning will be even.

Before sauteing meats, try sprinkling a small amount of sugar on the surface of the meat. The sugar will react with the juices, caramelize, and cause a deeper browning as well as improving the flavor.

Never overcrowd a pan that you are sauteing in. Overcrowding causes poor heat distribution resulting in food that is not evenly browned.

If the fat builds up from the foods that are being sauteed, remove the excess with a bulb baster.

Never cover a pan when sauteeing. Steam tends to build up and the food may become mushy.

Chapter 20

Herb and Spicy Facts

"SCIENCE AT ITS BEST"
Flavoring extracts come in two forms; pure extracts and imitation flavorings. The pure is derived from natural sources, then diluted with ethyl alcohol, while the imitations are artificially produced in a laboratory.

"USE IT OR LOSE IT"
Spices should never be stored near a microwave exhaust fan or range top. The heat tends to cause a loss of flavor, potency, and even color. All spices should be stored in a cool, dry location or in the refrigerator. If stored in the refrigerator, remove them 20 minutes before using. Herbs that contain oil readily oxidize and should always be stored in the refrigerator.

"ARTIFICIAL HERBALATION"
If your spices seem to have lost their potency, try rubbing them between your fingers for a few seconds to revive them.

"OLD WIVES TALE"
Hot or spicy foods do not irritate your stomach or aggravate ulcers in most people.

"GARLIC FLOAT"
Place a toothpick in a garlic clove if you wish to retrieve it.

Sour wines may be used in placer of vinegar.

The flavor of fresh herbs are milder than those from the supermarket that have been dried.

Dried herbs need to be stored in as airtight container as possible.

If you crush dried herbs before using them it will intensify their flavor. You can also intensify their flavor by soaking them for a few seconds in hot water, especially before adding them to a salad.

When doubling a recipe, never double the seasoning until you taste the dish.

ALLSPICE

Has the aroma of a blend of cinnamon, cloves, and nutmeg. Grown in Jamaica, Central America, and South America. Sold both whole and ground. Whole is mainly used in pickling, meats, fish, and gravies, while ground is used in baked goods, relishes, puddings, and fruit preserves. Allspice can also be found in a number of ready-to-serve foods such as, hot dogs, soups, and baked beans.

ANISE

Used in licorice and imported from Mexico and Spain. Marketed as anise seed and also use in candies, cookies, pickling, and as a flavor for beverages. Gives the liquor Anisette its aroma.

BASIL

Comes from a plant belonging to the mint family and is native to India and Iran. Also, known as "sweet basil" which is grown in the United States. Sold in the form of basil leaves and used in tomato paste, squash dishes and turtle soup. Commonly found in ready-to-serve products such as pizza sauce, soups, and dressings.

Fresh basil should be stored in the refrigerator in a slightly moistened plastic bag. It will last about 4-5 days.

Basil loses its flavor fairly quickly when cooked too long, especially on high heat or if subjected to boiling. For this reason it would be best to add basil after the cooking has progressed.

There are a number of varieties of basil which include; lemon and cinnamon basil which have green leaves and opal basil which has purple leaves.

BAY LEAF

Oblong green leaves, sold as leaves and used in stews, sauces, soups, French dressing, dill pickles, etc. Also, used in numerous ready-to-serve foods.

Remember to remove bay leaves from foods before you serve them. If someone eats a piece it will be like eating a mouthful of straw. Never crumble up a bay leaf when using it in a recipe.

The Turkish variety of bay leaf has a milder flavor than the California variety and is not as long and narrow.

CARAWAY SEEDS

Ripe caraway seeds are usually harvested at night before the dew evaporates. Most of the seeds come from the Netherlands. Used in rye bread, cabbage, sauerkraut, soft cheese spreads, sweet pickles and French dressing.

CARDAMOM SEED

Spicy, sweet seeds belonging to the ginger family. They are native to India and are sold whole or ground. They are widely used in Scandinavian dishes as well as pickling, a demitasse flavoring, grape jellies, marmalade, and frankfurters. The seeds are also used to cover up alcohol breathe.

CAYENNE PEPPER

Also, known as red pepper and is available in crushed, ground, or whole forms. Used in relishes, salsas, chili products, Italian and Indian foods, sausages, and dressings.

CELERY SEED

Celery seed and celery salt are used in salad dressings, fish dishes, salads, pickling, and many vegetable dishes. Celery flakes are made from dehydrated leaves and the stalks and used in the same dishes.

CHERVIL

A French herb, excellent for flavoring salad dressings and usually used in a similar fashion to parsley.

CHILI PEPPERS

To prepare them you must toast them with a long handled fork on top of the stove, making sure that they blister on all sides. As soon as the skin is evenly blistered and puffed away from the pulp, lay the pods on a cloth, sprinkle them with water and cover them with another cloth to produce steam. The skins will then pull away easily and the seeds and veins can be removed. All of the pulp can be used, but only use a few of the seeds.

Chili peppers and paprika are high in vitamin A and one teaspoon can supply you with 25% of your daily requirement.

CHILI POWDER

"BETTER GLUE YOUR HAT DOWN"
The major ingredients are cumin seed, chili peppers, oregano, salt, cayenne pepper, garlic, and allspice.

CHIVES

Chives are a member of the onion family, however, they have a milder bite than most onions. They are used to flavor dips, sauces, soups, baked potatoes, etc.

CINNAMON

Found mostly in China and Indonesia. Comes from the bark of the Laurel tree. The cassia variety is used in the United States in its whole form for preserving, flavoring puddings, pickling, and hot wine drinks. The ground form is used for baked goods, sweet pickles, ketchup, vegetables, apple butter, mustards, and spiced peaches.

CLOVE

Comes from a tree which is a member of the Myrtle family and was first discovered in Indonesia. Whole cloves are used for pickling, ham roasts, and spiced syrups. Ground cloves are used for baked goods, puddings, mustards, soups, hot dogs, sausages, and barbecue sauces.

CORIANDER SEED

Comes from a small plant of the carrot family and has a sweet musky flavor. It is native to the Mediterranean Area and sold in seed and ground forms. It is normally used in gingerbread, cookies, cakes, biscuits, poultry stuffing, and is excellent when rubbed on fresh pork before roasting.

CUMIN SEED

The flavor resembles caraway seed and is native to Egypt. Sold in both seed and ground forms. It is an essential ingredient in curry, chili powder, soups, stuffed eggs, and chili con carne.

CURRY POWDER

Curry powder is a blend of 20 spices, herbs, and seeds. Some of the ingredients include; chili peppers, cloves, coriander, fennel seed, nutmeg, mace, cayenne, black pepper, sesame seed, saffron, turmeric, etc. The turmeric gives many of dishes the yellow coloring.

DILL

Used for pickling, soups, sauerkraut, salads, fish, and meat sauces, green apple pie, and spiced vinegar. Great for livening up egg salad.

FENNEL

Has a sweet anise-like flavor and is available in seed form. Used in Italian sausage, sweet pickles, fish dishes, candies, pastries, oxtail soup, and pizza sauce. May also be brewed as an herbal tea and served hot.

When used in dishes fennel has a pleasant flavor and is sweeter than anise.

When you choose fresh fennel, make sure you choose clean, crisp bulbs that are not browning. The stalks and greenery should be removed before using.

Fennel bulbs and the base may be used raw in salads.

FENUGREEK

Has a similar aroma to curry powder and has a bitter flavor. Mainly used in imitation maple syrup.

GARLIC

Grown in the United States and a member of the lily family. It is sold as garlic salt and powder and is used in hundreds of dishes from pizza sauces to chicken pot pies. Historically, garlic has been used for centuries to cure illnesses such as high blood pressure, etc. Garlic is more nutritious than onions.

Americans consume 250 million pounds of garlic annually.

To peel garlic easily, place it in very hot water for 2-3 minutes. Garlic cloves should be stored in a small amount of pure cold-pressed extra virgin olive oil to avoid drying out. The oil can still be used and will have a pleasant garlic flavor.

When peeling garlic, try rinsing the garlic under hot water first. This will loosen the skin.

Before adding your salad ingredients to a bowl, rub a clove of crushed garlic on the sides of the bowl.

Garlic salt may contain over 900mg. of salt per teaspoon.

There are 300 varieties of garlic grown worldwide.

Elephant garlic has very large cloves, but is actually a form of leek with a milder flavor than most garlic.

If garlic is not peeled and the cloves separated it will store for 3 months in a cool, dark, dry location. If the garlic sprouts, the garlic and the sprouts can still be used for salads, etc.

If you nick a clove of garlic, it must be used or it will get moldy very quickly.

To make garlic vinegar, place 2-3 fresh cloves in each pint of white vinegar and allow to stand for 2 weeks before using.

Never freeze garlic, it will destroy the flavor.

Garlic products should contain an antibacterial or acidifying agent such as phosphoric acid or citric acid. If not the product should be under constant refrigeration.

Garlic butter should only be stored in the refrigerator for 10-14 days then discarded. Most products do not have a preservative. Once garlic has been processed it is more perishable than most people realize.

"WITH TONGUE IN CHEEK, NOT TEETH ON NECK"
Historically, garlic has been known to repel vampires. However, there are certain rules to follow which include; the garlic must be no more than 1 month old, made into a circle, worn around the neck with each whole garlic separated by 2 inches.

GINGER

Has a pungent spicy flavor and is grown in India and West Africa. Sold in whole or ground form and is used in pickling, conserves, dried fruits, gingerbread, and pumpkin pie.

MACE

Mace is a fleshy growth between the nutmeg shell and the outer husk. It is sold in ground form and used in pound cake and chocolate dishes. In its whole form it is used in pickling, ketchup, baked beans, soups, deviled chicken and ham spreads, and French dressing.

MARJORAM

Has a sweet nutty flavor and is an herb of the mint family. It is available in leaves and is imported from France, Chile, and Peru. Usually, combined with other herbs and used in soups, stews, poultry seasoning, sauces, and fish dishes.

MINT FLAKES

They are dehydrated flakes of peppermint and spearmint plants and have a strong sweet flavor. They are grown in the United States and Europe and use to flavor stews, soups, fish dishes, sauces, desserts, and jellies. For an instant breathe freshener, try chewing a few mint leaves.

MSG

Monosodium glutamate has no taste of its own but helps to bring out the natural food flavors as well as helping foods blend with each other. MSG has been implicated in adverse physiological symptoms, some of which include, light flashes and miner allergic reactions. Should be used in moderation only.

MUSTARD

Either yellow or white seeds will produce a mild mustard, while the brown seeds produce the more spicy variety. Powdered mustard has almost no aroma until mixed with a liquid. Mustard has hundreds of uses and is one of the popular spices worldwide.

Most mustards will last about 2 years if kept under refrigeration.

If a recipe calls for a particular type of mustard, it would be best to use that one. Using the wrong mustard will make a difference in the taste desired.

Mustard oil, which is pressed from mustard seed is extremely hot and sometimes used in Chinese or other oriental dishes.

TYPES

American Mustard
The typical hot dog mustard is produced from a mild yellow mustard seed, sweetener, vinegar, and usually colored with the herb turmeric. It has a fairly smooth texture.

Chinese Mustard
Found in small ceramic dishes in all Chinese restaurants. It is produced from powdered mustard, water, and a strong vinegar. The sweetener is left out and the mustard will only retain its bite for 1-2 hours.

Dijon Mustard
Originated in Dijon, France. Produced from brown mustard seeds, white wine, unfermented grape juice and a variety of seasonings. It has a smooth texture and is usually a grayish-yellow color.

English Mustard
This mustard is produced from both white and black mustard seeds, a small amount of flour, and turmeric for coloring. This is one of the hottest mustards sold.

German Mustard
Produced from a variety of mustard seeds. The color varies and the flavor is somewhat mild due to a small amount of sugar used in the production.

NUTMEG

Available in ground form and imported from the East and West Indies. Used in sauces, puddings, as a topping for custards, eggnogs, and whipped cream. Also, used in sausages, frankfurters, and ravioli. Best when used in ground form.

The most pungent is the freshly ground nutmeg. Special nutmeg graters are sold in kitchen specialty shops.

OREGANO

A member of the mint family, also known as origanum and Mexican sage. Available in leaf or ground forms. Used in Italian specialties such as pizza and spaghetti sauces. Try oregano on a grilled cheese sandwich and you will never eat another one without it.

PAPRIKA

Ground pods of sweet pepper. The red sweet mild type is widely used and grown in the United States. Used in a wide variety of dishes such as vegetables, mustards, dressings, ketchup, sausages, and fish dishes. Makes an excellent garnish.

PARSLEY

Grown in the United States and Southern Europe. Used as a flavor in salads, soups, vegetable dishes, chicken pot pies, herb dressings, and even peppermint soup. A favorite garnish and high in nutrients, especially vitamin E and K. Helps alleviate bad breathe and should be stored in a plastic bag in the freezer. Parsley can be dried in the microwave.

PEPPER

Pepper is the most popular spice in the world. It is sold in both black and white varieties and imported from India, Indonesia, and Borneo. Sold in whole or ground varieties and used in almost any dish.

After pepper has been ground, it tends to lose its flavor rather quickly. Best to use a pepper grinder so that your pepper will be fresher and more flavorful. Grind white pepper and you won't change the colors of your dish.

Szechuan pepper berries are harvested from the prickly ash tree and have a very tiny seed and a somewhat hot taste.

Cayenne pepper is produced from chili peppers. Pink peppercorns are harvested from the Baies rose plant and have a very pungent odor and a somewhat sweet flavor.

PEPPERCORNS

Peppercorns come in three colors; black, white, and green. Black has the strongest flavor, with the berry being harvested before it is ripe. The white peppercorns are ripe berries with the skin removed. The green are also underripe and preserved in a brine solution. Most are sold dried.

POPPY SEED

Has a nut-like flavor and used in salads, cookies, pastry fillings, and baked goods.

POULTRY SEASONING

The major ingredients are, sage, thyme, marjoram, and savoy.

ROSEMARY

A sweet fragrant spicy herb, imported from Spain and Portugal. It is used in stews, meat dishes, dressings, and Italian foods. Great in gin drinks.

SAFFRON

One of the most expensive of all herbs. It is derived from the stigma of a flowering crocus. It is imported from Spain and is used primarily in baked goods and rice dishes.

SAGE

A member of the mint family, it is available in leaf or ground form. Used in pork products, stuffings, salads, fish dishes, and pizza sauces.

SALT (Sodium Chloride)

While salt contains important minerals that are beneficial to the body, in excess may be detrimental. Body fluids and their distribution in the body depend on the location and concentrations of sodium and potassium ions.

Our kidneys regulate the blood sodium levels and provide the bloodstream with the exact amount as needed. When blood levels rise due to excess sodium ingestion, the body's thirst receptors are stimulated and fluid intake increases to balance the sodium to water ratio. The excess sodium and water is then excreted by the kidneys. When this balance cannot be maintained the result may be higher blood pressure and an increased deposition of atherosclerotic plaque material.

In the purifying process of salt, the native minerals are stripped away and it is then enriched with iodine and dextrose to stabilize it, sodium bicarbonate to keep it white, and anti-caking agents to keep it "free-flowing." Morton's Special Salt is one of the only salts that has no additives. Salt is used in almost every food that is processed.

It is estimated by the National Institute of Health that over 10 million people over the age of 65 have some degree of high blood pressure problems.

Since sodium is found in thousands of food items, it is recommended that "added salt" be avoided to help control your total sodium intake.

SALTY FACTS

40% of regular table salt is sodium, Lite salt has only 20% sodium content.

"SALT TEST"
A simple barometer of your salt intake is to eat a slice of bacon. If it doesn't taste salty, you are eating too much salt.

Excess sodium intake builds up in the bloodstream, kidneys are unable to clear the excess water it retains, an increase in blood volume occurs and the heart has to work harder causing higher blood pressure.

Fast food restaurants may use high levels of salt to hide the offensive flavors of low quality foods.

Kelp can be ground up and used in a shaker to replace salt. It only contains 4% sodium and the taste is very close.

Recommended maximum daily intake of salt should be 1/10 teaspoon per day. We consume 25 times that amount. One teaspoon of salt equals 2000mg. Americans consume 4000-8000mg. each day.

Mother's milk contains 16mg. of sodium per 3 1/2oz. Canned baby food may contain 300mg. per 3 1/2oz.

Canned peas have 100 times the sodium of raw peas.

"SALT OF THE EARTH"
The average person consumes about 4,500mg. of salt daily, which amounts to about 2 teaspoons. The body only requires 200mg. daily.

SODIUM IN PUBLIC WATER SUPPLIES

Milligrams of sodium in 8 ounces of water

Aberdeen, SD.........48.0	Bismarck, ND..........14.4
Biloxi, MS...........55.2	Crandall, TX..........40.8
Galveston, TX........81.6	Kansas City, KS.......23.6
Los Angeles, CA......40.1	Oklahoma City, OK.....23.6
Phoenix, AZ..........25.9	San Diego, CA.........12.0
New York, NY......... 0.7	Reno, NV............. 1.1

It is necessary to read labels and be aware that many foods contain ingredients that contain sodium, such as MSG. Many spices also contain sodium as a normal part of their makeup. The following list are some spices and flavorings that are sodium-free:

ALLSPICE	*ALMOND EXTRACT*	*BAY LEAVES*
CARAWAY SEEDS	*CINNAMON*	*CURRY POWDER*
GARLIC	*GINGER*	*LEMON EXTRACT*
MACE	*MAPLE EXTRACT*	*MARJORAM*
MUSTARD POWDER	*NUTMEG*	*PAPRIKA*
PARSLEY	*PEPPER*	*PIMIENTO*
ROSEMARY	*PEPPERMINT EXTRACT*	*SAGE*
SESAME SEED	*THYME*	*TURMERIC*
VANILLA EXTRACT	*WALNUT EXTRACT*	*VINEGAR*

SODIUM DIETARY RESTRICTIONS

*The following foods should be avoided, due to their high
sodium content:*

AVOID

Meats and Luncheon Meats

All pickled products
All smoked products
Ham/pork
Dried beef (jerky)
Pastrami
Sausages
Frankfurters
Luncheon meats
Canned meat/fish

Snack foods

Salted crackers
Salted nuts
Salted popcorn
Pretzels
Potato chips
Corn chips
Tortilla chips
Salt sticks
Candy bars/nuts

Soups

Regular broth
Bouillion/cubes
Canned soups
Dehydrated soups

Vegetables in Brine

Sauerkraut
Pickles
Olives
Pickle relish

Seasonings/Condiments

Soy sauce
All salts including "Lite"
Tomato juice
Prepared mustard
Steak sauce
Wocestershire sauce
Chili sauce
Meat tenderizer
MSG/Accent
Commercial salad dressing
Dried packaged seasonings

Miscellaneous

Instant hot cereals
Fast food sandwiches
Ready-to-eat meals
French fries
Processed foods
Commercial sauces
Commercial gravies
Softened water
Mineral water
Seasoned salts
Packaged pasta mixes

SODIUM CONTENT OF COMMON FOODS

HIGH SODIUM FOODS

FOOD ITEM	SERVING SIZE	SODIUM MG.
Dill Pickle	1 large	1935
Turkey Dinner (frozen)	1 large	1830
Macaroni & Cheese (frozen)	1 cup	1090
Pretzels	1 oz.	890
Tuna (oil packed)	3 1/2 oz.	800
Peanuts (roated in oil)	1 cup	662
Creamed Corn	1 cup	671
Beef Frankfurters	1 reg.	495
Tomato Soup	5 oz.	475
Bologna	2 slices	450

MEDIUM SODIUM FOODS

American Cheese (processed)	1 oz.	447
Pancakes (mix)	3-4" cakes	435
Mashed Potatoes (instant)	1/2 cup	375
Cheese Pizza (frozen)	1 med. slice	370
Carrots (canned)	1 cup	366
Tomato Juice	1/2 cup	320
Cottage Cheese (creamed)	1/2 cup	320
Corn Flakes	3/4 cup	305
Buttermilk	1 cup	225
Doughnut (packaged)	1 med.	210
Oatmeal (cooked)	3 oz.	175
Green Olive	1 large	155
Angel Food Cake (mix)	1/12 cake	130
Whole Milk	1 cup	120

LOW SODIUM FOODS

Graham Cracker	1 large	95
Mayonnaise	1 Tbl.	80
Egg	1 med.	70
Turkey (roasted)	3 oz.	70
Margarine (salted)	1 Tbl.	50
Cottage Cheese (unsalted)	1/2 cup	30
Fruit Cocktail	1/2 cup	7
Orange Juice (canned, fresh)	1/2 cup	2
Fruit (canned, most)	1/2 cup	1
Macaroni (cooked)	1 cup	1

Types Of Salt

Iodized Salt
Standard table salt with iodine added.

Kosher Salt
A coarse-grained salt that is used in many gourmet recipes. Has an excellent flavor and texture__as well as being additive-free.

Pickling Salt
A fine-grained salt that is additive-free and used in the preparation of pickles and sauerkraut.

Rock Salt
A poorly refined salt that has a grayish appearance with large crystals. Combines with ice to make ice cream.

Sea Salt
Has a fresh flavor and is available in fine or coarse-grained varieties. It is usually imported and preferred by chefs.

Table Salt
A highly refined salt that contains additives. Very fine-grained making it free-flowing.

SAVOY

Another member of the mint family, but one that has a sweet flavor. Available in leaf and ground forms and is primarily used to flavor meats, poultry, and fish.

SESAME

Has a nut-like flavor with a high oil content and used primarily as a topping for baked goods and in halavah.

TARRAGON

An anise-flavored leaf that is native to Siberia and imported from Spain and France. Used in sauces, meat dishes, salads, herb dressings, and tomato casseroles.

THYME

Belongs to the mint family and is available in leaf and ground forms. Used in soups, stews, sauces, chipped beef (an old army favorite), sausages, clam chowder, herb dressings, and mock turtle soup.

TURMERIC

A member of the ginger family, it is imported from India and Peru. It is used in meat dishes, dressings, curry powder, Spanish rice, relishes, and mustards.

VANILLA

Beans
Long, thin dark brown beans are expensive and not as easy to use as the extract. To use the bean, split it and scrape out the powder-fine seeds. The seeds from a single vanilla bean is equal to 2-3 teaspoons of extract. Beans should be stored in a sealed plastic bag and refrigerated.

Pure Extract
Comes from the vanilla bean, but the taste is less intense. Has excellent flavor and is similar to the real bean.

Imitation Extract
Made from artificial flavorings, tastes stronger and is harsher than pure vanilla. Should only be used in recipes where the vanilla flavor does not predominate the taste.

Mexican Extract
A possible dangerous extract. This poor quality inexpensive product may contain coumarin, a blood thinning drug and the product has been banned in the United States due to other possible toxins.

VINEGAR

Produced from ethyl alcohol. A bacteria, acetobacter feeds on the alcohol, converting it into acetic acid (vinegar). Vinegar can, however, be made from a number of other foods, such as, apples or grains. Distilled vinegar is best used for cleaning purposes and not for foods.

Balsamic vinegar is produced in Italy and is made from sugars that are converted to alcohol with the addition of boiled down grape juice. Best used in salad dressing and will bring out the flavor in many vegetables.

UNSAFE HERBS

The following herbs are classified as unsafe for human consumption and should not be used in any food or beverage. This is only a partial listing of the hundreds of unsafe herbs.

BITTERSWEET, WOODY NIGHTSHADE, CLIMBING NIGHTSHADE

Scientific Name: Solanum dulcamara

Danger: Contains the toxin glycoalkaloid solanine as well as solanidine and dulcamarin.

BLOODROOT, RED PUCCOON

Scientific Name: Saguinaris canadensis

Danger: Contains the poisonous alkaloid sanguinarine as well as other alkaloids.

BUCKEYES, HORSE CHESTNUT

Scientific Name: Aesculus hippocasteranum

Danger: Contains the toxin coumarin glycoside, aesculin (esculin).

BURNING BUSH, WAHOO

Scientific Name: Euonymus atropurpureus

Danger: The actual poisonous chemical compound has not been identified as yet.

DEADLY NIGHTSHADE

Scientific Name: Atropa belladona

Danger: Contains the toxic solanaceous alkaloids hyoscyamine, atropine and hyoscine.

EUROPEAN MANDRAKE

Scientific Name: Mandragora officinarium

Danger: Poisonous plant contains narcotic similar to belladonna, Contains the alkaloids hyoscyamine, scopolomine, and mandragorine.

HELIOTROPE

Scientific Name: Heliotropium europaeum

Danger: Contains alkaloids that may cause liver damage.

HEMLOCK, SPOTTED HEMLOCK, CALIFORNIA OR NEBRASKA FERN

Scientific Name: Conium maculatum

Danger: Contains a poisonous alkaloid (coniine). Slows the heartbeat and eventually coma and death.

HENBANE, HOG'S BEAN, DEVIL'S EYE

Scientific Name: Hyoscyamus niger

Danger: Contains the alkaloid hyoscyamine, and atropine.

INDIAN TOBACCO, ASTHMA WEED, EMETIC WEED

Scientific Name: Lobelia inflata

Danger: Contains the alkaloid lobeline.

JALAP ROOT, HIGH JOHN ROOT, ST. JOHN THE CONQUEROR ROOT

Scientific Name: Ipomoea jalapa

Danger: Usually found in Mexico, its resin contains a powerful poison.

JIMSON WEED, THORNAPPLE, TOLGUACHA

Scientific Name: Datura stramonium

Danger: Contains the alkaloid atropine

LILY OF THE VALLEY, MAY LILY

Scientific Name: Convalleria majalis

Danger: Contains the toxic cardic glycoside convallatoxin.

AMERICAN MANDRAKE, MAY APPLE, WILD LEMON

Scientific Name: Podophyllum pelatum

Danger: A poisonous plant containing a polycyclic substance.

MISTLETOE

Scientific Name: Phoradendron flavescens, Viscum album

Danger: Contains the toxic pressor amines B-phenylethylamine and tyramine.

MORNING GLORY

Scientific Name: Ipomoea purpurea

Danger: Contains a purgative resin. Seeds contain lysergeic acid.

PERIWINKLE

Scientific Name: Vinca major, Vinca minor

Danger: Contains toxic alkaloids. Can injure the liver and kidneys.

POKEWEED, SKOKE, PIGEONBERRY

Scientific Name: Phytolacca americana

Danger: Contains unidentified poisons.

SCOTCH BROOM, BROOM

Scientific Name: Cytisus scoparius

Danger: Contains the toxin sparteine and other alkaloids.

SPINDLE-TREE

Scientific Name: Euonymus europaeus

Danger: Produces violent purges.

SWEET FLAG, SWEET ROOT, SWEET CANE, SWEET CINNAMON

Scientific Name: Acorus calamus

Danger: Jamma variety is a carcinogen. Prohibited by the FDA.

TONKA BEAN

Scientific Name: Dipteryx odorata

Danger: Seeds contain coumarin. Can cause serious liver damage.

WATER HEMLOCK, COWBANE, POISON PARSNIP, WILD CARROT

Scientific Name: Cicuta maculata

Danger: Contains an unsaturated higher alcohol called cicutoxin.

WHITE SNAKEROOT, SNAKEROOT, RICHWEED

Scientific Name: Eupatorium rugosum

Danger: Contains a toxic alcohol substance.

WOLF'S BANE, LEOPARD'S BANE, MOUNTAIN TOBACCO

Scientific Name: Arnica montana

Danger: Unidentified substances. Produces violent toxic effects.

WORMWOOD, MADDERWORT, MUGWORT

Scientific Name: Artemisia absinthium

Danger: Contains oil of wormwood, an active narcotic poison. Never purchase the liquor Absinthe unless it is produced in the United States.

YOHIMBE, YOHIMBI

Scientific Name: Corynanthe yohimbi

Danger: Contains toxic alkaloids.

Chapter 21

Food Additives

FOOD ADDITIVES

"YOUR OVERWORKED LIVER"
The foods we consume today contains over $500 million dollars worth of additives. Americans eat approximately 6-9 pounds of these chemicals annually which amounts to over 1 billion pounds of additives consumed every year. Your liver is in charge of detoxifying this garbage. It is the major organ that must breakdown and dispose of these chemicals. In many cases it requires a number of nutrients to assist in their breakdown. Nutrients that would prefer to be useful in other roles.

White bread may have as many as 16 chemical additives just to keep it fresh. Some of these may be in the wrapper.

Almost 98% (by actual weight) of food additives that are used in food are corn syrup, pepper, mustard, baking soda, baking powder, citric acid, salt, or a vegetable coloring agent.

BETA-CAROTENE

A natural substance found in plants and animals. Has the ability to produce vitamin A. Found in many fruits and vegetables and has a yellowish-orange color. Used as a food coloring agent in numerous food products and cosmetics. Recent studies have shown beta-carotene to be a potent antioxidant. Since there is no toxicity involved with it, it is usually recommended over vitamin A.

BROMELIN

"A NEW BAR DRINK?"
Extracted from pineapple and used in meat tenderizers. A very effective protein-digesting enzyme. If a piece of meat is allowed to stand in bromelin for a prolonged period, the meat will totally liquefy.

CITRATE SALTS

Used in cheese spreads and pasteurized process cheeses. May tend to mask the results of laboratory tests for pancreatic and liver function and blood acid-base balances. If you are going for extensive blood work, try not to consume these cheeses for at least one week prior to the test.

CITRUS RED #2

Has been used for coloring Florida oranges, however, in recent years the use has been discontinued. The dye remained in the peel and did not enter the pulp. However, if the dye was ingested in quantity, it could cause serious visual, circulatory, and urinary problems.

COLORINGS

The majority of colorings presently being used are derived from coal tars (carcinogens). As the years go by, more and more of these colorings are being further tested and subsequently banned.

GELATIN

Derived from boiling the skin, muscle, and hoofs of animals. Mainly used as a thickener and stabilizer for fruit gelatins. Has been found to strengthen fingernails.

METHYLENE CHLORIDE

A gas used in the decaffeination of coffee. Residues may remain and coffee companies do not have to disclose their methods on the label. Best to drink decaf if the label states that it was decaffeinated with water.

NITRITES

One of the most dangerous additives presently used in our foods are nitrites and nitrates. They may be found in almost all processed meat products, especially hot dogs, bacon, lunch meats, smoked meats, canned meats, and sausages.

The chemical is used both for cosmetic purposes (to keep meats red) as well as to help retard bacterial growth and reduce the risk of botulism. Because of the risks involved with this chemical, the general concensus among scientists is that the food industry should be conducting exhaustive research to find a safer alternative.

Nitrite studies have shown that in laboratory animals malignant tumors have developed in over 90% within 6 months, and death approximately soon afterwards. Other incidents been reported and documented showing that high levels of nitrites in food has caused "cardiovascular collapse" in humans and even death from consuming hot dogs and blood sausage that were produced by local processors in different areas of the country.

In Israel, studies on animals discovered problems related to brain damage when they were fed an equivalent amount of nitrites that would be consumed by a person eating a large amount of processed meats.

The biochemical changes that occur in the food takes the following course; nitrites are broken down into nitrous acid which then combines with the hemoglobin of the meat or fish, forming a red pigment.

In humans there are two pathways that the ingested nitrites may take that could be harmful; The first involves the nitrites reacting with a person's hemoglobin to produce a pigment called meth-hemoglobin, which may seriously depress the oxygen-carrying capacity of the red blood cell. The second is the possible cancer connection when the nitrites are biochemically altered into a "nitrosamine."

The last reaction usually occurs in the stomach and requires the presence of "amines" and "gastric juices." Amines are usually in adequate supply, since they are a product of protein metabolism, and protein foods often carry the nitrites. The end result is the formation of the nitrosamine, which are classified as a carcinogen.

It is necessary, however, to clarify the two points; just because you eat meat containing nitrites it does not mean that you will automatically produce nitrosamines. If the nitrosamine is produced, your immune system (if not overworked) may render it harmless as soon as it is produced.

Vitamin C (ascorbic acid) has been found to neutralize the reaction that takes place in the stomach by interfering with the amine combining with the nitrite. Due to recent studies relating to this neutralizing effect, some manufacturers of hot dogs are now adding ascorbic acid to their product.

As a measure of protection it would be wise to chew a vitamin C tablet or drink a glass of orange juice before consuming foods that contain nitrites.

NOTE:
Many countries have already banned nitrites from food products, however, the USDA and the FDA will not prohibit its use until a good substitute is found that they approve of.

SORBITOL

Extracted mainly from berries and some fruits. It is an alcohol that produces a sweet taste and is used in dietetic products as a replacement for sugar. Also, it has numerous other uses as a food binder, thickener, texturing agent, humectant, and food stabilizer.

SULFITES

There are three types of sulfites that may be used as anti-browning agents; sodium, potassium, and ammonium. All may be used of any food except meats or a high vitamin B content food. Physiologic reactions to sulfites are numerous with the more common being an acute asthmatic attack.

Sulfites have been used for years to retard browning of fruits and vegetables, providing a level of preservation. The most common use was on salad bars. The outside leaves of lettuce should be discarded since they have been found to contain sulfites in some instances. The U.S. has limited the use of sulfites, however, imported produce may still be hazardous.

SULFUR DIOXIDE

A chemical formed from the browning of sulfur. A food bleach, preservative, antioxidant, and anti-browning agent. It is most commonly visible when used on "golden" raisins. Has a tendency to destroy vitamin A and should not be used on meats or high vitamin A content foods.

TYPES OF ADDITIVES

Flavorings

There are approximately 1,100-1,400 natural and synthetic flavorings available to food processors. Scientists are most concerned regarding the toxicity of a number of the ones that are commonly used. Flavorings give foods a more acceptable taste, restore flavors that have been lost to processing and improve some natural flavors, making them more intense.

Stabilizers/Gelling Agents/Thickeners

These are used to keep products in a "set-state" and are used for jellies, jams, and baby foods. They are also used to keep ice cream creamy. They improve consistency and will affect the appearance and texture of a variety of foods. The more common ones are modified food starch and vegetable gum.

Colorings

Ninety percent are artificial and do not contain any nutritional value. Some foods have a tendency to lose their natural color when processed and must be dyed to make them more eye appealing to the consumer. A good example of this is banana ice cream which is dyed yellow and maraschino cherries which are dyed red or green.

Sweeteners

The United States consumption of artificial sweeteners is estimated at approximately 6-9 pounds per person annually.

Aroma Enhancers

An example is the yellowish-green liquid diacetyl, which is used in some cottage cheeses to produce an artificial butter aroma.

Preservatives

Helps maintain freshness and prevents spoilage that is caused by fungi, yeasts, molds, and bacteria. Extends shelf life and protects the natural colors and flavors.

Acids/Bases

Provides a tart flavor for many fruits as well putting the "fizz" in soft drinks. The two common acids for soft drinks are citric acid and phosphoric acid.

Antioxidants

Reduces the possibility of rancidity in fats and oils. Natural ones are vitamins C, E, and beta-carotene. Synthetic one are BHA and BHT.

Taste Enhancers

Brings out the flavors of certain foods. MSG is a good example, but is not recommended.

Improving Agents

Humectants	Control the humidity of food
Anti-caking Agents	Keeps salt and powders free-flowing.
Firming/Crisping Agents	Used for processed fruits and vegetables.
Foaming Agents	Used for whipped cream and root beer.
Anti-foaming Agents	Keeps pineapple juice from bubbling over a filled container.

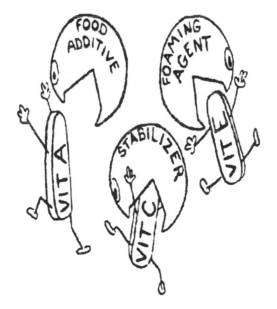

Emulsifiers

These help to keep foods and chemicals in solution. A good example is water and oil which can be kept in solution by using lecithin.

NOTE:

Keep in mind that you are rarely aware of the quantity of additives you consume. Almost all these additives require vitamins and minerals to assist with their breakdown, so that they can be properly disposed of, usually by the liver. These additional nutrients must be obtained from somewhere in the body that could use them more effectively.

Chapter 22

Sugar and Sugar Substitutes

HOW SWEET IT IS

American sugar intake per person in 1822 was 8.9 pounds a year. In the last 174 years, it has risen to a level 16 times that amount. Each day the average refined sugar consumption per person in the United States is over 40 teaspoons. This is over 3/4 cup, or 147 pounds a year!

It is hard to believe that we could eat so much sugar in a day, but it is hidden away in many places besides the sugar bowl. It can be found in soft drinks, candy, baked goods, toothpastes, cereals, etc. If you read the labels on foods you will be surprised at the foods that contain one form of sugar or another.

Sugar requires B vitamins and minerals to enable the body to metabolize it into glucose, yet it contains none of these. Therefore, it must take the nutrients away from other bodily sources where they may be needed more.

Sugar may also increase the rate at which we excrete the mineral calcium, making bones more fragile as well as weakening the heart action.

Sugar robs the body of chromium which is crucial for the regulation of blood sugar levels.

NATURAL SWEETENERS

Corn Syrup

Produced from a mixture of starch granules and is processed with acids or enzymes to convert it into a heavy sweet syrup. Corn syrup is artificially flavored and used for pancake syrups, etc. Used in place of sugar in candy making and ice creams. Honey would be a better substitute, but is too expensive for commercial use.

The fact that corn syrup tends to stop crystallization makes it a good choice for candies, preserves, and frostings.

Honey

The best honey will be labeled "100% pure unfiltered", "raw" or "uncooked." This honey will not be nutrient depleted by heat processing. To use honey as a spread, look for the labeling that says, creamed, spun, or granulated. Honey has many different flavors, depending on where the bee obtained the nectar. Blended honey is the least expensive and lacks a unique flavor.

Honey is sold in three varieties; liquid honey which is extracted directly from the "honeycomb", chunk-style honey which contains pieces of the honeycomb, and comb honey which contains a larger section of the honeycomb.

One pound of honey is equal to 1 1/3 cups.

Honey is a unique sugar in that it will not grow bacteria. It is the only food that has this unique ability. However it is twice as sweet as granulated sugar. Crystallized honey is easier to measure and spread, and can be liquefied by placing it into the microwave for 30 seconds to 2 minutes depending on the size of the jar. Do not allow to boil.

Maple Syrup

Read the label well! Make sure it doesn't say "maple flavored," "maple-blended," or use the word "imitation." The real thing is rare and does contain an excellent blend of natural nutrients, especially iron and calcium.

Pure maple syrup is sap that has been boiled down until most of the water content has evaporated. It is not as sweet as the artificial varieties. The highest grade is AA or fancy which has a lighter color.

Pure maple syrup should be refrigerated after opening to retard the growth of mold. It should last about 1 year. Should be used at room temperature or slightly heated.

Maple-flavored syrup is a blend of corn syrup or other low-cost syrup and a small quantity of the pure maple syrup for flavor.

The typical pancake syrup is almost pure corn syrup and artificial maple flavoring.

Molasses

Made from sugar cane which goes through a complex processing which removes all of the nutrients resulting in white sugar. The residue that remains after processing, is the actual blackstrap molasses product. Unsulfured molasses is actually produced to make molasses and not the results of the processing to make sugar.

Unsulfured molasses has a lighter, cleaner flavor than sulfured.

If a recipe calls for dark molasses, you can use light molasses without a problem.

When you bake with molasses, be sure and reduce the heat about 25^0 F. or the food may overbrown.

If you need to measure molasses for a recipe, try coating the measuring utensil with a spray vegetable oil before measuring the molasses, it will flow better and give you a more accurate measurement.

Molasses has a degree of acidity that can be neutralized by adding 1 teaspoon of baking soda to the dry ingredients for every cup of molasses the recipe calls for.

Molasses is best used in gingerbread and baked beans because of it's robust flavor.

Raw Sugar (turbinado)

Refined sugar, almost exactly like refined white sugar, except with the addition of molasses for color. No advantage over normal refined sugar, don't bother to pay the extra price.

ARTIFICIAL SWEETENERS

ACESULFAME K

A non-caloric sweetener, also called "Sunette" or "Sweet-One." It sweetens and does not breakdown in the body, but passes through and is excreted. Can also be used for high temperature cooking and baking unlike Nutrasweet (Equal). It is 200 times sweeter than sugar and used commercially in chewing gums, dry beverage mixes, candies, puddings, and custards. Received FDA approval in 1989 and has about the same sweetening power of Aspartame.

Presently, approved in 20 countries. The Center for Science in the Public Interest tested the product, but any negative results were inconclusive. Can be used in baked goods unlike aspartame (Equal).

ALLTAME

A super-sweetener produced from two amino acids and is 2,000 times sweeter than sugar. It is metabolized by the body normally, with almost no calories. A good all around sweetener that nay be used in almost any recipe and baked goods.

ASPARTAME (NUTRASWEET, EQUAL)

This approved sweetener is produced from phenylalanine, aspartic acid and methanol. It has been implicated in animal lab testing regarding nerve disease, however, testing is not conclusive and the studies were being conducted using high dosages which may skew the outcome. Aspartame may also lower the acidity level of the urine causing a reduces susceptibility to disease.

When Aspartame is heated, a percentage may turn into methyl alcohol. Best if it is not used in baked goods and any drink that requires boiling. Recent study results by leading universities and the Arizona Department of Health Sciences were regarded by the FDA as "unfounded fears."

Symptoms are becoming more frequently reported relating to Equal consumption and include; insomnia, headaches, vision changes, dizziness, and nervous disorders. A double blind study of diabetics using the products reported more adverse symptoms in the group consuming Aspartame. The study was conducted using a measured quantity of Nutrasweet equal to 14 diet drinks per day. However, even if you don't drink that many diet drinks, Equal is now found in hundreds of other products.

In 1980 when Aspartame was approved by the FDA, they set a maximum recommended amount at 34mg. per Kg. of body weight. This equates to a 140 pound person drinking 12 diet drinks per day or the equivalent in foods containing Aspartame, Nutrasweet, or Equal. The World Health Organization recommended a maximum of 40mg. per Kg. of body weight for adults. A child in an average day consuming an assortment of cereals, gum, candy, puddings, ades, soft drinks, etc. could easily exceed the adult maximum amounts. Future testing may prove very interesting.

Cyclamates

The FDA has now decided to reverse its original decision that cyclamates are carcinogenic. It may very well be back on the market at any time and commercially used in baked goods. It would be best to read the labels well and limit artificial sweetener intake.

L-Sugars

Contains no calories or aftertaste and may be used to replace a number of present day sweeteners. Can be substituted cup for cup for refined sugar in recipes. Still in the development stages.

Saccharin

Has been used as a sweetener since 1879 and is 300 times sweeter than sugar. Used in mouthwashes and lipsticks. The FDA has proposed additional testing and recommended limiting intake. Products containing saccharin have a warning label stating that saccharin may be hazardous to your health.

Sucralose

Produced from common table sugar but is 600 times sweeter and has no calories. A very stable product in foods and carbonated beverages.

SWEET FACTS

"A GOOD SWEETENER?"
Fruit is high in the sugar "fructose." However, all studies show that there is no risk factor involved with this sugar and consumption does not have to be limited. Fructose breaks down slower than most sugars giving the body more time to utilize it before it is completely broken down to glucose.

"WERE SUPPOSED TO BE SMARTER"
Adults purchase over 50% of all chocolate sold in the United States. Dark chocolate is the most sought after. Chocolate bars were invented by Fry & Sons in 1847 in England. Milk chocolate must contain at least 10% chocolate liqueur and a minimum of 12% milk solids. Dark chocolate must contain at least 15% chocolate liqueur and no more than 12% milk solids.

"DENTISTS RETIREMENT FOODS"
The annual per capita sugar intake of 147 pounds equals 246,752 calories of an "empty calorie" food forcing your body to find the nutrients to break it all down, especially B vitamins. This is enough calories to add 68 pounds to a person's weight each year.

"ZITS MAKERS"
Americans consume approximately $3.4 billion worth of candy per year and 1.3 billion pounds of chocolate candy bars. Over $630 million is spent on advertising junk foods in the United States every year.

"CHOCOHOLICS BEWARE"
Theobromine in chocolate may reduce the absorption of protein through the intestinal wall. Sugar also reduces the bodies ability to destroy bacteria. Oxalates in chocolate unite with calcium carrying it through the intestine as an insoluble compound, rendering it unusable.

"CREATING A LARGER PROBLEM"
Sucking on hard candy or lollypops causes a greater risk of tooth decay than consuming large quantities of cake, ice cream, or doughnuts. Hard candy dissolves slower and surround each tooth with a coating of sugar for a longer period of time.

"SEVEN MILLION MILES TO THE GALLON"
To produce a 1 pound jar of honey, bees have to forage over a flight path equal to three trips around the earth and burn only one ounce of honey for fuel.

"SHAKIN' SUGAR"
In Europe confectioners' sugar is called "icing sugar." Most recipes call for confectioners' sugar to be sifted. It is also used frequently for "dusting" and some should always be kept handy in a shaker.

"OVERWORKING YOUR LIVER"
Most candies, especially if they are multicolored contain a number of additives that may be suspect. These include; Red Dye #3 and #40, Green Dye #3, Blue Dye #2 and #12, Yellow Dye #5, glycerides, etc. Check out your favorite for any of these additives. Remember your liver is the organ that must cleanse these chemicals from the body.

"PRECISION COUNTS"
If your making candy, be sure and follow directions to the letter. Candy recipes are very exacting and variances can cause a poor quality product.

"BY THE BOOK"
Candy recipes must be cooked at the temperature that is recommended. Never try and speed up the process by increasing the heat.

"COOL IT"
The lower the final temperature of the candy after it is cooked will determine the softness of the final product. In fact, if the humidity of the kitchen is over 60% it will affect the candy quality.

"MAKING A SMOOTHIE"
To improve the texture of your fudge, try adding a teaspoon of corn starch when you start mixing the ingredients.

"BEAT ME, BEAT ME"
Fudge should be stirred or beaten with a wooden spoon. Beating the fudge is one of the most important techniques. Beat the fudge from its glossy, thin consistency to a slightly thick consistency. This is when you will need to add raisins or nuts and place into a pan to cool.

"A SMALL AMOUNT OF FUDGING"
If your fudge won't set-up, try returning it to the pot and adding a teaspoon of water, then continue cooking for a few more minutes.

If a candy recipe calls for water, always use hot water and your candy will be clearer.

Most freshly made candy will remain fresh for 2-3 weeks.

"DON'T TAKE A BEETING"
Cane sugar should always be used for candies, beet sugar tends to cause more foam.

"HOW SWEET IT IS"
Smokers tend to consume more sugar than non-smokers. Smokers tend to drink more sweetened coffee, which may account for the difference.

"WHOA, SUGAR, WHOA"
Fluid movement around the teeth is slowed to a crawl by a high intake of sugar and sweetened foods.

"IN THE BRITISH ISLES"
Studies are underway that may prove that sugar may raise cholesterol levels.

"SUGAR DISASTER"
Never freeze clear hard candies, jellies, cereal, popcorn candy, marshmallows or any candy that has been dipped in chocolate. Hard candies may crumble, jellies become granular, and the rest lose their original consistencies due to the expansion of their liquids.

"FRESH 'N FRUITY"
Purchase only jams and jellies made from the "real thing." Best if they were also labeled "lite." The commercial products usually only contain extracts of the real fruit.

If a dish is too sweet, try adding a small amount of salt or white vinegar.

"SNIP, SNIP"
Marshmallows can be stored in the freezer. If they become too hard to use, just cut them with a scissors as needed, Dip the scissors in hot water first.

When marshmallows become hard, try placing them into a plastic baggie with a slice or two of very fresh bread for a few days.

"THE REAL THING"
If the product is labeled "maple sugar" it must contain a minimum of 35% "real" maple syrup. The lighter the color, the higher the quality. Maple syrup should be stored in the refrigerator after it is opened. If it granulates and hardens, just heat it slightly.

"PERFORMING A LUMPECTOMEY"
To soften brown sugar that has developed a case of "lumps", try placing the sugar in the microwave with a slice of fresh white bread or 1/2 half an apple. Cover the dish tightly and cook about 10-15 seconds. The moisture from the bread or apple will produce just enough steam to soften the sugar without melting it.

To remove hardened brown sugar from a box, just add a few drops of water to the box and microwave on full power for a few seconds.

Brown sugar is chemically almost identical to white sugar.

Blackstrap molasses is higher in nutrients than any other type of molasses, especially iron, calcium, and potassium.

Ice cream sales in the United States in 1995 were approximately $2.1 billion dollars. We averaged almost 15 quarts of ice cream per person.

When you empty a jar of jam or jelly, place it in the microwave for a few seconds or place the bottom of the jar in very hot water to melt the rest of the jam or jelly. Save all the different ones in another jar until you need it to baste a ham, lamb, or other food that requires a sweet sauce.

When defrosting candy, the temperature should be raised gradually. Place the candy to be thawed, still in the wrappers, in a brown paper bag. This will absorb the condensed moisture that collects during defrosting.

Candy and chewing gum cause the salivary glands to produce saliva at a higher rate than normal, causing frequent swallowing. This is the cause of bloatiness and flatulence in many people.

Over $600 million dollars were spent in 1995 on sugar related commercials.

"HEAT KILLS"
Jams and jellies retain only a fraction of their vitamin C content after processing.

"IT'S NOT THE REAL THING"
White chocolate isn't real chocolate. It is made from sugar, milk powder and cocoa butter. When cocoa butter is pressed from chocolate liquor it loses its chocolate flavor.

Sugar is a natural product and may be labeled as such.

Candies when frozen fresh will retain a better flavor.

"THE NOSE, KNOWS"
Candies tend to pick up foreign odors and should be stored properly in a closed container.

To keep sugar from caking up in your canister, try placing a few salt-free crackers in the canister to absorb the moisture. Crackers need to be replaced frequently.

"BUBBLE, BUBBLE, TOIL AND TROUBLE"
If your candy tends to boil over, place a wooden spoon over the pan to break the bubbles.

Children as well as adults are subject to personality changes and hyperactivity problems from high sugar intakes. New studies are showing that there may not be much validity to this, however, I have seen too many instances where it has proven true.

Most cough drops contain over 50% sugar. This is necessary since the chemicals used are bitter tasting. Approximately 30% of all cough syrups are 25% sugar.

America's favorite desserts are pie, cheesecake, and ice cream in that order.

"POP A CUBE"
If you have the need to satisfy a sugar craving, try eating a sugar cube. They only contain 10-16 calories each and contain no fat or artificial chemicals.

"MINERAL ROBBER"
Sugar may also increase the rate at which we excrete calcium, making bones more fragile and may also weaken heart action. It robs the body of chromium, which is a critical mineral for the regulation of blood sugar levels.

"A VACATION AT YOUR EXPENSE"
High sugar intake reduces the effectiveness of the body's healing mechanism, causing a prolongation in the healing time. White blood cells which aid in the healing process tend to stay in the bloodstream and "lap up" the glucose, which is their preferred food source, instead of going to work.

Sugar And Sugar Substitutes In Foods

Glucose	Sucrose	Maltose
Fructose	Lactose	Dextrose
Xylose	Levulose	Dextrim
Beet Sugar	Corn Syrup	Brown Sugar
Molasses	Maple Sugar	Mannitol
Xylatol	Hexatol	Invert Sugar
Sorghum	Honey	Turbinado Sugar
Nutrasweet	Equal	Aspartame
Saccharin	Sucryl	Malt

"Surprises Galore" Foods That May Contain Sugar

Packaged Cereals	Mustard	Ketchup
Salt	Canned Soups	Fudge
Tomato Sauce	Canned Fruits	Soft Drinks
Canned Meats	Rolls	Cookies
Ice Cream	Puddings	Lipstick
Lip Gloss	Breads	Jam/Jelly
Canned Veg. Juice	Bacon	Lemonade
Pancake Mixes	Waffle Mixes	Canned Beans
Cough Drops	Apple Butter	Breathe Mints
Breakfast Bars	Canned Fish	Potato Chips
Bread Mixes	Sherbert	Stewed Fruit
Soup Mixes	Peanut Butter	Baby Foods
Yogurt	Prepared Sauces	Condensed Mill
Dried Fruit	Egg Nog	Licorice
Protein Powd.	Laxatives	Vitamins
Red Wine	Crackers	Mouthwashes
Chewing Gum	Soy Sauce	Pickles
Relish	Tooth Paste	Meat

Tenderizers
TV Dinners
Condiments
French Fries
Stamp Adhesives
Breakfast Drink

Meat Sauces
Medications
Food Seas'n
Envelope Adh.
Chewing Tob.
Hamburger Buns

Gravies
Packaged Nuts
Margarine
Pretzels
Fast Foods
Snails

Sugar Content In A Few Goodies

CANDIES	%
Candy Corn	59.5
Nestles Crunch	47.4
Mr. Goodbar	42.2
3 Musketeers	41.0
Mars	40.3
Milky Way	36.4
Tootsie Roll	36.1
Baby Ruth	35.3
Butterfingers	33.5
Snickers	33.2
Milk Duds	30.7
Almond Joy	25.6
Mounds	21.7

COOKIES	%
Oreo	40.1
Vanilla Wafers	32.6
Lemon Snaps	31.7
Oatmeal and Raisin	18.8
Peanut Butter	16.4
Fig Newtons	11.6

Sugar In Common Foods	%
Jello	82.0
Breakfast Cereals	up to 68.0
Cream Substitutes	up to 57.0
Shake & Bake	up to 51.0
Sara Lee Chocolate Cake	36.0
Russian Dressing	30.0
Ketchup	29.0
Ding Dong	25.0
Hamburger Helper	24.0
Cool Whip	22.0
Ice Cream	21.0
Libby's Peaches	18.0
Low-Fat Yogurt	14.0
Ritz Crackers	12.0
Most Peanut Butter	up to 12.0
Coffee	9.0
Ragu Spaghetti Sauce	6.0

SUGAR CONTENT OF BREAKFAST CEREALS

Product	Manufacturer	% Total Sugar
Honey Smacks	Kellogg	56.0
Apple Jacks	Kellogg	55.0
Fruit Loops	Kellogg	48.0
Super Sugar Crisp	General Foods	46.0
Cocoa Pebbles	General Foods	42.6
Lucky Charms	General Mills	42.2
Frosted Flakes	Kellogg	41.0
Cap'n Crunch	Quaker Oats	40.0
Bran Buds	Kellogg	40.0
Alpha Bits	General Foods	38.0
Trix	General Mills	35.9
Cocoa Puffs	General Mills	33.3

Fruit and Fiber	Kellogg	31.1
Post's Raisin Bran	General Foods	30.4
Golden Grahams	General Mills	30.0
Raisin Bran	Kellogg	29.0
Frosted Mini-Wheats	Kellogg	26.0
Just Right	Kellogg	25.7
100% Nat. Granola	Quaker Oats	21.5
All Bran	Kellogg	19.0
Life	Quaker Oats	16.0
Team	Nabisco	14.1
Grape Nuts Flakes	General Foods	13.3
40% Bran Flakes	General Foods	13.0
Product 19	Kellogg	9.9
Total	General Mills	8.3
Wheaties	General Mills	8.2
Rice Krispies	Kellogg	7.8
Special K	Kellogg	5.4
Corn Flakes	Kellogg	5.3
Kix	General Mills	4.8
Rice Chex	Ralston-Purina	4.2
Wheat Chex	Ralston Purina	3.5
Cheerios	General Mills	3.0
Shredded Wheat	Nabisco	0.6
Puffed Rice	Quaker Oats	0.1

Source: Analysis by the USDA in 1989 Manufacturer's   Information.

Chapter 23

Sauces, Soups, Stews and Gravies

"GO FOR PAUL'S"

Spaghetti sauce should be homemade, store bought sauces are for the most part high in fat and calories. Prego Extra Chunky with sausage and green peppers is 47% fat. Ragu Marinara is 40% fat. One of the best commercial sauces is Newman's Own. The mushroom sauce is only 22% fat.

Packaged sauces and gravies are all lower quality convenience items. They contain chemicals for flavor, coloring, freshness, and texture.

"EDIBLE OFFAL, AGAIN"

If you purchase spaghetti sauce, never buy the ones that already have the meat included. By law, companies only need to include meat that is 6% actual meat. Best to add your own meat and you will know what you are eating.

Use your blender to smooth lumpy gravy or sauces.

Add a teaspoon of peanut butter to cover up the burnt flavor of gravy. This will not alter the taste.

"ONE OF THE BIGGIES"

When using butter for sauteing, always use unsalted butter since the salt separates from the butter when heated and tends to give the food a bitter taste.

"OR USE A ROLLING PIN"

If you add a pinch of salt to the flour before mixing it with a liquid, it will help keep the gravy from becoming lumpy.

To obtain a richer brown color to your gravy, try spreading the flour on a cookie pan and cook over a low heat, stirring occasionally until brown. Adding a small amount of coffee to the gravy will also do the trick, without adding the coffee flavor.

"IN OLDEN TIMES"

A method used in the 19th century was to add onion skins to give the gravy while it is cooking to give it a brown color and then remove them after a few minutes and discard.

When making a white sauce, add a dash of nutmeg for a great taste.

If your Hollandaise sauce has curdled, try beating a tablespoon of cold water into the sauce to bring back the smooth texture.

A high-fat gravy (which should only be eaten in moderation) will have a better consistency if you add 1/4 teaspoon of baking soda to it. If it has a high starch content, don't add baking soda or it will turn it black.

"SHOE LEATHER, AU JUS"
When making stew, never add boiling water to the stew, if more water is needed, always use cold water. The boiling water may toughen the meat.

"JEWISH PENICILLIN"
When making chicken soup, use a quart of water to each pound of chicken.

Soups and stews should only be allowed to simmer, never boil.

"TV DINNERS"
Place leftover stews into individual baking dishes or small casserole dishes, cover with pie crust or dumpling mix and bake.

Store the liquid from canned mushrooms or vegetables, freeze it and use it in soups and stews.

Refrigerate cooked or canned stews and soups overnight before serving. The fat will rise to the top and can easily be skimmed off.

Read the label when buying soups. MSG, disodium inosinate, and guanylate are flavor enhancers you should probably avoid.

Many vitamins are lost to the liquid when cooking vegetables. The liquid should be saved, frozen and used in soups and stews.

Stews are usually best if prepared the day before allowing the flavors to be incorporated throughout the stew.

Bones from poultry and beef should always be frozen and saved for soups and stews. Allow them to remain in the soup or stew from the start of the cooking to just before serving.

When preparing a sauce that contains a milk product that has curdled, try placing the sauce in a blender for a few seconds.

"UP, UP, AND AWAY"
Basil is a common spice for use in soups and stews, however, basil tends to lose much of its flavor after about 15 minutes of cooking and should be added about 10 minutes before the food is done for the best results.

"CORNSTARCH TO THE RESCUE"
If you need to thicken stew or soup, be sure and remove as much fat as possible before adding a thickening agent for the best results.

Popcorn on top of soup makes it more appealing for children.

One of the best commercial canned soups is Progresso, however, still watch for the flavor enhancers.

Dry soup mixes are usually additive-free and only contain a few dried vegetables and seasonings.

"STRETCHING IT OUT"
Soup will go farther if you add pasta, rice or barley.

For an easy treat when making stew, take a stack of tortillas, cut them into long thin pieces and add them to the stew during the last 15 minutes of cooking. Remember corn tortillas are lower in fat than flour tortillas.

A good trick to avoid burning the peas in split-pea soup is to add a slice of fresh white bread when you are cooking the peas and liquid together.

When making stew, try adding a tablespoon of molasses for flavor.

If you add 1/2 cup of strong tea to the stew, it will help tenderize the meat and reduce the cooking time.

Leftover soup can be frozen in an ice cube tray and used in soups and stews at another time.

To thicken stews, try adding a small amount of quick-cooking oats, a grated potato, or some instant potatoes and onions.

If you are making vegetable soup, pour enough water into the pot to cover the vegetables by only two inches.

To reduce the saltiness of soups, add a can of peeled tomatoes.

Another method of reducing the saltiness is to use a small amount of brown sugar or adding a slice or two of apple or potato, mixing it in and then remove and discard.

If you would like a sweeter taste to your soup or stew, try adding a small amount of pureed carrots.

Never use dark-colored bones in soups, they are too old and have deteriorated.

"A MILK CURDLING EXPERIENCE"
To avoid curdling when you are making tomato soup with milk, try adding the tomato base/soup to the milk instead of the milk to the tomato base. If you add a small amount of flour to the milk and beat it, it would also help.

"A REAL WINNER"
The best method of making soup or stew stock is to use a metal pasta cooker basket. Place it into your pot and cook all your ingredients, including any food containing bones. Remove the basket and it will contain all the veggies or bones you may not want.

"THE PARSLEY MAGNET"
If you obtain too heavy garlic a flavor when cooking, place a few parsley flakes in a tea ball to soak up the excess garlic. Garlic tends to attracted to parsley.

"ON A CLEAR SOUP, YOU CAN SEE FOREVER"
To make a clear noodle soup, cook the noodles, then drain before adding them to the soup. When noodles are cooked in the soup, the excess starch will turn the soup cloudy.

When making a cream soup, try adding a little flour to the milk. it will make it smoother and it will work with 1% milk.

Chapter 24

Vegetarian Facts

VEGETARIANISM

An ever-increasing segment of the American public is choosing not to eat meat. Approximately 13 million Americans consider themselves vegetarians, or at least lacto-ovo vegetarians, those who still eat dairy products. This food trend is pursued for a variety of reasons, such as considering it wrong to kill animals, a waste of natural resources by using large quantities of grain to feed beef and hogs, religious reasons, and last but not least the fact that it is healthier.

While vegetarianism is a way of achieving a healthier diet for most of the public, it is a radical change and one that is not easily adhered to. There are sufficient studies and evidence that do provide us with proof, that even a modified vegetarian diet is beneficial and results in a healthier, longer life.

One of the major concern among non-vegetarians who wish to consider changing to vegetarianism is that they will lack protein. There are of course, many excellent vegetable sources that are capable of supplying all your essential amino acids needs.

One of the best plant sources of protein is soybean, which contains 30-40% protein and is closer to meat protein than vegetable when examined under amino acid pattern analysis. The question also arises regarding the lack of B_{12} in a vegetarian diet, but most vegans do eat some form of dairy product, which eliminates the problem.

TYPES OF VEGANS

True Vegetarian
Will never eat animal flesh from any living creature, fresh or processed.

Lacto-Ovo Vegetarians
Includes dairy products.

Ovo-Vegetarians
Will only include eggs in their diet.

Pesco-Vegetarians
Includes fish, chicken, eggs and dairy products, no red meat.

VEGAN FACTS

Meat is really not necessary for a healthy diet. B_{12} can be taken as a supplement if needed.

Most vegans have lower cholesterol levels than meat eaters and have a lower incidence of colon cancer and digestive problems.

Soy products contain high levels of phytoestrogens, which scientists now think will reduce the risks of breast and prostate cancer.

Tempeh is a chunky, chewy soybean product that has been mixed with rice or millet. Miso is a combination of soybeans and a grain. Has very little fat and usually used as a seasoning for soups, dips, and stews.

Iron and zinc are not as easily absorbed by true vegans and may have to be supplemented.

Read labels well when purchasing a vegetarian product, many are high in salt and sugar content.

Chapter 25

Water Facts

FLUID BALANCE

Water is the most abundant and most important nutrient in the body, it is as essential to life as the air we breathe. All body functions are dependent on water, thus the quality of our drinking water is of the utmost importance. Medical experts agree that a water from a good quality source with a good mineral balance is best.

Water in our bodies dissolves the foods, carries nutrients to various organ systems, leaves the body as perspiration, thus helping maintain normal body temperatures, cleanses our systems of wastes, and is then eliminated through the kidneys in the form of urine. We lose 3-8 pints of water per day. The average person requires about 6 pints of water per day to replace losses. The body absorbs cold water more quickly.

Humans are 60-70% water by weight. If you weigh 150 pounds, your body contains about 90 pounds of water. The following shows the percentage of water making up the tissues, organs, fluids, and bone:

Brain	*75%*	*Kidneys*	*83%*
Heart	*75%*	*Bone*	*22%*
Muscle	*75%*	*Blood*	*83%*
Lungs	*86%*	*Saliva*	*95%*
Liver	*85%*	*Prespiration*	*95%*

Every person drinks approximately 16,000 gallons of water in their lifetime.

WATER QUALITY

The quality of the water we consume is as diversified as the sources from which it is derived. Most tap water comes from streams, rivers, and lakes. If the water has flowed down a mountainside, for example, it may very likely come in contact with and a carrier of impurities in suspension.

Surface water may contain pollutants and agricultural wastes. Fertilizers and insecticide residues are frequently found when water is tested. Air pollutants that escape from automobiles and industrial chimneys can all end up in our drinking water supply.

Other chemicals, such as chlorine, fluorine, phosphates, alum, sodium aluminate, and others are frequently added to drinking water for purification. Fluoridation is considered by some to be the most dangerous of all methods of treating water. Sodium fluoride, one of the most poisonous of all chemical compounds is the active ingredient in rat poison and moth control preparations.

Water should not be relied upon as a healthy source of minerals. Frequently, it may also contain inorganic minerals which cannot be assimilated by the body, but rather are deposited in various parts of the body, with the possible end result of an arthritic condition, calcium-hardened arteries, and organ stones.

Since it cannot be taken for granted that the water we drink is beneficial to our health, a home filtration device or purchasing bottled water is a must. The following information will shed some light on a number of common systems:

WATER TREATMENT METHODS

Filtration

These units contain carbon, usually in the form of activated charcoal, very effective in removing odor, chlorine, pesticides, and organic matter. Not as effective for removing bacteria or heavy metals and hard minerals. Attracts particles from the water until it reaches the saturation point.

Chlorination

Designed to kill bacteria with chlorine. Has a tendency to leave objectionable taste and odor. It also may form a potentially dangerous element.

Microstrainers

Capable of removing bacteria and some chemicals from water, but cannot remove nitrates.

Reverse Osmosis System

Contains a sediment filter and an activated filter. Effective in removing 60-90% of most minerals and inorganic compounds. Does not produce a large amount of water in a 24 hour period.

Distillation

Boils water to produce steam, which is then cooled to produce a relatively clean water. However, this method will usually not clean the water of gasses.

Aeration

The best method of removing radon gas, which is one of the worst environmental hazards to man. The EPA estimates that over 8 million people may be at risk in the United States from high radon levels in their water supply.

Sediment Filters

Screens that filter out suspended particles, such as detergents.

Ultraviolet Radiation Purifiers

Effective for the removal of bacteria. Usually installed on wells with other types of filters.

Eletrohydrolysis Units

Demineralizes the water by passing a current of electricity through it to remove inorganic minerals. This method is not very effective in removing organic substances or bacteria.

Ozonators

Utilizes a highly active form of oxygen to burn up bacteria.

Water Softeners

Removes hard minerals such as calcium or magnesium and replaces them with sodium through a process of ion-exchange. The addition of the sodium softens the water and makes it more effective for washing clothes, bathing, and doing dishes. The high salt content does not make it recommended for drinking.

Ultra Filters

Uses membranes similar to those used in reverse osmosis units, but utilizing a different method of operation. The membrane is designed to collect relatively large organic molecules as well as remove dissolved organic solids or bacteria.

NOTE:

Water filters are only good if they remove the particular problem in your area and are serviced properly, this includes changing the filter at regular intervals.

TYPES OF WATER

Sparkling Water

Carbonated water obtained either through natural underground springs or made by dissolving CO_2 gas in water. Carbonation lasts longer in naturally carbonated waters.

Mineral Water

Contains dissolved minerals, Various brands will contain different levels of minerals. Some mineral waters are made from tap water, than minerals are added or removed as desired.

Club Soda

Usually tap water that has been filtered and carbonated. Minerals and mineral salts are added. Club soda will also take tomato juice stains out of your carpet.

Seltzer

Usually tap water, filtered and carbonated. No mineral or mineral salts added.

Soft Water

Low mineral content water. Usually comes from deep in the earth with its principal mineral being sodium. Will dissolve soap better, and won't leave a ring around the bathtub . Will dissolve minerals such as lead from pipes.

Hard Water

High mineral content water. Usually comes from shallow ground that has high concentrations of calcium and magnesium. Hard water leaves a residue of rocklike crystals.

Spring Water

Water without gas bubbles, usually tap water or natural spring water. Bottled "bulk" water falls into this category. When purchasing bottled water, try buying it in glass bottles labeled "natural."

Artesian Well

Water from a well that taps into a water bearing layer of rock and sand which lies above the normal water table.

WATER FACTS

There are more than 64 rare and different formulas for water utilizing hydrogen and oxygen isotopes. We still have a lot to learn about water.

Excess copper has been found in tissues of schizophrenic patients and have been traced to soft water eroding away the copper pipes. Private wells, as a result of using soft water for drinking may be the cause of mental illnesses in one out of every 10 families.

According to the National Cancer Institute, nine recent studies correlated water quality and cancer with drinking waters in Pittsburgh, New Orleans, a number of cities in Ohio, New York, and New Jersey. 66% of all households in the United States are using water that is in violation of EPA standards.

There are 50,000 water contaminants and only 100 are subject to regulation. These include organic compounds, biologicals, heavy metal salts, inorganic compounds, gasses, and suspended solid particles. In the United States every year about 30 outbreaks of diseases are traced to bacterial or chemical contamination of water supplies.

A 1994 survey showed that 75% of all Americans are concerned about the quality of their drinking water. Homes with copper plumbing that have no soldered joints may be a health hazard.

There are 55,000 chemical dumpsites in the United States according to the EPA that can leak contaminants into our water supplies in those areas. These are just the ones we know about! A study of 969 water systems in the United States showed that 41% has impure water that was being delivered to 2.5 million people.

Allow your water to run for three minutes each morning before using it, there may be lead from pipes in the first water that comes out.

In 1993 110 people died and 400,000 became ill from drinking tap water in Milwaukee, Wisconsin. The water contained the parasite cryptosporidium. The problem is usually caused by agricultural runoff and sewage leaks. In 1996 a report was released that listed 28 cities that may be at high-risk from the same parasite. Numerous other cities were listed at a lower risk. Some of the high-risk cities were Baltimore, Boston, Chicago, Houston, Los Angeles, Denver, New York, Portland, OR,, San Diego, West Palm Beach, FL, and San Francisco.

"THIRSTY, GET OUT THE BLOWTORCH"
97% of the earth's water is in the oceans as salt water, Desalinization is becoming more important as new methods are being found. Only 3% is fresh water and 75% of that is frozen in the glaciers.

"DON'T CHILL OUT"
Ice water may be harmful to persons with cardiovascular disease. Sudden drops in tissue temperature may cause a shock to the system and affect the heart.

"A ONE, AND A TWO, AND A...."
The colder the water we drink with meals, the slower the digestive process will work. Also drinking water with meals tends to wash some of the food down without it being chewed adequately.

Hot tap water is more dangerous than cold water due to the higher risk of contaminants.

If it were not for the water secreted by the salivary glands in the mouth, we would not be able to swallow, nor digest the food properly.

Americans spend $2.4 billion dollars on bottled water annually. $1.9 billion is being spent on home filter systems. Most filter systems only remove large particles and still leave the small ones, such as viruses. One out of twelve households in the U.S. use bottled water as their main source of drinking water.

All water is considered to be mineral water, even rainwater. The only 100% pure water is distilled water.

Rinsing vegetables in a sink filled with water (instead of under running water) will save about 200 gallons of water per month for the average family. Waiting for water to get hot wastes another 200 gallons per month. Try saving it for the house plants.

If you leave the water running, you will waste 1 gallon of water every time you brush your teeth.

A family of 5 uses about 326,000 gallons of water per year.

A carrot is 90% water.

A laundromat with 10 washing machines, uses 1,800 gallons of water per day.

A carwash handling 24 cars per hour uses 8,000 gallons of water per day.

47% of our nations water supply goes for food production.

To feed one person in the United States for one year, requires 1,726,000 gallons of water.

1 average baked potato requires 12 gallons of water to grow.
1 pat of butter requires 100 gallons of water to produce.
2 dinner rolls require 26 gallons of water before they hit your table.

Well water should be tested every 6 months, without fail.

It takes 325 gallons of water to produce 1 gallon of alcohol.

It takes 375 gallons of water to produce a 1 pound sack of flour.

Every person drinks approximately 16,000 gallons of water in their lifetime.

Mineral water from famous spas have no particular health benefit.

When water is called for in a recipe it should be between 60-80 degrees for the results.

Sugar lowers the boiling point of water.

If a recipe calls for water by weight, remember 1 tablespoon = 1/2 oz. and 2 cups = 1 pound.

It takes 100,000 gallons of water to produce one automobile.

To print one copy of the Sunday paper takes 280 gallons.

It takes 5 gallons of water to produce 1 gallon of milk.

In 1995 a report was released by the Environmental Working Group (EWG) stating that 1,200 water supplies in the U.S. had a high level of fecal coliform from animal wastes affecting 12 million people.

Radioactive contamination of water is a problem for 1.7 Americans. It is caused by natural radioactive elements such as radon and uranium seeping into groundwater. If you feel that this may be a problem in your area call (708)505-0160 for information regarding special filter units.

Greenpeace has reported that 1 million Americans are affected by chemicals and pesticides, some of which are now under investigation and may be phased out of use. The more serious problems are from atrazine and trichloroethylene.

Chlorine has become a problem. It does protect us from a number of waterborne diseases, however the latest findings are that it reacts with organic matter to produce a carcinogen called trihalomethanes (THM's). This problem affects about 650,000 Americans.

A new bacterium water contaminant, Helicobacter pylori is now being studied as a possible link to stomach cancers. Studies are ongoing in attempts to control it.

Call the **EPA SAFE DRINKING WATER HOTLINE 1-(800)426-4791** for a free booklet.

Additional water information and literature may be obtained by calling the following number:

Environmental Working Group – (202)667-6982
Greenpeace International – (202)462-1177
Natural Defense Council – (212)727-2700

FOOD TERMINOLOGY

A

ACIDULATED WATER Cold water which has had acid added to it to retard browning of fruits and vegetables. Made by adding either 1 1/2 tablespoons of white vinegar, 3 tablespoons of lemon juice, or 1/2 cup of white wine to 1 quart of water.

A LA MODE Means the addition of a food item to another food item. Pie a la mode is pie with ice cream.

ALLEMANDE A thick sauce made from meat stock with egg yolks and lemon juice.

ANGELICA Refers to a candied leafsteak, part of a European herb. Used for cake and dessert decorating.

ANGLAISE A typical English dish that is boiled or roasted.

ANTIPASTO An Italian word for an assortment of appetizers, such as, cold cuts, olives, pickles, peppers, and vegetables.

ARROWROOT A fine powder that is produced from dried rootstalks of a subtropical tuber. It is used to thicken soups, sauces, and pastes. Has 1 1/2 times the thickening power of flour.

ASPIC Gelatin made from concentrated vegetables and meat stocks. Usually contains tomato juice.

A BUERRE Either "with" or "cooked in butter."

AU GRATIN Usually refers to a dish that has a browned covering of bread crumbs, usually mixed with cheese and butter.

B

BABA A rum or fruit-juice flavored French cake made with yeast dough.

BAKE To use dry heat, such as an oven for cooking.

BARBECUE Using hot coals to cook meats or other foods on a grill.

BARDING	This is the process of covering meat or fowl with added fat to keep the meat moist. It is usually done to meats that only have a small coating of natural fat. It is done by basting with fat from another source most of the time.
BARQUETTE	A pastry in a boat shape.
BAR-LE-DUC	A French jam made with currents and honey. The French variety is best with the seeds removed, The American version leaves the seeds in.
BASTE	A process of moistening food while cooking, usually by spooning liquid over the food.
BATTER	A combination of a liquid and flour or other ingredients thin enough to pour or flow freely to coat foods.
BAVAROISE	A creamy custard that is set with gelatin.
BEAN THREADS	Translucent threads that are produced from the starch of mung beans. These are also known as Chinese vermicelli or glass noodles. They may be found in oriental markets.
BEIGNETS	Any food that has been dipped in batter, then deep fried.
BEURRE NOIR	A browned butter sauce.
BIGARADE	Food that has been cooked in orange juice.
BISQUE	A rich, creamy soup made from fish or game. May also refer to a frozen dessert.
BLANCH	Plunging food into boiling water, usually to remove the skin from fruits and vegetables.
BLEND	To mix thoroughly.
BOMBE	A dessert made using a melon-shaped mold and filling one layer of ice cream with another.

BORDELAISE	A brown sauce using a Bordeaux wine as one of the main ingredients.
BORSCHT	A soup made from beets and sour cream.
BOUILLABAISSE	A soup made from a variety of fish, usually containing different fish parts.
BOUILLON	A clear soup usually made from beef broth.
BOUQUET GARNI	Combines herbs in a cheesecloth and then used to season soups and stews.
BRAISE	Lightly browning the exterior of meats. Usually used for tough cuts of meat. The meat is then cooked in a covered pan with a small amount of liquid.
BREAD	Applying a light coating of bread crumbs, flour and eggs.
BRIOCHE	A sweet French breakfast yeast bun.
BROIL	Placing food directly under a heating element.
BRUNOISE	A generic term referring to a food that contains finely diced vegetables.

<u>C</u>

CAFE AU LAIT	Coffee with hot milk added.
CANAPE	A small piece of toasted bread topped with a variety of foodstuffs.
CAPERS	The unopened flower buds of the caper plant usually preserved in a vinegar solution.
CAPON	An emasculated male chicken.
CARAMELIZE	Melting granulated sugar over a medium heat forming a brown sauce.

CAVIAR	Fish eggs (roe). May be red, black or gold. Caviar is obtained from a variety of fish such as the sturgeon, The finest is called Beluga.
CHANTILLY	A name derived from a castle near Paris which refers to a dish that contains whipped cream.
CHAPON	A small crust of bread that has been flavored with garlic.
CHARLOTTE RUSSE	Sponge cake in a small cardboard cup with whipped cream and topped with a cherry.
CHORIZIO	A heavily seasoned Mexican pork sausage.
CHOWDER	A very thick, creamy soup, usually made from fish, clams, vegetables, potatoes, and onions, then cooked in milk.
CHUTNEY	A sweet relish made from a combination of fruits and vegetables.
CODDLE	A gentle simmering in a liquid for a short period of time.
COMPOTE	Usually, refers to a stew of mixed fruits cooked at a low temperature in a syrup, allowing the fruits to remain in their natural form.
CONDIMENT	A substance to make a food more appetizing, such as, ketchup, mustard, or a chutney.
CONSOMME	A clear broth, usually made from chicken or veal stock.
COQUILLE	A dish cooked in a scallop shell.
CRACKLINGS	The crisp remains of fat after lard has been cooked out of food.
CREAM	To blend shortening and sugar against the sides of a bowl, using a beater to blend thoroughly.
CREOLE	A heavily seasoned food containing a blend of peppers, onions, bell peppers, and tomatoes.

CREME FRAICH	A thickened cream that has a slightly tangy, nutlike flavor and a very rich texture. It can be boiled without curdling which makes it excellent for sauces and soups.
CREPE	A very thin pancake which originated in France.
CROQUETTE	A crisply fried, chopped meat patty made with a white sauce and coated with crumbs and egg.
CURRY	A dish that is cooked and flavored with curry, a combination of spicy herbs.
CUTIN	The process of adding fat into a flour mixture with a pastry blender or other mixing utensil.
CUTLET	A piece of meat cut from the leg or ribs and usually fried or broiled. Most popular dish is veal cutlet.

<u>D</u>

DAUBE	A piece of braised meat.
DEMITASSE	A small cup of after dinner coffee.
DEVIL	A preparation made with spicy seasonings or sauce.
DREDGE	To place a thick coating of a flour mixture on a food.

<u>E</u>

ECLAIR	An oblong-shaped pastry, filled with whipped cream or custard and usually topped with a chocolate icing.
EN BROCHETTE	To be cooked on a skewer.

<u>F</u>

FLAKE	To break up a food into small thin pieces.

FLAMBE	Setting a food afire, usually with brandy. A percentage of the alcohol does stay on the food, not all of it is burned off. Never use alcohol that is more than 80 proof, they may ignite and explode.
FOLD IN	The process of cutting into the center of a batter with a wooden spoon or spatula and adding ingredients then stirring them in gently and slowly.
FONDANT	A sugary syrup that is cooked into a small soft ball stage (234^0 F.) then cooked and kneaded to a creaminess.
FONDUE	A Swiss cheese dip for small pieces of bread.
FRAPPE	Frozen, diluted sweet fruit juice that has been made into a "mushy" consistency.
FRICASSE	To cook a meat by braising, chicken by stewing.
FRIZZLE	The process of pan-frying until the edges of the food curls.
FROMAGE	French for cheese.

G

GLACE	Coating a food with sugar syrup then cooking to the "crack" stage.
GLAZE	Coating a food with a sugar syrup or jelly to add luster. The food can then be heated or chilled.
GNOCCI	A very light dumpling made from flour, potatoes and egg.
GRITS	Coarsely ground corn that has been hulled.
GUMBO	A thick soup usually made with okra and a combination of other vegetables and seasonings. A Creole dish.

H

HACHE	Hashed or minced food.

HARICOT	A term used to describe a thick meat stew.
HOLLANDAISE	A sauce made from egg yolk, butter, and seasonings. Usually served hot over vegetables and fish.
HORS d'OEUVRES	A selection of different canapés and appetizers.

I

ICE	Usually, referred to as a frozen dessert made of fruit juice, sugar, and water.

J

JULIENNE	Foods that are cut into small narrow strips, usually vegetables.
JUNKET	A sweet milk dessert coagulated by rennet and flavored.

L

LARDING	The process of inserting long thin strips of lard into a piece of meat every inch or so with a small instrument. A method of tenderizing meat.
LEAVENING	Placed in baked foods to make them lighter and more porous by causing the release of gas during cooking.
LEGUMES	Beans, peas, and lentils.
LYONNAISE	Usually, means a dish that has been seasoned with onions and parsley.

M

MACEDOINE	A mixture of fruits and vegetables.
MAIGRE, AU	A dish prepared without meat.
MARGUERITES	A baked salty cracker covered with frosting and nuts.
MARINADE	Usually referred to as a meat tenderizer or flavor enhancer. An oil-acid mixture sometimes utilizing pineapple or papaya.

MARZIPAN	A candy made with the past of almonds and sugar, shaped into miniature fruits and vegetables.
MERINGUE	A stiffly beaten mixture of egg whites and sugar that is used for pies or made into small kisses.
MIGNON	The most tender cut of meat.
MORNAY	A rich, cheese sauce.
MOUSSE	A frozen dessert, usually made from whipped egg white or cream.

<u>N</u>

NAVARIN	A lamb stew.

<u>P</u>

PANADA	A thick sauce containing bread or flour.
PARBOIL	Partially cooking food in boiling water and then completing the cooking by another method.
PARCH	Browning with dry heat.
PARE	Removing the outer skin from apples or potatoes.
PARFAIT	Either an ice cream sundae or a frozen dessert made from whipped cream and eggs then cooked with syrup and flavored.
PATTY	Puffed pastry shell filled with a creamed chicken, meat, or fish dish.
PETIT FOURS	Small fancy cakes made by cutting a square sheet cake into different shapes and then decorating each differently.
PHYLLO DOUGH	A very thin pastry dough, usually sold in 1 pound cartons. Sold fresh in the Middle East and frozen in the United States. Must be kept wrapped, otherwise the dough dries out rapidly.
PILAF	A rice that has been specially seasoned and used as a bed under meat, chicken or fish dishes.
PIQUANT	Having a sharp flavor.

POACH	Cooking food by surrounding them with boiling water to retain their form.
POIVRADE	A strong peppery flavored dish.
POLENTA	A corn meal or farina mush, to which Italians usually add cheese.
POTTAGE	A thick soup.
PUREE	To press fruits or vegetables through a small sieve to reduce them to almost a liquid form.

<u>Q</u>

QUENELLES	Meat that is finely ground, mixed with eggs and shaped into ovals then poached.

<u>R</u>

RAGOUT	A very thick meat stew which is heavily seasoned.
RAMEKIN	Individual baking dishes.
RAVIOLI	Small squares of pasta shapes filled with cheese, meats, or chicken.
RENDER	The process of removing fat from meat, usually done over low heat.
RISSOLE	A mixture of meats encased in a pastry shell and deeply fried.
ROAST	Meat cooked in the oven or over a dry heat.
ROE	Fish eggs (caviar).
ROUX	A special cooked mixture of flour and butter, usually used to thicken sauces and stews.

<u>S</u>

SAUTE	Browning or cooking in a pan using a small amount of fat.
SCALD	Heating a semi-liquid until a skin forms on the top. Usually to a point just before the boiling point.

SCALLOP	A sea food baked in a sauce.
SEAR	A quick browning of the surface of a food, usually meat.
SOUBISE	A food that is strongly flavored with an onion puree.
SOUFFLE	A custard that is delicately baked and contains cheese, meats, vegetables or fruits.
STEEP	Allowing a food to cook just below the boiling point in order to extract the flavor.
STERILIZE	Using boiling water to kill microorganisms.
STOCK	A liquid in which meats and poultry have been cooked.

<u>T</u>

TARTARE	A sauce made from mayonnaise, capers, pickles, and mustard.
TIMBALE	A custard or white sauce, unsweetened, with vegetables, meats, fish, or poultry baked in individual dishes.
TORTE	A cake made from crumbs, nuts, and eggs.

<u>V</u>

VELOUTE	A rich sauce that is made with cream and a fish or poultry stock.
VINAIGRETTE	A dressing made from vinegar, oil, salt, pepper, and herbs.

<u>Z</u>

ZEST	The oil found in the outer yellow or orange rind of a citrus fruit.

INDEX

Dr. Myles H. Bader's Formulas to the Rescue!

Certain chemicals, vitamins, and minerals act as antioxidants to help the body's own scavengers destroy free radicals. The role of antioxidants is still being studied. However, in all reasearch to date,they are "highly recommended in over 60 diseases as a preventative measure or to reduce the severity of a disease in patients who already show symptoms."

Dr. Myles H. Bader's Formulas declare war on free radicals. A 100% natural product, it may help:
* **shield your cells against free radicals,**
* **dislodge existing free radicals from cellular tissue,**
* **flush free radicals from your body, and**
* **stimulate the natural biochemicals in your body to maximize their
   potential to fight free radicals and rebuild damaged cells.**

Dr. Myles H. Bader's Formulas combine, in one potent compound, the most effective antioxidants now known through research: proanthocyanidin, phytochemicals (powdered vegetables), selenium, and vitamins A (Beta Carotene), C and E.

TWO FORMULAS TO MEET YOUR NEEDS:

For Further Information Call:

1-800-717-6001

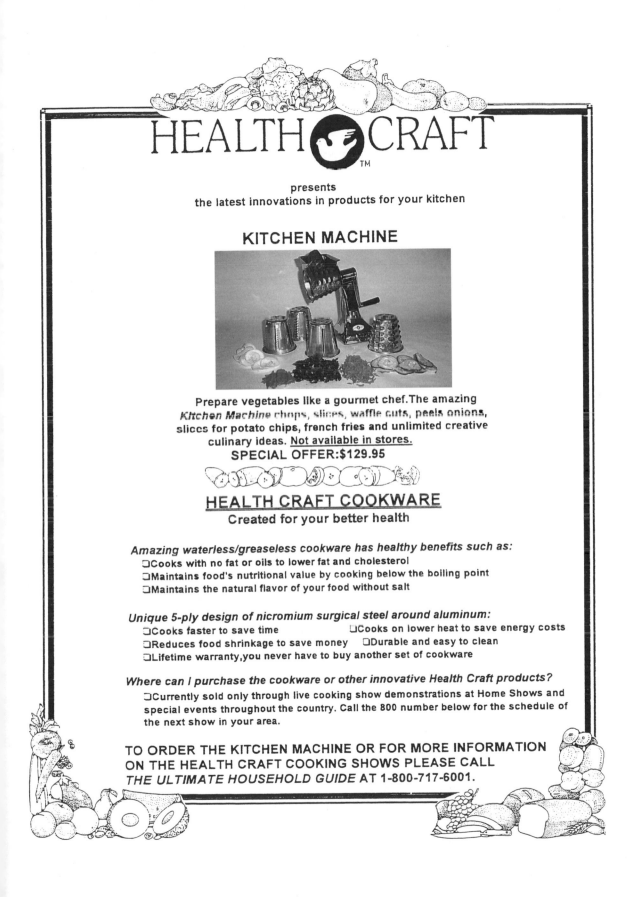

HEALTH CRAFT ™

presents
the latest innovations in products for your kitchen

KITCHEN MACHINE

Prepare vegetables like a gourmet chef. The amazing *Kitchen Machine* chops, slices, waffle cuts, peels onions, slices for potato chips, french fries and unlimited creative culinary ideas. <u>Not available in stores.</u>
SPECIAL OFFER: $129.95

HEALTH CRAFT COOKWARE
Created for your better health

Amazing waterless/greaseless cookware has healthy benefits such as:
- ❏Cooks with no fat or oils to lower fat and cholesterol
- ❏Maintains food's nutritional value by cooking below the boiling point
- ❏Maintains the natural flavor of your food without salt

Unique 5-ply design of nicromium surgical steel around aluminum:
- ❏Cooks faster to save time
- ❏Cooks on lower heat to save energy costs
- ❏Reduces food shrinkage to save money
- ❏Durable and easy to clean
- ❏Lifetime warranty, you never have to buy another set of cookware

Where can I purchase the cookware or other innovative Health Craft products?
- ❏Currently sold only through live cooking show demonstrations at Home Shows and special events throughout the country. Call the 800 number below for the schedule of the next show in your area.

TO ORDER THE KITCHEN MACHINE OR FOR MORE INFORMATION ON THE HEALTH CRAFT COOKING SHOWS PLEASE CALL *THE ULTIMATE HOUSEHOLD GUIDE* AT 1-800-717-6001.